W9-CFB-561

The making of the Edmonton Oilers

CHAMPIONS

The making of the Edmonton Oilers

CHAMPIONS

Kevin Lowe with
Stan and Shirley Fischler

Prentice-Hall Canada, Inc., Scarborough, Ontario

Canadian Cataloguing in Publication Data

Fischler, Stan, 1932–
    Champions : the making of the Edmonton Oilers

Includes index.
ISBN 0-13-235623-6

1. Edmonton Oilers (Hockey team). I. Lowe, Kevin.
II. Title.

GV848.E45F58 1988 796.96'26 C88-094535-4

© 1988 by Stan and Shirley Fischler and KCL Marketing Ltd.

ALL RIGHTS RESERVED. No part of this book may be
reproduced in any form or by any means without
permission in writing from the publisher and author.

Prentice-Hall Inc., Englewood Cliffs, *New Jersey*
Prentice-Hall International, Inc., *London*
Prentice-Hall of Australia, Pty., *Sydney*
Prentice-Hall of India Pvt., Ltd., *New Delhi*
Prentice-Hall of Japan, Inc., *Tokyo*
Prentice-Hall of Southeast Asia (Pte.) Ltd., *Singapore*
Editora Prentice-Hall do Brasil Ltd., *Rio de Janeiro*
Prentice-Hall Hispanoamericana, S.A., *Mexico*

Cover photo: Larry Wong/Edmonton Sun
Design: Gail Ferreira Ng-A-Kien
Manufacturing Buyer: Don Blair
Composition: Howarth and Smith Limited

ISBN:0-13-235623-6

Printed and bound in Canada by Gagné Printing Ltd.

1 2 3 4 5   G   92 91 90 89 88

Every reasonable effort has been made to obtain
permission from copyright holders of the excerpted
material. The publishers woud be pleased to have any
errors or omissions brought to their attention.

TABLE OF CONTENTS

Acknowledgments

As any teammate of Wayne Gretzky will attest, goals cannot be accomplished without good passes. Expert playmaking is often as important to the success of a team as goals. Which is why the NHL awards points for assists.

Likewise this book could not have been produced without solid assistance. If this book can be symbolized as a goal, then many significant assists are in order.

All members of the Lowe family — Jessie, Kenn, Nancy, Carol, Marianne, Barry Johnson and David Rendell — were enormously helpful. They graciously provided interview time and background material including valuable scrapbooks.

In Edmonton, Mark Hall, Dennis Glasgow, Jennifer Korol and Jessica Gilsdorf were helpful in many ways, not the least of which was research. Not to be overlooked were Edmonton journalists such as David Staples, John Short, Chris Cuthbert, Jim Matheson, Dick Chubey, Ray Turchansky, Terry Jones, Cam Cole, Norm Cowley, Mark Horton, and anyone else whose names we may have forgotten whose work supplied important insights for the book. Likewise Reyn Davis of the *Winnipeg Free Press* whose writing on the WHA was nonpareil, and Walt Marlow who supplied priceless information and inspiration as well.

Considerable help was required on transcriptions and other research. In this area invaluable help was supplied by Karen Jackson, Scott Decelles, Gabriel Price, Kay Ohara, Andy Schnieder, Mickey Kramer, Andrea Lehman, Kisha and Kell Ciabattari, Dave Katz, Elliot Polatoff, Joe Glus, Joe Dionisio, Neil Dovosin, Noam Cogen, Catherine Grace, Linda Olmstead, Adam Friedman, and Arthur Staple.

Needless to say, the book would not have been possible without the inspiration of the aces at Prentice-Hall Canada, Inc. — Ed Brewer and Tanya Long — who guided the project to its goal.

Special Thanks

While a number of people have been especially helpful in the development of the history section of this book, none has been of more assistance than Gary W. Zeman.

Author of the definitive work on hockey in the province, *Alberta On Ice*, Zeman was extraordinarily encouraging and thoughtful enough to provide us with vintage photos which appear in this book.

It goes without saying that anyone seeking more detail on hockey's development in Edmonton and its environs should obtain a copy of *Alberta On Ice*.

THE AUTHORS

PART ONE

1

Ancestors of the Oilers

When Glenn Anderson drilled a laser-like slapshot past Ron Hextall late in the third period of the seventh game of the 1987 Stanley Cup Finals, virtually the entire entourage of Edmontonians rose as one and saluted the Oilers. The score was 3-1 for the home club and, although a couple of minutes remained before the result would become "official," everyone sensed that Anderson's tally had sealed a third Stanley Cup championship for Glen Sather's sextet.

Adding yet a fourth Cup in 1988, making it four in five years, was an astounding accomplishment when one considers that Edmonton had not been incorporated into the National Hockey League until the 1979-80 season. No previous NHL club had ever won so many Stanley Cups so soon after entering hockey's major league. The feat has done much to dramatize the Oilers' contribution to The Game and yet the Stanley Cup events, for all their glitz and glamour, tend to obscure the less glittering pioneer days of hockey in Edmonton when the roots of championships present were originally planted.

For one to understand and appreciate the glory of the Oilers, one should first retrace the route through many calendars and many decades until one arrives at The Originals — those who made the present possible.

Many Canadians would be surprised to learn that hockey was not invented in North America, although the first professional league was founded in the United States shortly after the turn of the century. Surprisingly, a variation of the ice game we know and love so dearly was being played in Europe as far back as the Middle Ages and was actually being recorded on canvas. Hockey anthropologists are convinced that the first visual evidence of "players" with "sticks" can be found in a painting by the Flemish artist Pieter Bruegel. Dubbed "The Hunters," Bruegel's work was painted in the 1500s and depicted a group of men in a winter scene returning from a hunt with their catch. Trudging through the snow, the hunters are in the forefront of the scene; those who appear to be "hockey players" are in the background.

The "rink" is either a frozen lake, a river or possibly even a canal since the scene was one from the Low Countries. The "players" are carrying sticks of some kind (likely tree branches) and appear to be skating on what would be the obviously primitive skates of the era. "Their various poses indicate strongly that they are skating," noted Charles Wilkins in *Hockey: The Illustrated History.* "Because of the scale of the painting, it is impossible to see a puck though the presence of the sticks is powerful evidence that *something* is being shoved around on the ice."

Something *was* being shoved around on ice in various European precincts from that point and on through the early 19th century, but nothing approaching a rules-governed formal game existed. Then, hockey was a primitive pick-up game and remained so through most of the 19th century. Even in a seemingly sophisticated milieu like the McGill University campus in Montreal, hockey was still a "play-it-by-ear" pastime in the 1870s. "One of the first Canadian games on record," said Wilkins, "was a crowded fracas played in Montreal by 30 McGill University students, all of whom were on the ice at once. Some wore skates, some street shoes. The game was played with a ball."

Kingston, which like Halifax and Montreal has laid claim to having been the birthplace of hockey, featured a league in 1885 and within five years, organized puckchasing had moved as rapidly across the Dominion of Canada as tracks for the transcontinental railroad were laid. Lord Stanley of Preston had recognized hockey as a game so relevant to the populace that he donated a silver bowl to be contended for by the best teams available. When the Montreal Amateur Athletic Association annexed Lord Stanley's "cup" in 1893, the game of hockey was here to stay in Canada but still aborning in the distant land mass of Alberta — still considered uncivilized by most eastern Canadians.

There was plenty of ice and snow on the western prairie but not much in the way of people. Alberta itself boasted a population of less than 30,000 at the start of the 1890s and there were fewer than 1,000 people in Edmonton. Like their cousins in Calgary, Edmontonians had a liking for curling in winter and baseball in summer, not to mention lacrosse and soccer. Hockey would be a Johnny-Come-Lately, so to speak.

But once hockey fever took hold in the last decade of the 19th century, it did so with a fervor that has remained undiminished for almost a century. Alberta's initial sparks of enthusiasm were evident in Calgary where the first organized games were played, not in an arena, but rather on frigid ice patches of the Bow River. According to Alberta hockey historian and author Gary W. Zeman, Alberta's original three teams were the Tailors, the Northwest Mounted Police and the Calgary Town club. "These three clubs were playing on the Bow River," observed Zeman in *Alberta On Ice*, "while the top teams in Montreal had been playing in the comfort of Victoria Rink."

The landmark game for hockey in Alberta can be traced to January 3, 1893, when, according to the *Calgary Herald*, the first game in the territory was played. Final score: Town 4, Tailors 1. The site, in this case, was not the Bow River but rather the Star Skating Rink. Just two weeks later the Northwest Mounted Police team defeated the Town team, 4-0 on the Bow River rink. "By the spring of 1893," Zeman reported, "Calgary had two more teams and a number of other groups were engaged in training."

Within a year Edmonton had officially joined the hockey world. Facilities were available at the 102nd Street Thistle Rink and enthusiasm was generated by the likes of Syd Snyder, who would become captain of Edmonton's first organized hockey team. Known as the Thistles, Edmonton's original septet (hockey was a seven-man game in those days) enjoyed an auspicious debut, defeating Fort Saskatchewan, 3-2.

Early photographs reveal a player who would be foreign in the late 20th century hockey milieu. In the beginning no equipment — except, of course, for the obligatory sticks and skates — was necessary; no shinguards, shoulder pads, protective cup or even pads for the goaltender. Players in those antediluvian days had not mastered the art of lifting the puck nor was any of the violence that we know today evident, although that would come sooner than most would have liked. Sticks of the 1890s bore a faint resemblance to the present high-tech variety. Many were one-piece jobs with completely flat blades at the bottom. Interestingly, some players covered their stick blades with black tape even then.

The start of Canada's hockey equipment industry followed quickly on the discovery sometime in the late 1890s that it *was* possible to propel the puck off the ice and more goals could be scored this way. These first "lift" shots cost unprotected goaltenders black-and-blue marks beyond belief, not to mention the odd broken shinbone and ankle.

Those wounded goaltenders who had decided not to give up the sport opted for the best available protection, cricket pads. They made their debut in Edmonton toward the end of the 1890s. As for the rest of the playing uniform, it consisted of a sweater, sometimes but not always with the club logo, stockings and what appear to be scissored-off trousers which extended just below the knee. (One presumes that this style, unique in sports, was an adaptation to the speed of the game. The shorts enabled enough mobility while the stockings provided the necessary warmth.) As the games got rougher, more protection was deemed necessary. Thus, the advent of shinguards for forwards and defensemen, elbow pads and, much later, the shoulder harness.

A good reason why pads were unnecessary in the earliest games was the relative "cleanliness" of hockey at the start. Competition existed, to be sure, but it was less than keen. Players, for the most part, represented patricians of the community and sportsmanship (often considered dead in the NHL of today) was regarded as an integral aspect of the hockey atmosphere. Certainly, there was none of the harsh Edmonton-Calgary feeling that exists today among not only the players and management but the media as well.

As the number of teams increased and more attention was drawn to hockey in the newspapers of the day, so did the rivalries grow. Inevitably, one would spring up in Alberta between the teams from Edmonton and those in Calgary. Just when the switch from friendliness to ferocity took place is debatable, although Zeman has pinpointed the year as 1895. A touring Calgary all-star team visited Edmonton and defeated both the

Thistles and the Northwest Mounties. The double defeat was then followed by a match against a combined Thistles-Mounties squad and, again, Calgary prevailed. A year later Edmonton hosted the Calgarians once more only to be slapped down by the visitors in no uncertain terms. If that wasn't enough, Zeman pointed out, the *Calgary Herald* related that the victors "gloried at their supremacy over their northern rivals."

When Edmonton finally exacted revenge — 1899 was the year — it did so with a vengeance. The Thistles routed Calgary's Fire Brigade team, 15-2, amid rumors that the rooters for the host Edmonton squad had wined and dined the visitors on the eve of the game and had sufficiently softened them up for the ensuing defeat.

Outsiders who visited the booming Northwest Territories at the turn of the century grasped the intensity of civic pride that existed in both Edmonton and Calgary and also understood that the competition would be around for at least 100 years. One such individual was Ottawa law clerk T. G. Rothwell, who noted: "Calgary will not at any level allow itself to play second fiddle to Edmonton and will endeavor to keep pace with or even surpass the progress of their northern opponents in one of the greatest rivalries of modern time." The Flames-Oilers matches of 1984-1988 certainly underline Rothwell's theme.

Any Edmontonian who savored hockey in those early days understood that before the growing community could consider itself significant in a sporting sense, it had to have suitable arenas in which to play The Game. In this regard one of the more important structures went up in 1902 at the corner of 102nd Street and 102nd Avenue. The Thistle Rink, when completed, featured both a curling rink and a skating facility which had what was then the largest ice surface in the Northwest Territories (204 by 85 feet total, hockey and curling; hockey — 180 by 60 feet). Seating capacity exceeded 1,000. For its time and place the Thistle Rink was impressive. The ice was lined with boards four feet high as well as protective chicken wire. No less noteworthy was the design. Long before hockey fans complained about obstructed view seats, the Thistle Rink's designers anticipated the complaints and built the arena with an arched roof that obviated the need for pillars that often impinge on the spectators' sight-lines.

Meanwhile, the Edmonton-Calgary war began gaining

momentum as feuding spread to several levels. In junior hockey, for example, an Edmonton club got its collective nose out of joint after losing a Jackson Cup Challenge match to Calgary in 1904. As it happened, no less than three Calgary players were over-age and the Edmonton club vowed not to play Calgary again unless it complied with the regulations. The problem, at the time, was that no Alberta Junior Hockey Association existed to monitor the matches.

An oft-cried put-down of today's Calgary-Edmonton battles on the NHL level ("too much high-sticking") could have been heard 90 years ago during a match between Edmonton and the Calgary Fire Brigade. After releasing a shot, an Edmonton forward followed through and struck an opponent (Marshall) in the left eye with his stick blade. That night a doctor removed Marshall's injured eye. In the same match another Calgary skater received an arm injury while a third left the ice with a broken nose. Tim Hunter and Kevin McClelland should be amused.

Still another episode in the Nothing Changes department deals with the losers' view of officials. Gary Zeman reported: "Referees such as Dr. Sullivan were prominent citizens and were sometimes not very well versed in the rules of hockey. This caused problems. A February 25, 1903 game between Strathcona (now southside Edmonton) and Medicine Hat is a case in point. Medicine Hat went down to defeat 8-6 and protested that the referee, the Strathcona postmaster, favored his home team. The teams could not agree on a new referee so Strathcona went home."

As hockey interest grew, it was only a matter of time before demands would be made for a more formal organization to adjudicate disputes, develop uniform rules and arrange championships. The Alberta Amateur Hockey Association was merely waiting for some catalysts and they arrived in 1907 from almost a dozen communities including Edmonton and Calgary. The organizational meeting, on November 29, 1907, was held at Red Deer with R.N. Brown of the host town named first president of the AAHA. One of the group's first moves was to divide Senior hockey into an "A" and "B" class and two districts, Northern and Southern.

To the surprise of some — although not likely the Edmontonians — Calgary chose not to become a part of the AAHA. The alibi, if it was to be believed, had to do with exorbitant traveling expenses, although historian Gary Zeman theorizes otherwise: "Edmonton was a 'powerhouse' and perhaps Calgary did not want to compete in the same league." In time Calgary relented and was welcomed into the fold.

Shortly after the turn of the century the Stanley Cup had obtained a significant measure of recognition across Canada. *This* was a trophy that commanded more and more respect and, gradually, more and more challengers. When he originally had the trophy struck in his name, Lord Stanley had designated that *any* team in Canada could compete for his attractive hunk of silverware and, furthermore, the challenging team could do so anywhere and at any time during the ice season. In 1905, for example, before any Edmonton team had gone after the mug, a rambunctious club from the Yukon deemed itself worthy of Stanley Cup play and, thus, the prospectors from Dawson City trekked by dogsled, boat and, ultimately, train to Ottawa for a two-game series against the mighty Silver Seven champions. (Ottawa won the tourney, 9-2, 23-2.)

If teams from Dawson City or Rat Portage (another 1905 challenger) could get into the Stanley Cup action, why not a representative from suddenly hockey-mad Edmonton? It was a question asked by Fred Whitcroft, the Wayne Gretzky of early Edmonton hockey. Whitcroft was not only a player of more than passing repute, he was equally adept as an organizer and three years after the Dawson City expedition, Whitcroft rounded up a team which embraced not only Edmontonians but aces from all across Canada.

By far the most noteworthy Edmonton player of all was Lester Patrick, the son of a lumberman, who gained fame as a revolutionary defenseman playing for Brandon in 1902. Lester could never understand why forwards and *only* forwards were the puck-carriers. In those days, the defensemen had only one assignment — halt the attack. "Of course, at Brandon, Lester was expected to behave like a defense player," said Elmer Ferguson, the longtime Montreal historian-journalist, "but instinct and temperament proved too strong for Lester Patrick."

Before anyone could consult a rulebook, Patrick became the first defenseman to make a practice of rushing headlong toward the goal, à la Paul Coffey. He soon scored a goal and thereby set a precedent that much later was followed by the likes of Bobby Orr, Denis Potvin and, of course, Coffey. But Patrick had just begun to innovate.

In the early 1900s it was traditional for defensemen to stand in front of each other, like the point and cover-point player in lacrosse. Patrick thought that was foolish and suggested that defensemen line up abreast. Not only that, he implemented his idea and, once again, hockey tradition was changed.

After revolutionizing defensive hockey in Brandon, Lester returned to his father's lumber business in Montreal where he was signed by the strong Montreal Wanderers hockey club. In March 1906, Patrick led the Wanderers to a 12-10 two-game, total-goal win over the previously unbeatable Ottawa Silver Seven. Lester scored the 11th and 12th goals for Montreal en route to the Stanley Cup.

Patrick's star had climbed so rapidly that he was sought by just about every Canadian club with a big bankroll. He next signed with the Renfrew Millionaires at a salary of $3,000 for 12 games — astronomical for the time. A year later, December 14, 1908, Patrick and Tom Phillips, another high-class player, were inked by the Edmonton club which Whitcroft was preparing for the city's first Stanley Cup challenge.

The opponent would be the famed Wanderers, for whom Patrick had previously played. As befit a "first" in Edmonton history, the initial Stanley Cup challenge was treated with pomp and circumstance, right down to "The Glencairn," the private Canadian National Railways car which was lavished, for the occasion, with black and orange paint, the official colors of the challengers.

As was the custom of that earlier sporting era, challenge series often were decided by total goals scored rather than games won and such was the case with the Edmonton-Montreal conflict. In any event, the favored Wanderers discovered early on that they were facing a formidable foe, especially since Patrick was at the very top of his game.

Certainly, the Edmonton squad gave every pound of flesh available — as the injury list clearly indicates. Phillips suffered a broken ankle, made light of the injury to others on the club, and played 45 minutes on the wounded limb. McNamara hurt his knee, Petrie suffered a lacerated mouth and nose, while Vair was sliced on the head. (So, how bad were the 1988 finals in comparison?)

Despite their medicinal heroics, the Edmonton skaters came

up short on the scoreboard. They lost the opening match, 7-4, which meant that they would have to win the second by at least three goals to earn a tie and four goals to win the total-goals series. With a revised lineup, Edmonton came close — but got no cigar!

The injured Phillips and McNamara were replaced with Deeton and Miller. In the view of some second-guessers, the new player made a significant difference as Edmonton took the game, 7-6, but lost the series, 13-11. In what might have been the first example of 20-20 coaching hindsight, Whitcroft accepted some of the blame for Edmonton's defeat, pointing out that had Deeton, who scored a three-goal hat trick in Game Two, and Miller, a two-goal man, played in Game One, the series might have gone the other way.

Despite the defeat, nobody in the western entourage returned home embarrassed by the two-game series. They were rather encouraged and immediately laid plans for yet another Stanley Cup challenge. This would come in January 1910, the opponents being the Ottawa Senators. As he had in the previous expedition, Whitcroft was the prime organizer while remaining one of the star players. Among the players returning from the first challenge were Harold Deeton, Hugh Ross and Jock Miller. The new goalie was Jack Winchester.

If the thrill of being immersed in ''big-time'' eastern hockey prevailed in 1908 during Edmonton's first Stanley Cup foray, it was even more evident the second time around and not simply because the contest was played in the nation's capital. Hockey was now truly big-time in the Dominion. Important matches received coverage in all major newspapers — and minor journals as well — and the public and power brokers responded in kind.

This hockey fever was evident at the Ottawa Arena where nearly 6,000 onlookers — including Canada's Governor General Earl Grey — took in the fray. To the dismay of the home crowd, the brash westerners jumped into the lead and were ahead, 3-2, when a bizarre episode took place. ''One of the Edmonton players 'lost his trousers' — and had to go to the dressing room,'' reported Gary Zeman. The game was stopped for ''lost trousers repairs'' and halted again, later, when a smog comprised of tobacco smoke, cold air and warm bodies enveloped the arena.

The breaks in the action did nothing to enhance Edmonton's

chances. Ottawa soon overcame Edmonton's one-goal lead, pulled ahead and took the game, 8-4. When the teams met again two days later, on January 20, 1910, Edmonton managed to score seven goals but Ottawa beat Winchester 13 times and annexed the series, 21-11. If there was any consolation for the visitors, it was the fact that several of their players — Whitcroft in particular — won critical acclaim as well as offers from some of the better eastern clubs.

Acclaim notwithstanding, Edmonton's pro team would soon go into mothballs, so to speak, because it had run out of funds. For the moment, at least, the quest for the Stanley Cup would have to remain in a state of suspension, although hockey on other levels continued to gain popularity as it did throughout Canada.

By far the biggest strides were made on the amateur level and, not surprisingly, the dignitaries once again got in on the action. Lord Stanley's Cup remained pre-eminent, to be sure, but new Sir Montague Allan came forward and donated another handsome trophy, the Allan Cup, which would be awarded to the best purely amateur team in the country. (In later years the Allan Cup would to to the best "Senior" amateur team whereas the Memorial Cup was given to the champion "Junior" amateur squad.) Within the province of Alberta another trophy, this one sponsored by two prominent dailies, the *Calgary Herald* and *Edmonton Journal*, was designated for the winner of the AAHA championship. Edmonton's entry, the Deacons, lost the first match in 1911 to Calgary's St. Mary's, 10-8, in the two-game total goal series.

With the soaring popularity of hockey, new arenas sprouted from one end of the country to the other and in the northern United States as well. (Ironically, the first artificial ice indoor arenas appeared in major American cities before Canada began seeing them.) By far the most emphatic impetus for Canadian rink construction came from the brothers Lester (who had played for Edmonton) and Frank Patrick. After their father had moved his lumbering business to the Pacific Northwest, Lester and Frank took one of the biggest gambles in sports history.

The Patricks decided to construct a chain of ice rinks throughout the Pacific Northwest and operate a professional hockey league with teams in each city. With the aid of a $300,000 note from their father, Lester and Frank poured all their savings into what was to become the Pacific Coast Hockey League. They faced not only the uncertainty of public opinion but also the skepticism of hockey players and others who couldn't envision a league embracing Seattle, Edmonton, Victoria, Calgary, Regina, Vancouver and Saskatoon.

But in 1911 the Pacific Coast Hockey League was born and, for the first time, a truly major hockey league embraced teams on both sides of the border. A Patrick enclave was established in British Columbia with Lester taking over the Victoria septet while Frank ran the Vancouver club.

Any doubts about the wisdom of creating a major hockey league in the west were erased as soon as the schedule began. Starved for evening entertainment, the citizens of Seattle, Vancouver and the other cities in the league welcomed Patrick's organization. Lester and Frank responded by working overtime to improve the brand of hockey being displayed.

In order to host top-grade hockey, Edmonton needed a first-class rink and on December 25, 1913, a building that would become a city landmark, the Edmonton Arena, opened to the public. Not only was the rink handsome by standards of the day but it boasted an ice surface that measured 220 feet long (20 feet longer than the present standard NHL surface) and was considered the longest in the Dominion.

Opponents in the Edmonton Arena premier were the Dominion Furriers and the Edmonton Eskimos. The Dominions won the match, 4-2, and Edmontonians would pour into the Arena, eventually renamed Edmonton Gardens, for decades thereafter to view the likes of future Hall of Famers Eddie "The Edmonton Express" Shore, Frank Boucher, Duke Keats and Glenn Hall, to name a few.

The Patricks, meanwhile, did everything they could to keep western hockey on a par or above that played in the rival east. It was Lester and Frank who introduced the penalty shot to hockey, as well as numbers on players' jerseys and the "new" offside rule that enabled a player to pass the puck from behind the opponent's net to a teammate skating in front of it.

Speeding up the flow of a hockey game became an obsession with the Patricks. They were particularly appalled by the way a referee could slow the game down to a virtual halt by an endless series of penalties. At times each side could be reduced to two men *including the goaltenders* and the games then became a bore. As a result, the Patricks invented the "delayed-penalty" system that insures four skaters on the ice no matter how many infractions are called.

They then legalized kicking the puck in certain areas of the rink and also introduced the assist (which Wayne Gretzky greatly appreciates) to the scoring records. "Practically every forward step taken by professional hockey between 1911 and 1925 can be traced to the keen mind of Frank Patrick and the practical knowledge of Lester who tried out every rule first to prove its soundness," said Arthur Mann. "Between the two they just about made the game what it was before it hit the big cities below the border."

Thanks to Lester and Frank, the blue lines made their appearance in the Pacific Coast League during the 1914-15 season. To preview the fans, Lester informed the local newspapers and detailed explanations of the purpose of the blue lines were printed in each league city.

Not that everyone immediately grasped the changes. Defenseman Ernie "Moose" Johnson was one who couldn't quite figure out the Patrick plan. When a fan asked Moose to explain the blue line rule, he replied: "What's the blue line all about? Don't ask me, Bud. As far as I'm concerned there's only one rule in hockey — you take the puck on your stick and you shoot it in the net!"

Once, Lester was forced to put on the goalie pads when his regular netminder Hec Fowler was ejected from a game. Patrick not only played well, but learned a lesson about goaltending that would inspire him to write yet another rule. He decided that it was ill-advised to retain a rule that forced goaltenders to remain on their feet when making saves. The Patricks promptly changed the regulation and from that point on goaltenders began flopping, splitting and doing *anything* possible to keep the puck out of the net.

The Patricks' attempt to challenge the easterners was significant in many respects. For one thing it produced a player war that would not end until the National Hockey League expanded in the mid-1920s and absorbed whole teams and players from the western clubs. For another, it impelled promoters such as Frank and Lester to continue upgrading The Game. And, finally, it provided later inspiration for another band of westerners to take on the venerable NHL in the 1970s. Led by Winnipegger Ben Hatskin, the World Hockey Association borrowed several pages from the books of the old Patrick league — they innovated, stole players and challenged the NHL — and competed against the NHL a lot longer than the established league had believed possible.

Of course, the NHL had not even come into existence, as we knew it, back then. (It wasn't officially the NHL until 1917.) But the eastern leagues — the National Hockey Association in particular — had been dispensing a highly entertaining and competitive brand of stickhandling at high salaries for the better players.

"By 1910," said Fred "Cyclone" Taylor, "I was receiving $5,260, the most ever paid a hockey player until that time. And if I'd been smart I could just as easily have gotten $10,000, because they wanted me that badly."

Raiding parties from the Pacific Coast League frequented the east in search of talent. Taylor explained:

> Once, Frank Patrick went east in search of some 20 odd players for the western clubs. The easterners claimed they had no players to spare. Frank said, 'Okay, that's all I wanted to know; I'm free now to go out and get them.' And he went out and found twenty-five of the best hockey players from around Montreal, Toronto and Quebec. That shortened the supply of players in the east and so the league decided to play six men instead of the regular seven. Meanwhile, we in the west continued to play seven-man hockey from 1911 to 1925.

The west also continued to compete for the Stanley Cup with first the Pacific Coast Hockey League and later the Western Canada Hockey League (organized in 1922) sending representatives up against the eastern champs.

Patrick's Pacific Coast League struggled through its first decade of existence and yet managed some remarkable accomplishments, not the least of which was a PCHL team from the United States becoming the first non-Canadian team to win the Stanley Cup. Seattle did just that in 1917, defeating The Montreal Canadiens. Seattle reappeared in the Stanley Cup matches both in 1919 (the series between Montreal and Seattle was tied 2-2-1 when the championship round was cancelled because of a worldwide flu epidemic which had felled several players and would take the life of Montreal's Joe Hall) and 1920 when Ottawa defeated Seattle, three games to two.

All of these Cup events were enjoyed vicariously by Edmontonians who had no Stanley Cup team to cheer for since Fred Whitcroft's outfit had returned from Ottawa in 1910. In the decade-plus that followed the Edmonton eastern challenge, most of the Cup play involving westerners entailed either Vancouver or Seattle.

When the NHL began sending a representative to Stanley Cup play beginning in 1918 (Toronto), Vancouver provided the western entry three times and Seattle twice. During that era senior hockey boomed in Edmonton while the pro game suffered by comparison. The onset of World War I in 1914 put a crimp in everyone's plans as Canada sent soldiers and sailors overseas by the thousands; among them were innumerable Alberta hockey stars.

Soon after the end of hostilities on the western front in 1918, the Canadian forces headed home and with them came the players who were needed to stock the assorted hockey leagues. One who would have tremendous impact on both Alberta hockey and the NHL was Mervyn "Red" Dutton, an accomplished defenseman who had served overseas with the Princess Pats division. Dutton nearly lost both legs when an artillery shell exploded a few feet away from him. At first doctors prepared to amputate, but decided against such a measure and Dutton returned to Canada to recover and later star for Calgary. In time he would become president of the NHL.

When Frank and Lester Patrick conceived the Pacific Coast Hockey League in 1911, they envisioned a circuit that would embrace all of western Canada's major centers but, as luck would have it, their original plan failed. Like the World Hockey Association in 1970s, the PCHL did a lot of scrambling from city to city attempting to stay in business. Patrick ultimately concluded that the prairie cities were not large enough to support major pro hockey, although innumerable attempts were made to include them in some top competitive situation or another.

One such grouping was known as The Big Four, which included two Calgary teams, the Canadians and the Tigers, and a pair from Edmonton, the Dominions and the Eskimos. Among the stars for the Eskimos were Duke Keats and Barney Stanley. The former would emerge as one of the most colorful characters ever to grace the Edmonton hockey scene.

The PCHL did not look kindly on The Big Four to the extent

that Frank Patrick put the *kibosh* on any Big Four teams competing for the Allan Cup when he disclosed that no less than ten Big Four players were professional (thereby disqualifying them from Allan Cup play). Furthermore, Patrick offered a $1,000 "reward" if it could be proven otherwise. In fact, The Big Four closely resembled senior "amateur" teams that flourished after World War II. While the players operated under an "amateur" banner, many were receiving salaries which, technically, qualified them as professionals.

Since Calgary and Edmonton filled out The Big Four, it should surprise no one that the league had more than its share of feuds. In one classic incident, the two Calgary teams protested that Eskimos goalie Bill Tobin had failed the league's residency rules. Although president Allan McCaw ruled in Edmonton's favor, the protest continued flaring until the disgusted and eminently frustrated McCaw ruled that the season here and now was concluded and no championship series would be played.

Upon hearing that, the astonished protestors finally huddled and agreed to play a championship under their own aegis. Bitterly fought and fraught with incidents, the series concluded with Calgary the winner, two games to one.

If nothing else, the competitive zeal displayed by the Big Four would have a positive result and this, in turn, would eventually put Edmonton back into the Stanley Cup hunt once more, albeit on a much grander scale than in 1908 or 1910.

2

Edmonton's First Golden Era

A tour of the corridors of Hockey's Hall of Fame instantly tells a visitor something about the high-grade level of stickhandling available in Alberta at the start of the Roarin' Twenties. Hall of Famers Red Dutton, Barney Stanley, Duke Keats, Dick Irvin and "Bullet" Joe Simpson were among the regulars to grace the rinks in Edmonton and Calgary and they were just part of a grand group that would soon have enormous impact on The Game.

Anyone with just a passing knowledge of hockey soon realized that The Big Four was offering a product that ranked just below the NHL level and almost on the scale of the PCHL. Just as the WHA would someday decide that it could compete with the NHL, so too did the prairie folk decide that *their* time for major professionalism had come.

The date was August 9, 1921. That was when The Big Four officially gave way to the Western Canada Professional Hockey League. E.L. Richardson, manager of the Calgary Exhibition Board, was named to head the WCPHL and, furthermore, the new circuit brazenly announced that it would go head-to-head with the established leagues in an annual bid for the Stanley Cup.

This, of course, meant that the Stanley Cup playoffs would take on a new form. Rather than merely a single round involving a team from the east and a team from the west (NHL vs. PCHL), the playoffs now would include a preliminary round in which the NHL club would meet one of the western representatives and the winner then would play the other west entrant for the championship.

Without question the three-league arrangment represented the first golden age of major professional hockey on the continent, both because of the geographical scope of the teams involved and the number of top-quality players participating. It also meant that full-scale raiding would be the order of the day as clubs vied for the superstars needed to fill the rinks.

Surely, the fans had no complaints about the intensity of competition. Edouard "Newsy" Lalonde, who bolted from the NHL's Montreal Canadiens for the Saskatoon Sheiks, once described a collision between Dick Irvin of Regina and Cully Wilson of Calgary:

> The referee gave Wilson a five-minute major penalty for high sticking but this didn't satisfy Irvin at all. He skated over to Wilson who was on his way to the penalty box, and smashed Cully right over the head with his stick. Knocked him out cold; in fact, Cully took enough stitches in him to weave an Indian blanket. Of course, I was no angel either. One night Joe Hall nearly crushed my windpipe and I came back and almost broke his collarbone. And if you think that was bad, you should've seen Sprague Cleghorn. He said he once knocked out three players in one night!

The first WCPHL season embraced a 24-game schedule and concluded in a promoter's dream. Edmonton and Regina were tied for first with 29 points apiece. To produce a first-place team, a one-game playoff was arranged and played at Edmonton. It was no contest. Edmonton took the match, 11-2. But in the playoffs that followed, Regina defeated Calgary and faced the Eskimos once again.

In the playoff final opener at Regina, the Capitals held the Eskimos to a 1-1 tie and then defeated the Eskimos 2-1 at Edmonton in what was a shocker for the Alberta fans. In the next round to determine a Stanley Cup finalist, Regina was defeated by the Vancouver Millionaires 5-2 in the two-game total goal series.

If the WCPHL did not produce a champion immediately, it did offer a stimulating brand of hockey with some of the most colorful characters ever to step on a sheet of ice. And this included the referees as well. Mickey Ion, later to be one of the earliest great NHL referees, was one of them.

Thoroughly fearless, Ion also possessed a rapier wit and was never reluctant to deliver a squelch when necessary. Once during a WCPHL game he was being berated by Newsy Lalonde over a call. To emphasize his point, Lalonde waved his stick in Ion's direction. Nonplussed, Ion counterattacked by waving a large and solid handbell in Lalonde's face.

Lester Patrick, who was there at the time, remembered the episode. "A slight lull occurred in the battle of words," said Lester, "and Clem Loughlin butted into the argument to inquire quite mildly — it was always mildly, if they knew Ion — 'Why are you using a bell tonight, Mickey? You've always had a whistle'."

"Ion ceased his scrap with Lalonde long enough to make a simple statement in a tone which inferred that Loughlin wasn't very bright. 'Hell! You can't wallop anybody with a little whistle'."

Another remarkable character who graced the Edmonton sports scene in the WCPHL days was Gordon Blanchard "Duke" Keats, the grand old centerman of the west. How good was Keats? Frank Patrick once put it this way: "Keats is the possessor of more hockey grey matter than any man who ever played the game. He is the most unselfish superstar in hockey. I have watched him innumerable times. In one game, I specially checked up on his play. He gave his wingmen 30 chances to score by perfectly-placed passes. He's the brainiest pivot that ever pulled on a skate because he can organize plans and make passes every time he starts." (If that doesn't sound like a description of Wayne Gretzky, what does?)

Others who watched Keats in action with Edmonton during the early 1920s reflected the praise uttered by Patrick. Although he wasn't a native Albertan (Keats was born in Montreal), Keats is most closely associated with Edmonton. However, he got his big-league hockey start in the east with the Toronto Arenas (also known as the Blue Shirts) of the old National Hockey Association.

Keats became involved in one of pro hockey's first major feuds in 1915, playing for the Blue Shirts. With World War I flaring in Europe, Keats joined the 228th (Sportsmen's) Battalion of Toronto. Interestingly, the Battalion also had a team in the NHA and since Keats was a member of the battalion and also a playing-member of the Blue Shirts, the fur began to fly. The NHA ruled that Keats would play for the Blue Shirts for the rest of the season. Ah, but what happened when the Blue Shirts were supposed to play the Battalion team? Defenseman Babe Donnelly, who played at the time, remembered well: "The upshot was that when these teams faced each other, Keats was often missing because of 'extra army duties.' On the day of an important final game he was put in the clink, but he got out just in time to get into that night's game."

The tug-of-war for Keats' services became a big story in the papers and it was only after every newspaper in Toronto had printed the story on the day of the game that he was released and allowed to play against his Battalion mates. In time, the Army guys got even with Duke when Keats was sent overseas. "Nearly every time Duke happened to get a relatively cushy army duty," recalled Donnelly, "some officer or sergeant-major would make it a point to find some tougher duty for him to do. Keats did more latrine-duty than any dozen other men, but that failed to daunt Duke. Upon his return to Canada, he became a far greater hockey player than ever in Edmonton."

Keats was the balance-wheel of the 1922-23 Edmonton Eskimos team and would prove instrumental in guiding Edmonton to the WCPHL title. But Keats was just one of many outstanding players on the squad which included Ty Arbour, Hal Winkler, Bill Tobin (who later would become president of the Chicago Blackhawks) and "Bullet" Joe Simpson.

A member of the Hockey Hall of Fame, Simpson was rated by Newsy Lalonde as "the greatest living hockey player" of the 1920s. Simpson's moves reminded one of a jackrabbit prancing through the grass and inspired the nickname "Bullet" Joe. Like many a WCPHL player, Simpson served overseas in World War I and performed a number of heroic feats on the battle-scarred Belgian countryside. Twice wounded, he received the Military Medal as a member of the 43rd Cameron Highlanders. At the conclusion of hostilities, Simpson returned to Canada and began what was a spirited climb to hockey's crest. It began in his home town of Selkirk, Manitoba, but blossomed in Edmonton with the Eskimos.

Paced by Keats and Simpson, the Eskimos proved to be the class act of the WCPHL in 1922-23 and edged Regina, 4-3, to take the league pennant while 7,000 cheered at the Edmonton Arena. However, the decision wasn't sealed until sudden-death overtime when Keats scored at 30 minutes and 25 seconds of overtime. Having eliminated Regina, Edmonton thus qualified for Stanley Cup competition in Vancouver. According to the playoff arrangements, the Eskimos would play the winner of the Ottawa Senators (NHL)-Vancouer Maroons (PCHL) preliminary match for the Stanley Cup.

Edmontonians were as much interested in the Vancouver-Ottawa match as in any previous game of the season because of the eventual impact on the Eskimos. The wires from Vancouver revealed an exceptionally tight playoff. In Game One neither team scored for 55 minutes until Harry Broadbent beat Vancouver goalie Hugh Lehman and the game ended 1-0 for Ottawa.

Vancouver rebounded for a 4-1 triumph in Game Two, setting the stage for an exceptionally exciting third match which drew more than 10,000 fans to the Vancouver rink. Frank Nighber scored the winner as Ottawa nipped Vancouver, 3-2. Although battered, the Senators wrapped up the series with a 5-1 decision and, thereby, qualified to meet Edmonton for the Stanley Cup.

Despite the obvious power displayed by the Senators, hopes ran high in the Edmonton camp. The Eskimos knew that their foe had been well battered in the Vancouver series and Edmonton had the advantage of a best-of-three series which figured to tire the easterners more than themselves. The Senators opened the finals with but one substitute, Lionel Hitchman. Edmonton boasted five substitutes.

Sensing victory, the Eskimos jumped to the attack and, despite their skating advantage, were held scoreless in the first period. But Edmonton took the lead on Crutchy Morrison's goal in the second period, only to be forced into overtime when Hitchman came off the bench to tie the count for Ottawa in the third. For some inexplicable reason, the Vancouver fans were rooting passionately for the easterners and they cheered lustily when Cy Denneny squirmed through the Edmonton defense to beat Hal Winkler at 2:08 of sudden-death overtime.

A feature of the opening match was the confrontation of two exceptional centers, Duke Keats for Edmonton and Frank Nighbor, the gentlemanly pivot from Ottawa. "Keats was supposed to chase Nighbor out of the rink," wrote Charles L. Coleman in *The Trail of the Stanley Cup*, "but he made little headway against the peerless Ottawa center."

The opening game victory gave Ottawa inspiration and for Game Two the injured Eddie Gerard (bad shoulder) and

George Boucher (ankle) returned to the lineup. Several times during the match Gerard returned to the bench for adjustments to his shoulder but invariably returned to action and played throughout the game.

Edmonton's problem was goalie Clint Benedict, who played a flawless game, stopping Keats, Arbour and Art Gagne, the usually fearsome forward line. As he had been in a 1-0 playoff victory over Vancouver, Harry Broadbent was the hero once more for Ottawa. His goal was all that was needed and the Senators defeated Edmonton, 1-0, to win the Stanley Cup. "There was no doubt," wrote Coleman, "but that this edition of the Ottawas were real champions."

They had to be because they overcame more adversity than the Eskimos. Like the Islanders did to the Oilers in 1983, the Senators demonstrated that a solid defensive team could shut down a speedier offense-oriented club. Ottawa accented defense from the start and remained tight-checking through the final minute of the final period. On top of that the Senators also stymied an unusual Edmonton "power play." During the second period of Game Two, Ottawa's goalie Benedict was penalized for two minutes. (In those days the goalie sat out his penalty.) With Benedict in the penalty box, King Clancy took over in goal — and still Edmonton could not score!

The Senators playoff payoff was $116 per player. (Compare that to the Oilers, who received more than $20,000 a man for winning the 1988 Stanley Cup). But the loss hardly dimmed enthusiasm for hockey in Edmonton. Hockey had become *the* game in the city and nothing says it better about the ambience of WCPHL hockey in Edmonton in the early 1920s than the following description offered by journalist Ken McConnell.

> Soft, large snowflakes are falling, drifting lazily onto the ground. Our car is rolling over the hard-packed snow on the road. We are near the centre of a long line of automobiles, all containing shivering, but determined hockey fans. Snow, ice and 20-below-zero weather just put them in the mood for hockey at Edmonton. We enter a big, barn-like arena. The management has previously announced that the "arena's three big furnaces" will be in operation. While waiting for the game to start, we wonder whether or not the management has run out of coal.
>
> Then, the battle gets underway. There are some close-in shots on goal, some dazzling stickhandling, a few hair-raising

saves in our team's goal, and the first period ends at a lightning clip. Our feet, hands and ears that were cold only a few minutes ago are now tingling. We feel warm. We can defy the cold. Hot blood is coursing joyously through our veins. We are "sitting in" on the greatest game in the world, ice hockey. In particular, we are watching the play of Duke Keats, one of the greatest of them all.

Unlike today's sophisticated NHL, the WCPHL still was imbued with Canada's frontier spirit and its players betrayed a certain joie de vivre that no longer is apparent in the modern game. One of them was Amby Moran, a favorite in Edmonton and other western arenas.

Frank Boucher says, "If there was anything Amby loved more than playing hockey, it was painting the town in the company of other hockey players after the games. He was the soul of good nature until he spotted a police officer and then, if he'd had a drink or two, he was a holy terror. He usually ended each night of fun tangling with a cop, then landing in jail to sleep it off. But once the cops got to know him they began overlooking his amiable assaults, and eventually he became friends with most of them."

Moran's antics never seemed to end. Prior to the start of the 1923-24 campaign, Charles Coleman reported, Moran once again was A.W.O.L. from the WCPHL. "Moran managed to land in the Brandon jail for assaulting a policeman," noted Coleman. "After a couple of months of training there, he rejoined the WCPHL early in January."

The Edmonton club altered its championship lineup somewhat, selling Art Gagne to Regina for $1,500 and Spunk Sparrow. But the nucleus — Winkler, Keats, Simpson, Arbour — remained the same and most observers figured that Edmonton would win the title once more. The critics notwithstanding, Edmonton did much worse than expected and trailed the pack from the opening weeks of play. It was apparent that they missed Gagne more than anticipated and the fans showed their displeasure in some very obvious ways.

On New Year's Day 1924, Keats, who had spent a lot of time in the penalty box, was incessantly hooted by one fan and finally wound up fighting the heckler. Keats was tagged with a $50 fine while teammate Sparrow was sent down with a two-game suspension for belting referee Skinner Poulin. (Times don't change, do they?)

As a rule WCPHL referees were more liberal in their handling of games than the current crop of zebras. Frank Boucher remembers:

> One night I tried to lift Herb Gardiner's stick and steal the puck. But my stick flew up and caught Gardiner's face, inflicting a small cut. I apologized but that wasn't good enough for Gardiner. He threatened to get me. Well, now it was my turn to get hot because the cut really had been an accident so I told Gardiner he'd have his chances the next time I got the puck. The referee, Mickey Ion, overheard all this, and at the next faceoff he gave me a sly wink and dropped the puck in such a way that I had no trouble getting it. I headed straight for Gardiner. I saw he was ready to let me have it, so I pushed the puck through his feet and sailed into him with my elbows, knees and body, knocking him flat on his back. Ion blew his whistle and penalized *Gardiner* for charging. And then he gave me another sly wink of approval!

Those who complain of goon hockey in the NHL of today will find its roots in the WCPHL of the mid-1920s. On the same night that Keats battled the Edmonton fan, a riotous game was taking place between Regina and Saskatoon. Charles Coleman recalls, "A lot of time was taken up making repairs to Red McCusker who was the target of the Crescents led by Newsy Lalonde. Following the game, manager Wes Champ of the Capitals announced that his team would not play Saskatoon again unless president Richardson took some action. He accused Lalonde of being the leader in a deliberate attack on McCusker. Newsy was given a one-game suspension."

Edmonton finished the 1923-24 season far behind league-leading Calgary. Regina and Calgary met for the league playoff championship and the Albertans prevailed. This enabled Calgary to move into a curious playoff for the Stanley Cup. After Calgary beat Vancouver two games to one, NHL President Frank Calder ruled that the Montreal Canadiens also had to beat Vancouver before playing Calgary. Montreal swept Vancouver in two games and then whipped Calgary 6-1 and 3-0 to annex the Cup.

Although nobody could foresee it at the time, a chain reaction of events would soon take place that, within two years, would forever change the complexion of professional hockey in North America. The turnabout began in a Montreal hotel room in 1924 when the NHL governors voted to grant the first American franchise to New England grocery magnate Charles F. Adams. Only a few months earlier Adams had watched the Canadiens play at Montreal's Forum and became enamoured of pro hockey. Adams' movements were being closely watched by other sports entrepreneurs in the United States. If the Bruins became a success in Boston, other arena owners would want to jump on the puck wagon and, soon, there would be another player war. As it happened, Bruins manager Art Ross immediately went west and began signing such well-known PCHL and WCPHL names as Spunk Sparrow, Bernie Morris, Bobby Rowe and Alf Skinner.

By this time the Patricks' dream of big-league hockey on the Pacific coast had drowned in red ink, disbanded before the start of the 1924-25 season while its surviving Vancouver and Victoria teams were welcomed into an expanded WCPHL. There was no shortage of talent and some very interesting new faces, not the least of whom was Eddie Shore, a defenseman signed by Regina but who would achieve his initial fame with the Eskimos where he was nicknamed "The Edmonton Express."

The Eskimos had a better season than they had had in 1923-24, but still finished fourth behind Calgary, Saskatoon and Victoria. Victoria beat Saskatoon in one playoff round while first-place Calgary drew a bye. Victoria then defeated Calgary in a two-game playoff final and qualified to go up against the Canadiens for the Stanley Cup. In many ways the Cup final was a landmark series. For one, it was the last time a Victoria team would compete for the trophy and for another, it marked the last Stanley Cup captured by a representative of the WCPHL.

Directed by Lester Patrick, the Cougars defeated Montreal 5-2 and 3-1 in the first two games, lost 6-2 to the Habs and then brought glory to the west with a resounding 6-1 rout.

Unfortunately, the WCPHL was not as healthy as the Victoria franchise. Regina could not support big-league hockey and finally lost its franchise to Portland, compelling the league to change its name to Western Hockey League. Even more ominous were the player raids conducted by the expanding NHL. Following the Bruins' success in Boston, two new American teams were added in New York City (the Americans) and Pittsburgh (Yellow Jackets) and others were on the way. Edmonton lost "Bullet" Joe Simpson to the Americans as well as Crutchy

Morrison. On the plus side was the Eskimos' acquisition of Eddie Shore and the return of Art Gagne.

Few athletes have had greater impact on their sport than Shore had on hockey in the 1920s and 1930s, but his first intimations of superstardom were visible in Edmonton, where he blended the toughness of a rhino with the speed of a gazelle. Rarely did a player skate with such impudence. Shore was brash beyond belief and just as mayhem-oriented.

Al Silverman, editor of *Sport* magazine, once observed about Shore, "It has been written that man is the cruelest of the animals and also the most maligned; that man is capable of dealing out merciless, inhuman punishment, and yet is just as capable of absorbing such punishment. Man endures all, say the philosophers. Well, in real life this is true only of certain extraordinary men. Men like Eddie Shore."

The toughness that Shore displayed as a member of the Eskimos was acquired on the family farm in Fort Qu'Appelle, Saskatchewan, where he engaged in his first real passion — breaking wild horses. It was an interest that supplied fuel for his competitive fire and taught him that doing the things one loves may involve great risk and can be the cause of great physical pain.

Shore had never even entertained the thought of playing hockey until his brother Aubrey challenged him to try out for the school — Manitoba Agricultural College — team. "Anybody can be a hockey player," Eddie replied and in his indefatigable way he set out to teach himself the game. For weeks he spent every free moment on an outdoor rink, often in temperatures of 40 to 50 degrees (Fahrenheit) below zero; a challenge had been offered and it was not in Eddie's nature to turn it down. Hockey was just a game at first — only a college game at that — until family financial reverses demanded that Eddie leave school and look for a job. The job he chose was that of professional hockey player, and it was in Edmonton that it reached full flower.

While toughness was Shore's trademark, speed was an asset that he employed to better advantage than any defenseman in the league. In an era when defensemen were still confined to playing defense whenever necessary, Shore nevertheless went on many an offensive foray and scored 12 goals in 29 games in the 1925-26 season. Only three other Edmonton players —Art

Gagne (22 goals), Duke Keats (19) and Barney Stanley (14) — scored more than Shore.

The profusion of talent carried Edmonton to the top of the WHL standings and in the homestretch the Eskimos won 12 of their last 16 games to edge out Saskatoon for first place. In so doing, Edmonton earned a bye in the upcoming playoffs.

Victoria opened the post-season round with a 3-3 tie against Saskatoon, but in the decisive second match an overtime goal by Gordon Fraser gave Victoria a 1-0 triumph, setting the stage for the Edmonton-Victoria finale. Normally, the series would have been played on the Eskimos' home ice, but the ice was unavailable at the Eskimos' rink so the teams agreed to play one game in Victoria and the other at Vancouver.

Whether home ice would have made a difference in the final result is a moot point but this much is certain, Victoria had the goods and Edmonton did not. The Cougars took a two-goal lead in the opener and cruised to a 3-1 win. Since this, too, was a total goals series, Edmonton needed at least a two-goal advantage in Game Two to tie and three to win. But Victoria goalie Nap Holmes allowed only two Eskimos' goals while Victoria scored twice against Edmonton and the teams played to a 2-2 tie, giving the playoff to Victoria.

The dénouement was relevant in many ways, not the least of which was the ice failure at Edmonton Arena. This was symbolic of the problems afflicting pro hockey in the west and was particularly pertinent in view of the fact that mammoth modern arenas were rapidly being built in the east, all with up-to-date artificial ice-making facilities. Poor attendance at Calgary during the season set in motion rumors that the WHL was in trouble and rumors that NHL players were receiving much higher salaries than their western counterparts added to the unrest in the WHL.

Meanwhile, the NHL decided to add still more teams for the 1926-27 season and these included a second club for New York, the Rangers, as well as a team from Chicago and Detroit. Seeing the handwriting on the wall, the westerners, led by Frank and Lester Patrick, began auctioning off excellent players at reduced prices. Boston's Charles Adams purchased Eddie Shore, Duke Keats and Frank Boucher in a seven-man package for $50,000 — half of it in cash. Boucher, in turn, was sold to the new Rangers team. Others were dealt to the new Detroit team that had joined the NHL.

The NHL had an American Division composed of the Rangers, Boston, Chicago, Pittsburgh and Detroit as well as a Canadian Division made up of Ottawa, the Canadiens, Maroons, New York Americans and Toronto Maple Leafs.

The Western Canada League was dead and with it went big-league hockey in Edmonton for a long, long time.

3

The Depression Years

There were those in the west who nurtured the hope that the National Hockey League's "American experiment" would fail and that The Game on the big-league level would return to its rightful place — in Canada. They had the illusion that Americans would not support hockey on a long-term basis and, as the crowds dwindled in the States, promoters would return to Edmonton, Calgary, Vancouver, Victoria and Regina.

Some American teams did fail. The NHL representative in Pittsburgh was poorly received and eventually folded after the 1929-30 campaign, but this was the exception rather than the rule. In addition to New York's new Madison Square Garden, spanking fresh arenas were built in Boston, Chicago and Detroit, where the citizens welcomed the great ice game. When it became apparent that at least four American cities had major league hockey mania, all hopes for returning top-grade stickhandling to the Canadian west were dashed.

The success of NHL hockey in the States didn't wipe out hockey interest in western Canada although the death of the WCPHL and subsequent WHL was hard to take. Nevertheless, promoters realized that a market for pro hockey existed as well as a talent pool. A year after the WHL expired, the Prairie Hockey League took its place with franchises in Edmonton (Eskimos), Calgary (Tigers), Saskatoon (Sheiks), Moose Jaw (Maroons) and Regina (Capitals). The theme was "minor league but mighty good!" and rosters were sprinkled with names that had appeal to western fans, not the least of whom was Spunk Sparrow, now playing for Calgary. The Tigers, winners of the 1926-27 championship, also featured Norman "Dutch" Gainor who would later achieve NHL stardom with the Bruins, Rangers, Senators and Maroons.

While the quality of hockey was good on the minor league level, the quantity of fans was not and during the summer of 1927 an S.O.S. was flashed to the various supporters of the clubs. In Edmonton the Eskimos were helped, in part, by a group called Edmonton Fans Hockey Limited. The financial bath was too hot for them and their fiscal support was withdrawn, spelling the doom of pro hockey in Edmonton for the next few years.

The city was well represented on other levels and in November 1932, a senior amateur club sponsored by Gainers entrained for Montreal where they then boarded the steamship *Duchess of Athol* for an exhibition tour of Europe. Formally known as "The Superior Hockey Club," the Gainers outfit began its expedition in Scotland, made its way to England and then across the English Channel for a two-game series at the Palais des Sports in Paris. The club was criticized for rough play in Paris, but was well received in Prague and St. Moritz. A team comprised of French-Canadians representing Paris was the only club able to defeat the Edmonton club. The French club won 3-0 for Gainer's lone loss in 38 games which also included a single tie.

By this time Canada, like the rest of North America, was plunged into The Great Depression. Finding a job was a big deal and having enough extra cash to purchase hockey tickets was *really* something special. Yet, somehow, there were promoters who were willing to test the pro hockey waters in the midst of these dismal days. In 1932-33 the Western Canada Hockey League made its appearance with virtually the same city roster as those in the defunct Prairie Hockey League. Not only were the Edmonton Eskimos revived, but the lineup was graced by the immortal Duke Keats and his venerable sidekick Art Gagne. The club had a sprinkling of youngsters as well, including goalie Earl Robertson, a Saskatchewan boy who later would play in the NHL.

The blend of oldtimers and aspiring big-leaguers produced quality hockey, yet a sense of futility enveloped the circuit. Much of it had to do with the antiquated facilities used by the teams. At a time when modern ice plants were being built throughout the continent — even in sunny California — the province of Alberta still lacked an artificial ice rink.

An early thaw could ruin the best part of the season, the playoffs, and sometimes did. Yet Edmonton's minor pros struggled along in one way or another through the 1933-34 season when the circuit was called the North Western Professional League and embraced teams from Seattle, Portland and Vancouver. So bad were ice conditions in Edmonton at playoff time that the Eskimos (and Calgary Tigers) had to schedule "home" playoff games in Vancovuer and Seattle. The North Western League lasted one more season and, in fact, collapsed before the 1934-35 schedule had run out. In the midst of the Depression even a small financial nut was too difficult for the minor pro teams to crack. (In the NHL the St. Louis franchise went under at the end of the same season.) The Depression would last until the outbreak of World War II, so it is hardly surprising that pro hockey was non-existent in Alberta until the post-war years.

When pro hockey died, the senior brand took its place and almost immediately proved as big a draw as the play-for-pay variety. During the 1930s the Allan Cup had reached a level of eminence that placed it just below the Stanley Cup in terms of fans' respect. What's more, several senior stars and members of Allan Cup championship teams moved right into the pro ranks and up to the NHL. One of the most prominent was Dave "Sweeney" Schriner who starred for the Calgary Broncs and later became one of the foremost scorers with the New York Americans and later the Toronto Maple Leafs.

Hard as it may be to believe, Edmonton still did not have an artificial ice plant in 1937 — Calgary had already made the leap into the modern age — and, too often, the natural ice surface at Edmonton Arena would turn to slush. When the Edmonton Dominions edged the Drumheller Miners, 3-2, to win the Alberta Senior Six championship in 1937, the ice was so poor that Andy Purcell of the victors said the Dominions should also have been crowned water polo champs!

Senior hockey thrived until the players began donning khaki and heading for the European theater of war once again. As was the case in other provinces, Alberta became a haven for a quasi-major league brand of hockey embracing the Army and other branches of the Canadian Armed Forces. A number of NHL stars suddenly popped up on the service teams, one of them being Tommy "Cowboy" Anderson who had won the Hart Trophy with the Brooklyn (actually New York) Americans and was now with Calgary Barracks. Ironically, three of Edmonton's finest hockey products, the Colville Brothers, Mac and Neil, and Ken Reardon, wound up playing service hockey for the Ottawa Commandos and helped defeat the Victoria Army team for the Allan Cup in 1943. The Colvilles, who had played for the Rangers 1940 Stanley Cup-winning team (New York's last, by the way), would return to the Broadway Blueshirts after the war, while Reardon signed on with the Montreal Canadiens.

"The calibre of hockey in Alberta, as can be judged by the type of player, would have matched the NHL," commented Gary Zeman.

It would be difficult to dispute the claim. Max Bentley, a future Hall of Famer, Ed Slowinski, Alex Kaleta and "Sugar" Jim Henry either had already started in the NHL or would return after the war to have a significant impact on the big league.

At war's end normalcy returned to the hockey front, although the face of pro hockey had changed considerably. The Great Depression had reduced the NHL to six teams, two of them (Toronto and Montreal) in Canada and four (New York, Boston, Detroit, Chicago) south of the border. Minor pro hockey was booming in the States where the American Hockey League expanded on the east coast while the United States Hockey League sprouted in the midwest and the Pacific Coast Hockey League grew in an area first prospected by Lester and Frank Patrick.

Likewise, senior hockey enjoyed prosperity in many parts of Canada, including the prairies, where the Western Canada Senior Hockey League linked Edmonton (Flyers), Saskatoon (Elks), Regina (Caps) and Calgary (Stampeders). Calgary beat Edmonton, four games to one, and advanced to the Allan Cup finals, knowing full well that an Alberta entry had never won the Allan Cup since it was placed in competition early in the century. The drought was ended when Calgary nipped the Hamilton Tigers 1-0 in the spring of 1946.

Edmonton finally got its taste of Allan Cup champagne two years later. The Flyers, a melange of over-the-hill pros and soon-to-be NHLers, was crafted by Frank Currie and featured two tall men who would emerge as the first and second lines of defense. Big Bud MacPherson, a 6 foot 3, 205-pound defenseman, was a native of Edmonton and as superb a backliner as ever grew up in the city's hockey program. He would eventually wind up with the Montreal Canadiens. Behind Big Mac camped 6 foot 2, 175-pound goalie Al Rollins out of Vanguard, Saskatchewan. Rollins, who later would win the Hart Trophy as the NHL's most valuable player, ranks among the most underrated top goalies of all time.

Rollins and MacPherson were surrounded by a talented crew that started off slowly in the Western Canada Hockey League but gained momentum at playoff time. They advanced through the preliminary rounds until the finals loomed ahead with the powerful Ottawa Senators and the Quebec Senior Hockey League providing the opposition. With the series opening in Regina, Edmonton set the tone of the series with a persuasive 6-2 victory. The Senators produced one win — a 3-2 decision at Edmonton Arena — before dropping the next three and the series.

The only "downer" was the fact that Game Five, the finale, was played in Calgary where the fans rooted against the Edmonton skaters. On the up side was the reaction in Edmonton when the victors returned. A V-E Day and V-J Day aura engulfed the city which welcomed the Flyers with a parade that drew at least 60,000 citizens.

Edmonton would host yet another Allan Cup tourney but not with a home town entry. The Flyers were knocked out of the playoffs following their championship season by an upstart Regina Capitals club and a year later Calgary's Stampeders went to the Allan Cup finals. The eastern representatives, Toronto Marlboros, played their "home" game at Edmonton Arena and it was there that the Marlies defeated Calgary in the fifth and deciding game to take the trophy.

By now senior amateur hockey had taken on an image which was not quite consonant with what Sir Montague Allan had in mind when he offered the trophy in his name to the best amateur club in Canada. In fact the term "amateur" had become something of a joke in journalistic circles, at least when it came to hockey. In the United States, for example, the Eastern Amateur Hockey League was in full bloom yet everyone knew that its players — many of them farmhands of the New York Rangers and Boston Bruins — were being paid. The same held in Canada with a wink coming from the authorities.

When the 1950s arrived, the "amateur" situation had gotten so out of hand that a move was made to separate the paid senior "amateurs" from the Simon Pure skaters. To do so a new Major Senior level was created and World War II hero Sir Harold Alexander, Governor General of Canada, donated the Alexander Trophy to the winner of the championship series between the Dominion's top leagues.

4

The Second Golden Era of Edmonton Hockey

Until major league hockey — if you can call the World Hockey Association "Big League" — arrived in the Canadian west during the early 1970s, the most glorious era of post-World War II hockey took place in Edmonton two decades earlier. For that Edmontonians can thank two utterly contrasting characters, Hall of Famers Jack Adams and Al Leader. The ebullient and tempestuous Adams stamped a snarly and slick style on the city's professional club in 1952 and for years to come.

In many ways Adams did for the face of Edmonton hockey what Glen Sather has done in the present era. The diffident leader would influence hockey's growth in an organizational way, quietly and efficiently. Curiously, both Adams and Leader did their job for Edmonton from a distance — Adams in Detroit, where he masterminded the Red Wings and Leader in Seattle where he craftily manipulated the Pacific Coast Hockey League.

Adams was by far the more fascinating personality and to understand him one has to examine his background. A former NHL player of note (Toronto Arenas, Toronto St. Patricks and the Ottawa Senators), Adams treated hockey precisely the way Sather does today; he would do anything to win and rarely concerned himself with the consequences.

Once, during the 1918-19 season, Adams, playing with the Arenas, became engaged in a wild fight with Sprague Cleghorn, another robust skater. The Governor General was a front row spectator at the match and one whose criticism could have meant Adam's expulsion.

"It was a great slugfest," Adams later recalled. "Funny, I never did hear what the Governor General thought about it, but I thought I saw a distinguished-looking man clapping his white-gloved hands."

Adams brought to Detroit the successful style of play that had made him an outstanding hockey player through the years, a brand of hockey that frequently enraged his foes.

"Adams," said Alfie Skinner of the Toronto Arenas, against whom Adams played for many years, "was an awful slasher. Some fellows would slash and you'd hardly hear it through your pads. But when Adams swung his stick at a vulnerable part of your anatomy, he swung hard. He meant to hurt! On the other hand, he'd take punishment, without a murmur. He'd never complain when anyone whacked him. A guy like that you had to admire."

NHL president Frank Calder must certainly have admired Adams when Jack walked into the NHL office prior to the 1927-28 season and asserted that he was the man for the vacant Detroit coaching job. Calder agreed and telephoned club president Charlie Hughes to set up an appointment.

Adams then met Hughes and revealed the same brashness, a characteristic for which he was renowned. "I'd been involved in winning the Stanley Cup for Ottawa," said Adams, "so I told Hughes that he needed me more than I needed him."

Hughes must have agreed, because he signed Adams to a contract and told him to get started building a winner. A year later Hughes knew he had taken the right course. From a dismal 12-28-4 record, the Detroiters climbed to the .500 mark, winning 19, losing 19 and tying 6 games. It wasn't a good enough record for a Stanley Cup berth, but there was no question that the road to the cup had opened for Detroit. With a new nickname, the Falcons, the team finished third in the American division.

Adams soon discovered that building a winner required more than enthusiasm. Money was necessary to buy and sign players, but the Depression had hit the motor industry and loose cash was as distant as the Stanley Cup. One night Adams allowed a fan into Olympia Stadium in exchange for five bags of potatoes.

"If the greatest star in the game was made available to us for

$1.98," said Adams, "we couldn't have afforded him."

The turning point toward better times for the teams was reached in 1933, when the franchise was bought by James Norris Sr., a grain millionaire with a fervent love of hockey. Norris had played hockey for the Montreal Amateur Athletic Association's famous Winged Wheelers. He suggested a new team name, the Red Wings, and an insignia symbolic of the industry which dominates the city.

A no-nonsense type, Norris was even brasher than Adams. He laid it on the line with the manager. "I'll give you a year on probation," Norris warned, "with no contract."

Adams may not have had a written pact with Norris, but he quickly gained the millionaire's confidence as well as access to his bankroll to sign superior players. He bought Syd Howe (no relation to Gordie) from the St. Louis Flyers for $35,000. Howe was soon playing the brand of hockey that eventually put him in the Hall of Fame. Hec Kilrea was purchased from Toronto for $17,000, and the Wings were off, flying toward the top.

By the 1935-36 season, the Adams-Norris combination was the best in Hockey. The manager was not only off probation, but had become so friendly with his awesome boss that he referred to Norris as "Pops."

Adams put it this way: "Pops was the bankroll and the boss. After he took over, Detroit hockey never looked back."

By March 22, 1936, the final day of the 1935-36 season, Detroit was perched atop the American Division with a record of 24 wins, 16 losses and 8 ties for 56 points, the best record in either division. In Marty Barry, Herb Lewis, and Larry Aurie, the Red Wings boasted the best offensive unit in the league. Their distinguished efforts were reinforced by the exploits of Syd Howe, Johnny Sorrell, Hec Kilrea, and a big broth of a shooter named Ebenezer Goodfellow.

"Goodfellow," a member of the Detroit family recently commented, "was Gordie Howe before Gordie Howe came along!"

In the prime of his career, Normie Smith provided Detroit with more than adequate goaltending, fronted by capable defensemen like Bucko McDonald and Doug Young. However, the Red Wings had yet to bring the Stanley Cup to Detroit, a fact that was fast becoming a negative obsession with its fans.

To win the Cup in 1936 first required that the Red Wings dispatch the strong Montreal Maroons in the opening playoff round which began March 24, 1936, at the Forum in Monteal. To this day the game remains a classic among classics. It was the longest hockey match ever played in the NHL. Exactly 116 minutes and 30 seconds of sudden-death overtime was required, almost two additional full games. The winning goal was scored by Modere "Mud" Bruneteau of the Red Wings at 16:30 of the sixth overtime period.

Adams was actually the genius behind the victory. He realized that his regulars were fatigued beyond replenishment of their energy, and he knew that young legs would make the difference, no matter how inexperienced. So Bruneteau, who had scored only two goals and no assists all season, became Detroit's ace in the hole. He had not been used until the twelfth minute of the ninth period, when Adams sent him over the boards with simple instructions, "Let's get this over with; it's now or never."

Bruneteau launched the historic play with a crisp pass to Kilrea, who faked a return pass as he approached the Maroons blue line. By this time "Mud" had caught up with his teammate, and as Kilrea crossed into Montreal territory, the speedy Bruneteau easily raced behind the Maroons defense. Kilrea found an opening and ladled the pass to his young linemate, who was face to face with veteran goalie Lorne Chabot.

"Thank God," said Bruneteau, "that Chabot fell down as I drove the puck toward the net. It was the funniest thing. The puck just stuck there in the twine and didn't fall on the ice."

Although the Red Wings had triumphed 1-0 on foreign ice, the Forum fans, who remained until the H-hour (2:25 A.M.), cheerfully saluted Bruneteau. In a rare display of philanthropy, strangers pushed dollar bills into Bruneteau's glove, under his arms — wherever they could.

"I grabbed money from every direction," said Bruneteau.

In that Depression era, when a dollar bill meant infinitely more than it does today, Bruneteau collected $22 for each member of the team including the trainer, the stickboy, and Jack Adams. More important, the Red Wings collected a very special confidence as a result of the win. It showed in the weeks to come.

Adams eventually molded a Detroit powerhouse which was based on major league baseball's farm system theory. Jack realized that if his big club was going to thrive in the competitive post-World War II NHL which was dominated by the Toronto Maple Leafs and Montreal Canadiens, he would have to develop a far-flung farm system. In each city where the Red Wings planted a team (Indianapolis, Indiana, Omaha, Nebraska, Galt, Ontario) Adams implanted a system. "The way Jack wanted it then was just like Glen Sather wants it today in Edmonton," said former Red Wing farmhand Larry Zeidel. "He wanted fast, clever, and tough hockey players. And he made sure everybody in the system was instructed the Red Wings' way."

Fortunately Adams selected Edmonton as the site for his primary Candian farm team — and that's where Al Leader came in to enhance the second golden era of Edmonton hockey. A thoughtful hockey devotee, Leader helped spawn interest in the ice game throughout the Pacific Coast in cities such as San Francisco, Los Angeles, Seattle and Vancouver. His Pacific Coast Hockey League was a big hit in the late 1940s and soon embraced Edmonton, Calgary and Saskatoon. In 1952-53 the League changed its name to Western Hockey League and visionary that he was, Leader had dreams of improving the quality of play in his organization and eventually establishing it as a second major league which would compete on a level with the NHL. "I foresaw the day when large, new arenas would be built in the west coast cities as well as those in Alberta, British Columbia and Manitoba," said Leader. "I thought with prudent planning we could develop our own players and eventually produce a second major league."

In terms of Edmonton, Adams cooperated by dispatching some of the finest talent in North America, many of whom would have been NHL stars had there been more teams in the majors at the time. Glenn Hall and Johnny Bucyk, aces with Adams' Edmonton Flyers, eventually made their way to Detroit and the Red Wings and ultimately to the Hockey Hall of Fame. Other NHL-ers in the making were Al Arbour, Lorne Davis, Jerry Melnyk, Bronco Horvath and the extremely turbulent Larry Zeidel.

If any single player symbolized the spirit of Edmonton hockey in the early 50s it was Zeidel. Although he was originally from Montreal, the Jewish defenseman moved to Edmonton, settled in and married a local girl. He fell in love with Marie and Edmonton simultaneously and he was the quintessential disciple of Jack Adams-type hockey. "Although Adams was a couple of thousand miles away," said Zeidel, "I knew the way he wanted me to play. He'd open up the gate and say 'sic 'em'."

Adams had appointed former NHL sharpshooter Norman (Bud) Poile to run his Edmonton club. "Poile gave all the Edmonton players personal attention," Zeidel recalled. "He'd get them in the right frame of mind, one on one in his office, psyche them up a bit, build up confidence. He gave a lot of attention to developing skills, too, so one of the things I heard from Poile was, 'When all these guys come in on you, don't give up the blue line.' But he'd always point to someone with a certain skill that he thought would help one of his players, and he said, 'You know, sometimes when a guy is coming in on ya, you've got to tie them up.' A lot of kids nowadays could learn from that. So I tried it. We took pride, as defensemen, in getting shutouts for our goalies. So it worked, it worked good."

NHL hockey was tempestuous in those days, but pantywaist compared with some of the Pier Six brawls that spiced up the WHL. In addition to Zeidel, the league over the years featured such bad men as Harry Dyck of Vancouver and Jack Evans of Saskatoon. Fist fights were commonplace. "We were all battling to make it up to the NHL," recalled Lou Fontinato, who rocked plenty of jaws while playing for Saskatoon and Vancouver. "If you backed up too far, you were in big trouble."

Edmonton's Zeidel never backed up. Some of his WHL bouts have become permanently etched in hockey scriptures. Exhibits A and B are: (A) The Gory Phil Maloney Punchout and (B) The Savage Tex Evans Stick-Cracking Bloodbath. Zeidel, now a successful Philadelphia stock broker, has a vivid recollection of both encounters.

"Jack Adams made sure that every team in the Detroit system used the same plan for face-offs in our own zone. He always wanted defensemen to take the face-off, to take out the center man. In this instance I went up against Phil Maloney who was a slick quarterback-type center I usually bodied out of the play." Zeidel did not realize that Maloney had become increasingly angry at him and had decided to exact revenge.

"I moved in to take him out as the ref dropped the puck, and he didn't even go for the puck, he was so pissed off. He had both hands on his stick, and he pitchforked me between the legs, hit me right in the balls. So right away I started to fight with him. And it was very brief."

The bout was interrupted by the officials and both players were sent to the penalty box. Just when it appeared as though Zeidel had calmed down, Harry Dyck of the Canucks took a run at one of Edmonton's rookies.

"The kid was scared and started running away," Zeidel remembered. "It was embarrassing, especially when the fans started laughing. So I hopped over the boards and went after Dyck. We had a go of it and then I wound up standing by the Vancouver bench and I challenged the whole team. Meanwhile I remembered how Maloney had hit me in the nuts and suddenly I just hammered him right in the eye. It was pretty bad. The ambulance came and had to take him to the hospital. That really made headlines."

It's noteworthy that Winnipeg Jets general manager John Ferguson had been a stickboy for the Canucks when Zeidel challenged the Vancouver team. Ferguson often said that he made a mental note of the episode and vowed never to let that happen to a teammate if he ever became pro.

Zeidel's encounter with Jack Evans was not as one-sided as his devastation of Maloney. The lantern-jawed Evans, who eventually played for the New York Rangers and Chicago Blackhawks, was the strong silent type on the ice. The devastation that ensued on the Edmonton ice was ignited (what else?) by a high stick. Although there is still some debate about the perpetrator, Edmonton columnist Jim Brooke indicated that Evans was the culprit. The following is Brooke's description, which appeared January 31, 1953, the morning after the uprising.

> The Roman gladiators were a genteel collection of lounge lizards in comparison with Leapin' Larry Zeidel and Jack (Smiler) Evans, a pair of pugnacious defensemen in any league, A.D. or B.C.
>
> Evans, in the general opinion of the Edmonton fans who witnessed the contest of skill and science (perhaps we abuse the word?) between the Quakes and the Flyers at the Gardens last night, is strictly "The Goon of Saskatoon."
>
> The Smiler, who performed with New York Rangers last semester, and Zeidel staged a bloody, medieval war in which hockey sticks were the weapons and no quarter was sought or given.

The only difference between Evans' head and a baseball after the game last night was that a baseball has fewer stitches and less hair. Zeidel looked as if he had been necking with a meat grinder.

The boys didn't wait too long to begin the ball. It started after five minutes of the first period. Evans cracked Zeidel, who had rushed out of his own end, on the bridge of the bugle with his stick. Larry, easily one of the best defenders in the league, was momentarily befuddled but recovered in time to bastinado the Smiler right on top of the noggin. Evans replied with a mashie shot to Zeidel's forehead and the latter quickly connected with a round-house clout to the Saskatooner's temple. By this time there was more blood on the ice, boards, and combatants than the Red Cross ever gets on a bumper day at the donors' clinic.

It was a savage and entirely unnecessary bit of brawling.

Your agent took a look at the Smiler in the Saskatoon dressing room after the game. He had been creased squarely across the crown. If Zeidel was a barber he couldn't have parted Evans' hair more neatly. All told, Evans took eight stitches, one less than the Edmonton defenceman.

The Smiler, who is usually about as garrulous as Rodin's statue "The Thinker," but not quite as meditative, had nothing derogatory to say about the fine league president Al Leader will undoubtedly levy.

"He was coming at me and I just raised my stick up to defend myself," Smiler said, as sombre as a 19th century tombstone. "That started it. I guess this just about clinches the league's badman title for me, eh? I wonder if I'll get fined for $25 or $50."

Although he actually weighs only a little more than 170 pounds, the Smiler has always been a brash young bruiser. When still a junior up from the Lethbridge Native Sons on a tryput with the old Lethbridge Maple Leafs in the late lamented Western Senior League, he had a barney with Pug Young, of fond Edmonton memory. Evans dumped the big Edmonton defenceman. On the next rush they had another brush and again Young went down. Looking up at Evans from his position on the ice, Pug uttered dire threats and questioned the rookie's ancestry. Smiler gave him a long smouldering glance and then shouted from deep in his throat, "I'll eat ya, ya bum, I'll eat ya."

From then on the boys were almost friendly.

Johnny Mitchell, Detroit Red Wings roving reporter, was pretty indignant about last night's incident.

"How do you like that Evans? What kind of a way to play hockey is that?" he demanded. "I saw the celebrated Kenny Reardon-Cal Gardner stick-swinging duel and it was nothing compared to this."

Bud Poile was somewhat distressed by the whole thing. He said both Evans and Zeidel are potential National Leaguers but that the former is hurting his chances by taking stupid penalties.

"Jack is really only hurting himself," the maestro concluded.

And that's just about the definitive word on the subject, thank you!

The Edmonton Flyers could score as well as fight. "Bronco Horvath was as clever a playmaker as you'll ever find," said New Jersey Devils vice president Max McNab, who had played and coached in the WHL with Vancouver. "And Johnny Bucyk was tough and fast. If you took the whole Edmonton team and went right down the line player for player, you'd have one of the best clubs of any era. How do you get better than Glenn Hall in goal?"

Edmonton's entry was not the only class team in Alberta. The 1952-53 edition of the Calgary Stampeders oozed with talent as well. The rivals met in the 1953 playoffs, a best of five series which was tied 2-2 after four games. In the deciding match at Calgary Corral the Flyers trailed by three goals with eight minutes remaining in the third period. Methodically, Edmonton then picked apart the enemy defense, trimming the score to 5-4 in the closing minutes. Poile then lifted goalie Hall and the Flyers pressed to the attack. Zeidel orchestrated the tying goal, sliding a pass to Bill Hughes who flipped home the rubber with eight seconds remaining. Edmonton then won the series on Ray Hannigan's goal in overtime.

Poile's warriors then took the league championship, otherwise known as the President's Cup, defeating the Saskatoon Quakers four games to two in the playoff finals.

Back in Detroit Jack Adams was all smiles. He knew that several plums were ripening on the Edmonton tree, not the least of whom were Vic Stasiuk, Earl Reibel, Al Arbour, Larry Wilson, Glenn Hall and Larry Zeidel.

Better still, two native Edmontonians would make it not only to Motor City and the NHL, but to even greater hockey acclaim, the Hockey Hall of Fame. One of them was Norm Ullman; the other, John Bucyk.

5

An Edmonton Boy Makes Good — And an Earlier Gretzky Comes to Town

Of all the modern, post-World War II hockey players developed in Edmonton who eventually made it to the NHL and the Hockey Hall of Fame, none has a more rags-to-riches story than John Bucyk. Born in Edmonton — he grew up at 12941 65th St. — Bucyk evolved as the young, quintessential Edmonton hockey player who would eventually turn pro.

Like many products of the Great Depression years, Bucyk had little in the way of material assets. "You've heard about the kid who grew up on the bad side of the tracks, the bad part of town . . . well, that's me," said Bucyk. "I lived in the north end of Edmonton and everybody used to call it the rough part of town. We weren't all that rough, at least I didn't think so, but it had that brand name. Actually, as a youngster, I lived in four houses at one time or another, but they were all in the same general area."

Canada already was immersed in the war effort when Johnny started stickhandling at the start of the 1940s. In his autobiography, *Hockey in My Blood*, Bucyk details his early efforts at learning the game in 1942 and 1943.

> I can remember playing street hockey when I was a kid, maybe seven or eight years old. In those days you couldn't afford to buy hockey sticks, nobody in our group could. I was from a

poor family and I really didn't know what it was to own a hockey stick, so I didn't care. I played a lot of street hockey and we used brooms for sticks. We couldn't afford pucks either, so we'd follow the milk wagon which was pulled by a couple of horses, waiting until the horses did their job, dropping a good hunk of manure. Usually it would be a cold day, anytime between the start of October through the end of April, and we'd let it freeze up solid. We'd use it as a hockey puck.

Most of the time we were able to use a softball or a tennis ball for a puck. The horse manure was only in case of an emergency. I didn't get my first pair of skates until I was about 10 years old. It was a pair of my older brother Bill's, which he outgrew. That's when I finally started skating. I wasn't any Bobby Orr, either.

The holidays weren't very exciting for us and I can remember that Christmas wasn't too grand either. We used to have a big Christmas dinner and perhaps get a couple of presents.

I always wanted a present to do with hockey. I can remember as a youngster we couldn't afford shin pads, so I'd get magazines and roll them up and put them underneath my pants. We didn't have gloves either, just ordinary mittens. I never really had any good hockey equipment until I got into organized hockey.

The best present I ever received was my first pair of skates. You see, up until then I was using an old pair of my brother's or I'd borrow a pair from somebody. It was just something else to get a Brand New pair of skates. Imagine, not having a used pair of skates or not having to borrow skates from somebody else. It sounds funny now, but at that time it was the biggest thrill of my life.

One of Bucyk's earlier teammates was Norm Ullman, who displayed even then the leadership he would show later as a big leaguer. Ullman was captain and center on the Edmonton Maple Leafs, a juvenile-age team, with Bucyk on left wing and Ron Tookey on the right. Bucyk recalls,

When I was playing juvenile hockey I played in more than one organization. I played for an intermediate team that was competing just in tournaments. Then I played with the juvenile league, and when I found time I'd play three or four hours a day with the kids after school. My mother always knew where to find me if I wasn't home. I was always at the rink just three blocks away from our home.

I was playing so much hockey I was missing a lot of school.

When the time came, during Grade 11, that I had the chance to play junior league hockey, I had to make a big decision. Detroit offered me a contract which wasn't very much money. $1,500 for a season, and they also found me a job. So I told my mother I thought I should quit school. She said it was my decision, but something I would always have to live with. She wasn't working then, she couldn't work because of her health and I wanted to help the family as much as I could, so I decided to become a professional hockey player and that's what I did.

The goal for any young Edmontonian was to climb the local hockey ladder to the professional ranks. This meant first graduating to the junior Edmonton Oil Kings and then, best of all, to the WHL Edmonton Flyers.

"My ambition had always been to play for the Edmonton Flyers," said Bucyk. "It was my hometown team. Frankly, I didn't even think about making it to Detroit."

Bucyk, of course, became a pivotal member of the Flyers organization in 1954-55 along with Ullman. They were to be complemented by yet another gifted stickhandler named Bronco Horvath. Eventually Bucyk, Horvath and Vic Stasiuk would make up the "Uke" line. Horvath was a deft stickhandler who frequently upset his coaches with wisecracks. Hall of Famer Gump Worsley describes him thusly:

> Bronco would be considered a flake today; he joked around a lot and didn't always take the game too seriously. But he was a good goal-scorer with eyes in the back of his head. He'd stand there with his back to the net, take a pass and flip it past the goaltender. Never looking.
>
> I used to ask Bronco how he mastered that trick and he'd wink and say, 'Practice Gump. Lots of practice.' Bullshit. He hated practice as much as I did.

The Edmonton Flyers in that 1954-55 season dazzled just about everyone with their footwork. "If there ever was a good reason for NHL expansion," said Max McNab, "that Edmonton team was it. They had second and third liners like Ray Hannigan, Jerry Melnyk, and Eddie Stankiewicz, who were good enough to play in the big time."

Another good one was forward Enio Sclisizzi. Enio was one of only two professional hockey players to have his name changed for the benefit of broadcasters. Sclisizzi's name was changed to "Jim Enio." (Interestingly, the other player whose name was changed was also a Detroit farmhand. Stephen Wojciechowski had his name changed to Steve Wochy.)

Not surprisingly, Edmonton reached the WHL playoff finals and knocked off Calgary with ease. In those days minor pro hockey had been lifted to the highest pro level in Canada and the western champs headed east to play their counterparts in Quebec for the Edinburgh Cup. This was a best of nine series which the Flyers lost five games to two, but not without a gallant effort from all hands. A number of Edmonton skaters had been riddled with injuries but fought valiantly to return. Typical was Larry Zeidel, who had been hit in the head by a puck and badly dazed. Zeidel recalled:

> Suddenly a guy walks in and it was the trainer, Tiger Goldstick. He looked at me and said, 'They don't call you Larry the Rock for nothing.' When I heard that I got up, even though my head was throbbing like crazy, and went back out on the ice. After the game, Tiger suggested that I go to the hospital to have my head examined. It turns out I played the game with a fractured skull, and brother was it ever serious. I wasn't even allowed visitors in the hospital and I lost my appetite which used to be huge.
>
> After the sixth day in the hospital I got very hungry all of a sudden and said 'the hell with this; I want to get back and help the team.' I got my clothes, sneaked out of the hospital, then went to a steakhouse and found my teammates. Meanwhile the doctors at the hospital didn't know what the heck had happened to me.

As it happened the Flyers realized that it would be ridiculous to allow anyone with a fractured skull back in the lineup. Zeidel was told thanks but no thanks and returned to Edmonton for further repairs. "It took me about two months to get over it," Zeidel recalled. "But I couldn't wait to get back into the lineup. Naturally we all had our hearts set on getting into the NHL. That was the ultimate. But we also realized that some of the best hockey in the world was being played in Edmonton in those days and some of the best players I've seen were in the WHL. They talk about Wayne Gretzky today like he's God and I can understand that. But we had a Wayne Gretzky of sorts in the old Western League and he had to be seen to be believed. His name was Guyle Fielder."

Like Gretzky, Fielder didn't look like a hockey player. Someone once said he had "the chest of a tubercular cadaver." Fielder was only 5 foot 9, 165 pounds, but his forearms and wrists were thick and strong as were his calves and ankles.

"He always looked like a guy who was about to break into a house," *Vancouver Sun* columnist Denny Boyd remembered. "He never shaved. He was gaunt, his face was an unhealthy color. Maybe the greatest stickhandler I've seen next to Gretzky. No speed, No speed at all. The rap on him was that he lived an unhealthy lifestyle. He drank whiskey."

More than that, he was a goal scorer and a playmaker supreme. He piled up over 2,000 scoring points and led the WHL in scoring eight times, and was selected to the All-Star team a dozen times. He scored more points in pro hockey than Gordie Howe and Rocket Richard, yet he never amounted to a hill of beans in the NHL.

"Lord knows the Red Wings sure tried to make an NHL star of him," said Zeidel, "but a lot of things worked against him."

One of them was Bud Poile who was running the Edmonton Flyers when Jack Adams dispatched Fielder to Edmonton in 1952. Unfortunately for Edmontonians, Fielder had more trouble with a personality collision off the ice than he did with any on-ice body check.

"Mr Poile and I didn't see eye to eye." Fielder said, adding that his problem with Poile could be traced to a party in Fielder's hotel room in Edmonton one night, when some friends from Nipawin dropped in with a few cases of beer. Poile's room was next door.

That did it. Poile moved Fielder to St. Louis of the American League and he never returned to play for Edmonton again, although he frequently visited during his long career, most of which was played in Seattle. Ironically, he had his best NHL chance in 1957 when Jack Adams elevated him to the Red Wings and had him center for Hall of Famers Gordie Howe and Ted Lindsay. While most professionals would have given anything to skate with Howe, Fielder suggests that the NHL immortal just about ruined his chances.

"It might have been a bit different if I had been able to play on the line without Howe. You see, he's the same type of player that I am. He liked to have control of the puck, make the plays, set up the others to score when he couldn't score himself. There wasn't much point in having both of us out there on the same line."

Fielder returned to the minors where he became a legend to those familiar with his play. *The Canadian Magazine* once described him as "The world's greatest hockey scorer — and you probably have never heard of him."

While Fielder starred in the minors, the likes of Bucyk, Horvath, and Ullman moved up to the NHL. The Flyers' crack goalie Glenn Hall — rated in *Hockey's 100* as the greatest goalie of all time — eventually moved up to the Red Wings, replacing Terry Sawchuk. Zeidel was signed by the Chicago Blackhawks, but played most of his career in the Western and American leagues. When the NHL expanded in 1967, he was a Flyer again, only this time in the NHL with Philadelphia.

Max McNab, who played center for the New Westminster Royals, has said that the Edmonton team, led by Hall, Bucyk and Horvath, was as good as any he's seen in its class.

"I had the pleasure of playing against the Edmonton Flyers for quite some time," says McNab, "and I can assure you that they were a remarkable group of athletes. And I don't mean just the Hall of Famers. I'm talking about people like Al Arbour, Hughie Coflin and Steve Hrymnak. All good men and solid performers."

Despite the high quality play, interest began lagging in the WHL and the Flyers were never to reach the plateau they achieved during the Hall-Bucyk era, although Edmonton did deliver quality teams through the early 1960s and captured the league title in 1960-61 with future Red Wings Billy McNeill, Eddie Joyal, Howie Young and Len Lunde in the lineup.

In many ways Howie Young was as colorful and tough as Larry Zeidel. Young, who played defense on the 1961-62 Flyers, was the *enfant terrible* of pro hockey. Columnist Dick Beddoes once said that Young would be the guy most likely to start the Third World War. "Not only would Young start the war," one critic has said, "after he got her lit, he'd run around looking for some gasoline to fling on the flames."

Although he was a native of Hamilton, Ontario, Young adopted Edmonton as his home. Upon his arrival he bought himself a pair of black cowboy boots, a black ten-gallon hat and a blue pair of Levi's. He palled around with a rodeo clown who owned a pet elephant. As one observer put it, "Howie Young adopted Edmonton and Edmonton adopted him."

Sometimes the love affair took some weird turns, as it did in the spring of 1962.

After helping the team win the WHL playoffs, Young returned to his Hamilton home and a few days later put on his cowboy clothing and drove to nearby Kitchener. The Edmonton Oil King Juniors, an affiliate of the WHL team, were playing the Hamilton Red Wings there in the Memorial Cup playoffs for Canada's coast-to-coast junior hockey title.

Young was rooting for Edmonton: so much so that during the time-outs he would climb onto the sideboards and act as a cheerleader. This infuriated Eddie Bush, the Hamilton coach. When Young strolled by the Hamilton bench they both began swinging.

Out of the crowd came a plainclothes detective to break up the fight and escort Young from the arena. Young began swinging again. The next day he was up on a charge of assault, causing bodily harm. The detective had a black eye and facial cuts, an ailing back and a bruised elbow. "All I knew," Howie says, "is that he was coming at me. I didn't know he was a cop." Young was fined $100 in lieu of a ten-day jail sentence. Red Wings coach, Sid Abel, who had witnessed the battle while scouting with his farmhands, shook his head and just about gave up on reforming his bellicose badman.

"It was embarrassing," Abel said, "seeing one of our players acting like that. But I knew I had to give Howie another chance. He has too much natural ability. And he really nails a guy. You need somebody like that on a hockey team."

Young straightened out long enough to work his way up to the NHL, although he remained a turbulent character throughout his lengthy hockey career. Meanwhile the Flyers gradually lost their hold on the Edmonton community. The ultimate irony occurred in 1962-63, the Flyers' last in the WHL. They were eliminated from the playoffs in sudden-death overtime by the Seattle Totems. None other than former Flyer Guy Fielder orchestrated the winning goal.

6

Down Go the Flyers — Up With the Oil Kings

The demise of the professional Edmonton Flyers had a pendulum effect on Edmonton hockey. While the pro game went down, the junior amateur game was on the rise. Again the Red Wings of Detroit had a hand in this, since they were directly linked with the Edmonton Oil Kings (let's not forget that Jack Adams was overseeing Edmonton's junior club back in the early 50s) for decades.

In fact, many a starry-eyed skater got his first big break with an Edmonton junior club even before World War II, although Edmonton failed to win the Memorial Cup until 1963.

"If you check the rosters of the pre-World War II teams in Edmonton," said Max McNab, "you'll find some big names in hockey. A lot of people have forgotten that two-thirds of one of the NHL's finest-ever lines — the Colvilles and Shibicky — had its roots in Edmonton."

Neil and Mac Colville eventually teamed up with Alex Shibicky to help the Rangers win the 1940 Stanley Cup, the last ever seen on Broadway. But to reach the NHL, the Colvilles cut their puck teeth on outdoor ice rinks in Edmonton. The brothers starred for the Edmonton Athletic Club in 1933-34 and were eventually spotted by Ranger scouts. Their style was reminiscent of the Cook brothers, Bill and Bun, of an earlier era.

Hall of Famer Frank Boucher, who played alongside the Cooks and who later became Rangers coach and manager, was one of the first NHLers to view the Colvilles in Edmonton.

"They knew their routine perfectly," said Boucher. "They swooped over the ice with the precision of a flying circus."

While the Colvilles performed like twins, they had contrasting personalities. Boucher recalled,

> Neil, the center, was the spearhead, a fine puck-carrier and playmaker who employed a very deceptive body movement to throw the defense off balance. He was a handsome, prematurely grey-haired fellow, very pleasant and outgoing. Mac, his brother, wore a frown as his normal expression, was reserved and remote. We called him our Dour Scot. He was a blond and blocky rightwinger of 5 foot 8, a tough little fireplug and a tireless worker.

The Colvilles were not only sharpshooters, they were inventive. In fact, one of big league hockey's most innovative moves was credited to Neil. During his early NHL career, it was Neil Colville who devised the idea of offensive rather than defensive penalty killing when the Rangers were shorthanded. Why go on the defensive, Colville reasoned, when attack could turn out to be the best defense.

"This was a most unusual concept", Boucher said, "which grabbed my imagination, and we practiced it very carefully a number of times, working out each man's logistics. Of course, it might backfire, and we could look ridiculous. We chose Art Coulter as an anchor man, instructing him to play the whole length of the opposing team's blue line while three forwards — the Colvilles and Shibicky — prowled like nightfighters inside it. The tactic was enormously successful, partly because it was so unexpected and partly because of the men involved — each swift, a tough checker and a good shot. Over the season we outscored our opponents almost two to one when we were shorthanded.

"With this system we also developed a box defense for our own end which we used when we were trapped there. Our players formed a loose square in front of Kerr and diverted incoming attackers to the sides so that any shots on goal were from bad angles and Davey needed only to play those angles. The system is still the basic concept of man-short defense in the NHL."

The Colvilles left Edmonton in the mid 1930s, playing first for the Rangers' Eastern League farm team, the Crescents, and then the Rovers, both in New York. Then they moved up to the big club, starring alongside Shibicky. They were a fascinating trio but, as good as they were, they never reached their potential. Some observers thought the problem was that Shibicky, who packed a dynamite shot, often failed to convert the excellent passes supplied by the Colvilles.

Boucher commented, "Often, though, Alex would hold it too long, seeking a little better position, and you'd hear the gang on the bench go through a ritual when Alex waited, 'Shoot, Shibicky . . . Shoot, Shibicky . . . Ah, shit, Shibicky.' He got his share of goals; we just felt he could have scored more."

The Edmonton junior scene continued to sparkle through the war years and through the post-war era. Hall of Famer Bill Gadsby, for example, starred for the Edmonton Canadians in 1945-46. Another member of that team was Cy Thomas, who was the forgotten player in one of hockey's greatest trades. In 1947 the Maple Leafs sent five players, Gaye Stewart, Bud Poile, Ernie Dickens, Bob Goldham and Gus Bodnar, to the Chicago Black Hawks for the immortal Max Bentley. Cy Thomas was the throw-in along with Bentley. (And for good reason; he simply couldn't cut it in the NHL and disappeared in a short time.)

It was the source of continued annoyance to the Edmontonians that the city simply could not produce a Memorial Cup winner, although Calgary had won the Cup in 1926. The 1953-54 Oil Kings came close with Norm Ullman and Johnny Bucyk leading the way to the finals against the St. Catharines' Tee Pees. But the western skaters couldn't compete, losing 8-1, 5-3, 4-1, tying 3-3 and losing the finale, 6-2. In a sense, the loss was difficult to swallow for Ullman and company. They had more stars than the easterners, but a two-and-a-half week lay-off forced upon Edmonton because the Eastern play-offs were dragging left the Oil Kings jaded. Whatever the case, the Memorial drought continued through the start of the next decade. But it finally ended in 1962-63 when an Edmonton club coached by Buster Brayshaw encountered the Niagara Falls Flyers, a club oozing with talent. After dropping the first two games, the Oil Kings thundered back to defeat the easterners. Among the Edmonton stars were the Oilers' current boss Glen Sather and his Vancouver Canucks counterpart Pat Quinn.

After waiting more than three decades to grab the junior hockey crown, the Oil Kings would win a second Memorial

Cup within three years, this time with Wild Bill Hunter at the helm. (It's noteworthy that the Edmonton Oil Kings Alumni paid tribute to Hunter on April 15, 1988.) Several of the Oil Kings would, in time, follow Hunter into the World Hockey Association with his Alberta Oilers.

The alternate captain of the junior squad, Al Hamilton, would go on to captain the Oilers. In addition, Jim Harrison would emerge as the club 's premier forward at the start of the WHA run. Hunter's stint with the Oil Kings would establish him as one of North America's most arresting hockey people and guarantee that Edmonton would be represented in any major league venture if a second top-of-the-line hockey league emerged to challenge the NHL.

In the meantime, Hunter continued to produce star-laden outfits. While he was busily engaged in formulating the WHA, Wild Bill still had time to devote to a club that reached Memorial Cup finals in Ottawa. However, they were edged out by both Cornwall and Peterborough. The Cornwall Royals went on to win the Memorial Cup.

While this was a blow to Wild Bill, he was ready to take on the biggest challenge of his life, the creation of a hockey league that would compete with the almighty NHL. Even in the minds of optimists, this was an absurd undertaking.

"But one thing we've learned over the years in hockey," concluded Max McNab, "is never to underestimate the persuasive powers of Bill Hunter."

The words would prove prophetic, although there was a large bloc of power brokers who remained convinced for a long, long time that the concept of a World Hockey Association was an enormous joke.

Most of these powerbrokers were owners of National Hockey League teams. If there was anything that they believed impossible, it was that cities such as Winnipeg, Quebec and Edmonton could support major league hockey.

And Edmonton was at the very bottom of their list.

7

The Big Break — Birth of the WHA

As far as the National Hockey League was concerned — and the U.S. media, which helped influence NHL policy — Edmonton was a distant spot on the North American map which could be reasonably equated with Lompoc, California, Split, Yugoslavia and Clermont L'Hereault, France. It was nice to know that it existed, but any chance of its acceptance into the real world of big-league hockey could only be found in comic books.

The long and seemingly endless maze which eventually ended at the NHL's doorstep began for Edmonton's hockey promoters in the early 1960s, specifically the night in 1961 when former Edmonton Flyers Glenn Hall and Al Arbour paced the Chicago Black Hawks to the Stanley Cup. Not only did the occasion mark the first Chicago hockey championship since 1938, but it also signalled the beginning of an NHL renaissance that was almost a decade in the making.

Just ten years earlier the entire foundation of the six-team league was trembling to the very core. Both the Black Hawks and the Bruins were suffering terrible losses at the gate and there was serious talk of the NHL losing at least one, if not two, franchises. Realizing the need for bolstering their American cousins, the more successful Montreal Canadiens and Toronto Maple Leafs agreed with the weaker teams that a "Help The Poor" movement was necessary. The Canadiens, for example, virtually *gave* Chicago top notch young forward

Ed Litzenberger just to keep the Black Hawks in business. Litzenberger, in turn, became team captain and was a key factor in the 1961 Cup win.

The NHL governors also agreed that a more vigorous approach was needed in building The Game, especially in the weaker cities. Taking the cue, the Wirtz family, owners of the Black Hawks, launched an energetic movement, luring Tommy Ivan away from the Detroit Red Wings where he had been a successful coach, naming him manager and starting a far-flung farm system.

It worked. In a few years such future luminaries as Bobby Hull, Stan Mikita, Elmer Vasko and Pierre Pilote were developed on the Black Hawks' farm and graduated to the big club. At about the same time the Maple Leafs' system was producing the likes of Frank Mahovlich, Bob Pulford, Carl Brewer and Bob Baun, complementing a number of other young stars glittering around the league firmament.

As a result the NHL's attendance curve took a dramatic turn upward — the Bruins remained a terrible team through the first half of the 1960s, but were bolstered by a loyal following and the knowledge that soon young Bobby Orr would be the club's saviour — and when Chicago won The Cup in 1961, just about every professional connected with The Game realized that he stood on the brink of a bonanza not unlike the one in 1924 when big league hockey invaded the United States in a big way.

The difference in NHL thinking in 1924 and 1964 when arenas were bulging at capacity is fascinating. During the early 1920s, NHL leaders leaped at expansion, whereas two decades later their successors regarded expansion as some mystifying threat, like leaves which resemble poison ivy, yet *could* be harmless. Conn Smythe of Toronto, James Norris, Jr. in Detroit and Arthur Wirtz of Chicago all opposed expansion, and they represented the power base of the league.

"I find it very difficult to sell myself on the idea to get even two new teams in the NHL," said Norris in 1965. "That would mean we'd lose four games with the Canadiens and four with the Maple Leafs and I find it difficult to believe that I'm going to substitute eight games with Los Angeles or San Francisco for eight games with the Canadiens or Maple Leafs."

Conn Smythe concurred, "New York and Boston keep drawing because there are only six teams in the league. So you've always got an attraction coming in. But if you had two more teams that couldn't win games, it would be different. If you had four rotten teams in the league, you'd have a hell of a time getting people in the rink. They wouldn't buy season tickets for thirty-five games a year, knowing they had to take fifteen or twenty lousy games. Two more bad teams would make ten more bad games."

Smythe and Norris invariably were seconded by the most important non-owner, league president Clarence Campbell, who, as one NHL critic noted, "held his job by reflecting accurately the sentiments of the NHL owners." When Smythe and Norris said nix to expansion, Campbell quickly fell into step. "Expansion talk," said Campbell in 1965, "is newspaper talk. There's nobody who can create a new league faster than a columnist."

But Campbell didn't bargain for some executive changes in the league power structure that would forever alter his influence. A New York lawyer named William "Bill" Jennings had become president of the Rangers in the early 1960s and by 1965 had become a formidable league power broker. At the same time Conn Smythe, aging and less interested in hockey than ever before, retreated from the Toronto scene and delivered the reins to his rambunctious son, Stafford. To everyone's amazement, Stafford ignored his father's wishes and began campaigning for expansion, as did Jennings.

Since two out of six is not a majority, the Young Turks, as they were known by now in league circles, needed more allies. The decisive personality was J. David Molson, president of the Canadiens, who sided with the Turks. With a three-three deadlock, the expansionists looked to Boston for help. Bruins' owner Weston Adams, Sr. was from the old school, but he sympathized with Jennings, *et al* and so did his heir, Weston Adams, Jr. In Detroit, James Norris' son, Bruce, had taken over and, almost overnight, the Turks found themselves in command. Even Clarence Campbell, sensing change, began moving closer to the expansion bloc.

The final turnabout occurred late in 1965 when the Turks, at a league meeting in New York, produced a blueprint for expansion. No fewer than *six* new teams would be welcome in a new, second division of the NHL. Old Jim Norris was appalled, but he was now in the minority. Both he and Conn Smythe — still around but less influential — made one last lobbying effort. Their theory was that expansion would seriously dilute the talent base and cause a severe loss of fans. To that, Molson replied: "Expansion wouldn't dilute interest, it would increase it."

Less than a year later Smythe was pushed off his power base at Maple Leaf Gardens and Norris was dead. For the first time even Campbell began talking as if the 12-team NHL was not a bad idea. "I'm not anti-expansionist," said the league president, "but I'm solid for the economics, and I think that's my primary responsibility."

Not long afterward — early in 1966 — the green light was given to double the NHL's size. Publicly at least, Campbell gave the move his enthusiastic backing and the impossible happened — Los Angeles, St. Louis, Oakland, Philadelphia, Pittsburgh and Minnesota were welcomed to the club. The Kings, Blues, Seals, Flyers, Penguins and North Stars would form the West Division for the start of play in 1967-68.

After a year of play both the skeptics and optimists had something to crow about. Conn Smythe's concerns about dilution of talent were valid. Some of the new teams looked like glorified — if that — American Hockey League teams. The West Division Stanley Cup finalists turned out to be the Blues, a club that looked pathetically inept in losing four straight games to the Cup-winning Canadiens.

But the expansionists could point to growing fan interest in most of the six new cities and promise that there would be better days and nights ahead. Although Oakland proved to be a sore point and proof that NHL hockey doesn't guarantee success *everywhere*, representatives from other cities clamored for new NHL franchises. A good reason for this was the arrival of Bobby Orr and the emergence of his "Big, Bad Bruins" as Stanley Cup champions in 1970. Orr, Phil Esposito, Gerry Cheevers and Derek Sanderson converted the once hapless Bruins into the NHL's new glamor franchise. In addition Bobby Hull, now known as "The Golden Jet", was dazzling fans with his slapshot, Mahovlich had become a living legend in Toronto while Rod Gilbert, Ed Giacomin and Jean Ratelle were turning heads in Manhattan. NHL hockey had gained a foothold on U.S. network television and the price of franchises began climbing from the original $2 million tab affixed in 1966.

Buffalo and Vancouver bidders were tickled to pay more and be welcomed to the NHL in 1970. The addition of two teams, fattening the league to 14 clubs, did not satisfy all those clamoring for a big-league team, but NHL moguls didn't seem to mind. The new clubs were gaining in attendance and all signs pointed to long-term success in Minnesota, Philadelphia, St. Louis and Pittsburgh, while Los Angeles was a bit on the iffy side and Oakland remained a migraine.

That hardly deterred entrepreneurs in Cleveland, Houston, Providence and St. Paul, not to mention Canadian centers such as Edmonton, Winnipeg, Quebec City and Ottawa. Once Vancouver joined the NHL fold — and was an instant hit, gatewise — many Canadians believed that it was their divine right for other cities to follow into the big time.

At this juncture there were two conflicting views within the league. One bloc urged another massive expansion along the lines of the 1966 decision to add a half-dozen teams at one time, while more conservative elements suggested that a gradual long-term growth be the mode.

In the end the conservatives won and because they did, Edmonton ultimately obtained a big-league franchise; not, however, because the NHL *wanted* Edmonton (or Winnipeg or Quebec City, for that matter), but rather because the only major league at the time was determined to keep the Canadian cities out!

Some Canadians had the insight to realize that the anti-Edmonton, etc. feelings would do the NHL damage in the long run. They foresaw a dramatic move from *without* that would directly challenge the established league. They remembered how Al Leader had tried to promote a major league in the west when he urged the NHL to accept major cities of the old Western Hockey League and have two circuits. The NHL ignored Leader and expanded on its own, but Leader's motive was not forgotten.

Said David Molson, the most prophetic of all the NHL leaders,

> If we keep matters as they are, a new league could start on its own, and we'd have a lot of headaches. You just can't tell people forever and ever that they're going to be minor league and there's nothing they can do about it, because there *is* something they can do about it. They can say, 'Well, why shouldn't we class ourselves as major league hockey? We'll start our own league. We'll raid the NHL. We'll sign their players. We'll offer these guys *x* hundred thousand.' There's nothing to stop them.

Then you get into lawsuits, anti-trust actions, and everything else. This is all a definite possibility.

To this day NHL bosses, stung for millions of dollars by lawsuits and anti-trust actions, among other headaches, rue the day they ignored Molson's warning. As Molson spoke, plans were afoot to re-shape the big-league hockey map, although it would take considerable time, haggling, *more* haggling and agony before the blueprints were finally put in place.

Actually, one must flip the calendar back two decades to better understand the NHL arrogance which helped the World Hockey Association come into being. In May 1952 Jim Hendy, general manager of Cleveland Barons, thought that his club was on the verge of leaving the American Hockey League to become the NHL's seventh member. It had taken six months of beaverish activity to reach this point. A Cleveland sports columnist was so optimistic, he wrote: "Our city has been awarded a franchise in the NHL. This is the most pleasurable news of the year."

But the NHL works in funny ways, as Hendy would discover to his lifetime dismay. Despite all indications that the Barons were "in," two months later they were rejected. Frivolous reasons were offered in the rejection and when they weren't frivolous they were fatuous. Hendy was furious, but he had no recourse at the time. Some 20 years later Nick Mileti, another Cleveland sportsman, *would* have recourse.

Mileti had come to NHL expansion meetings certain that he would gain an NHL franchise for Cleveland where a new arena was being built. "Instead," said one of Mileti's friends, "he was treated rudely and looked elsewhere to place a hockey team." Multiply the Mileti experience by ten and you have an idea why the World Hockey Association's time had come.

Certainly, Gary Davidson and Dennis Murphy sensed the moment. It was to these Californians, of all people, that Edmonton would owe a lasting debt when it came to the birth of the Oilers. Neither the slim, blond attorney Davidson nor the chubby Murphy knew the difference between a hockey puck and a piece of pasta, but they did know plenty about promoting.

"They had watched the NHL expansion and decided that it wasn't doing enough," said Marty Blackman, a lawyer who helped organize the WHA in 1971. "Their ignorance of hockey was irrelevant. What mattered was that they were willing to fill a void that needed to be filled. They saw how Edmonton, Winnipeg, Cleveland and other potential NHL cities were being by-passed. Unlike the NHL, they were willing to gamble."

And gamble they did — in spades. Granted, they weren't "hockey men," but each had the personality and energy to make their project move. Murphy had once been mayor of the 68,000 citizens of Buena Park, California, and later a general manager in the American Basketball Association. A graduate of UCLA Law School, Davidson was once a four-sport letterman in football, baseball, basketball and track in high school and eventually became a founding partner in the ABA. On a brisk afternoon in January 1971 Murphy phoned his pal, Davidson, and said it was time they took their ABA expertise and applied it to the ice.

"The National Hockey League has had the run of things," said Murphy. "It's about time *we* formed a league and took a run at them."

Davidson begged for time, said he wanted to think about it. Three months later he phoned Murphy back and said the plan made sense. They convened and ordered a feasibility study to determine whether there was room for another major league of hockey. When the survey was completed, it reported in the affirmative. The articles of incorporation were filed in Delaware on June 10, 1971, for the World Hockey Association. The pair then began a series or flights crisscrossing North America in search of backers. Their first break came when Los Angeles tax expert Charles Abrahams, who negotiated for many NHL players, endorsed the Murphy-Davidson plan. "Don't sign anything but a one-year contract," he warned his NHL clients, "a new hockey league is on the horizon and you may be able to make a lot more money in it than in the NHL."

After contacting Abrahams, Murphy and Davidson had the wisdom to realize that their hockey ignorance would be a shortcoming in the months to come. "They understood," said Marty Blackman, "that the place to go for hockey know-how was Canada and that's what led them to Bill Hunter in Edmonton."

It would be a fateful meeting for all parties.

8

A Baby League Grows in Spite of the NHL

If the character, Bill Hunter, were created in Hollywood, the critics no doubt would say it was too much of a put-on. "Wild Bill," as he is affectionately known to friends and foe alike, is a combination huckster, showman, supersalesman — skeptics would call him a con man, others would say super optimist — and consummate lover of hockey.

"There isn't an actor in Hollywood who could play Bill," said Larry Zeidel. "He would have to play himself." *Edmonton Journal* columnist John Short, who goes back with Hunter to Bill's days as a junior Hockey entrepreneur, is no less enthralled by Wild Bill.

Hunter's life has been the stuff of legends, said Short. "No television serial in history provided more entertainment than his morning news conferences. Except, maybe, his afternoon news conferences or those he conducted in the evening. My all-time favorite was a function he designed in Moscow in 1974, after questionable officiating left the WHA's Team Canada with no chance to win an eight-game series against the Soviet Union.

Hunter called the news conference in the bowels of Luzhniki Arena to explain he was taking his marbles — er, his players — and going home. He asked, no instructed, me to file my game-over story as quickly as possible to the Canadian Press because 'the sports fans of our great country deserve to know exactly what's going on over here.'

I followed orders.

By the time I returned, Hunter insisted the final two games

would not be played. Money was no object. There was a principle involved. He did not identify it. One question begged to be asked: How could the financially-strapped WHA survive without guaranteed television revenues? What kind of bleep are you, Hunter thundered. Some kind of Communist?

He thundered and blustered as only he could, then declared the news conference over.

The series went on, of course, just as Bill Hunter does. None of that would have been possible without a WHA and those who were there at the very start insist that there never — *absolutely* never — would have been a WHA were it not for Wild Bill's energy, confidence and salesmanship. One could safely say that Wayne Gretzky would no doubt be skating today for the New York Rangers or Chicago Black Hawks had there not been a Bill Hunter to hitch his wagon to this new league which ultimately would bring Edmonton — and Gretzky — into the NHL.

Ironically, Hunter did not even know the plans for the WHA were afoot when Davidson and Murphy planted the WHA seeds on a California beach. Curiously, it was a transplanted Edmontonian (by way of Viking, Alberta) who was directly responsible for luring Hunter into the WHA fold and thereby getting the league on track. The chief protagonist, although he received very little credit, was *Los Angeles Herald Examiner* sportswriter Walt Marlow who had been a hockey nut since his teenage years in Edmonton. Marlow was working in his newspaper office when he saw the original communique for the WHA.

"It was just one paragraph about a second major hockey league," Marlow recalled. "There was no detail, but it intrigued me and I chased down Davidson and Murphy to get more information."

In no time at all Marlow was having regular meetings with the entrepreneurs. The more he heard about the venture, the more he liked it. Most of all, he was intrigued by the WHA's plan to bring big league hockey to western Canada.

"Right off the bat I knew they knew nothing about hockey and I knew plenty," Marlow asserted. "What they needed most of all was a good western Canadian contact. It so happened that I was heading to Edmonton for a visit with my father and I decided to see what I could do when I got there."

When Marlow got to Edmonton he sought a meeting with

Bill Hunter, although the two had not worked together before. Still, Marlow was smart enough to realize that Wild Bill was the hockey prince of Edmonton at the time, although his roots went back to Saskatoon. After leaving Saskatoon for Edmonton, Bill became immersed in the Alberta junior hockey scene. As co-owner of the Edmonton Oil Kings, Wild Bill had become one of the most prominent power brokers — and the most vocal — in western Canada.

"To my amazement," Marlow recalls, "Bill had not even heard of the WHA. But once I explained it to him, he became more and more interested and everyone knows what happened from there — Bill was as responsible for putting the league on the map as anyone."

With Marlow's help, of course. The newspaperman jetted south from Edmonton and became the liaison between his California pals Davidson and Murphy, and the great mover and shaker, Hunter. "Once I got them together," Marlow explained, "Gary and Dennis suddenly had the benefit of a hockey promoter who knew the ice game inside out. Better yet, they had a Canadian right from the heart of hockey country. And on top of that from a city that was dying for big-league hockey."

With Hunter in the fold, Davidson and Murphy sought other Canadian contacts and got them in Calgary and Winnipeg. R. "Bob" Brownridge was the pivotal personality in Calgary. He had been active and involved in the oil industry for 23 years and was associated with Bow Valley Industries. He was also the manager of Hi Tower Drilling Company and organized the Calgary Junior Centennials of the Western Canada Hockey League. He guided the team, together with his partner Scotty Munro, to four years of outstanding success. In addition, Brownridge played hockey for 13 years and in 1945-46 was a member of the Calgary Stampeders team which had won the Allan Cup. His sidekick Munro had entered the management and coaching end of the hockey business in 1942 after being a dedicated player as a youngster.

In Winnipeg the WHA promoters cultivated the friendship of wealthy Ben Hatskin who had once been a center for the Winnipeg Blue Bombers back in 1941 and since then had gone on to establish himself as one of the most important businessmen in Canada. He had also been involved with the Winnipeg Esquires and the East Kildonan Bisons, both successful hockey teams. He was president of Lodge Investments Limited, Wildwood Investments Shopping Centers, Hatskin Timber Company, Hatskin Containers, Universal Music Manitoba, Triangle Acceptance, Southland Management and James Realty, and president of the Winnipeg entry in the Western Canada Junior Hockey League.

"If we hadn't gotten Hunter, Brownridge, and Hatskin," said Murphy, "it would have been unlikely the league would have survived beyond that point."

Hunter was important because of his limitless hockey contacts. Hatskin and Brownridge were vital because of their money. By now the WHA concept was out in the open and was openly scorned by the NHL, its hirelings and friends. Davidson and Murphy were unconcerned. They had lined up interested parties in New York, Miami, San Francisco, Dayton, Chicago, Los Angeles, St. Paul, Winnipeg, Calgary, and Edmonton.

By October 1971, the WHA was producing a chain reaction of news stories to compete with the opening of the NHL season. One of the biggest was delivered on October 20, when Davidson announced that the WHA would operate without a reserve clause or "any substitute therefore, such as an option clause," in all player contracts.

On November 1, 1971, the WHA made its first big splash with the national media, following two days of meetings at the Americana Hotel in New York. It was then the WHA was formally organized and, following a gala luncheon, Davidson, Murphy, and Hunter told the audience that the new league was "here to stay."

Only a handful in the audience took them seriously. The skeptics said there were too many problems. Many of the cities had inadequate arenas. Others were in relatively small metropolitan areas. But mostly the question was asked: "Where are they going to get the players?"

Without saying so, the WHA owners made it abundantly clear they intended to get them from the NHL. At one of the meetings each owner put four players on his negotiation list. "I hope nobody else has Bobby Hull," said Hatskin, "because I've got his name on my list." Then, a warning to his colleagues: "Don't any of you try for Bobby. I can get him and you can't."

Later, Hatskin confided that his bravado was not fully supported by the facts. "I wasn't sure I could get Hull. But I had to show confidence."

It was precisely Hatskin's and Hunter's brand of confidence that inspired several of the other less confident franchise holders. Shortly after the Manhattan meetings, Steve Arnold, who had been a partner in the sports representation firm of Pro Sports, Inc., was signed as WHA director of player personnel. Lee Meade, former sports editor of *The Denver Post*, was named public relations director.

A month later the first former NHL employee signed with the new league when Vern Buffey signed as referee-in-chief. In the meantime, Hatskin was doing what few people ever thought he would do; he went after Bobby Hull. They met at the Hotel Vancouver when the Chicago Black Hawks were on a road trip in the B.C. metropolis. Hatskin offered the Golden Jet $1,000,000 for five years. "I just pulled the figure out of my head," Hatskin later confessed. "The figure $1,000,000 always gets a lot of attention."

Hull was privately enthusiastic because he had experienced several annoying contract problems with the Black Hawks front office. But he was also cautious. "Let's wait on it," said Hull, who then contacted his financial adviser Harvey S. Wineberg.

"If Hatskin is serious," said Wineberg, "you'll hear from him again."

He did, but Hull referred Hatskin to Wineberg. The financial adviser wanted more money for this client. By February 1972 the figure had climbed to $2,000,000 and was still climbing.

Davidson and Murphy were also busy trying to consolidate the franchises, which was not easy. The Dayton franchise was switched to Houston; San Francisco was moved to Quebec City; and Milwaukee dropped out of the picture altogether. But the biggest noise of all was heard on February 27, 1972, when Toronto Maple Leafs goaltender Bernie Parent jetted to Miami to announce that he ws going to leave the NHL and sign with the Miami Screaming Eagles. For the first time, the NHL was in a state of shock.

The fact that Parent, one of the NHL's best young goaltenders, would dare leave his team in mid-season, fly down to Florida, and announce he was prepared to quit the NHL suddenly lent credence to the rumors that Bobby Hull was, in fact, thinking of leaving the NHL too.

"I'd like to stay in Chicago," said Hull, "but I don't expect the Wirtzes to match the offer Winnipeg is making. The new league might need me a lot more than the Black Hawks will."

The race for Hull's signature symbolizes the WHA's *élan*. Unlike conservative NHL types, the WHA promoters were flamboyant to a fault. For example, when Marty Blackman, who was involved with the original New York WHA team, wanted a manager, he thought big. The first thing he did was ask a hockey writer for advice.

"You need a big name," the reporter advised. "Go for the best. Phone Rocket Richard. See if he's interested."

Blackman got on the blower to Montreal. Hello, Maurice Richard, would you be interested in managing the New York team in the World Hockey Association? "What da hell," asked the Rocket, "is da World Hockey Association?"

After listening to a brief explanation, Richard said in so many French-Canadian words thanks-but-no-thanks, and added that he wanted to see it to believe it. (A few years after the WHA was born, The Rocket was hired to coach the Quebec Nordiques. He quit after a week; it was too hard on his nerves.)

It appeared that Alberta would have two WHA representatives, Edmonton and Calgary. But in April 1972, just a week before a WHA meeting in Chicago, Scotty Munro announced that Calgary was dropping out of the WHA picture. (Brownridge had been forced to step down from his post as president of the Broncos and Centennials because of health reasons.)

"I have made up my mind that I'm personally not interested in world hockey," he said. "I've worked for many years to get a major junior hockey league in the west and for it to be a development league for professional players . . . that's what we have now. And it's a great product."

This was a cruel blow, viewed by citizens of Winnipeg and Edmonton as a double cross. *Edmonton Journal* columnist Wayne Overland described the move as calamitous. "The WHA was in its most serious crisis yet," said Overland.

Dennis Murphy agreed. "If somebody wanted to torpedo our league," Murphy stormed, "they couldn't have picked a better time to do it. The week of the bonding meeting."

But the WHA survived Calgary's exit and continued threats from the NHL. Wild Bill Hunter was now leading the charge and with evangelical fervor; he would counterattack every NHL assault. "I had always thought that there was no such thing as a healthy monopoly," said Hunter. "For 36 years before Vancouver entered the NHL there were only two cities in all of Canada represented in major pro hockey. Now, good young players have a choice between the two leagues."

Perhaps the most persuasive argument in *favor* of the WHA came from NHL president Clarence Campbell who uttered the deathless comment, "the new league will never get off the ground."

Hunter scoffed at Campbell and began putting together "Alberta's first major league team" and he did so in his typical frenzy. "Bill had two men helping him at the start," Marlow recalled. "One was Zane Feldman and the other was Doctor Charles Allard."

Dr. Allard was a practicing medical doctor in Edmonton who held vast real estate and investment interests not only in Canada, but in the United States. Feldman was president of Crosstown Motor City, Canada's largest Dodge Chrysler Dealer, and president of numerous related automotive service companies. He was vice-president of Allarco Developments, a diversified public company listed on the Toronto stock exchange, and the North West Trust Company.

Hunter realized that Edmonton could not get by with its antideluvian 5,800-seat arena. But the WHA concept had already set the sporting juices flowing throughout the city. "Once Bill got the team in motion," said Marlow, "everyone knew it would be only a matter of time before Northlands Coliseum went up. And it wasn't a very long time at that."

The speed of Edmonton's development as a big league hockey town was in direct relationship to Hunter's speaking pace. One observer remarked that Bill developed the press conference "into an art form resembling a cross between a pep rally and a sales meeting. Consequently, there is usually little news value in a Bill Hunter press conference. However, the entertainment and propaganda content is high."

The essence of Hunter is comprehended in a Walt Marlow comment: "Bill Hunter would call a press conference just to announce a press conference." Digest for a moment the content of one of his typical press conferences. A transcript of a 1972 edition follows.

Bill Hunter on Criticism of the WHA

I welcome criticism. I expect heaps of criticism. Criticism is healthy. But there's a hell of a lot of people with that "can't do" in their blood and they are going to be left in the dust of our success.

On WHA Finance

I find finance the dullest subject in the world. The game is the important thing. Does anybody ask about NHL finance? I know of NHL contracts that haven't been paid. Does anybody remember that Pittsburgh and Oakland went bankrupt and the NHL had to guarantee the salaries? Alan Eagleson [NHL Players' Association executive director] has publicly stated before myself and other witnesses that he is satisfied our contracts will be paid. Our league office will have $1.2 million bonding those contracts.

On WHA Franchises

A writer from Sports Illustrated asked me how many disasters we were going to have. I told him not to worry about disasters, everybody will be amazed at our success. After 50 years the NHL had six franchises. In our first year we will have 12 franchises. Even if we had eight, wouldn't that be outstanding success?

On Questions

You can ask any questions, and I'm not afraid to answer them. But don't ask any foolish questions, because I don't answer foolish questions.

On Signing Players

I am confident we could almost name our lineup right now. And I guarantee you this, it will be major league hockey at its best. There are two challenges in signing players. First, every man fears change, so that man must be sold. Secondly, the easy thing would be to go bankrupt. You have to be realistic signing players. Any player who talks to me about placing the money for a three-year contract in the bank before he signs won't be talking to me 10 minutes later. Who pays before they get performance? This is a business. Does the storekeeper pay for his goods three years in advance?

On an Edmonton Arena

The WHA can't exist in the Gardens for any number of seasons. This must be the smallest arena anybody ever entered major league sport with. If the city of Edmonton doesn't announce an arena in the next two months, we'll build one ourselves. Because no community needs an areana more than ours.

On WHA Coaching

We'll put our team together first and attend to the coaching later.

On Season Ticket Sales

There can't be many disbelievers, because people are buying our season tickets like hot cakes, and we aren't out making calls yet. Just this morning somebody phoned the office for 10. We won't sell more than 20 to one individual or organization, because we only have 4,500 season tickets available. We've sold or invoiced about a third of those.

On Free Tickets

Gentlemen, tell your companies to buy their season tickets now, because with only 5,200 seats in the building, there will be no free tickets. Even Bill Hunter will pay to get in.

While Hunter charmed many with his gift of gab, there was just as significant a bloc of skeptics who were convinced that the redhead was full of apple sauce. When Hunter was busy spreading the WHA gospel in January 1972, dissenters such as Dale Eisler of the *Moose Jaw Times-Herald* were just as quick to dismiss Bill as a con man and the WHA as a joke. Eisler, in one of the most devastating put-downs of Wild Bill and his still unborn league, put it this way in a column on January 19, 1972.

If you were wondering about the World Hockey Association, don't.

Bashful Bill Hunter, a general manager of the Edmonton organization which hopes to have a squad in the new circuit next fall, was in the middle of some more publicity-seeking speculation Tuesday.

In a published report Edmonton was said to have placed Norm Ullman of the Toronto Maple Leafs, Bruce McGregor of the New York Rangers and Cesare Maniago of the Minnesota North Stars on its negotiation list.

The purpose of the negotiation list is to gain sole bargaining rights with a player that a team is interested in. With the person's name on the scroll, no other team can court the same player until he is removed from all ties with the interested employer.

Edmonton's move is all on the horizontal, but it sounds more impressive than it is practical.

What National Hockey League player whose threads haven't worn thin on his bolt would consider gambling with the WHA? The credibility gap between the two leagues is too great for an established NHL-er to consider seriously taking the leap.

Publicity

By making statements like the aforementioned, the WHA receives all kinds of publicity which in turn creates an air of plausibility.

The twist to the latest WHA ploy is found in a statement by Hunter regarding the announcement: "Any speculation or publicity at this time could damage our chances of signing players. However, I guarantee Edmonton sports fans that we will announce major names in hockey before the puck drops next October."

Why wait until October, Bill? I can announce major hockey names now, as for example — Bobby Hull, Robert Orr, Yvan Cournoyer, Jean Claude Tremblay, Jean Ratelle, Rod Gilbert, ad infinitum. Announcing these names and having them as members of the WHA are birds of a different feather — just ask the Miami Screaming Eagles, also a prospective league member.

Is Hunter afraid the players in question will only laugh at the news statement?

Players are only one problem the league faces. Where are the officials going to come from? It's common knowledge that the NHL is having problems with a 38-man officiating team. To date the WHA has signed one official, that being Vern Buffey, and his role is strictly in an off-ice administrative capacity.

With the retirement plan offered to National League officials not too many will be anxious to break the ties.

Doom Spelt

If the WHA gets off the ground, one can only wonder what will become of the minor professional leagues in the United States. The biggest looting job will have to be done on the American, Central and Western Leagues, which can only spell doom for the same loops.

Much to Bill Hunter's chagrin, the skeptics far outnumbered the media optimists when it came to evaluating the WHA's chances of actually getting into the business of playing hockey. Dale Eisler's sentiments were echoed across the face of North America. Wild Bill and his Winnipeg ally, Ben Hatskin, realized that they had to pull off a truly extraordinary feat if the WHA was to gain any credibility in 1972.

True to form, Wild Bill and his more sedate partner in Manitoba came through — in bigger and better fashion than anyone had ever expected. But to do so, they had to land the NHL's biggest fish of all, Chicago Black Hawks superstar Bobby (The Golden Jet) Hull.

9

Wild Bill and Gentle Ben Get the Show on the Road

"It was a shame how underpaid big league hockey players were in the days preceding the WHA," said Bobby Hull.

The Golden Jet was aptly named. He glowed like no other hockey player before him. Certainly, Maurice (the Rocket) Richard of the Montreal Canadiens was charismatic, but off the rink The Rocket glowered. He was difficult with the English media and often surly to just about any newsman who caught him in a bad mood. Bobby Orr, who entered the NHL in 1967, created an imposing image on the ice, but once he stepped into the dressing room, shyness overcame him and he was virtually inarticulate with the journalists until late in his career.

Not Bobby Hull. Until Wayne Gretzky arrived, The Golden Jet was not only the NHL's most exciting single product, but a one-man public relations campaign for hockey. His smile was infectious; his quotes a reporter's dream; and his availability to the autograph-seeking public virtually limitless. "Bobby was the one player the NHL dared not lose," said *Chicago Tribune* columnist Bob Verdi, "because he was so valuable to the league in so many ways. If the NHL had a *total* treasure, this man was it!"

And that is why Wild Bill Hunter of Edmonton and Gentle Ben Hatskin of Winnipeg took dead aim at Bobby Hull. Like lions on the prowl for wildebeests in the Serengeti, Hunter and Hatskin sniffed out their prey and soon sensed that there was, in fact, a festering wound on the enemy that could be exploited for the eventual kill. Hull was underpaid and unhappy and the Black Hawks high command, for some masochistic reason, was totally unbending in their dealings with The Golden Jet.

"It was as if the Wirtz family didn't believe a WHA was out there being organized, waiting — just waiting — for a player like Bobby Hull to become disenchanted and jump to a new league," said Marty Blackman. "Perhaps they still felt the new league was just a put-on and would go away in a month or two."

But it wouldn't go away; Hunter saw to that. As more and more whispers were heard about Hull's rift with the Wirtzes, Hunter and Hatskin zeroed in on the target. "I instigated the plan to bring Hull to the WHA at a league meeting," said Hunter. "The Hull deal was the best move we made."

To say the least, it was revolutionary. Hunter understood that big money — really BIG money — would be necessary to inspire The Golden Jet to leave the sanctity of the NHL for an unknown league with dubious prospects for success. He also realized that there wasn't a single team in the prospective WHA that possessed such capital. What was, therefore, proposed turned out to be a masterful cooperative effort. Each member of the WHA fraternity was asked to ante roughly $200,000 to provide Bobby with his booty.

"What was so remarkable," recalled *Toronto Star* columnist Milt Dunnell, "is that this happened before any team had collected a nickel. Hockey had never done anything like it before. Basketball had taken that route in order to get a player who would give the whole league prestige, but it usually happened after the owners had picked up a few quid at the box office.

"The Hull venture was a severe test of the new league's sincerity and its willingness to gamble. In its favor were optimists like Bill Hunter. Nothing could ever be quite as good as Wild Bill would profess to see it. The Leaning Tower of Pisa would have been twins if Bill had been the architect."

The Hunter optimism proved a catalyst to the Hull money-collecting plan. But even after the WHA moguls had agreed to produce $1 million in up-front money for Hull, there still was the matter of actually getting him to leave Chicago. "I don't think the NHL thought we could do it," said Howard Baldwin, who orchestrated the New England Whalers' entry into the

WHA and later became the league's president. "But while the Black Hawks fiddled, Bobby burned — and we took advantage of the situation."

By now the WHA had become a byword to hockey fans and the talk of the continent. In its June 19, 1972 issue, *Sports Illustrated* magazine featured Bobby Hull on its cover wearing a Black Hawks uniform with an accompanying caption: THE MAN THEY WANT TO STEAL.

In the article that followed, "Hockey's Turn to Wage a War," the question of Hull's potential switch was amply debated. It concluded with Hull's basic statement: "The name of the game now is money."

The Black Hawks finally sensed touble, big trouble, and offered Hull $1,000,000 for five years. It was too little, too late. Hatskin had produced a 40-page contract which included $1,000,000 for Hull to sign; $250,000 a year for five years as player, or if he wished, as player-coach; $100,000 a year for another five years as a Jets' front office executive. All it needed was Winnipeg's seal of approval. "It's a fantastic contract," the adviser told Hull, and that was all Bobby had to hear.

On June 27, 1972, Hull rode a Rolls Royce through St. Paul, Minnesota, to autograph the WHA portion of his contract for the first $1,000,000. Then the motorcade headed for the airport, where a chartered airliner took Bobby, his family, Hatskin, and Wineberg to Winnipeg for a tumultuous celebration. "I have no regrets about leaving Chicago," said Hull. "The whole thing has made me wonder what the hell the Black Hawks were thinking. They must have thought I was bluffing or they must have been gambling that the Winnipeg offer would fall through."

Hull's signing opened the floodgates, and one by one, other NHL players moved to the new league. Larry Pleau left the Montreal Canadiens for the New England Whalers; André Lacroix left Chicago for the Philadelphia Blazers; George Gardner quit the Vancouver Canucks for the Los Angeles Sharks.

Davidson and Murphy completed their end of the franchise work when Nick Mileti, whose bid to put Cleveland into the NHL had been rejected, was granted the 12th WHA franchise. Mileti promptly pursued players and signed Gerry Cheevers of the Stanley Cup champion Boston Bruins, who also lost Johnny McKenzie to the Philadelphia Blazers.

In July 1972, the Quebec Nordiques signed defenseman J.C.

Tremblay who had been a Montreal Canadiens fixture, and New England captured Bruins defenseman Ted Green. But the biggest contract of all was signed by Derek Sanderson, the Bruin, who jumped to Philadelphia for an estimated $2,325,000. The skirmishing with the NHL was over. The war was on.

When Rosaire Paiement left the Vancouver Canucks for the WHA's Chicago Cougars, Canucks manager Bud Poile warned that his club would go to court to retrieve Paiement. "We have instructed our lawyers to go ahead and pursue the legal aspect of Paiement's contract," said Poile. "Let's test the contract and find out if it's good or not. This is the one we should hang our hat on. Losing a Paiement would be a very harmful thing to our hockey club."

With Hull in the Winnipeg fold, Hunter was determined to produce a prize of his own for Edmonton. He decided to obtain Jim Harrison of the Toronto Maple Leafs, who had been a hero to Alberta fans during his Junior days and was a native of the province. The big forward had gained attention in the spring of 1972 when he stood up and challenged the big, bad Boston Bruins during a series of confrontations between the clubs. Harrison had emerged as the Leafs' only leader.

What's more, Jim was regarded as a potentially big star — unfortunately, that was only half right. Harrison was big all right, but never displayed the overwhelming talents predicted of him. No matter. Hunter was tickled to get him, because he realized that his competitors were moving rapidly.

"If we made a mistake," Hunter admitted, "it was when we held off in our recruiting. We signed more NHL players than we expected to get, but we could have got more."

The reason the WHA was able to lure athletes from the security of the old and established National Hockey League, Wild Bill maintained, was that the players discovered easier communication with the owners in the new league and their contracts did not contain the detested reserve clause.

Eternally innovative, the WHA bosses constantly probed for weaknesses in the NHL infrastructure. WHA president Gary Davidson realized that the reserve clause infuriated NHL players, but that the old league would never strike it. That made things very easy for Davidson. With a few pecks at the typewriter he simply abolished the reserve clause with these words:

The WHA plans to operate without a reserve clause or any substitute for the reserve clause, such as an option clause, in its players' contracts. This innovative decision, which WHA feels should and will revolutionize professional sports, is based on the conclusion that the reserve clause as used today will not long withstand the scrutiny focused on it by players, players' associations, the Congress, the public and even yesterday, the Supreme Court of the United States. By abolishing the reserve clause altogether, the WHA is setting a trend that all of professional sports must inevitably follow.

The reserve clause is a particular provision in a player contract which binds that player to sign with the same team year after year after year, with only the salary being negotiable. In theory, this clause was designed to serve as an equalizer among teams in a professional league and to prevent the best financed franchise from cornering most of the top talent and thereby dominating the league. In practice, however, the reserve clause has not achieved this result. Instead, because it is in direct opposition to the principle of freedom of choice, it has served more as an obvious affront to individual rights and dignity than as a credit to professional sports.

A highly competitive and well balanced league, which is sadly lacking in major professional hockey today, can be achieved without the use of a reserve clause. Thus, the WHA will soon conduct a universal draft among professional, semi-professional, college, junior, amateur and European hockey players. In the event that a player chosen is unable to reach agreement on a contract with the team drafting him, he has the right to take his dispute to arbitration. The arbitration procedure will operate uniformly and fairly, and, in the event of a final impasse, will result in placing the player involved into a special draft pool which will enable him to play for another team in the league.

Once Bobby Hull emigrated from Chicago to Winnipeg and signed a multi-million dollar deal with Hatskin's Jets, press conferences sprouted all over the continent with announcements of signings. Some NHL clubs accepted the raids with a frown and others fought back. One afternoon the New York Raiders held a media event to boast that Dave (Hammer) Schultz and Bill (Cowboy) Flett were about to sign with them. Both were the property of the NHL's Philadelphia Flyers. Unnoticed, sitting in the back of the room, was Gil Stein, the Flyers attorney. A few weeks later Fleet and Schultz were back in the Flyers fold.

Amazingly, the NHL leaders *still* doubted that the WHA actually would operate. Such normally intelligent NHL leaders as Frank Selke, Sr. figured Bill Hunter and his fraternity members for buffoons and continued to propagandize against the baby league. "I think they are just waiting for the National Hockey League to pay them off," said Selke.

The former Montreal Canadiens boss was not all wrong. A small group of NHL leaders led by New York Rangers president Bill Jennings believed that it was important to negotiate some settlement with the WHA, but Jennings was rebuffed by most of his intransigent colleagues and the WHA marched into the fray, with Hunter and Hatskin leading the way.

Hatskin recalled, "Al Eagleson tried to kill us from the beginning. We couldn't get any of his players to sign with us. Clarence Campbell said we'd never drop the first puck. When we started, it seemed as though nobody was going to be a friend of the WHA's."

But start the WHA did, with the following colors and arenas:

ALBERTA OILERS (Royal Blue, Orange and White),
Edmonton Gardens (5,800).

CHICAGO COUGARS (Blue and Gold),
Chicago International Amphitheatre (9,000).

CLEVELAND CRUSADERS (Blue and White),
Cleveland Arena (9,500).

HOUSTON AEROS (Powder Blue, Navy Blue and White),
Sam Houston Coliseum (9,300).

LOS ANGELES SHARKS (Red, Black and White),
L.A. Sports Arena (14,700) 34 games,
Long Beach Auditorium (11,325) 5 games.

MINNESOTA FIGHTING SAINTS (Royal Blue, New Gold and White),
St. Paul Auditorium (8,000) until January 1973,
St. Paul Civic Center (16,180) after January 1973.

NEW ENGLAND WHALERS (Green and White with Black),
Boston Garden (14,994) 19 games,
Boston Arena (7,000) 20 games.

NEW YORK RAIDERS (Blue and Orange),
Madison Square Garden (17,250).

OTTAWA NATIONALS (Red and White with Blue),
Ottawa Civic Centre (9,355).

PHILADELPHIA BLAZERS (Burnt Orange and Yellow),
Philadelphia Convention Hall (9,000).

QUEBEC NORDIQUES (Blue and White),
Quebec Coliseum (10,000).

WINNIPEG JETS (Red, White and Blue),
Winnipeg Arena (11,300).

Needless to say there were glitches all over the place, but none was more embarrassing than that which befell the Blazers in Philadelphia. Taking on the Flyers in the City of Brotherly Love was a gamble to begin with, but the WHA club had obtained enormous publicity upon signing sexy Boston Bruins center Derek Sanderson to an obese contract.

The debut of Sanderson and the Blazers at Philadelphia's Convention Hall symbolized the future of that team. "We couldn't play our first game," Sanderson remembered, "because they didn't know how to make ice. It cracked wherever we skated so the game had to be called off." A hockey game called because of no ice. What next?

In point of fact, "What next?" became a veritable byword around WHA cities. The league's Los Angeles entry, the Sharks, actually played a game at 11 a.m., which is likely the one and only major league hockey match that ever started before noon. It was done because of a television commitment geared to prime Sunday afternoon time in the east.

Then there was the WHA's Ottawa entry, which turned out to be the rarest of the big-time franchises; it sold standing room even though the rink wasn't sold out.

Club president Doug Michel explained: "Ottawa was a heavy 'walk-in' town, with people often waiting until the last minute to buy tickets, so we'd get a frantic rush before game time. That's why we sold standing room even though all the seats weren't gone!"

Michel was responsible for introducing one of the zaniest characters ever to put on the goaltender's pads — one Gilles Gratton. In time, Gratton would play for the Ottawa Nationals, Toronto Toros, Team WHA and, eventually, the NHL's St. Louis Blues and New York Rangers. In each case he would cause his bosses to wonder whatever was the demon spirit that possessed them to sign Gilles in the first place.

At first, Michel believed that he had come up with a netminding prodigy. "We signed him straight out of Junior hockey on a two-year contract for $25,000-$30,000 with a $20,000 bonus," said Michel. "Gilles originally was going to be our 'second' goalie behind the old pro, Les Binkley. But Bink got hurt early in the season and was to play in only 30 games. The bulk of the goaltending was to fall upon the narrow and callow shoulders of 20-year-old Gratton."

Gilles appeared perfectly normal at first and Michel believed he had found the second coming of Georges Vezina. But Gilles did not maintain complete decorum for very long in his career. A few of the more bizarre moves of the man they called "Grattoony" follow:

— He announced that he hated goaltending and was vastly overpaid. "When summer ends, a hockey player gets itchy," said Gilles. "I feel like killing myself."

— While playing for the Toronto Toros in the World Hockey Association, Gilles once skated onto the ice with nothing on his skinny body but a face-mask.

— During a Toros playoff series Gratton disappeared, leaving his team with a second stringer before a critical game.

— As a member of Team Canada 1974, which was preparing for a series with the Russian National Team, Gilles posed nude with a female masseuse in a sauna bath.

— Following a game in San Diego, Gratton was interviewed over the arena public address system. "You have a great building here," he told the audience, "It's too bad you don't have a hockey team."

— Appearing on a Canadian network radio show, Gilles announced that he usually wakes up horny and that one of his goals was to pose nude in *Playgirl* magazine.

Grattoony's life was guided and governed not by logic but rather by astrological charts. In fact, the Gratton ice saga never would have soared or sagged were it not for a pivotal meeting Gilles had with his personal astrologer in 1970. At the time, Grattoony was playing for the Oshawa Generals of the Ontario Hockey Association Junior A Division, the foremost Canadian breeding ground for professional players. But Grattoony wasn't sure he should be a hockey player. The one person he went to for guidance was not his coach, or his manager, or his brother Norm, but his astrologer.

The "incredibly different" Grattoony did not really emerge until the Nationals moved to Toronto and became the Toros in

1973. That was when he skated out for practice one day attired solely in his facemask. Next day's headlines proclaimed: GRATTON, HOCKEY'S FIRST STREAKER.

"Big deal," said Gilles, recalling the episode. "Streaking was the fad at the time, so I did my thing and it got into the papers. At first the league fined me ten thousand dollars because they thought I'd streaked in a game. When they found out it was just a practice, the fine was dropped. I wouldn't have done it in a regular game because I knew I'd get thrown right out of the league."

Some WHA officials insisted that Grattoony was worth his salary in publicity alone. In September 1974, when Team Canada was in Stockholm enroute to its Moscow series with the Soviet National Team, Grattoony's photo made every Canadian sports page. While his teammates sat around, Gilles visited the local public sauna. By some strange coincidence, a photographer happened to be there as Grattoony disrobed and a female masseuse arrived. The next day's headlines said: TORO'S GOALIE POSES NUDE WITH MASSEUSE. And there was a picture of the bare Gratton, his hands covering his groin, while Mademoiselle Svenska looked on approvingly.

Gilles allowed a small smile as he recalled this incident. "I was taking my shower and a broad happened to be standing there," he said. "Big deal! It didn't matter to me. I put my hand in front. All they did was take a picture of me with nothing on."

Unlike all WHA players, Gratton was relatively lucky in that he usually received his paychecks on time. Others, such as André Lacroix, could not always make that statement. "When I joined the New York Golden Blades," Lacroix revealed, "the league owed me $20,000. For some reason the check was sent to the team instead of me, and before I could get it from them, the owners of the Golden Blades spent the money on a team song. As for the song, I never got a chance to hear it; we were gone out of New York before it came out."

According to hockey writer Reyn Davis of the *Winnipeg Free Press*, Lacroix was the WHA record holder for "teams (6), homes (8), games (551), assists (547) and total points (798)."

Davis, who followed the WHA better than any other writer from Day One of its existence to its demise, delivered an interesting commentary on the zany league for *Sports Illustrated*.

Of the 33 buildings used by the WHA, perhaps the worst facility was the Cherry Hill Arena, where the New Jersey Knights played the 29 home games of their brief existence. There were no showers in the visiting team's dressing room, so the opposition had to dress at the Holiday Inn two miles up the road. . . . Most arenas have a long player's bench for each team, but in Cherry Hill the players' section consisted of three rows of five seats. The teams looked like choirs. There was little room for a coach in Cherry Hill, so one night Winnipeg coach Nick Mickoski sat in the first row of the stands. But every time he stood up to make a line change or give instructions to a player, the fans would complain so loudly that he would have to shout his orders sitting down!

Various WHA coaches employed an assortment of good luck charms to inspire poeple to come to their buildings as well as collect victories. Easily the most unusual token of good fortune ever used by a team was a half-eaten cob of corn which was spotted outside the Ottawa Nationals' dressing room one night. The club trainer, Peter Unwin, discovered the cob, picked it up, walked into the Nationals' dressing room and tossed it at the first player he saw — Gavin Kirk. "Hey," said Unwin, "here's a good luck charm I got from an old Indian."

Kirk smiled. "If that's a good luck charm then I guess I better hang onto it." Instead of tossing the cob into the trash can, Kirk placed it in the palm of his glove, which was on the dressing table behind him. Sure enough the Nats won, 2-1, that night on a screwy goal by Bobby Leduc which deflected off the stick of Bob Wall of the Oilers.

Nats coach Billy Harris was not about to dismiss the cob. "Maybe the lucky lady's going to start smiling in our direction. She's sure as hell been looking the other way."

Following the victory, Kirk returned to the dressing room, spotted the corn on the cob and placed it carefully in the bag. Who knows, maybe it would work its magic again!

Sure enough, the Nats beat Cleveland, 2-1. Following that, they whipped Chicago, 6-4, for their fourth straight victory, their longest streak of the year. "That dumb corn cob," said Nats owner Doug Michel, "became the focal point of a pre-game ceremony. Before going on the ice Kirk would solemnly remove it from his glove on the dressing table, have six players rub it for luck, and then pry out one single kernel and throw it to Ken Stephenson. Then everybody'd hoot and holler and charge out on the ice."

The Nats did so poorly at the gate that there were rumblings the franchise would be removed from Ottawa. Then Bobby Hull and the Winnipeg Jets came to town and 9,424 people showed up (a near sellout) and prompted a needling from the local critics. "The Nationals feel a little uncomfortable," said Ottawa hotelier Sam Koffman; "this is the biggest crowd they've seen all year!"

Hull not only *was* the Winnipeg franchise, he also kept the league together in its first year, drawing large crowds wherever he skated. This, however, was impossible in the Cherry Hill (New Jersey) Arena, home of the Jersey Knights, because how can a rink seating fewer than 5,000 draw a large crowd? The Cherry Hill Arena was a bandbox among bandboxes and, according to Hull, featured the most uneven ice in captivity. "It's the only arena I've ever been to," said Hull, "where the visiting team had to skate uphill for two periods of every game. There was also a huge dip in the ice."

Reyn Davis reported that a Knights' player, Ted Scharf, once was awaiting a pass when the puck hit the dip, "shot straight up and struck him between the eyes."

Meanwhile, a lot of people affiliated with the WHA were getting hit between the eyes and falling by the wayside, but the Alberta Oilers withstood the early blows and gushed upward.

10

The Oilers Hang Tough and Survive

Stability was not the Oilers' byword during their early years in the WHA. Bill Hunter frequently changed coaches and the personnel turnover was rapid. Known as the Alberta Oilers in their first season, Hunter's skaters were competitive if not superior. They finished the season one game above .500 (38-37-3) and presented an interesting lineup topped by Jim Harrison who led the team in scoring with 39 goals, 47 assists, 86 points (Bobby Hull went 51-52-103). Other Oilers included large defenseman Allan Hamilton, who at one point was considered to have Norris Trophy potential in the NHL, and Billy Hicke, who was once mistakenly labeled "The next Rocket Richard" in Montreal. Significantly, there wasn't a single Oiler leading in any of the major departments (goals, assists, etc.), although Alberta's goalie Jack Norris finished second to Gerry Cheevers in the Goals Against department. Cheevers led the league with a 2.84 Goals Against average. Norris' mark was 3.06. The Oilers' biggest problem wasn't *on* ice, it was *the* ice. The antideluvian Edmonton Gardens held 5,200 seats and was as far from being major league as Timbuctu was from the WHA. "No problem," exclaimed Bill Hunter, who had plotted for the monumental addition that was to come. "We'll be fine once the new building goes up."

Sure enough the Edmonton Exhibition Association, with Hunter's WHA acting as a catalyst, approved plans for a 17,498-seat arena. Naturally, conservatives believed it would be too large for a city like Edmonton, but Hunter was not among them. Wild Bill was sure that his adopted city could fill the new building at the drop of a WHA puck.

"Edmonton is as big now as Toronto was when Conn Smythe built Maple Leaf Gardens," he reasoned. "I have no doubt we'll sell out the new building.

"We'll strengthen our club at least 25 percent by signing at least five new players. Signing Jim Harrison [of the Leafs] last season was an important move. In our league, the players get a chance to enjoy hockey. We're going places."

But not without many changes. Hunter fired his first coach Ray Kinasewich before the first season was over, only to become the replacement coach himself. Although the club was above the .500 mark, they failed to make the playoffs. For the 1973-74 season, Hunter hired Brian Shaw as the new coach. The setbacks did not disburb Hunter one bit. Like the man who could find sermons in stones and books in running brooks, Wild Bill found good in the 1972-73 infant season.

"The best thing we did," he opined, "was that we went for 12 franchises and finished with 12." With construction of the new Northlands Coliseum underway, hockey interest crescendoed in Edmonton. Although the team finished with exactly the same record as the previous season, the difference this time was that the Oilers made the playoffs. It was, however, a brief run. The Minnesota Fighting Saints eliminated Edmonton four games to one, sending Hunter back to the drawing board. Coming off the drawing board, however, was the coliseum, which opened November 10, 1974. The new rink was hailed as state of the art, which was more than could be said for the Oilers.

The 1974-75 season found Edmonton under (36-38-4) for the first time despite Hunter's attempt to sprinkle stars through the roster. Detroit Red Wing ace Bruce McGregor was on right wing and Hall of Famer Jacques Plante was in goal. Jake the Snake opened with a flourish but his play cooled down and he finished with a 15-14-1 record and a 3.32 Goals Against average.

"While it's true that Jacques didn't set the world on fire," said Howard Baldwin, "it's also true that we landed another big name in our war with the NHL. Every time we signed a high-quality player like Plante, we moved closer to the NHL and, no less important, we won another skirmish on the publicity front."

If Plante was one of the greatest goalies of all time, surely Gordie Howe was the preeminent forward. Like Bobby Hull, Howe had been mistreated by his NHL team, the Detroit Red Wings, and was tickled to accept a big contract from the WHA's Houston Aeros. Even more sensational was the fact that Howe brought his sons Mark and Marty along with him, forming the only father-son trio in hockey. They turned Houston into the League powerhouse while the Oilers remained closer to the outhouse. Brian Shaw eventually was replaced behind the bench by Clare Drake who came by way of the University of Alberta. But the coaching merry-go-round in Edmonton proved more laughable than useful. Even the new Calgary WHA team outdistanced them in 1975-76. Calgary finished with a 41-35-4 mark to Edmonton's embarrassing 27-49-5 record. Compounding the humiliation for Hunter and company was a four-straight shellacking at the hands of Winnipeg in the playoffs.

"The Oilers were bad," recalled Larry Zeidel, who had retired as a player to become a WHA broadcaster, "but unlike the Raiders, Golden Blades and Knights, they were at least alive. Hey, it was 1976 and nobody ever figured the WHA would get this far." Certainly hockey fans in Edmonton kept their fingers crossed whenever another rumor about the WHA's demise surfaced. They realized that if the new league failed, any chance Edmonton had of making it to the NHL would go out the window. And there still was considerable cause for concern after four years of survival. Checks were bouncing, top NHL players were looking twice before jumping, some began defecting back to NHL, and in the 1975 final between Quebec and Houston, uniforms and equipment were seized under a Quebec Supreme Court order because the WHA owed the Canadian Amateur Hockey Association $195,000 (Houston $35,000 alone) for signing underage juniors.

By the end of the 1976 season the losses were staggering. The Toronto Toros had lost $2 million, San Diego Mariners $1 million, Calgary $500,000. Nobody was making money.

Meanwhile the NHL was being bled white. The old league had run up millions of dollars in legal fees in its attempts to stymie the WHA and player contracts had skyrocketed beyond anyone's imagination. Howard Baldwin had become the new WHA president and he spearheaded negotiations with the NHL to produce some kind of merger, but they failed and the WHA continued to plod along, picking up franchises wherever they could find them. One of the most unusual sites was Birmingham, Alabama where the Baby Bulls iced one of the most awesome collection of goons on record —Gilles (Bad News) Bilodeau, Steve Durbano, Frankie Beaton, Serge Beaudoin, Phil Roberto and Dave Hanson. The Bulls coach Glen Sonmor never favored pantywaist hockey. One night after the local Baptist minister urged the skaters to maintain decorum, Sonmor's goons immediately jumped Robbie Ftorek of the Cincinnati Stingers. League president Baldwin summoned Sonmor and his goons to his office for a hearing. The coach was, as always, well prepared.

"I told the guys to go out and buy the most conservative suits they could find," said Sonmor. "They're usually not as rough on you if you're all dressed up. I still have my suit. It's robin's egg blue. I wear it to weddings, funerals and hearings."

There seemed to be a funeral for a WHA team at every turn of the calendar. In all, 26 cities had WHA teams, but 22 of them were abandoned.

Roster stability was for the most part non-existent. Only one Oiler, Al Hamilton, was with the club from start in 1972 to the WHA's finish in 1979. Norm Ferguson paid the price for his loyalty. He launched his WHA career with the New York Raiders who later became the New York Golden Blades, the Jersey Knights and the Mariners. Ferguson lasted five years with the franchise and it folded five times.

Analysts offer any number of reasons for the WHA's instability. Winnipeg Jets owner Ben Hatskin had this theory, "In the end, it wasn't arena troubles, money troubles or the NHL which hurt the league. It was circumstances. In 1974, when the WHA made up Team Canada and played the Soviet Union, if we had won that series, we would still be around. We would have been accepted as a big-time league. Then things got really bad when we lost Vancouver Blazers, Toronto Toros and Phoenix."

The Oilers high command suffered considerable turbulance yet the club plowed through the rough waters. Bill Hunter, once the darling of Edmonton, was eventually pushed out of his job as the Oilers continued to flounder. The 1976-77 season found real estate entrepreneur Nelson Skalbania running the show. Skalbania, in turn, added self-made millionaire Peter Pocklington to the masthead as an equal partner.

11

Hail Sather, Hail Gretzky, Hail the NHL

hose who had a superficial view of Glen Sather, the big-
·ague hockey player, were never especially impressed. And
·hy should they be? At best he was a journeyman left wing
·hose arithmetic was less than impressive. His best NHL sea-
·n, 1973-74, was with the St. Louis Blues when he totalled 44
·oints in 69 games (15-29-44). He launched his career with the
·oston Bruins in 1966-67 and bounced to the Pittsburgh Pen-
·uins, New York Rangers, Blues and Montreal Canadiens
·efore winding up his NHL career with the Minnesota North
·tars.

But arithmetic can be very deceptive. Sather had two special
·ualities that made a difference: grit and savvy. He was both
·reet smart and cerebral in his approach to hockey and peo-
·le. And brother, was he tough. "I can't remember him ever
·sing a fight," said veteran broadcaser Bill Mazer. "Slats came
·i at 5 foot 11, 180 pounds but he'd go with the biggest guys in
·ie league without flinching."

In 1976 Sather was acquired by the Oilers and enjoyed his
·est ever season. The team captain, he scored 19 goals and 34
·ssists for 53 points. Most significant was the transfer of
·ower. Armand (Bep) Guidolin coached the team through 63
·ames and they put together a desultory 25-36-2 record. Even
·orse, the Oilers seemed destined to blow a playoff berth to
·ie Calgary Cowboys. But with 18 games remaining, Guidolin
·as replaced by Sather who turned the team around with a 9-

"Nobody knew it at the time," said Jim Brov
administrator of the WHA, "but Pocklington's ar:
herald a complete turnabout in Edmonton's hocke
Peter was followed by two of the biggest and mos
names in the business — Glen Sather and Wayne G:

7-2 mark. Edmonton edged Calgary by three points for the last playoff spot where they were knocked out of the playoffs by Houston in the first round.

Meanwhile, Pocklington had solidified his hold on the team while Skalbania purchased the Indianapolis Racers. The key elements were rapidly falling into place but there was still the matter of the League staying alive long enough to allow a merger with the NHL. Fortunately, another significant personality had entered the scene to hasten a merger — John Ziegler.

Having succeeded Clarence Campbell as president of the NHL in the late 1970s, Ziegler, unlike his predecessor, was committed to hammering out some sort of armistice with the WHA. Syndicated columnist Jim Coleman put it this way:

> John Ziegler, well into his second season as president of the National Hockey League, is an expansionist. Thus, there can be no doubt that personally he will welcome the day when such Canadian cities as Winnipeg, Edmonton, and Quebec have franchises in the NHL.
>
> As far as Ziegler is concerned, the key word which ultimately will settle the off-again on-again negotiations between the NHL and the WHA is expansion. He disdains such terms as merger or accommodation.
>
> As this season progresses, Ziegler is making a tour of major cities, holding informal conversations with groups of media commentators and explaining his views on the present state and the future state of professional hockey.
>
> What is the major league hockey future for the cities of Edmonton, Winnipeg, and Quebec?
>
> Well, those cities have a friend in Ziegler.
>
> Ziegler's comments in Toronto this week were on the record but because of the informality of the discussions, no one was writing notes or attempting to quote him directly. What emerged from the meeting was an over-all impression of what Ziegler believes will be the future of professional hockey. In stock market terminology, Ziegler is "bullish" as he looks into the future of the sport.
>
> His expressed views can be paraphrased as follows: Major league hockey presently consists of 24 teams, 17 in the NHL and seven in the WHA.
>
> Ziegler doesn't see any good reason why the NHL can't be expanded initially to 22 teams. And he can envision the possibility of further expansion when the financial climate

improves and when professional hockey arouses some of the national fervor in the U.S. which it long has aroused in Canada.

Ziegler is a frank man and he's quick to acknowledge that there are still some NHL club owners (a few, he emphasizes) who resist expansion which would include WHA cities. Those holdouts are emotionally motivated. They can't forgive the WHA teams for taking players away from them when the new league came into existence.

Still, time heals most wounds. Initially some NHL club owners insisted: "We can just sit here and wait for those WHA guys to go broke." Ziegler believes that type of thinking began to fly out the window in 1974 and 1975.

Ziegler is no pollyanna and he is keenly aware that even an initial NHL expansion to 22 teams cannot be accomplished without causing some serious business dislocations and fan heartburn.

Pro WHA types such as Coleman were fervently hoping that there would be a halt in the WHA franchise dropouts. In Indianapolis, for example, the Racers were projecting losses of $1.3 million for the 1978-79 season. On the plus side was the arrival in Indiana of a Lanky Lad with a remarkable hockey pedigree; his name was Wayne Gretzky and if ever there was a prodigy, this young man was it. At his 42 Varadi Avenue rink in Brantford, Ontario, Wayne was skating with a stick in his hands at the age of three. Under his father's watchful eye, he practiced skating and stickhandling drills and learned how to play defensively.

Wayne was so advanced for his age that when he turned five he was good enough to play for a team that normally did not accept lads until they reached their tenth birthday.

At age six, his second year playing in the Novice A division, Gretzky scored 27 goals. His routine was constant; upon return from school he headed directly for his hockey equipment, laced on his skates and played until dinner time. After dinner, he returned with his companions and resumed playing.

An asset that many youngsters of a similar age lacked was the gung-ho attitude of both parents. Wayne's did everything possible to encourage him. In 1971-72, 11-year-old Gretzky scored 290 goals, reguarly stuffing five or six goals in the net while playing a complete 45 minutes of nearly every game.

When Wayne was still 11, he met his idol Gordie Howe and the NHL's most durable superstar posed with him, curving a stick around Gretzky's left ear, mocking a hooking infraction. Wayne was very amused. Gordie was very impressed. "God," said Howe, "he's got talent."

At age 13, in April 1974, he had already scored his 1,000th career goal and was already suffering the emotional pains of a professional superstar. He was, quite simply, too good for his peers and the parents of those children resented him.

Yet Wayne remained polite and patient, traits he retained into adulthood.

"Since I was six years old," he explained, "I've had a lot of media attention. I was brought up to believe that when people are interested in you you have a responsibility to them, that you have to watch what you say and do whenever you're in the public eye."

Wayne later went on to play junior hockey in Toronto where he became friends with Murray Howe, Gordie's youngest son. At the time, Howe was rooming with a Torontonian named Gus Badali who would in time become Gretzky's agent.

Gretzky was drafted by the Sault Ste. Marie Greyhounds in June 1977 (third overall in the draft). He had hoped to play for Peterborough of the same Junior A division which was closer to home. Badali escorted him to Sault Ste. Marie and Gretzky decided to stay.

Gretzky had hoped to obtain uniform number nine — the same as he had in Brantford and the same worn by his idol, Gordie Howe, but it was already spoken for so he picked number 99 and nobody complained. Tough as it had been billed, the Ontario Major League turned out to be a piece of cake for The Kid.

Wherever he played, the results were at the very least superlative. In Montreal, he participated in the World Junior championships and paced the pack with eight goals and 17 points in six games. He broke the Greyhounds scoring record with 70 goals and 182 points and excelled in virtually every department including shorthanded goals, where he led the league with seven. To nobody's surprise he was voted the rookie of the year (he had set records for most goals and points in a season by a freshman). As an appropriate finale he was presented with the William Hanley Trophy for quality and gentlemanly play.

In a coaches poll Gretzky took honors as the finest playmaker, the most dangerous in the goal area, and the smartest player.

In June 1978, when Wayne Gretzky was 17 years old, the World Hockey Association was ready for The Kid and he was ready for the WHA.

Stalking Gretzky — although Wayne didn't know it at the time — was Nelson Skalbania who dared to march where others had feared to tread, in the market for underage aces. Badali, who was not only Gretzky's agent but also the representative of other junior stars, had no compunctions about talking contract with the very brash Skalbania.

"Nelson called me and asked me how much it would take to sign Gretzky and I told him," Badali revealed. Shortly thereafter Badali was invited to Vancouver with Wayne, his mother and father. "We had dinner on a Saturday night," added Badali, "talked about it and on Sunday morning he told me we had a deal." Then they piled into Skalbania's private jet aircraft and, while it cruised eastward from British Columbia, Gretzky and his parents signed a four-year personal services contract with Skalbania.

Badali explained that the deal called for "slightly less than $1,000,000" and gave Skalbania a further three-year option at numbers to be negotiated or set by an independent arbitrator. Badali allowed that his end was five percent or approximately $50,000.

Wayne handled the signing, and the questions thereafter, with the same aplomb that he has when ladling a pass to one of his wingmen. "All my life people kept telling me I couldn't make it," he said. "If I'd listened I'd still be back in Brantford. All my life, I've worked to become a professional hockey player. If I didn't take this opportunity, and broke a leg or something back in the Soo, it could be all over."

Gretzky, with his youthful candor, admitted that he would have liked to have signed an NHL contract and both he and Badali made no secret of the fact that they anticipated that the NHL and WHA ultimately would merge. "There'll be one league sometime during the life of the contract," said Badali. "It's only sensible."

Reaction to the signing was immediate and harsh, particularly in junior hockey circles. Greyhounds president Jim McAuley hinted that he might fold the team without Gretzky, although a league clause provided that his club would receive $20,000 for every player who turned professioinal before his junior eligibility was over. "So we get $20,000," snapped McAuley. "Look what we stand to lose in gate receipts with the likes of Gretzky gone."

Badali wasted no time counterattacking. "There's a war between two leagues and I'm an agent with a client. How can I tell Wayne that he should not take nearly a million dollars from Indianapolis but go back to the Soo for $75 a week? What happens if he gets hurt? Better it should be $200,000 a year. Skalbania came to me. I did not go to him."

Still undetermined was Gretzky's ability to withstand the heavier checking from the more robust professionals. Badali had an answer to that, too. "I'm not arguing he shouldn't play junior another year but he's been tested and he's strong enough (5 foot 10, 155 pounds). He was named the best center in the World Junior Tournament over Bob Smith of Ottawa, who'll be the NHL's number one draft choice. And, playing with a fifth place team, he scored ten points less than Smith who was with a first place team."

Wayne seemed still to have his head in the clouds. "I guess," he smiled, "the master plan worked — the dream's come true. I never thought a player should be restricted from advancing because of his age. That's why I'm grateful to the WHA for giving me a chance to turn pro early."

By sheer coincidence, the WHA's annexation of Gretzky took place precisely when the NHL was conducting its annual meeting in Montreal. When the shock waves of Wayne's signing reached Montreal, they drew a mixed reaction from the old guard. Some tried to ignore the event as if it had transpired in some mythical land beyond the sea. Others pooh-poohed its significance, while some said they couldn't blame the lad one bit.

"You can't blame the kid for getting a big offer and taking it," said Boston Bruins general manager Harry Sinden. "But you have to wonder what effect it will have on his overall hockey career. Gretzky is 17 with one year of major junior experience. He has great talent, but he's not that big. He's going to take a pounding around in pro hockey. I think it was proved when we went through the underage thing before that it wasn't the best move."

There were sour grapes from the likes of Montreal Canadiens managing director Sam Pollock. "The signing of one 17-

year-old player by the other league won't cause any ripples. If the NHL can't survive the loss of one teenaged kid, then we're in pretty rough shape."

Of course, Skalbania could be in pretty rough shape if Gretzky failed because, based on the personal services deal they signed, Wayne would get paid whether he succeeded or failed. "If he can't play hockey," quipped Skalbania, "he's going to be the most expensive handball partner I've ever had!"

An equally relevant question was raised by many who probed Gretzky's psyche. How would becoming a millionaire at age 17 affect Wayne? There were those who recalled how in 1974 the Vancouver Blazers of the WHA had signed a 19-year-old defenseman named Pat Price to a six-year $1,300,000 deal. "He was," wrote Jim Taylor, a *Vancouver Province* columnist, "the biggest bust since Dolly Parton."

Taylor noted that the gamble being taken by Skalbania was nothing short of enormous. "While there are those in hockey who insist that Gretzky is the next Bobby Orr, there are others who say he isn't: that he is too slow, that he's not big enough, that he controls the puck well and has some dazzling moves — but that once the pros see the moves a couple of times they'll shut them off. . . . There will be an acceptance problem for Wayne Gretzky — and quite possibly a talent problem."

If Skalbania had read those words, he wasn't letting on. As he began hyping the arrival of The Kid in Indianapolis, he preferred going over the *Sports Illustrated* reviews which noted that "without question Gretzky is the most exciting player since Guy Lafleur. . . . Right now Gretzky has a knack with a puck equal to anyone's at any level."

To which Wayne added: "I know now I have to go out and prove myself again. The challenge is there."

Before meeting that challenge, Wayne headed for a northern Ontario hockey school that specialized in power skating. "I'm going there as a student," he chuckled, "not to teach."

The folks who operated the Indianapolis Racers awaited The Kid as eagerly as schoolboys at the circus ogle cotton candy. Racer's general manager Don LeRose launched the ticket-selling campaign with a relatively modest hype. "We're billing him as The World's Best Junior, on the basis of what he did in the world tournament. The people here are aware of him —

don't forget, there was a feature article on Wayne in *Sports Illustrated* and that's the Bible."

Whatever testament the folks following the Racers read, the gospel according to Wall Street indicated that the Indianapolis hockey club, like others in the WHA fraternity, was not in the best of financial health. LeRose insisted that Skalbania could handle all potential debts. "Don't worry," LeRose asserted, "Nelson can afford it. All the players are signed to him and not to the Racers."

Nelson could afford it — for the first week at least. Skalbania needed crowds averaging 11,800 each game to stay above the fiscal waves in Indianapolis. Otherwise he was in trouble, big trouble.

Despite the hoopla, the story in "the Bible," and his general competence while skating alongside the more mature — physically at least — professionals, Gretzky was no big box office. The Racers drew crowds averaging fewer than 5,000 persons at home games. After eight contests, Wayne had scored three goals and three assists and Skalbania was panicking.

The NHL had been well aware of Gretzky for years but with the special brand of officiousness displayed by the senior league, NHL leaders disparaged the 17 year-old. "They said that what he had done until then would mean nothing in terms of big league success," recalled Howard Baldwin. "Naturally, they said he was too skinny, too light to last in the NHL. Obviously, our people were quite willing to take their chances with him."

It is to Skalbania's everlasting credit that he was the first to take the plunge with Gretzky. Unfortunately for Skalbania, he had to bail out, never to reap the benefits of Gretzky's greatness. On November 4, 1978, following consummation of the Skalbania-Pocklington deal, Gretzky boarded a chartered Lear jet for Edmonton. Pocklington had paid only $800,000 for Gretzky, forward Peter Driscoll and goaltender Ed Mio. In addition, Pocklington swallowed their contracts. Gretzky's arrival in Edmonton would be a monumental media event and Oilers public relations director John Short did all he could to properly organize the arrival of The Kid. On the ninth anniversary of the event, Short recalled the circumstances preceeding Gretzky's arrival. Short penned these words for the *Edmonton Jounral*:

The biggest difficulty for the public relations director of that time was to figure out exactly when Gretzky and his travelling entourage would arrive. At first, we were told the plane would touch down at the international airport in late afternoon.

Good. We wanted maximum coverage on early-evening telecasts.

Then we were told to expect a delay until early evening. So we got special clearance to land the new players at the municipal airport, close to downtown, for the convenience of the broadcasters.

If we couldn't get detailed coverage to the public at suppertime, we wanted them to have the information by bedtime, at least.

Coverage by daily newspaper wasn't a problem. Not at that time. Not until we encountered delay after delay.

Finally, the aircraft arrived. Close to midnight. So late that all our promotional preparation went down the drain.

Worse, the weary Mio hinted that he might not be able to play the next night. He did, though. Pretty well too. His stress, we learned, was caused mostly by the fact he hadn't been allowed to leave the plane with his credit card. The pilot took it.

"I'm a long way in debt until this gets straightened out," Mio moaned. "Can I get a check for $6,000 right away?"

He got it the next morning.

Radio and television broadcasters were both hungry and tired. They lamented that they couldn't get the truth, the whole truth and nothing but the truth onto film that night.

Driscoll insisted he was anxious to play, no matter how weary he might be.

Gretzky, too. During the long-awaited news conference, he was asked whether he could recover from the ordeal in time to play the next night.

"If I'm going to be at the Coliseum anyway," he grinned with some shyness, "I might as well get into the game."

Gretzky's arrival was a tonic for Glen Sather but the Oilers coach realized that it had to be diluted with a dose of discipline. If anything, Sather would have to be especially diligent in dealing with Gretzky's defensive flaws, the only obviously weak part of his game. During a match with the Cincinnati Stingers, a Gretzky defensive blunder provided Cincinnati with the puck and the Stingers promptly converted it into a goal. The Kid returned to the bench and awaited his next turn on the ice.

The turn never came. Sather deliberately bypassed Gretzky

and kept him on the bench until he felt that the lesson had been learned. A period later The Kid got the high sign and returned to action.

"He could have pouted and sulked," said Sather. No way, not the Brantford Bullet. He scored a three-goal hat trick, enabling the Oilers to overcome a 3-2 deficit and triumph 5-2. "That," added Sather, "was the turning point in his career. Not just anyone could keep the motivation with a contract like his. But he wants to be the best."

Although they pretended otherwise, many NHL moguls kept looking over their shoulders at the WHA and in particular at Gretzky. The WHA, still struggling for survival — and hoping fervently for a rapprochement with the NHL — exploited Gretzky for all he was worth. Typical was an advertisement in *The Hockey News* with a large photo of Gretzky accompanied by the caption: "Many of the brightest young stars in hockey are thrilling fans in WHA arenas."

The Kid was catching on and drawing crowds partly because of his curiosity value and partly because of his ability. By now wise in the ways of public relations, the WHA worked the young man at every turn. Once, even though the league no longer had a team in New York City, they imported Gretzky and his boyhood idol Gordie Howe to Manhattan for a midtown press conference just to show off their jewel.

"It was a splendid move," said popular New York sportscaster Marv Albert, "because everybody in the sports world adored Howe and it was clear from one meeting with Wayne that everybody was going to love him as much or even more. He was, even as a teenager, as wonderful a WHA salesman as Bobby Hull."

After six years, Hull had managed to keep his cool through one bizarre WHA season after another; it was amazing that The Golden Jet didn't go bonkers with all the franchise changes and crazy travel arrangements. Edmonton columnist Terry Jones recalled: "If you covered the WHA, you couldn't possibly fail a geography exam. I remember one road trip I was on. Two games. One in Phoenix. One in Cincinnati. There were take-offs and landings at 13 different airports.

"Every time I went to a new rink in the WHA I stopped at the souvenir stand and bought a puck with the team logo on it for my son Shane. Someday his collection is going to be worth a fortune."

Hull was fortunate in one respect: the Jets were prescient

enough to see the value of having classy European players on the roster. Skaters like Lars-Erik Sjoberg — a splendid little defenseman — complemented Hull's attacking style. "Lars was one of the best skaters I've ever played with," said Hull, "and that goes for any league, any time."

Incredibly there were several WHA players who vigorously campaigned against — and sometimes attacked — the Swedes.

San Diego had a few stickhandlers who were particularly anti-Scandinavian. Reyn Davis of the *Winnipeg Free Press* once noted:"The Mariners led by André Lacroix hated the Jets because they had seven Europeans in their lineup. Lacroix contended they were depriving Canadians of jobs and once, along with ancient Harry Howell, he had tried to convince the WHA Players' Association to force owners to introduce quotas in their hiring of Europeans. It seemed that everybody wanted to fight the Swedes. Lacroix was the worst. He used his stick and let the other Mariners do the fighting."

Fortunately, Lacroix and his troublemakers had little impact on the Swedes, but they weren't as big an attraction as Hull and Gretzky — not to mention the Howe family, starring Gordie, Mark, and Marty. At one time they actually skated on the same line together, but Mark and Marty frequently played defense. One of the amusing aspects of watching the Howes in action was papa Gordie's wife Colleen. She was in the stands one night when the Oilers and Aeros engaged in a free-for-all. The actions of her gray-haired hubby brought a smile to her face.

"The Aeros had the win wrapped up, 6-2, but the fight was still undecided. From the stands you could see a gray head bobbing through the mob of forty players, all squared off and flailing away," Colleen remembered.

"From the middle of the pack, Mark's head surfaced. 'Over there, Dad,' he yelled at Gordie, pointing across the ice. 'Some guy's on top of Marty again.'

"But it wasn't just Gordie looking after the boys. We were all mother hens — even Cathy. From the stands she would shout down to the rink, 'Don't you dare hit my brother.' I can't imagine what it would be like if Mark and Marty ever wound up on opposing teams. Rooting for both, having to watch one check the other."

The Howes moved en masse to the New England Whalers for the 1977-78 season and finished their WHA careers in Hartford. The Whalers had become a solid fixture in Connecticut and Hartford thirsted for an NHL team. It didn't hurt that the club president Howard Baldwin also ran the WHA and it helped cement the coupling with the NHL.

"I can remember the first meeting we had at the Americana Hotel off Times Square in 1971," said Baldwin. "We were the laughing stocks of sports at the time. But as that old song goes, 'Who's got the last laugh now'."

Baldwin, for one, was laughing. Even though he no longer would be president of a major sports league, he had steered Hartford into the WHA.

Peter Pocklington was laughing because he had Wayne Gretzky.

The Quebec Nordiques were laughing because their city would be represented in the NHL for the first time since 1920.

Ben Hatskin was laughing because by the spring of 1979 the Winnipeg Jets had sold more NHL season tickets for 1979-80 (about 10,500) than the Jets averaged in the 1978-79 season.

"We were ready to close our league with pride and dignity," Baldwin concluded, "and we hoped that our last playoff would be a good one."

Thankfully it was — but not for Edmonton.

12

Good-Bye WHA, Hello NHL

The WHA passed from the sporting scene with all the grace and artistry that Wayne Gretzky displays on the ice. This was partly because the Great One had become a presence along with the Howe family and Bobby Hull. What's more, the Jets had infused even more artistry into the league by signing the gifted Swedes Ulf Nilsson and Anders Hedberg. "When Hull, Hedberg, and Nilsson were on the ice," recalled WHA president Howard Baldwin, "it was like watching a ballet."

Appropriately the Jets and Oilers marched to the WHA finals. Edmonton was favored, having topped the WHA over the regular reason with 48 wins, 30 losses and 2 ties. Winnipeg's 39-35-6 mark placed the Jets third, 14 points behind the Oilers. The finale offered a bittersweet scenario. On the sweet side was the delicious brand of hockey being served to the customers. On the bitter side, there was the knowledge that the fans would never see WHA hockey again. Many newsmen, such as Jeffrey Goodman of the Toronto *Globe and Mail*, sensed the drama of the moment and articulated it in print:

> In Edmonton and Winnipeg throughout the WHA championship final, it is evident that hockey fans have a strong allegiance toward a league they have sometimes loved, sometimes endured in its brief existence. But the prevailing interest is in that other series, the one between the Montreal Canadiens and the New York Rangers, the one which everyone else in the country is concentrating on.
>
> In Edmonton, during the first two games of the best-of-seven series, the Oilers have not drawn as many fans as they averaged

during the regular season. In Winnipeg, for the third game and with the Jets up two-zip, the arena is not sold out. On top of that, it's as though the series is being played under quarantine, shut off from the outside world.

Not surprisingly, journalists like Goodman descended on the remaining founders of the WHA for post mortems. One who was delighted to talk happened to be the man who had teamed up with Wild Bill Hunter eight years earlier to blueprint the new league. Ben Hatskin no longer had Hunter at his side but he was thinking about Wild Bill as he recalled the utter craziness of the circuit.

"There is no doubt we were living on a day-to-day basis," said Hatskin. The Jets owner was recalling the days when checks were bouncing and top NHL players looked twice before jumping to the WHA.

Perhaps the saddest aspect of the WHA's exit was the fact that two of the final six franchises — Cincinnati and Birmingham — were cut adrift. As part of the deal with the NHL, only four franchises would be allowed into the Senior Circuit. Both Birmingham and Cincinnati were attractive hockey towns but unlike Edmonton, Winnipeg, Quebec, and Hartford, they had not displayed the same staying power.

"The Oilers, Jets, and Nordiques stayed in the same cities right from the start," said Howard Baldwin. "The only move the Whalers made was from Boston to Hartford (by way of Springfield until the Hartford Civic Center opened). These teams paid their dues." Baldwin, the outgoing WHA president, John Ziegler and Bill Jennings, along with Winnipeg's Ben Hatskin, all deserve considerable credit for hammering out the armistice.

Hatskin said, "I always thought we'd merge. Let's face it. The people in Edmonton, all over the west, are NHL people at heart. When you've been watching Hockey Night in Canada for 25 years and all you've heard is NHL, you don't want to be part of something secondary. But we killed ourselves by talking merger so much instead of consolidating, then expanding. In the final analysis, however, one thing should be noted. This merger, first and foremost, isn't a victory for the WHA. It's a victory for Canadian hockey. Calgary could have been in it too if it had built an arena. They were foolish. But it must be remembered, and it will be out here, that although it is a victory for Canadian hockey, there would not be NHL hockey in Quebec City, Edmonton and Winnipeg [and Hartford] next season if it wasn't for the WHA."

Although he was a Peter-Come-Lately, Pocklington was also a major factor in the merger. The Oilers arrival in the NHL obviously gave fans what they wanted even before the 1978-79 season had ended. In Edmonton, they sold 14,200 NHL season tickets in a four-day period and could have sold at least 16,000 if they had wanted to.

"Let's fact it," said Pocklington. "There's a lot of disposable income in this city and sports is one of the few items it can be spent on."

The idea that Edmonton *really* was going big time touched a sentimental nerve with hard-nosed journalists like Terry Jones. As he covered the final WHA series of all time, Jones reminisced:

> Was it only seven years ago when Wild Bill Hunter rented the Steak Loft and gathered the flowers of local sports journalism together to meet Gary Davidson and Dennis Murphy and to first announce to the world their plans of forming the World Hockey Association? Only a couple of us thought it would ever see the light of day.
>
> Remember the first exhibition game in the Gardens? Los Angeles Sharks were the opposition, I think. There have been bigger crowds in a phone booth. But here we are today, thanks to Bill Hunter and that mob of rogues, with a major league arena which will be sold out for 1979-80 by this time next month and in a city which before a game is played is one of the four or five top franchises in the NHL. You've come a long way, baby.

Suddenly all of the hardships endured by such forgettable clubs as the Indianapolis Racers, Vancouver Blazers, Philadelphia Blazers, Jersey Knights, New York Golden Blades, New York Raiders, Ottawa Civics, Ottawa Nationals, Toronto Toros, Houston Aeros, San Diego Mariners, Phoenix Roadrunners, Los Angeles Sharks, Michigan Stags, Baltimore Blades, Calgary Cowboys, Denver Spurs, Cleveland Crusaders, Chicago Cougars, and Minnesota Fighting Saints I and II became romantic in the telling.

"One night, the Chicago Cougars chartered an old DC-3 to take them the 893 miles to Quebec City," recalled Reyn Davis. "The plane took off before midnight, and the players curled up in their seats and went to sleep. Rod Zaine woke up and glanced at his watch. It was 5 A.M. and they were still in the air.

"At long last the plane began to settle down. The landing was smooth and the players reached for their coats to go outside when one of them noticed the sign under the control tower. *Bienvenue à Mont Jolie, P.Q.*

"The pilot had landed in the wrong city. He had missed Quebec City by 200 miles!"

The Winnipeg-Edmonton Avco Cup final was disappointing to Pocklington who had promised the players and their wives an all-expense paid trip to anywhere they desired if the team went out champions. Despite the presence of Gretzky, the Oilers lost the first two playoff games, May 11 and May 13, 1979 at Northlands Coliseum.

Several opinions were offered about the Oilers modest play in the finals. One theory had it that the general disbursement that would follow the merger was going to break up that old gang in Edmonton. One of the most outspoken was Oilers defenseman John Hughes, a top-flight performer in the WHA.

It's obvious the players don't care about the series. Some are aggravated because the winner's share will only be $10,000 and not the $12,500 we were promised. They can understand the cutback because the schedule was shortened but a deal is a deal. It's just a strange circumstance in which to play a final.

The players who can play and are confident about their ability are delighted about the merger. But there are others in the opposite position on both teams. When everyone went wild about the NHL merger, it also affected the players. The attitude seemed to be one of let's get this over with.

One thing I did learn out there is that anything east of Manitoba is either a bad word or doesn't exist. I heard about it but didn't believe it. Now that I've lived here I do. Harold Ballard's name, for example, is mud. Hockey fans can't believe the terms of the merger. They're upset and understandably so.

How are we going to sell hockey in the U.S. if the teams they're admitting aren't the strongest in the first place but are still going to get torn apart? Why the NHL would want the WHA's players is bewildering. There isn't one who will turn a franchise around. There probably won't be more than five guys taken so why bother in the first place?

All these things are getting to a lot of guys. That's why there isn't any intensity in the series, but I'd like to see how Colorado, Minnesota or the Leafs would react to this.

Wayne was prominent in game three, an 8-3 triumph for the Oilers. The Great One scored the opener in game four and set up the go-ahead 2-1 goal in the second period, but Winnipeg put two past Oilers goalie Dave Dryden in the third period to hand Edmonton a heartbreaking 3-2 defeat. Edmonton had one last gasp, a 10-2 joy ride in game five. It looked for a brief time like the Oilers could pull off an amazing rally.

According to Jeffrey Goodman of the *Globe and Mail*, Pocklington sensed the movement. "He even went into the dressingroom and dangled in front of each player a bathing suit and a bottle of suntan lotion — a not so subtle reminder of the reward ahead."

It didn't work. Winnipeg jumped into a 2-0 lead in the first period and made it 5-0 before the game was half over. The final score was 7-3 and Gretzky didn't have a single point. Winnipeg reigned as the final WHA champion, which was perfectly appropriate since the Jets leader Bobby Hull had made the League possible.

The glee which was shared by the WHA teams was also tinged with bitterness. Not only was the NHL socking each of the WHA clubs $6 million dollars to gain entry but the four new teams were being permitted to protect only two goalies and two skaters for the expansion draft that would take place. This was a source of great annoyance to WHA executives like Larry Gordon of the Oilers.

"The more I think about it, the more it bothers me," Gordon said. "Why would the NHL do this? You'd think they'd realize that fans in Montreal and Boston for example, are tired of seeing teams like the Colorado Rockies and St. Louis Blues coming to their city. You'd expect that they would want a more competitive league. But I guess they've been telling their fans for so long that the WHA is a bush league that it would be embarrassing if the WHA teams went in and beat them.

"But, if it's so bush, why would they want our players? We've been a bush league for seven years and all I know is, when you look at the NHL final you see Napier, Hickey, Nilsson, Hedberg, and where did they come from?"

It was clear that the absurdly inequitable protected list was a one-two punch to the solar plexis of every hockey fan in Edmonton, Winnipeg, Quebec, and Hartford. But by the same token the WHA over seven years, through 26 cities and 35 owners, had made an undeniable mark on the face of professional hockey. It turned Edmonton into a major league city and did what the NHL refused to do — gave Wayne Gretzky a place to play the professional game.

The league was all things to all people associated with it but nobody put it better at the final closing than Randy Smith who covered the Whalers for the *Journal-Inquirer* of Manchester, Connecticut.

To our friends in Boston and Toronto the WHA was "Send in the Clowns," a second-rate league with second-rate talent. Clarence Campbell, then the head of the NHL, said seven years ago that the WHA "won't make it till Christmas." Campbell, Harry Sinden, Harold Ballard and innumerable others said many things — all of which were derogatory — but somehow the league survived.

To others the league was "A Place in the Sun," a glorious chance to make big bucks and big headlines. Youngsters on the way up and veterans on the way down pulled on the same colored sweaters and played out "Rocky," parts one, two, three and four.

The WHA was a million to one shot which made it, thanks to some sound leadership, most notably Howard Baldwin, and some sound financial support, most notably Aetna Life & Casualty out of Hartford.

It would be the height of hypocrisy if I slammed the league because it took me places I hadn't been and permitted me to meet people I had only read about. To me the WHA was "An Affair to Remember", a collection of priceless memories. And I'd like nothing better than to take a ride on the carousel one last time.

Thanks to the WHA, I had breakfast with Gordie Howe, a drink or six with Dave Keon, John McKenzie and Glenn Hall, and an unforgettable night with Don Blackburn in an Indianapolis snowstorm.

There were the colorfully-named teams: the Calgary Cowboys, the Chicago Cougars, the Toronto Toros, the Phoenix Roadrunners, the Minnesota Fighting Saints, the Philadelphia Blazers, the San Diego Mariners and the New York Golden Blades.

There were the joints: Sleep-Out Louie's in Cincinnati, the Teller's Cage in Indy, the Cobblestone in Birmingham, the Keg in Springfield, Eddie Webster's Peanut House in Minneapolis, the Old Bailey in Winnipeg and the Hotel Frontenac Piano Bar in Quebec City. Yes, there was drinking, but there was also a camaraderie, a loyal and warm feeling among friends and associates tossed together into a glamorous and yet totally unglamorous lifestyle.

There were the magnificent old-timers: Gordie Howe, Bobby Hull, J.C. Tremblay, Norm Ullman, Ralph Backstrom, Keon and McKenzie.

And the young turks, extended a chance to play that they wouldn't have received otherwise: Mark Howe, Réal Cloutier, Robbie Ftorek, Wayne Gretzky, Mark Napier, Gordie Roberts, Terry Ruskowski, Rob Ramage, Scott Campbell and Morris Lukowich.

And, of course, there was Marc Tardif, who deserves his own paragraph. The Quebec winger surfaced as one of the best two or three players in North America and that's including the NHL.

There were poignant moments: a sellout crowd at Market Square Arena in Indy standing and applauding for the last three minutes in a seventh playoff game which the home team would lose, 6-0; Ulf Nilsson and Anders Hedberg skating around Winnipeg Arena with the Avco Cup to the strains of "Auld Lang Syne." Harry Neale, then coach of the Raiders, said it best. "Those two kids did the impossible, they got out of Winnipeg without ever hearing a boo." Then there was Backstrom, at the very end of a 19-year career, standing at full attention for "O Canada" at Le Colisée in Quebec. Backstrom didn't dress and watched the Whalers play from the press box.

There were the tough guys: Jack Carlson, Cam Connor, Kim Clackson, Dave Hanson, Steve Durbano, Gilles Bilodeau, Curt Brackenbury and Frank Beaton.

And the genuinely nice people: Tom Earl, Danny Bolduc, Backstrom and no less than five New England goaltenders — Louie Levasseur, Cap Raeder, Bruce Landon, John Garrett and Al Smith.

I saw "House Calls" with Neale, "An Unmarried Woman" with Raeder and Bolduc, "Coming Home" with PR man Dennis Randall and "The China Syndrome" with broadcaster Bob Neumeier.

There were the real pros: Keon, Rick Ley and Larry Pleau.

And the cut-ups: Carlson, Brad Selwood and Bill Butters.

There were airplane rides and changing coaches and shifting personnel and racetracks and movie houses and more airplane rides. There were great moments like beating the Russians in Hartford.

"It's the only puck that I've ever kept," said Raeder, the winning goaltender.

There were memorable quotes: Does this mean you have to

win the next one, Neale was asked. "You don't HAVE to win any of 'em," he said.

I took a tour of the Houston Astrodome with Freddie O'Donnell, a walk along the St. Lawrence River with Doug Roberts and a midnight cab ride through Indy with Mike Antonovich.

My favorites were Neale, Keon and Blackburn and it's exciting to think that all three will hook up in the NHL next season. I'm looking forward to it, just like you, but before the Canadiens, Bruins and Islanders land in Hartford, light a candle for the WHA.

The league took very little and gave us a lot.

Especially me.

While Glen Sather may have waxed just as sentimental as Randy Smith, the Oilers boss also realized that he could not waste his time on nostalgia. Since his WHA roster would be decimated by the NHL, Sather would have to be extremely insightful when making his selections for 1979-80. Of the four players he decided to protect, Gretzky and Bengt Gustafson were the forwards while Eddie Mio and Dave Dryden manned the goal.

Now came the essential decision on who to draft. The Oilers would pick 21st. The draft went as follows:

No.Player	Claimed By	Last Amateur Club	Position
1. RAMAGE, Rob	Colorado	London Knights	D
2. TURNBULL, Perry	St. Louis	Portland Winter Hawks	C
3. FOLIGNO, Mike	Detroit	Sudbury Wolves	RW
4. GARTNER, Mike	Washington	Niagara Falls Flyers	RW
5. VAIVE, Rick	Vancouver	Sherbrooke Beavers	RW
6. HARTSBURG, Craig	Minnesota	Sault Ste. Marie Greyhounds	D
7. BROWN, Keith	Chicago	Portland Winter Hawks	D
8. BOURQUE, Raymond	Boston	Verdun Black Hawks	D
9. BOSCHMAN, Laurie	Toronto	Brandon Wheat Kings	C
10. McCARTHY, Tom	Minnesota	Oshawa Generals	LW
11. RAMSEY, Mike	Buffalo	University of Minnesota	D
12. REINHART, Paul	Atlanta	Kitchener Rangers	D/C
13. SULLIMAN, Doug	NY Rangers	Kitchener Rangers	RW
14. PROPP, Brian	Philadelphia	Brandon Wheat Kings	LW
15. McCRIMMON, Brad	Boston	Brandon Wheat Kings	D
16. WELLS, Jay	Los Angeles	Kingston Canadians	D
17. SUTTER, Duane	NY Islanders	Lethbridge Broncos	RW
18. ALLISON, Ray	Hartford	Brandon Wheat Kings	RW
19. MANN, Jimmie	Winnipeg	Sherbrooke Beavers	RW

| 20. GOULET, Michel | Quebec | Quebec Remparts | LW |
| 21. LOWE, Kevin | Edmonton | Quebec Remparts | D |

Who was this Kevin Lowe and why did the Edmonton Oilers pick him as their first selection? It was a question that would pique the curiosity of Edmonton fans until the young man from the French-Canadian town of Lachute, Quebec, would make his debut at Northlands Coliseum.

(Photo courtesy *Alberta on Ice.*)

Women's Lib was way ahead of its time in Edmonton. Mrs. Mary Deeton, wife of center Harold Deeton (front row, right) accompanied the city's hockey team to Montreal for a crack at the Stanley Cup in 1907. This photo, taken in January 1909, also includes: Top (l to r) Oscar Hetu, Jack Miller, Bill Crowley, Ernie Chauvin, Hugh Ross. Front: Fred Whitcroft, Mary Deeton, and Harold Deeton.

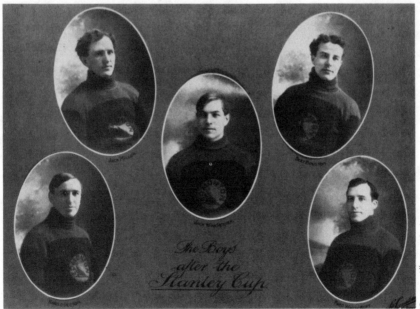

(Courtesy *Alberta on Ice.*)

Our second Stanley Cup challengers journeyed to Ottawa in January 1910 for a crack at the Ottawa Senators. They didn't quite win it but the Edmonton hockey team sure takes a good picture (l to r) Harold Deeton, Jack Miller, Jack Winchester, Bert Boulton, Fred Whitcroft.

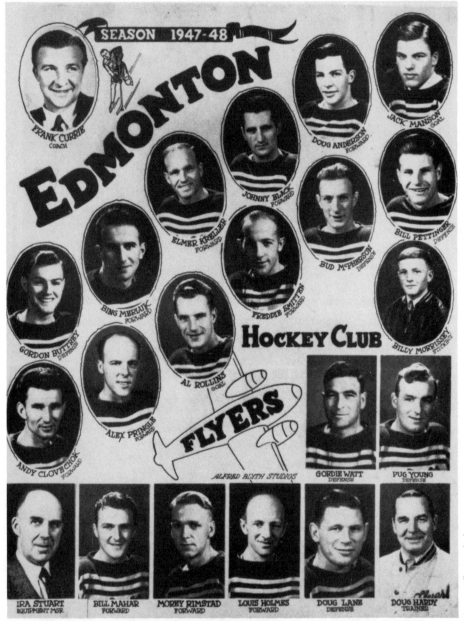

SEASON 1947-48

EDMONTON

HOCKEY CLUB

FLYERS

FRANK CURRIE
COACH

DOUG ANDERSON
FORWARD

JACK MANSON
GOAL

ELMER KRELLER
FORWARD

JOHNNY BLACK
FORWARD

BUD McPHERSON
DEFENSE

BILL PETTINGER
DEFENSE

BING MERLUK
FORWARD

FREDDIE SMITTEN
FORWARD

BILLY MORRISSEY
STICKBOY

GORDON BUTTREY
DEFENSE

ALEX PRINGLE
FORWARD

AL ROLLINS
GOAL

GORDIE WATT
DEFENSE

PUG YOUNG
DEFENSE

ANDY CLOVECHOK
FORWARD

ALFRED BLYTH STUDIOS

IRA STUART
EQUIPMENT MGR.

BILL MAHAR
FORWARD

MOREY RIMSTAD
FORWARD

LOUIS HOLMES
FORWARD

DOUG LANE
DEFENSE

DOUG HARDY
TRAINER

(Courtesy Alberta on Ice.)

The quality of minor pro hockey improved significantly after World War II. Our Flyers oozed with talent, particularly in goal where Al Rollins starred. He eventually won a Vezina trophy with the Toronto Maple Leafs and a Hart with the Chicago Blackhawks. He didn't do badly in Edmonton, helping the Flyers to the Allan Cup.

(Courtesy Alberta on Ice.)

If there was a "Gretzky" in Edmonton during another era it would be Eddie Shore, otherwise known as the Edmonton Express. He's to the right of the man with the Homburg, who happens to be Manager Ken McKenzie. A member of the famous Boucher clan, Bobby is in the front row on the right. Others include: Back row (l to r) Leroy Goldsworthy, Barney Stanley, "Duke" Keats, Kenny McKenzie (Manager), Eddie Shore, Spunk Sparrow, Lloyd McIntyre. Front: Bob Boucher, Bobby Benson, Herb Stuart, Art Gagne, Ernie Anderson, Johnny Sheppard.

One of Edmonton's most popular defenseman ever was Larry "The Rock" Zeidel, who was a combination early-day Dave Semenko–Marty McSorley. As you can see, he later played for Chicago in the NHL.

(Courtesy Stan Fischler Collection.)

111

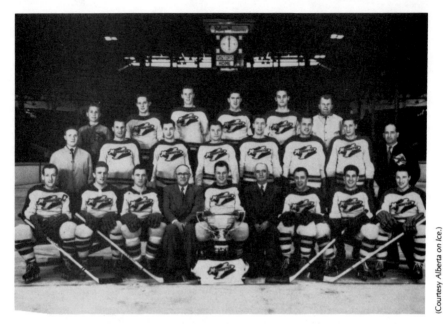

(Courtesy Alberta on Ice.)

That's Bud Poile with the Allan Cup between his knees. The Red Wing bosses in Detroit must have been beaming because fellows like Earl Reibel (top row, far left) and Glenn Hall (middle row, third from left) soon would be in Red Wing uniforms.

(Courtesy Alberta on Ice.)

The Rock and friends were about as good as most NHL clubs with Hall of Famers like Johnny Bucyk (upper left), Norm Ullman (upper right) and Glenn Hall, to name a few winners.

112

(Courtesy Alberta on Ice.)

Another reason for Edmonton to be proud, the 1961-62 Flyers were Western Hockey League Champions with one name quite familiar to current fans — Messier. That's right, Mark's dad Doug (second row, third from left) was a key member of the local club. On his right (your left) was hockey wild man Harry Young. Others include: Back Row (l to r) Don Chiz, Billy McNeill, Lionel Dewis (trainer), Eddie Joyal, Keith Walsh. Second row: Robert Merkle, Howie Young (#15), Doug Messier, John Miszuk, Len Lunde, Lloyd Haddon, Roger Dejordy, Bob Edwards. Front row: Warren Hynes, Lou Marcon, Ed Yuzda, Gilles Boivert, Bud Poile, Chuck Holmes, Don Poile.

(Courtesy Alberta on Ice.)

They don't call William Hunter "Wild Bill" for nothing. Amazingly, his energies kept pace with his ideas and Bill brought "Big League" (otherwise known as World Hockey Association) Hockey to Edmonton in 1972.

There never would have been an Edmonton team in the NHL if Bobby Hull (second left) didn't put the WHA in business. That's Brett Hull behind the check.

(Courtesy Walt Marlow Collection.)

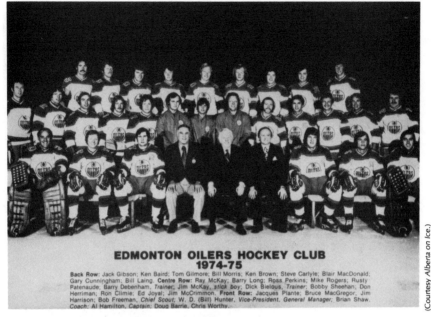

EDMONTON OILERS HOCKEY CLUB
1974-75

Back Row: Jack Gibson; Ken Baird; Tom Gilmore; Bill Morris; Ken Brown; Steve Carlyle; Blair MacDonald; Gary Cunningham; Bill Laing. Centre Row: Ray McKay; Barry Long; Ross Perkins; Mike Rogers; Rusty Patenaude; Barry Debenham, Trainer; Jim McKay, stick boy; Dick Bielous, Trainer; Bobby Sheehan; Don Herriman; Ron Climie; Ed Joyal; Jim McCrimmon. Front Row: Jacques Plante; Bruce MacGregor; Jim Harrison; Bob Freeman, Chief Scout; W. D. (Bill) Hunter, Vice-President, General Manager; Brian Shaw, Coach; Al Hamilton, Captain; Doug Barrie, Chris Worthy.

(Courtesy Alberta on Ice.)

This WHA club was hardly short of experience. Take the first two fellows in the front row on the left. The goalie was none other than Hall-of-Famer Jacques Plante. Right next to him is Bruce McGregor, currently our assistant GM (photo page 87).

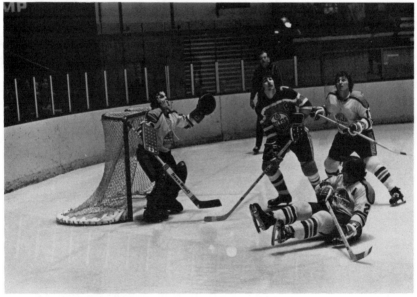

(Courtesy Alberta on Ice.)

The WHA Oilers weren't exactly world beaters but they did play entertaining hockey. That's Jim Harrison looking for a high pop fly while surrounded by three members of the New York Raiders.

(Courtesy *Alberta on Ice.*)

You're looking at a genuine antique — Edmonton's last WHA entry, the 1978-79 Oilers. We had several winners in this line-up including Dave Langevin (standing, far right), Dave Semenko (fourth from left, top row), and a thin young chap on the right in the middle named Wayne Gretzky.

PART TWO

13

NHL, Here I Come

I was not a peacenik as far as hockey was concerned. There was a war on and I had a lot to gain from it in 1978.

I'm talking about the war between the World Hockey Association and the National Hockey League. It was a conflict that I had viewed with enormous fascination ever since my fourteenth birthday, when the WHA was just getting underway.

My interest grew during my junior hockey years with the Remparts in Quebec City. After all, I was playing in a WHA town, Quebec also being the home of the Nordiques. The longer the WHA lived, the longer the Nordiques would be around. And the longer they played, the more I got to see some very interesting professional hockey at the big rink, Le Colisée.

But my interest in the war involved economic as well as artistic gains. Since I had developed into a competent defenseman in my late teens, both NHL and WHA scouts had been eyeing me. You didn't have to be an Einstein to figure out that the longer there was intense competition between the two leagues, the higher salaries would remain for hockey players. And since I've never had an aversion to money, there was every reason for me to hope that the WHA would last a very long time.

My links with the league extended far beyond the Quebec City limits. At one time, it even went below the Mason-Dixon Line. Think of it. Kevin Lowe, Edmonton Oiler, at one time could have been Kevin Lowe, Birmingham Bull. It's hard to believe today but there once had been a flourishing WHA team in the deep south operated by a Toronto sportsman-entrepreneur named John Bassett. Not only that but Bassett contacted my agent at that time, Alan Eagleson, and made it clear that he wanted me to join his team. I was 19 years old at the time — and very tempted.

Who wouldn't be? The talk was that I'd wind up with a four-year contract worth anywhere from $300,000 to $600,000. This for a kid who had never played a game of professional hockey in his life.

Not that I was naive about the business. I had seen how teenagers like Rick Vaive, Kenny Linseman and Michel Goulet, a teammate of mine in junior hockey, had been signed to six-figure contracts by Bassett and they hadn't had any more experience than I had at the time. What was even more tempting was the fact that the contract would have given me financial security in the event of a WHA-NHL merger. Officials from the two leagues were about to begin talks on that subject. "We want protection between now and the NHL draft in case of a merger," said Bill Watters, Eagleson's associate.

Plenty of talk was exchanged between Watters, Bassett and Bulls general manager Gilles Leger. Meanwhile, I found myself the center of attention, not just in Quebec City but also in Montreal where reporters began questioning me about my intentions.

Frankly, I wasn't sure which way to turn. Merger talk had heated up to a point where the union of the two leagues seemed only a matter of days away. Meanwhile, the Bulls offer was on the table and Watters was in the Soviet Union on business. Should I sign with the Bulls and fatten my wallet in the belief that the merger would not be ratified? *That* was the question.

Herb Zurkowsky, who covered junior hockey for the Montreal *Gazette*, phoned to get my decision. "I don't know what to do," I told him. "With these new merger talks, will Bassett try signing me and then screw around and sell me?"

It all became academic very soon By late March 1979, the two leagues had made peace and I lost what would have been a bundle of cash. That was the bad news. The good news was that I would now have much less to worry about and could concentrate my efforts on finishing as powerfully as possible with the Remparts in the hopes that some NHL teams would express as much interst in me as the Bulls.

My preference was the Nordiques now that they were to be a part of the NHL. It wasn't just that I had played all my junior hockey in Quebec; there was a matter of strong family ties to the province. The Lowe family and the province of Quebec had been intertwined for a long, long time and I felt very close to the land where I was born — not very far from Le Colisée.

My father, Clifford Lowe, was very much a man of the land and had a very powerful influence on me both as a person and as a hockey player. Dad, who had six brothers and two sisters, helped operate our family business — *Lowe's Dairy* — in the French-speaking town of Lachute. All of my dad's family was born in nearby Grenville but they moved to Lachute, launched the dairy and settled there.

Jessie, my mother, was born in Montreal. When she was four a curious thing happened; she visited an aunt and uncle who lived in Lachute. Mom had planned to stay there for about a week — but she never went home! Even though her brothers and sisters were still in Montreal, my mother remained with her uncle and aunt and grew up as an only child. If that sounds as if my mom ran away from home, it really shouldn't. Her true father had been a very sick man and her true mother was having a very difficult time making ends meet. Jessie's mother actually was very generous. She realized that her sister in Lachute couldn't have children but that she was a very loving person so she decided that it would be much better for mom to grow up in Lachute, which is where she met my dad.

"I chased him," she told me. "I did a lot of the running but I caught him."

Mom met dad when she was 15 years old and married him five years later. "In between," she said, "he tried to persuade me to date others. I had seen all his brothers but I zoomed in on him right away. I wanted him to be my future husband. I can be as determined as any Lowe can be."

Carol was their first child, followed by Nancy and Kenneth. My mom insists that when I was born, April 15, 1959, it was her most difficult birth of all: almost 24 hours of labor. For some reason, she had decided that instead of breast-feeding me, she would do it with bottled milk.

The day after I was born they brought me into the nursery and my mom gave me the bottle. But each time she fed me with it, I vomited. (Mother thought it was because she had been five years out of practice!) This happened so many times that the nurse told her that they would have to switch me to canned milk.

"This is ridiculous," my mother announced. *"We own a dairy; I'm not putting my son on canned milk. I want Lowe's milk!"*

Sure enough, they got some milk from our dairy and I drank the whole darn thing without bringing anything up. After we got home, mom checked it out and learned that the nursery was using another brand of milk. Lowe's Dairy had not been delivering there — until I came along.

Lowe's Dairy not only supplied milk for the community but it also provided refrigeration for the Lachute ice rink which was operated by the local Lion's Club. In fact it was named "Lowe's-Lion's Club Rink" and my dad was deeply involved with the operation; so much so that on the day that he drove mom home with me from the hospital, dad informed her that he would have to attend a rink meeting that night.

"What do you mean," she demanded. "I'm arriving with our new son and you're going out. Does hockey mean more to you than your new son does?"

Give dad credit, he had the answer: "Look at it this way; Kevin may grow up and want to skate. Most of his cousins are already skating. I'm working for them all."

Later, mom confessed to me, "Kevin, little did I know how involved I would become with hockey."

Although mom was around the house quite a bit when I was growing up, it was my sister Carol, who is nine years older, who spent a lot of time raising me. Once, my grandmother gave me a huge plush teddy bear which became my favorite stuffed animal. I'd take it to bed with me every night, but then one day it disappeared. I was beside myself with grief. We looked high and low but couldn't find the teddy. I was so upset that Carol had to cuddle up in bed with me that night. (The following summer, my sister opened her music bench to find some sheet music. There was teddy!)

Our family was closely knit as far back as I can remember. I had 31 cousins in the immediate vicinity and they always were involved with sports. Whenever there was a tournament, we'd stock up with pots of soup, sandwiches, cakes and homemade buns, pile into the cars and trucks and away the whole family would go.

When we kids weren't playing, we had to work. The dairy

provided jobs for just about the entire second-generation Lowe family so that a young fellow couldn't get into trouble even if he tried. On the few occasions that I really did get into hot water, I usually managed a light sentence because, after all, I was the baby of the family.

Once, when sister Carol was around, I hit my older brother Kenny with a baseball bat. By the time Carol turned around all she saw was Kenny's retaliation so, naturally, she gave him the business. "I'm only defending myself," Kenny shouted. "That kid gets away with everything."

Actually, I was very shy during my pre-teen years. Hockey was a part of my early life but my first ambition was to be a dentist. Kenny was the hockey player in the family at the time. He was an excellent goalie and was watched closely by dad who always strove for the best. Dad would tell Kenny that if he wanted to be a professional, now was the time to train.

"You have to eat, drink and sleep hockey," he would say. "First comes school, then church and then hockey."

Dad began taking me to the rink by the dairy two or three times a week and let me skate all by myself. After a while, a woman who worked for the dairy was under orders to tell me to stop. Then, she'd take off my snowsuit, dry me off and have a coloring book for me in one hand and an ice cream cone in the other. I was only three years old at the time and while I didn't know it then, my hockey career was officially underway.

Nor surprisingly, hockey was *the* sport in Lachute. When the cousins were playing, all the fathers would drive the cars and bring their sons to the rinks while the mothers, friends and their smaller kids would pile into a bus and head for the game. It was nothing for them to have 50 people jamming into that bus and, you can be sure, it was encouraging to the kids to know that they had such a big family behind them.

As big as we were, the fact remains that the Lowes were a minority of sorts in Lachute. We were one of a handful of English-speaking Catholic families in town and one of the few English-speaking families in the community. Yet, until I reached the peewee level of hockey-playing I spoke very little French. At the time I thought it was the hardest thing in the world to do but that changed quickly when I was named captain of the team.

That's when I learned the true meaning of leadership. It was one thing being the captain because I was one of the Lowes and the dairy paid for the hockey team. But my father would tell me that since I was the captain, it was up to me to phone the kids — and just about all of them were *French*.

There were no ifs, ands, or buts about it with my dad. He forced me to get on the telephone and call the kids and it was then that I *really* learned to speak French. The equation was made simple by my father; this was *my job* to do and I did it. I spoke their language and I learned it. Everything I learned in hockey since those childhood days goes back to what my father pushed me to do. I owe him a lot and that's why his death, when I was 13 years old, was such a blow to me.

My whole life changed with dad's passing. For one thing, the relationship with Kenny — he had been away at the University of Montreal at the time — became tighter. (After the wake, when it was time to return to university, Kenny opened the clothes closet and found me sitting in the corner. I told him then that I didn't want to play hockey again because of dad's death.) For another, I was helped a lot by a cousin, Carmen, who also took my father's passing very hard. When Kenny was ready to return to Montreal, Carmen put his arm around me and told my brother reassuringly, "Go ahead, Kenny. Get packing. Kevin and I will be okay."

He was right. Once I realized that I didn't have the grades to become a dentist, I began concentrating more seriously on hockey and moved up from the peewee to midget leagues in Lachute. I couldn't have been too bad because my next stop was the Remparts in Quebec City where I became the team's first English-speaking captain.

At first I had my problems in the Quebec Major Junior League. Without question, it was (and is) one of the fastest amateur hockey groups on the continent. Facing me were talents like Denis Savard and Ray Bourque who were dazzling even then, but I studied the older players and learned. When Mario Marois graduated from our club, it was my time to take over the leadership and I did so without hesitation. Surprisingly, (at least when you think of my *defensive* defense these days) I did plenty of puck-carrying and there were those who said that I lived dangerously. But I always felt confident that I could recover in time on any attack and get back to the defense.

Actually, I didn't think I was *that* good until someone from the Remparts front office cornered me early in my second season with Quebec and suggested that I get myself an agent because "all the scouts are coming to see you play." Oddly enough, Barry Fraser — the Oilers scouting director — phoned Al Eagleson, the agent and head of the NHL players' union, suggesting that The Eagle handle me.

It was apparent even then that hockey was more than just a pastime, that there was serious business involved. I didn't have to look very far to find out. My teammate Michel Goulet left the Remparts after his second season to play for the Birmingham Bulls and it was clear that the WHA clubs would sign whomever they thought could help them, age notwithstanding.

The lure of Birmingham was strong right from the very first offer, but there were other considerations to make. For one thing, my family was not crazy about my moving to the south. They figured I would be better off finishing my junior career with Quebec and then, assuming that my play was at a high caliber, I'd be picked in the first round of the NHL draft. Another factor was that, had I gone to Birmingham at that relatively young age, I might have played badly in the pros and thereby damaged my future in the eyes of the NHL scouts. Once the WHA-NHL merger was complete, I simply had to await the 1979 draft and hope that I would be a relatively high pick. When Irving Berlin wrote "All Alone By The Telephone," he could have had Kevin Lowe in mind.

For some strange reason the NHL decided in 1979 to have a telephone draft and my information — via Al Eagleson — was that it would start at 10 A.M. and The Eagle would contact me at about 10:15 A.M. to let me know where I was picked in the first round. Naturally, I sat by the phone — waiting, waiting, waiting.

By 10:45 A.M. the phone still had not rung and the hollow in my stomach was getting larger and larger. My mom said, "My God, they're not drafting him."

We didn't know it at the time, of course, but a mixup had developed on the phone lines which caused a major delay in the selection process. It was 11 A.M. and the phone still hadn't sounded. I was, to say the least, a basket case, staring at the walls, wondering where I had gone wrong.

Ten minutes later, *brinnggg!* I grabbed the receiver. A woman's voice was on the other end. Eagleson's private secretary told me that the Edmonton Oilers had chosen me —21st. (The

Montreal *Gazette* had speculated that I would be picked 12th in the first round. That distinction went to Paul Reinhart of the Flames, then in Atlanta.)

Mom remembers my deathless quote when I hung up. "Edmonton? I'm going to Edmonton? *That's even colder than Quebec!*"

I didn't know whether to laugh or cry at the news. What could be farther from the civilization that I had come to know and love than the province of Alberta? That was the bad news. The good news was that, yes, somebody wanted me and this bit of information was re-confirmed with a call from Glen Sather after I had gone out for a walk. He spoke to my mom and told her, "I couldn't believe that a player of Kevin's talents and potential was still unpicked by the time it came for our selection. I'm thrilled to have him."

When I returned home and mom relayed the message, I felt somewhat better. That night Eagleson reinforced Sather's message. "You're going to be starting out with a fresh, vibrant organization," he said. "It's a small city but there's money there and the club has a lot of potential. It'll work out to your advantage."

The words sounded nice but, truth to tell, I was a disappointed kid that day. I really had my heart set on Quebec — the Nordiques, ironically, picked my old teammate Michel Goulet — but I wasn't going to pout very long. There were reasons to be optimistic. For one thing, there was the knowledge that the Oilers had rated me a lot higher than 21st. Matter of fact, Barry Fraser would say, "We had him eleventh on our list. We liked his composure on the ice and he never seemed to get into too much trouble. When his name came up, we didn't think about it for a minute."

For another thing, I had fulfilled a childhood dream, if you will, and one that my father had nurtured from the earliest days when he'd watch me, a three-year-old, skating on my ankles around the Lowe Dairy Rink.

Clifford Lowe would have been mighty proud and if it was going to be Edmonton where I would play my pro hockey, so be it. As dad would have wanted me to be thinking, I switched to positive.

As the summer of 1979 unfolded, I riveted one thought in my head: NHL, here I come!

14

Edmonton, I Am Here

13/9/79

Hi Mom,

Just a little note to tell you things are going just fine. I'm getting a lot of attention from the press, T.V. media and coaches. In the scrimmages I'm playing well, picking up a couple of assists every game.

The reason there is no picture of me signing my contract is because I haven't signed it yet. I have it sitting here in my room with me. We're just waiting for Larry Gordon to get back so he can witness it. Everything is as we had discussed, as far as money goes.

Bryan Watson, the assistant coach, is a great guy. He's always joking with me, saying that first-round picks have to be treated with white gloves, and saying I'm not worth anything close to what I'm getting. He's also helping me a lot with my game, giving me hints every so often.

The guys here are a pretty good bunch. We usually go out and have our meals together at various restaurants. The beef out here is just great. I've had a steak or two just about every day.

Tomorrow we are playing an exhibition game against Great Falls, a junior team. Things are just fantastic. Charlie says hi. Bye for now.

Love,
Kevin.

The letter to my mother was written in the middle of training camp. There still was no guarantee that I was going to make the big team but I had no intentions of missing the opportunity. During the summer I did plenty of running and attended two hockey schools. Then, I went to a power skating class and learned that since I have long legs, I wasn't using the proper knee bend.

But once camp began I decided that the best course was to follow the path that had gotten me to the NHL, play the way I had in Quebec, and let the chips fall where they may. Besides, Sather had made a considerable investment in me and then made an admission that gave me even more confidencee. "We could have traded our first pick to St. Louis and even obtained [NHL ironman] Garry Unger," said Sather. "Garry certainly has two or three good years in him, but Lowe could turn out to have ten or twelve good years."

Wow! That was nice to hear.

Sather had me on defense with Lee Fogolin, Jr., whose dad, Lee, Sr., had played for the Detroit Red Wings and Chicago Black Hawks during the early 1950s. Pat Price, Al Hamilton, Doug Hicks, Colin Campbell and Risto Siltanen rounded out the defense.

They were an interesting bunch, both serious and humorous. Campbell, who wound up as assistant coach with the Red Wings, was the clown of the crew. One of his specialties was puncturing the bottom of a styrofoam coffee container with a tiny needle. The hole would be big enough for liquid to seep through but small enough to be invisible to the naked eye. Colin preferred singling out coach Sather as his victim because Glen was such a classy dresser. Once Sather began drinking, the coffee would make its way down his chin. Of course, he soon realized he had been had but then he'd try to make like nothing was happening.

Another Campbell specialty was the "Why Don't You Get Out Of The Toilet" routine which he'd orchestrate in the locker room after a workout. Colin would take a pair of pants, attach them to socks and then insert the socks into a pair of shoes. He'd arrange it so that someone from the outside would think one of the guys was sitting on the can. Sooner or later the guys would be pounding on the door, trying to get into the john themselves. Since there were so many kids on the team, we weren't wise to Campbell's capers, so he had quite a few victims to play around with for a while.

I did a lot of my playing with Wayne Gretzky. Sather had decided at training camp that it would be a good idea to have the Oilers first-ever draft choice room with their high-scoring hopefully-great hockey player. Up until then, Wayne had been living with families wherever he played — Sault Ste. Marie, Indianapolis and even his first seasons in Edmonton. He was tired of that routine and wanted a place of his own.

When Sather suggested (perhaps "ordered" is the more appropriate term) the Lowe-Gretzky union, I phoned my mom and mentioned it to her. "Oh, Kevin," she said, "what if you two are not compatible? What if you like different kinds of music? What if you don't get along well together? You're the newcomer, the new boy on the block. If you two have a falling-out the papers aren't going to take your side."

Mother was aware that Wayne already had gotten so much hype that he was known all over the continent. She was looking out for her son but I told her that everything would be all right. Not to worry. And with that, Wayne and I became the Felix and Oscar of the Oilers. Edmonton's "Odd Couple."

Despite mom's concerns, Wayne and I got along famously from Day One in our south side apartment. One reason for our compatibility was the fair decision-making process. Gretz realized right from the start that I was a better cook and the Lowe roasts began to be a staple of *Chez Kevin-Wayne*.

And if my mother was concerned about Wayne's ego and all the attention affecting him, she need not have had any worries along that score. From the very start, I could sense that he was a down-to-earth, unaffected young man with a clear grasp of what was happening to him and what he had to do. On top of that, we were both on the same wavelength. He was dedicated to becoming the best possible hockey player in the shortest amount of time, a dedication which I shared.

In time the Mutual Admiration Society would be expanded to include fellow neighbors Doug Hicks, Dave Lumley and Mark Messier. Dave and Doug had moved into our building while Mark, who had been staying at his parents' place a half-hour from downtown Edmonton, would often wind up tenting with us.

Each was a significant personality in his own way and although Hicks has long been forgotten by most fans, those of us who had the good fortune to play alongside him remember him well. Doug was a seasoned pro — Minnesota, Chicago — by the time he reached Edmonton and knew the meaning of teamsmanship. One of the first bits of business he initiated was "The Original Team Beer." Dougie decided that every couple of weeks it was mandatory for *everyone* to go to a certain place, have a steak sandwich and a couple of beers. It was like a fraternity bash where we could unwind, hash out any problems and, most of all, cultivate the team spirit that would very soon be evident on the Edmonton Oilers.

The subject of "The Original Team Beer" would vary from meeting to meeting. Sometimes we'd talk about a game just played or about girlfriends, wives, whatever. Hicks and another veteran Bill (Cowboy) Flett convened our first-ever Oilers team beer in Vancouver before the 1979-80 season had even started.

When Flett informed me that there was to be a "team meeting," I had no idea what he was talking about but all he would say was, "Follow me, kid." So, I followed.

He proceeded to lead me to an old hotel, a tavern-type place that, to be kind, looked rather shabby from the outside and was even frumpier inside. I said, "Cowboy, I thought we were going to a *team meeting*. What the heck are we doing here?"

Flett stared me down and replied, "This *is* where the team meeting is, and where did you think you were going?"

Cowboy then led me inside and what do I see but the entire Oilers squad sitting at the bar, downing a few beers. The only problem was that I didn't drink very much, so I had a couple and left it at that. Maybe that's what Dick Chubey had in mind when the headline on one of his columns about me read: WHOLESOME KID HITS BIG TIME.

If being wholesome was a virtue, Sather had a surplus of goodness on his original NHL squad as he prepared for opening night of the 1979-80 season. As Jim Matheson of the *Edmonton Journal* noted as we wound down training camp, "Unless Sather has a sudden change of heart, he will play baby-sitter to a gang of fuzzy-cheeked kids this winter."

Of course this was to my advantage. Slats had to fill in gaps with older players but his accent was strictly on youth and that's why youngsters like myself and Mark Messier were so fortunate to be Oilers at that time. Sather made no secret about it.

"I don't think there will be too many guys over 30 on the club," Sather pointed out. "Not that that's exactly a sin. If we're going to struggle in our first year, and that's a possibility, I'd rather do it with kids than guys say, 32 or 33, with only a few years left in their careers. I plan on building with youth — like the Islanders."

Slats found himself in an interesting situation. On the one hand he had some 14,000 season ticket-holders lined up who wanted to see a winning team, just as they had the previous year when the Oilers finished first in the WHA. On the other hand, there was the knowledge throughout the city of Edmonton that the NHL, because of the severe restrictions it had placed on the four former WHA clubs, had made it almost impossible for us to ice a contender in 1979-80. The Oilers had lost 13 players from the previous roster. The team captain, Paul Shmyr, had gone to the Minnesota North Stars and improving defenseman Dave Langevin was grabbed by the Islanders. John Hughes went to the Vancouver Canucks and Risto Siltanen to St. Louis. In order to get Siltanen back to Edmonton, we traded another good prospect, Joe Micheletti, to the Blues. On top of that, we had an NHL ruling turn Bengt Gustafson over to the Washington Capitals after Sather thought he had had him and Doug Berry was lost to Colorado.

The old man of the team was goalie Dave Dryden who had just turned 38 with the start of training camp. He had won the WHA's most valuable player award in 1978-79 and Sather designated Dave as his main man between the pipes.

"We've got the guy to build a team around," said Gordon. "Now we've just got to give him some help."

Gretzky, who still hadn't played his first NHL game, obviously would be the club's nucleus although there were still plenty of doubters throughout the league who wondered whether the skinny kid from Brantford would be able to survive — let alone thrive — in this supposedly higher-quality, higher-pressure atmosphere.

Wayne would be centering right wing Blair MacDonald, otherwise known as "BJ," and Brett Callighan on the left. We called it our "GMC Line" and it clicked right from the start in spite of people like Vancouver scout Larry Popein who went on record saying, "MacDonald won't be able to score in the NHL."

After 19 games, BJ had 14 goals and 10 assists and his center, under a microscope wherever we went, was proving that the transition for him from WHA to NHL was as easy as exhaling. "I try to stay out of trouble," said Wayne. "I'm hard to hit. A lot of players took shots at me when I first got into the WHA and a lot are taking shots at me now in the NHL, but I can take it. I'm not a fighter, but I practice self-defense."

Within a month, Wayne was leading the Oilers in scoring and amazing the opposition and teammates alike. BJ summed up our thinking when he said, "The puck follows him around."

But as magnificent a scorer as Wayne turned out to be, he still cannot lay claim to a distinction which I will have for the rest of my life — scoring the first-ever Edmonton Oilers NHL goal. The milestone occurred in Chicago Stadium on October 10, 1979, our opening game of our premier season.

Scoring was the farthest thing from my mind as we suited up in the ancient building located in a Chicago slum area. Like the rest of the gang — especially Wayne — I was fidgety in the dressing room as we awaited the call to the ice. To a man we were determined to make a good first impression, particularly because the fans were wondering whether we were going to be that awful.

And for a few minutes it looked like we *were* going to be as bad as the people expected. John Marks and Rich Preston scored for Chicago before two and a half minutes had elapsed and the Stadium was going wild. But in no time at all, we seemed to pull ourselves together. At 9:09 Terry Ruskowski of Chicago was sent to the penalty box and we went on the power play with Yours Truly one of the point men. Just 40 seconds later I lifted a 15-foot backhand past Tony Esposito and felt that very special surge of stomach energy one experiences when the red light flashes behind the net. (My mom has had a bit of trouble describing the goal because the pictures that ran the next day showed Wayne, who got an assist on the play, with his arms upraised in front of the net. The puck, by the way, was placed on a plaque and hangs on the wall of mom's house. Once, when Wayne visited, he kidded her and said, "Isn't that my plaque on the wall?" Mom shot back, "Like hell it is. You'll have a million of them before you're through but that one is Kevin's.")

We lost the game, 4-2, but didn't look all that bad. "They are a good-skating hard-working team," said Stan Mikita, the outstanding Black Hawks center.

"If they continue to play like that," added Tony Esposito, "they're going to surprise a lot of teams."

As for myself, there was no doubt that opening night was not all that bad — and in many ways commendable. Sure, I was in a bit of a daze at the start (who wasn't?) but I got over the jitters soon enough. The goal wasn't exactly the kind they write textbooks about but, what the heck, it wasn't so bad either. The shot deflected off one of the Chicago defensemen and floated over Esposito like a knuckleball. When I returned to the bench, I remember thinking that I wished my mother had been in the stands to see it first hand.

More important was my defensive work. ("It's hard to believe the kid has so much poise," said Sather.) I held my own and even managed to come out even in a fight with Chicago's big forward Grant Mulvey late in the game. It had started when he was trying to dig in around Dave Dryden. I knocked him down about six times and then turned around in time to see him take off his glove and swing at me. Maybe that's what Sather meant when he said later, "Kevin really stuck his nose in there!"

Like the other WHA clubs which had moved into the NHL, we stumbled and sputtered through the first half of the season. By January 14, 1980, we had the third-worst record in the league, only a point more than the Washington Capitals and Colorado Rockies. Gordon had a good line on our problems when he said, "Inconsistency is what's hurting us most and that's attributable to inexperience. But people love to watch the young guys on this team develop. In every city we go they're all keen to see our youngsters."

They didn't see all that much of me. I suffered an ankle injury in Atlanta which sidelined me for more than a month. (The longest I had ever been out as a junior was six games with a separated shoulder.) If that wasn't bad enough, I cracked up my brand new Thunderbird on the way to a practice.

I wasn't the only one struggling. Dave Dryden was having his troubles between the pipes and it was evident that Father Time was catching up with this great guy. Luckily we had Eddie Mio in reserve and Steady Eddie would prove to be invaluable for us until those two wonderful kids, Andy Moog and Grant Fuhr, arrived on the scene.

What made life so fortunate for all of us — no matter how dreadful some of the losses or depressing the injuries — was the rapid evolution of Gretzky. His brilliance was evident even then and it deflected a lot of the potentially negative attention which might have been directed at players like myself and Mark who were trying to find ourselves.

How good was Wayne? Only two players, Guy Lafleur of the Canadiens and Marcel Dionne of the Kings, were pacing him in the scoring race by mid season. Behind Wayne were such big names as Bryan Trottier, Mike Bossy and Gil Perreault. Soon, Wayne would pass Lafleur and duel with Dionne in a neck-and-neck race for the Art Ross Trophy.

After Gretzky, we counted on two other centers, Stan Weir and Ron Chipperfield, and this produced an interesting bit of drama and pathos as the season unfolded. Of the two, Chipperfield would have seemed to be the better bet to excel. During his WHA years he scored more than 30 goals in three different seasons and twice totalled more than 85 points. When we started the 1979-80 season, Ron was only 25 years old and was voted captain by the players. (Lee Fogolin and BJ were the alternates.) At the time his captaincy was made public, Sather added, "Ron is mature, sensible and will lead by example."

Unfortunately, the example — at least when it came to goals and assists — was not encouraging. To put it kindly, Ron struggled through the first three months of the season and in 17 games failed to come up with a single point. The double failures of Dryden and Chipperfield worried Sather and he soon proved — as he would do so many more times in the future — that he would not allow a team wound to fester without treatment for very long.

Trades were never pleasant but the deal which sent Chipperfield to the Nordiques taught me early on that Slats, no matter how difficult it might be for him emotionally, can manage to bury sentimentality when it comes to improving his hockey club. Just before the trade deadline, he dealt Chipperfield to Quebec for goalie Ron Low. At the time our captain had been in Winnipeg with his dying mother.

"It was the toughest thing I had to do in years," said Sather, who didn't stop trading with that move. He also moved forward Cam Connor to the New York Rangers for controversial scorer Don Murdoch.

Whether we were to make the playoffs or not, Sather had irrevocably made his decision to go with the youngsters for better or worse. Naturally, Wayne would be the scoring leader but Slats also wanted me and Mark Messier to eventually take over. He told us straight out, "Hey, you guys take charge. You tell 'em when they're screwing up." I feel that Mark and I would have been leaders eventually, but Sather pushed us into the leadership role. Some guys were meant to be leaders and I feel I have that quality.

Certainly, Mark would prove that he was as much a catalyst as anyone who wore Edmonton colors but he lagged a bit in the discipline department during that rookie season. For one thing he was late for practice a few times and was duly reprimanded by Slats. Yet, it kept happening and happening until Mark delivered the *coup de grace* prior to a trip from Edmonton to St. Louis where we were scheduled to play the Blues.

Our flight was to leave from the *international* airport but, for some reason, Mark was under the impression that the plane would take off from the *municipal* airport. There was, as he would learn, a big difference.

For starters, Mark made the mistake of leaving his house late. Next mistake was heading downtown to the municipal airport. Naturally, when he arrived there he was informed that there were no planes for St. Louis and if there were, none of the Oilers would be on them. As quickly as possible, he turned his car in the direction of the international airport — as he tells it, driving on the wrong side of the road because there had been an accident, facing traffic for about two or three miles — almost killing himself and his mom.

They arrived at the international airport just in time to watch the TWA flight climbing into the sun.

Mark headed for the nearest phone and called Bruce MacGregor who by now was assisting Slats in the front office. "I missed the flight to St. Louis," Mark announced.

"That's all right," MacGregor replied. "I have one for you."

"Good," said Mark with the utmost naivete. "Can I catch the team?"

MacGregor paused momentarily. "Yeah, you can catch the team. But the team you're catching is the Houston Apollos."

Mark Messier was sent to the minors and we all learned a lesson from that little comedy of erroneous airports.

It wasn't funny to Mark at the time but, in the end, it would do a lot to help us in our stretch drive for a playoff berth.

15

The Oilers and Gretzky: A Pair of Stretch Runs

The demotion of Mark Messier was a superb example of Glen Sather's sense of discipline and was one of several which would chill the players and emphasize Slats' no-nonsense approach to orchestrating his hockey club. Still another was *"L'Affaire Bobby Schmautz."*

A smallish, wiry forward (a bit nasty with the stick as well), Schmautzy had played his best hockey for the Boston Bruins during the heydey of coach Don (Grapes) Cherry in Beantown. When Cherry was fired by general manager Harry Sinden, a few hearts were broken inside the Bruins locker room and one of them belonged to Schmautz.

By the time I had reached the NHL Cherry had moved to Denver where he had become coach of the Colorado Rockies. Naturally, any player who had been a member of the Cherry Marching and Chowder Society wanted to play for him — if it could be arranged. One such player was Schmautz.

However, getting to Colorado was not all that easy. Cherry and Sinden had become bitter — and I mean bitter — enemies. (To show how intense the dislike was, more than ten years have passed since their split and they *still* don't talk to one another.) There was no way Sinden would accommodate Cherry by sending a player *directly* to him but there were avenues for getting around this problem. (Doesn't it remind you of the diplomatic arena where two warring nations communicate through the Swiss Embassy?) One route would be through a third party, in this case the Edmonton Oilers. And that is precisely what happened. On December 10, 1979 Schmautz was traded to us for Dan Newman, a forward who had had little impact on the club. Schmautz did have an impact on the Oilers but in a negative way, usually with story-telling.

From the minute Schmautzy arrived in Edmonton to the moment he left, all he did was tell stories about Don Cherry, or so it seemed. By the time Bobby got through, you'd have thought he was talking about St. Grapes. I mean he portrayed Cherry as the greatest thing since the invention of the puck. He simply couldn't stop telling us how good it was playing hockey in Boston. (If a player came to our team today and started telling stories about how wonderful his other club was, we'd tell him to get the tattoo off his rear end, quick, or he'd be out the door.)

The younger Oilers didn't mind listening to Schmautz because, in a way, he was charming and besides, we were entranced by tales about the big league but Schmautzy overstepped his bounds when we went to Denver for a game with Cherry's Rockies. The incident happened before one of our practices just after our arrival at the rink.

Instead of heading for our dressing room, Schmautz headed for the Rockies' end, sought out their trainer and got himself a Colorado jersey. (Mind you, he *still* was an Edmonton Oiler.) Meanwhile, our players dressed and skated out onto the ice for the workout, all of us, that is, but Schmautzy.

Slats had herded us all on the ice when, from the other end of the rink, who should skate out but Schmautzy, wearing the Colorado jersey. We thought it was hilarious. Sather thought otherwise.

On February 25, 1980 Schmautz was traded to the Rockies for Don Ashby. As far as Slats was concerned, the deal came not a moment too soon.

From the very start of training camp, Sather had one main rule: *don't at any time embarrass me — or the team.* After that, just about anything goes. And, believe me, a lot of madcap stuff goes on, some of it involving Sather himself.

From the very start Slats was in on the pranks. I haven't got enough fingers to count all the times I saw him running through the dressing room with a bucket full of cold water, heading for the shower where he would douse one of his victims. (He also nailed many a target with cold water in the sauna.) Another of his ploys was to find a player's hair brush, fill it with shaving cream and then turn the brush upside down so the cream isn't readily seen. When the guy grabs the brush and puts it to his hair, he finds himself with a head full of shaving cream. (Shaving cream is also useful in shoes.) For variety, he'll unobtrusively fill a player's hair dryer with powder. The storm of talcum that accompanies the flicking of that hair-dryer's switch is positively awesome.

Naturally, Slats expected to be the victim as well — and he was. Dave Semenko, who was with us in 1979-80, would victimize Glen with "The Flexible Stick Routine." To understand this — if you're not a hockey player — first picture the whole hockey stick, from tip of blade to end of the neck. Then, focus half-way down the shaft. On just about every stick the manufacturer adds a bit of "chrome" in the form of shiny foil, sometimes silver, sometimes black.

What Semenko did was carefully remove the foil, saw Sather's stick in that precise spot, and then replace the foil over the sawed portion of the stick. He then put the stick on the top of Glen's other sticks which sat on the stick rack so that when Sather went to get a stick he would take the one that was easiest to obtain.

Sure enough, a few minutes later Slats grabbed the stick off the rack and headed for the ice and our workout. As all the players knew, the first thing you do when you get on the ice is either test the stick by pressing the blade (flexing it) on to the ice with considerable force or take a big slapshot. Glen took the (ahem!) slapshot; the stick buckled at the sawed-off point and the coach fell on his face. (Naturally, Slats would get retribution with cold water, shaving cream in the shoes or any number of shampoo pranks.)

Now all of this Three Stooges kind of stuff may sound contradictory to the "Don't Embarrass Me . . ." theme but Sather's point was that tomfoolery was permissible. In fact, we could go very far with it but it had to be in the right place and the right time. The timing was very important. Obviously, Schmautz had chosen the wrong time and place and, furthermore, was trifling with a major no-no and that is Oilers loyalty. Pride in the team was stressed from the very beginning with Slats. The jersey represented our team. When Schmautzy donned the enemy colors, that was tantamount to treason.

There was another gray area of pranksterism that I, for one, could never abide although I knew that it had been a part of hockey tradition for years and that was the infamous "Shave," a ritual that could best (or perhaps worst) be compared to college fraternity hazing in its most degrading form.

The Shave was designed to bring rookies into the fold through the vehicle of embarrassment. Many techniques have been employed over the years but, essentially, it consists of cornering a rookie (several veterans are needed because resistance is often fierce) pinning him down (a training table is extremely practical for this purpose) with rope if necessary and then applying scissors and razor (a barber's professional razor is preferable). In its most extreme (and painful) form, The Shave is perpetrated *without* shaving cream and with enormous anguish.

I speak firsthand since I was a victim although my attitude when it finally happened perplexed a lot of the veterans and, I imagine, disappointed them. As it developed, my mother was involved in a tangential way and, to that extent, it did bother me.

My initiation to The Shave developed on our first eastern swing of the season, a time of special excitement for me because I was, in effect, returning home, although our first stop was Maple Leaf Gardens in Toronto. The thrill of coming east was such that mom decided to leave Lachute and meet me before our game with the Maple Leafs.

Needless to say, everyone on the team sensed how excited I was to see my mother and play in familiar country. It was then that a few of the Oilers veterans began plotting to get me. They decided to perform the operation immediately after a morning practice at the Gardens. All of the guys knew I was in a hurry to get dressed and see mom after the workout. They watched me rush off the ice into the dressing room. I quickly removed my equipment and was heading for the shower when they nabbed me.

At this point many rookies try to get away and, in the process, cause more hurt to themselves than they otherwise would absorb. Not me. I was so happy being part of the team that I basically said, "Here, take me. This is great! You fellows are accepting me as one of the guys." That annoyed them. They wanted a bit of a struggle so they could get physical with me but they didn't get any of that. Then they shaved me, daubed me with vaseline and black ink, and left me quite a mess.

That didn't bother me nearly as much as the realization that

mom was in the stands, waiting. I ended up spending an hour
— after all the executioners had left — getting cleaned up.

I can't say that The Shave had a particularly negative effect
on me although I have been told that other players on other
teams have been traumatized by the ritual. (The late Pelle
Lindbergh of the Philadelphia Flyers was one who reportedly
was seriously affected by The Shave.)

To my way of thinking, The Shave is obsolete. It's silly.
There are lots of other ways to accept a younger player and,
fortunately, the Oilers have slowly but surely gotten away
from it. The process was slow but it became less and less abusive. Finally, we stopped it altogether which was good,
morale-wise, because it degraded the rookies and set them
apart from the other players.

Doing that made no sense since we were working together
to achieve one goal: so why have rookies in one corner and veterans in the other, plotting against each other? In the long
haul, one secret to the Oilers success has been the fact that all
players are treated equally. Consequently, we haven't had the
gap between rookies and veterans that other clubs do. The
rookies are woven into the club fabric in various ways, not the
least of which is "The Rookie Round." That's where the newcomer takes the rest of the club out for a night and buys them
all a round of drinks, even if the drinks happen to be orange
juice. Believe it or not, the tradition makes the rookie feel a
part of the team.

Naturally, you'll always find collisions between the kids and
the oldtimers and our club suffered through those pains as
well. One of the inevitable problems surfaced around Gretzky
who, by this time, was receiving enormous attention wherever
he went. Nobody quite knew for sure just how great Wayne
would become and he certainly hadn't achieved the superhu-
man, although he and Marcel Dionne were now duelling for
the scoring championship in the final month of the season.

I mention this because there was one player on our team
who had a confrontation with Gretzky and that was our veteran defenseman Pat Price, a man not known for withholding
his opinions. It was Pricey who had managed to talk his way
off the Islanders and now he was having a go at our one and
only crown jewel.

Whether he meant to degrade Wayne or make him look bad,
I'm not sure, but Pricey was trying to make a point. Wayne

and BJ MacDonald were scoring lots of goals, getting lots of points, but we were also losing games and not looking like we were going to make the play-offs — unless there was an awfully good run in March.

One day Pricey pointed at Wayne and said straight out, "Listen, Wayne, you have to start playing better defense."

Wayne got the hair up on the back of his neck as if to say, "Pricey, I'm doing my best to help the team — I can't do it any other way."

So, there was a conflict there but it was resolved, in part, by our fantastic run to the finish line and Sather's leadership combined with his intuitive way of handling Wayne.

Slats was willing to bend with a particular player if he felt the club would benefit overall and that's the way it was with Sather and Gretzky. Slats compensated. He knew that Wayne was lacking defensively. He knew that 80 percent of Wayne's efforts were concentrated on offense and the other 20 percent might have been defense. Glen turned his back to that. He knew that this guy was a great player. Sather used what I call "The Stallion Theory." If you have a stallion that wants to run, you don't rein him in, you want to let him go. Same with Wayne. He had all the natural talent in the world, so let him do what he does best.

Occasionally, Sather would pull the reins back and tell Gretz, "All right, standing up at the red line is not going to help the team. So, make it half way between the red line and the blue line." In that way, Sather allowed Gretzky to develop in a manner that a stricter disciplinarian — such as a Scotty Bowman — might not have done. Under a Bowman, Wayne might not have emerged as the enormous star that he is, and Wayne might even say the same thing. Whatever the case, more and more people around the league were learning mighty quickly not to trifle with Gretz. One of them was Jim Craig, the 1980 American Olympic hero.

As the goaltender for Herb Brooks' Olympians, Craig had returned from Lake Placid as a national hero. He was not only the talk of the continent but also the subject of much conversation around the NHL, particularly after he had been signed to a contract by the Atlanta Flames right after the Winter Games had ended and just in time for the stretch run.

Whether or not Craig was a good goalie is a moot point. History has shown that he didn't last very long in the NHL but he

sure was cocky in that short run and we — I should say Wayne
— got a taste of Craig's wisecracking during a game at the
Omni in Atlanta.

We had fallen behind a couple of goals and were not having
a particularly good game up until this point when Wayne
skated near the crease. "Gretzky," snapped Craig, "just who
do you think you are anyway?"

Wayne didn't say a word to Craig but in the next 30 minutes, Gretz did score three goals including the eventual game-
winner. That silenced Jim Craig awfully quick.

With six games left in the regular schedule Wayne was
seven points behind Dionne in the scoring race and we were
trying to beat out Washington, Detroit and Quebec for the last
playoff spot. In those days, the playoff berths went to the 16
teams with the best point marks no matter what division.

There's no way we would have made the playoffs had Glen
not executed a couple of key moves. First of all, there was the
disciplining of Mark Messier. Another coach might have
insisted that Mark remain in the minors for the rest of the season but Glen wasn't pig-headed that way. He allowed Mark to
get a taste of the Central League for two weeks during which
Mark burned up the league. Then, he brought him back to the
NHL. But more than scoring punch, we needed better goaltending to make it.

Dave Dryden had retired by now and neither Eddie Mio nor
our other goalie, Jim Corsi, seemed to be the answer. Getting
Ron Low from Quebec was the ideal move. Not only could
Ronnie stop the puck, he added an intangible factor. "He's a
tremendous competitor," said Bryan Watson, "and he doesn't
lose his composure or get rattled."

He didn't. The Oilers reeled off win after win until we
wound up against Colorado for our final game of the season.
Going into it, we knew we needed a victory to put ourselves
into the playoffs but in the first six minutes of the game good
old Schmautzy scored two goals to spring Colorado to a 2-0
lead. But then Gretz got going and rallied the club. He assisted
on the tying goal in the second period and scored the game-
winner in the third — his 51st goal of the season — not bad for
the WHA kid they said wouldn't cut it in the NHL!

By this time the Gretzky-Dionne scoring race was the talk of
the league and the two were neck-and-neck on that final night
of the season. The difference was that Dionne's game in Los

Angeles was going to be played later so we all went to a restaurant to celebrate our entrance into our first-ever NHL playoff.

While we were at the table Wayne looked at his watch and said, "The game should be over in Los Angeles; I'm going to phone to see what happened."

Naturally, Gretz wanted to know whether Dionne had caught him. Wayne had finished with 137 points. Marcel was two behind before his game was in progress. When Wayne returned to the table he had a long face on and it was obvious he hadn't won the title. "We tied," he said.

According to the NHL rules, if there is a tie — Wayne was 51-86-137 and Marcel 53-84-137 — the player with the most goals gets the Art Ross Trophy, no questions asked. Dionne was the winner.

Wayne was devastated by the news. At the time he thought that this would be his one and only shot at the scoring championship. (By the way, Dionne was thinking the same thing; only Marcel was the one who turned out to be right.) But Wayne got over his depression very quickly because we had a playoff on our hands and the opposition was none other than the Philadelphia Flyers who would, eventually, make it all the way to the Stanley Cup finals that year.

None of us had any illusions about Philadelphia. How could we? The Flyers had finished with the best point mark of all the playoff teams, 116 points, and we were last of the 16 teams with 69 points — a fat 47 point difference. But this much is certain; we weren't the least bit intimidated by them despite all the hoopla about the Broad Street Bullies and the Flyers domination at The Spectrum.

I must admit that when I was on the ice for the National Anthem, I did feel moved. That's when the Flyers tradition became apparent to me and I had memories of Kate Smith singing "God Bless America" in person there for the seventh game of the 1975 playoff against the Islanders. I was still thinking about the Flyers I followed as a kid when Paul Holmgren ran my face into the glass. Suddenly, reality set in and I realized there was a game to win.

All things considered we didn't do as badly as some Edmontonians may have feared. In the opener, we fought back from a 0-2 deficit to tie the score, courtesty of Gretz, and then we went ahead, 3-2, in the third. Ronnie Low was standing on his head just as he had in the stretch. We knew we had to play way above our heads just to stay alive but, with less than a minute and a half left in the third period, Rick MacLeish tied the score and Bobby Clarke won it for Philly in sudden-death.

The loss hurt but it didn't dampen our spirits because if there was one outstanding trait about our club it was the phenomenal spirit. In fact there were times during the season when Glen simply had to put his foot down and cool our fires. We never wanted to fall into the mold of being a "typical NHL team" so we'd do silly things like wear ball caps in practices and other capers that showed we had a special joie de vivre. But when it got out of hand, Glen stepped in and put on the brakes.

There was little Slats could do about the Flyers because they already were a top-drawer established team and we were still just a bunch of players assembled to play hockey and many of us were still trying to make it in the NHL. The difference was evident in Game Two, a 5-1 Flyers blowout. But then we returned to Edmonton and made them work. Gretz opened the scoring and we opened with a 2-0 lead.

But there was no denying that the Flyers were superior to the tune of their having a differential of seven quality players whereas we had a bunch of guys fighting for our lives. None of us would concede it at the time — we gave them a good run for their money — but to beat them would have required a miracle and none was forthcoming. The Flyers tied the score, sending it into overtime once again.

After 20 minutes the score still was tied but in the second sudden-death Ken Linseman (later to be my teammate) beat Low at 3:56 and the season was over — just like that.

Many observations were made in the next few days but the most telling of all came from the Flyers captain Bobby Clarke. He pointed out that the 16th place team had given the first place club quite a run for its money. He wasn't being flippant when he added that the Edmonton Oilers would be heard from for a long, long time.

16

The Kid Learns the Ropes

If I learned anything that rookie season it was that I still had a lot to learn. The playoff knocked me down a peg. For the first time I felt I was in over my head; it seemed, at least momentarily, that I was out of my league. I learned what it was like to ride the bench but, most important, I learned. I learned not only what the big leagues are like on the ice but outside of the arena as well.

In the early days Gretz and I were dazzled by big-league life. Wherever we went out our standard dinner was shrimp cocktail or *escargot*, a Caesar salad followed by a big piece of prime rib with baked potato and all the trimmings, then cheesecake for dessert. In between we might add a little bit of wine and a liqueur and coffee to finish the meal. We did that just about every time we had dinner.

Then, Dougie Hicks, who had been around a bit longer, broadened our horizons. From him, I learned that there's more to a meal than meat and potatoes — sushi, for example. Dougie was the first one to get me to try sushi. The next morning we were on the team bus and one of the guys asked me what I had for dinner. I said I went for sushi. "What's sushi?" somebody asked. I said it's a Japanese dish — raw fish. "Well, just say 'fish,' you don't have to make up a name for it," one of the fellows snapped.

Hicks also taught me all about the instant vacation. Right after the Flyers knocked us out of the playoffs, Dougie said, "Come on, let's go to Hawaii." Just like that!

Hawaii. Why, I had never been off the continent in my life.

"Geez," I said, "I don't know about that. Don't you have to plan for those sorts of things?"

"Hell, no," he pointed out with the tenderness that comes with dealing with greenhorns. "You just get an airplane ticket, pack a few things, take a little money and you go."

I was amazed at the simplicity of it all. Hicksy not only persuaded me but he also added Mark Messier, Wayne Gretzky and Dave Lumley to the entourage. And to say the least, I was excited since I had never really traveled on a vacation before. (The traveling around the NHL wasn't like a vacation.) Going to Hawaii seemed tantamount to flying to the moon so I packed appropriately with no less than four suitcases. Mark had the right idea. He brought nothing more than a little tote bag, a pair of jeans, a T-shirt, running shoes and about $4,000 stuffed into the top of his pocket. Which only proved to me that you never stop learning.

The vacation was wonderful if for no other reason than that we escaped the pressures of that first season and what was to be the endless regimentation of traveling from city to city for seven months of the year. Mind you, I'm not complaining — far from it — but it was good to escape the curfews, for example, and we had plenty in that 1979-80 season.

Sather had imposed an 11 P.M. curfew when we were on the road that year and every once in a while he'd do a room check at our hotel. At first it would be a surprise but, after a while, I could tell when he'd call. I learned to read Glen and know when he was going to check and when he wasn't going to phone the room. Sometimes he might even warn us in advance. "You guys had better be in because I might be checking tonight." One night Dave Semenko discovered that Slats wasn't kidding after all.

Dave arrived back at his room an hour late. When he opened the door he chuckled to himself, thinking he had made an hour on the deal without the coach knowing. He also wondered whether Glen had called. But he didn't have to wonder very long; sitting in the chair right in front of Dave was the coach himself. All Slats uttered was one sentence: "And did you have a good night?"

Slats had been around and frequently he'd tell us about the greats and near-greats he had had as teammates and opponents. One of them, of course, was the immortal Gordie Howe who just happened to have been my idol when I was growing up in Lachute. Although just about everyone in our town had been a Montreal Canadiens fan, I always picked the underdog and when it came to the NHL, I rooted for the Detroit Red Wings, Howe's original team.

Once Gordie and his Red Wings played an exhibition game just up the road from us in St. Jerome and my dad took me to see the game. I was all of four years old at the time but I went down to the bench while the game was going on, tugged at Howe's jersey and asked for his autograph. Great guy that he was (is), Gordie turned around, looked at me, laughed and signed my program. From that moment on, he was my idol, my hero.

Now, he was my opponent. He was playing out his career — a grandfather by now — with the Hartford Whalers and was only a shade of the former super-superstar he had once been. Interestingly, I had no stars in my eyes when he bore down on me and it only indicated that right at the start of my NHL career I had not a bit of sentimentality in my blood when it came to the opposition. An enemy was an enemy in my eyes no matter how much I had once idolized him as a youth.

Gordie was leading a rush down the ice and kind of looking behind him for a pass. In that moment when the predator (me) prepares to attack his prey, there wasn't a single thought about *not* hitting him because he was Gordie Howe. It didn't matter whether he was my idol or my brother, I was going to hit him as hard as possible. In this case, I nailed Gordie with my shoulder and sent him flying.

When Howe recovered, he had a look in his eye that could only be described as menacing and, fortunately for me, he hadn't exactly seen who had laid him out. What he did see was Dave Lumley hovering nearby. Lummer was looking at Howe in such a way as to suggest that *he* was the perpetrator. Gordie got up and took a swing at Lummer. I was lucky enough to sneak away.

Another lesson I learned early on was never to get caught up in conversation with the enemy, especially the older players who seem to enjoy gabbing. I recall once coming around the net while Bobby Hull was coming off the boards to forecheck me since I had the puck. Instantly, I detected an opening between his legs that was wide enough for me to send a pass through. I faked a pass to the side and put the puck right through his legs to our right winger.

Too late, Hull realized what was happening and tried to close his legs all in one motion as the puck went through. As he skated by, Hull turned to me. "I knew you were going to put it there, kid," he said. "I'm just not quite as quick as I used to be." I got a kick out of that — coming from the one and only Golden Jet.

In a sense, I felt sorry for legends like Hull and Howe. Each was playing out the string — that was Hull's last year and Gordie retired the year after — and seemed to be hanging in just to promote the league. Not that they were out of place, but they were no longer the dominant players who had earned that special niche in the Hall of Fame.

Another lesson I learned off the ice was the ways and means of dealing with the media and, most of all, not to expect the press to be nice to us all the time. In our first season we did an admirable job in making the playoffs but there was criticism, to be sure. It was then that the confrontation between Terry Jones and Slats got started and lasted for some time thereafter.

Jones wrote a sports column for the *Edmonton Journal* at the time although he would later move over to the rival *Edmonton Sun*. Unlike the beat writers — Dick Chubey of the *Sun* and Jim Matheson of the *Journal* — Terry wrote more subjectively than objectively. Jones was particularly critical of Glen and a number of guys on the team.

That's where Slats' brilliant handling of the media came into play. He became the buffer between the critics and the team, the front man who gladly bore most of the criticism. He wasted no time discussing the press with the guys on the club and made it obvious from Gretzky down to the lowest fourth-liner that we were all in this thing together. "We can't wash our dirty laundry in the press," he'd insist.

He didn't have any problem with us arguing with each other inside the private confines of the dressing room, "as long as it's behind closed doors." He wanted us to be as diplomatic as possible with the media and continually emphasized the concept of team. It was clear that Glen was heavily influenced by his experience with the Montreal Canadiens where he had played alongside Jean Beliveau and some of the other classy Canadiens.

In a lecture to us on teamsmanship, he once mentioned an episode that had occurred in the Canadiens locker room one night after a game. A young player angrily stormed into the clubhouse and threw his sweater in the direction of the trainer, but it landed on the floor.

Beliveau walked across the room, picked up the sweater and carried it back to the rookie. "Do you see this sweater?" he said to the youngster. "From now on, this sweater *never touches the floor*." Beliveau, Sather pointed out, was filled with enormous pride in his Canadiens. Slats wanted us to have as much pride in being Edmonton Oilers.

In time we did. If the Canadiens had Beliveau, we had Wayne Gretzky who became as prideful an athlete as ever graced the continent. Even in those early days of the Oilers, Gretz had become the symbol of Edmonton. He carried himself with a majesty and grace that reflected positively on the entire hockey club. "Without Gretzky," said Bill Fleischman of the *Philadelphia Daily News*, "the Oilers might as well be a soccer team."

Wherever we traveled, be it Philadelphia, Vancouver, Los Angeles or Quebec City, Wayne held center stage with the media after every game. Sure, there were 18 separate egos in that dressing room but everyone was willing to defer to Wayne. The guys felt that it was nice to have the pressure off them and on Wayne because they knew that Wayne was capable of handling it. I don't mean pressure in the sense to produce but in the sense of media attention.

Sometimes we'd get annoyed for him. We felt sorry for a guy whose time had such heavy demands made on it. Selfishly, we were thankful it was him and not us but there was no jealousy directed at Gretz whatever. It was hard for us to imagine that we could even deserve any of that attention. Remember, at this point in our careers we were just a bunch of kids playing in the NHL and we recognized that Wayne was a different part of the team itself. It wasn't "Wayne Gretzky and the Edmonton Oilers." It was just "Wayne Gretzky" at this point. *He* was the show.

One of the most amazing aspects of Wayne's development was that he never turned to the media — ever! — and said, "Enough of this applesauce, leave me alone." Interviews had become such a part of Wayne's life it was like having dinner. He had been doing them since he was ten years old and, from that point on, he had more media attention than any athlete in the world. It was all second nature to him and he knew even then, as a young teenager, that it was always going to be that way so there was no sense fighting it.

Finding some peace and quiet was a problem for Gretz.

When Brett Callighen was his roommate in the early days, Wayne would have Brett answer his phone at the hotels. This was a bit unusual since Brett was almost ten years Wayne's senior and everyone on the club bugged Brett about being the guy who had to answer the phone but he understood that if Wayne was going to get any sleep, he had to be kept away from the telephone.

Slats' attitude toward Wayne and the media was that Gretz already had the experience and intelligence to handle it. Sather understood that Wayne had to have a press conference here and there but every once in a while the coach would supply a little reminder about who he was and what he was doing. "A commercial here and there is acceptable," Slats would point out, "but I don't want you doing too much stuff." Sather handled the off-ice Gretzky in the same manner he handled him at the rink. He let him run with the ball, let him have free rein, but every once in a while, he'd tug back a bit, just to make him aware of what was going on.

If Gretz needed any further reminders, there were always a couple of teammates ready to give him what-for, or kid him along while making sure that he was always one of the boys. This never was a major problem, not when we had a character like Dave Lumley on the club in those formative days.

Although Lummer had played earlier for the Montreal Canadiens, he was still, like Gretz and myself, developing in the NHL. Dave was a perfect counterpoint to Wayne because of his natural enthusiasm and his ability to say the right thing at the right time. If ever there was tension in the hockey club — *is* there a team without tension? — Lummer would be the safety valve.

In many ways Lumley was a young Sather. Dave played the same way Slats played (with a bit more talent) and he was incredibly spirited. Off the ice, his outstanding virtue was his sense of humor, followed closely by his story-telling ability.

Spontaneity was his forte as was the case one afternoon when our team bus was traveling from LaGuardia Airport on the outskirts of New York to our hotel in Manhattan. The Grand Central Parkway was jammed to the gills with rush-hour traffic and, incredibly, three hustlers had established a stand *in the middle of the highway*. (Only in New York, eh!) You name it, they were selling it, from jewelry to flowers to socks to magazines. For some reason, their specialty on this day was socks.

This captured Lummer's imagination and with the bus stuck in traffic, he pushed back the window, thrust his head outside and began wheeling and dealing with the highway entrepreneurs. Since the bus wasn't moving, Dave had plenty of time to haggle and he did that very well to the tune of six pairs of socks for only $1.25 in American money. The troops in the bus were both amazed and vastly amused.

Lumley was the perfect example of a less talented player who boasted that intangible the French called *élan* which binds a team together. It didn't bother him that Slats might sit him out for 58 minutes of a game but then send him out for two. In those two minutes Lummer could ignite the club and put us back on the right track. And if he didn't do it in a game he'd do it in the dressing room or around the dinner table regaling us with stories, the most memorable of which was his tale about taking a ferry ride to Toronto's Centre Island.

As Lummer put it, there was a seagull with one heck of a bombsight. From way up high he managed to drop a load that plopped right on Dave's eye.

Lumley was one of the original ingredients in our developing chemistry. The concoction was bubbling nicely but it was also apparent that if the Edmonton Oilers were going to move up in the standings we would need more talent to surround Wayne Gretzky. Fortunately for us, that man with the Argus eye for hockey talent, Barry Fraser, was out there unearthing stars where other NHL birddogs had never tread.

17

Fraser Applies
the Finnish–ing Touches

"Bub Slug," an *Edmonton Journal* comic strip which occasionally poked fun at the Oilers, once portrayed our chief scout Barry Fraser at the breakfast table up to his elbows in bacon and eggs and answering all questions with "Grrrrrrrrr!" At one point in the strip assistant coach John Muckler cautioned owner Peter Pocklington: "Don't bug him while he's eating breakfast."

The fact of the matter is that *nobody* in the Oilers organization should bug Barry, considering the job he's done for Edmonton, which is to turn us into a powerhouse with skillful moves. It was Fraser who persuaded Sather to select me in the 1979 draft and it was Barry who helped fortify the Oilers nucleus with late-round finds, ranging as far from Edmonton as Finland.

Even before the Oilers moved from the WHA to the NHL, Fraser and Sather were eyeing the Scandinavians. They admired the artistic play of Winnipeg's Anders Hedberg, Ulf Nilsson and Lars-Erik Sjoberg and felt the era of Philadelphia's bully brand of hockey was on the wane. "We felt the game was going to go in the direction of speed and finesse," said Fraser.

He was right.

But there was one major problem. Many of the NHL teams already had scouts swarming over Sweden, from whence Hedberg and Nilsson had come. Fraser made a daring and, as things turned out, insightful decision. He left the Swedes to the other clubs and concentrated on the virgin territory of Finland. "We could have scouted both countries in a half-assed way," Barry explained, "or we could have done a good job just in Finland. So we hired the best scout in Finland, Matti Vaisanen, on a permanent basis."

As we would later learn, Finns like Esa Tikkanen exhibit many of the traits that we're accustomed to seeing in Canadian hockey players. (I've often said that Tikkanen should have been born in Thunder Bay or Moose Jaw.) This was not all that surprising, at least not to Fraser. "The Finns have a harder lifestyle than the Swedes," Barry pointed out, "and I'm from the old school. I still think that most of hockey talent comes from the working classes."

The first Finns to arrive in Edmonton, Matti Hagman and Risto Siltanen, both were gifted hockey players but neither was to have the major impact of a Jari Kurri. Part of the problem with the trail-blazers was their newness to North America and the NHL. "The Finns," said Fraser, "are basically a very shy people and they didn't have the confidence at first. They needed one player to break through the barrier to become a star and Jari Kurri did it for them."

One might say that the discovery of Kurri — a major *major* move in the ascendency of our franchise — was a combination of smarts and luck, in this case a training camp in Finland, which was a rarity for NHL clubs. While the Oilers were there, exhibition games were scheduled against Finnish teams including one against Kurri's club, Jokerit. Fraser was very impressed with Jari and advised our scouts to follow his progress; he was drafted in the 1980-81 season.

That, in terms of Barry's genius, was just for starters. He had a game plan, worked out with Slats, that was precise and they followed it without deviation. "In our estimation," said Fraser, "the only way to build the Oilers for the 1980s was through the draft. As for style, Glen and I liked what we had seen in Winnipeg — fast play and quick transition from defense to offense. My qualifications, when I went scouting, were speed and good puckhandling ability."

And that is how we wound up landing three of the greatest players ever to grace an Edmonton Oilers jersey, Mark Messier, Paul Coffey and Glenn Anderson.

We were fortunate that Fraser had previously scouted for the WHA's Cleveland Crusaders and Houston Aeros before joining the Oilers. That enabled him to get a line on a young-ster who had been overlooked by everyone because of his awk-ward (at least then) appearance and failure to produce anything of consequence on the scoring sheet.

As far as the rest of the hockey world was concerned, Mark Messier was a tall, husky nobody with the Cincinnati Stingers and the Indianapolis Racers. In 52 WHA games he had but one goal and ten assists, hardly the inspiration for any scout, yet Fraser saw enough future in him to make the pick. Barry also knew that Mark's father, Doug, had been a very competent professional himself, starring for the old Edmonton Flyers in the Western League. On the Fraser checklist, Messier got high points on physique, skating and family tree. The rest would fall into place.

"A lot of work went into shaping Mark up as a big leaguer," Fraser remembered. "After he joined the Oilers, Slats got him to cut down on the slapshot (1979-80) and that alone took a year. But it didn't take long for us to realize we had a winner."

A big winner and the 48th pick the same June I was drafted. With me and Mark among the original assets, Barry went back to the draft a year later, in 1980, looking for more speed. As Fraser put it, "You have to know how to *see* the speed. I mean the stride, the balance, the posture, the lateral movement. Those things constitute a God-given talent and Paul Coffey possessed them."

Knowing what we do now about Paul it is hard to believe that there were those who counseled against picking him. A former NHL defenseman named Rod Seiling knew Paul from his days with the Kitchener Rangers and vigorously counseled against selecting Paul. Ultimately, the decision would rest with Fraser because Slats wanted it that way.

"Barry sees so many more games than I do," Sather explained, "so it would have made no sense for me to chal-lenge him. He's our head of scouting and I trust his opinion."

We picked sixth in 1980. The Canadiens were first and took Doug Wickenheiser. Winnipeg then decided on David Babych and the Black Hawks followed with Denis Savard. With the fourth pick Los Angeles went for Larry Murphy and then Washington, just ahead of us, bypassed Paul for Darren Veitch, also a defenseman. Without blinking an eyelash, or worrying about Seiling's veto, Fraser told Slats that it should be Paul and Coffey it was, to our eternal gratitude.

Alongside the doubters were people like Blues (now Red Wings) coach Jacques Demers, who viewed Fraser with a mixture of admiration and envy. "Barry is one of those rare individuals with a great eye to pick the right people," he said. "With most clubs, it's a gamble. You can draft a guy first and he flops. Not with Barry. He's building the perfect hockey team."

The Glenn Anderson selection reinforced Demers' comment. Here we have one of the genuine talents of the 1980s and yet he was a *69th pick*! Can you believe that?

What persuaded Fraser, in this case, was the word of former NHL player Lorne Davis, who had then been coaching the Canadian Olympians. Davis clued him in on Glenn's speed and intensity and that was enough for Barry.

And while Mark, Lummer, Hicksy and I were vacationing in Hawaii during that spring of 1980, Fraser was plotting one of the most important picks in the history of the Oilers until then — and one of the all-time long-shots, Andy Moog.

As effective as Ron Low had been in the late winter of 1979-80, Fraser realized that we would need goaltending strength down the line. Kelly Hrudey and Don Beaupre were the highest rated at the time but Barry had Moog graded directly behind them. With that in mind, he expected Andy to be selected relatively high but pick after pick was called and still nobody called out Moog. Incredibly, Andy went untouched for 131 picks until Fraser made his move.

(I should point out that Barry did even better a year later after Dale Hawerchuk (Winnipeg), Doug Smith (Los Angeles), Bobby Carpenter (Washington), Ron Francis (Hartford), Joe Cirella (Colorado), Jim Benning (Toronto) and Mark Hunter (Montreal) were selected in the first seven. With the eighth pick, Fraser called out "Grant Fuhr" and, with that, our goaltending problems for the rest of the decade were over.)

I like the way Toronto *Globe and Mail* columnist Trent Frayne put it about Barry: "Fraser must own a sixth sense when he assesses an adolescent's worth because there's nothing mysterious about the yardsticks he looks for."

Over the years Barry has used a Player Evaluation Report which is divided into 15 chapters and 72 lesser sections. On a one-to-nine scale (nine is tops), he rates everything imaginable. In the skating category there are subdivisions for change of pace, stride, posture, speed, balance, lateral right, lateral left, turn right, turn left, cut right, cut left and stay on feet.

Here's what he said about me: "I have Kevin down as the tenth-rated player so when he was still untouched (21st) when we got to pick, we grabbed him. Since we were very interested in a good skater, we had checked out Kevin's skating ability. In those days the Quebec Junior League was very big on skating so if he could skate there, he could skate anywhere."

Thank you, Barry.

One of Barry's first rules of scouting was that the accent on overall ability took precedence over the significance of a one-night starring effort. "What the player can or can't do overall is more important than what he does on a single night," is the way Fraser put it.

With Sather's blessing, Fraser examined the "iffy" free agent market and steered a pair of excellent stay-at-home defense-men — Charles Huddy and Randy Gregg — to Northlands Coliseum and few teams can boast a more valuable low-key pair. Apart from Gretzky, Edmonton's top franchise players have been Messier, Anderson, Kurri, Fuhr and, until 1987-88, Coffey — all Fraser choices, myself included.

(I might add that he pursued the Finnish connection through 1983 by selecting Esa Tikkanen *in the fourth round*. And when someone asked Barry how far Tikkanen was from play-ing in the NHL, he correctly replied, "About 4,000 miles!" Tik-kanen arrived at Northlands late in the 1984-85 season and dressed for us in the Stanley Cup finals against the Flyers. Not bad for a young man picked 80th overall.)

P.S. One of our 1988 Cup-winning stars was Steve Smith. Barry picked him 125th overall in 1982.

Now you know why they say, "Don't bug him while he's eating breakfast."

18

The Characters Emerge

Say what you will about Glen Sather — and *much* has been said about him — there is no denying that he is, for better or worse, a *character*. That, as much as anything, explains why he always has stocked our hockey club with characters, some outrageous, some unusual in subtle ways — what other team has had a full-fledged medical doctor as a defense regular but us with Dr. Randy Gregg on the blue line? — some inexplicable.

Being a character, Sather has a feel, a tolerance and an understanding for other characters and where more conservative general managers would turn away from a Craig MacTavish, a Glen Sather would welcome him to our club with open arms on the grounds that we are all human and all susceptible to mistakes once in a while. Glen has brought in more players over the years that others have quit on than any leader in the NHL and the results have been, on the whole, positive.

From Day One we've had characters on the club and some of them have been truly rich personalities. One of the most appealing — and deceptive — was Dave Semenko, an original Oiler. Sammy, as we called him, terrorized the opposition for several years and, as you might expect, was viewed by opposition fans as some kind of gorilla. Unfortunately, they didn't know the *real* Dave Semenko, a rather tender fellow, given to wonderful bursts of wit and, believe it or not, hardly the meany that people thought he was although his image was otherwise.

But he knew that there was a job to be done. He was in the

lineup because he was a big, tough guy and every NHL team needed a big tough guy. He understood that if he wasn't there, Slats would have obtained another big tough guy, so why not Sammy? He was there to protect not only Wayne Gretzky but also the other smaller players.

The question has often been asked, how tough was Sammy? Pat Price would tell stories about the Gassoff brothers and Lee Fogolin had a few about Battleship Bob Kelly. Slats never forgot John Ferguson, when Fergie roamed the ice for the Canadiens and then there was Dave Schultz and the Broad Street Bullies. But the general consensus had it that Sammy was the toughest of all. He was in a class of his own; he didn't beat guys up, he destroyed them. He employed a combination of sheer strength, sheer power, and sheer quickness, but mostly power. He wasted players with just two or three punches. And this, although he never really had a mean streak in his body.

Interestingly, Semenk would fight maybe only once in 15 games but the results were so devastating that word would spread like wildfire around the league — *Leave this guy alone! don't even touch him!!* When Sammy would fight, not only was the opposition devastated, *we* were devastated. The reaction of the guys on our bench after he had withered yet another victim was "Holy . . . I can't believe it." We almost felt sorry for the poor saps he laid out. To me, Sammy was the Gretzky of the tough guys.

Yet even in the heat of battle Sammy never lost his rapier wit. Once Dave (Killer) Carlson, a short-term NHL bad guy, made some menacing gestures at Semenko. Sammy just dismissed him out of hand with this squelch: "How'd you get your nickname, Killer; did you shoot your dog?"

Dave wouldn't pick his spots when it came to put-downs. Once, after having been benched for a few games, Sammy was returned to the lineup. After suiting up, he ambled over to Wayne and snapped, "Well, Gretz, now people are finally going to get their money's worth!"

Former NHL coach Harry Neale, himself a wit, described Dave as The Regulator. He went around ensuring that peace reigned. Sammy had three objectives in his life as an Oiler. He wanted to be on the cover of *The Hockey News*. He wanted to be one of the players Slats told to take a day off. And he wanted to be told to replace the first guy who came to the bench on a line change.

Another specialty act, as it were, was Glenn Anderson, a player who we wondered about quite a bit during 1979-80 because there had been an aura of mystery surrounding him even before he ever donned an Edmonton jersey. It all developed when he was 19 years old, an underage right winger who had been a fourth-round draft while he was at Denver University.

At the time nobody had heard of Glenn but by the time I was ending my rookie season stories began breaking in *The Hockey News* and Edmonton papers about another one of Sather's "steals." Glenn even told the media that several teams had suggested Anderson be included in trades. "Every time teams call us," Slats pointed out, "they throw Anderson's name into the conversation." By the time he joined us, I could see why. His skating was brilliant, to say the least, and he had the natural scoring touch.

As a hockey personality, however, he was atypical and the older players on the club had difficulty understanding him. Consequently, they nicknamed him "Mork," which was a take-off on what was then a popular television show called "Mork And Mindy," starring Robin Williams portraying an alien. The veterans called him "The Spaceman" and other nicknames suggesting that Glennie was far out and, truth to tell, there always has been a mystique about him. From the start he impressed us as happy-go-lucky but in a mysterious kind of way and this baffled the Old Guard. They'd pass remarks to the effect, "Mork is from his own planet; I wonder what he's doing today."

In this case you could see the social split on the team because younger guys like myself didn't appreciate the Mork nickname the vets hung on him because we thought it was degrading and, furthermore, we knew that Glennie didn't like that because, in his eyes, he wasn't that type. Actually, he wasn't a spaceman and we younger fellows *knew* that he wasn't a spaceman. More important, Slats appreciated Glennie and never fell into the spaceman trap.

Sather was willing to accept the fact that Glennie had an even more nonchalant attitude toward life than Mark Messier did — as long as he did his hockey work and, Lord knows, the minute he joined the team he began producing for us. Slats, employing his intelligence and background in psychology — few realize that he studied it extensively in college —

understood that behind Anderson's loose and relaxed facade was a very keen mind. No matter how you shake it, he *is* a particularly intelligent guy. (When he was with Canada's Olympic team in 1980, Glennie listed his ambition as starting a chain of small restaurants! In due time he did emerge as quite an entrepreneur, dabbling in horses and assorted other businesses, and doing very well, thank you.) I soon learned that there was a link between his on-ice image and his off-ice trademark. In each case he *seemed* not to be in control but he was. Teammates would tell him to get some control on the ice or his wild skating style would kill him one day. To that Glennie would shoot back, "I'm *not* out of control; I know what I'm doing."

What Slats grasped was Anderson's background and how it had influenced his thinking. Glennie, literally, was influenced by the sea. "Anderson has the sense and soul of a sailor," said David Staples of the *Edmonton Journal* and truer words were never spoken.

Nor was a more accurate assessment made about Anderson than by Glennie himself when he said, "I've always had a carefree spirit and attitude about whatever it might be but when it comes down to the nuts and bolts of things, I'll be there. Always. It's a great feeling to know that. I think I'll always have that feeling wherever I go, as long as I live."

He got that way because of the sea. Magnus Anderson, his father, began to fish as a means of livelihood at the age of 15. Glennie's dad once explained: "I was never intimidated by anything. I found that that was a point of my character that I don't mind having when I look back on it. Glenn might have inherited some of that."

Slats knew all about Magnus early on and contacted the elder Anderson to find out what kind of boy he had. Sather asked Mister Anderson whether Glenn liked hockey. He replied: "Glenn has a great desire for winning hockey games. I'm afraid he loves hockey more than anything else. And I enjoy hockey myself."

What I saw in Magnus' influence was the freedom of the fisherman's life; the ability to chart the unknown. What other occupation also has that relaxation, that live-your-own-life, be-your-own-man kind of quality than that of someone who lives by the sea. Then, Glennie went to Denver University in the Rockies. Now, where are people more relaxed than in the Rockies? So, Glennie brought this whole attitude to the team and the old guys just couldn't understand where this Glenn Anderson was coming from.

There were times, however, when even Slats was baffled by Andy. One of his better off-the-wall classics involved an Oilers practice, or should I say, practice that Glennie missed. He had gotten up one day in plenty of time for the practice which was at eleven in the morning. Glennie was up at 8 A.M. and realized that he still had plenty of time before practice, so he just started doing things in his apartment. He turned on the television, poured himself a cup of coffee and began cleaning up.

That done, he sat down on the couch and started watching the tube. Pretty soon, he fell asleep. At some point his mind-clock awakened him and he tore over to the rink, considerably late for our scrimmage.

Nothing was said until after practice when Glennie was on the training table. A bunch of us were wondering how Slats would handle this. Finally, the coach walked in and approached Anderson. "Glennie," he said, "where were you?"

Anderson looked up from the training table and matter of factly explained: "You know, Slats, I was up real early and I was cruising around my apartment, having a good time. And I dozed off!"

That was his explanation. No more, no less.

Those of us within earshot were stupified. So was Sather, who thought he had heard everything. Slats just kind of looked at him as if to say, "Glenn, that's your explanation?"

"You were cruising around the apartment having a good time," the coach blurted. "Why didn't you say your alarm clock broke? Say you had an accident, say your dog died. Say anything but don't say you were cruising around your apartment having a good time."

Still astonished by what he had heard, Slats turned around and walked out. He simply didn't know what to say or how to handle it. In one of the rare moments in coaching history, Glennie gave Slats a momentary case of lockjaw.

Few had that impact on Sather but, as we would later discover, Paul Coffey could cause Slats to walk away shaking his head — to the point of eventually being traded. Like Glennie, Paul often was misread by other players. He was extremely shy (his shyness often was misinterpreted as a kind of snootiness, which hardly was the case) and extremely low-key.

When he joined us in 1980, Paul was a jeans man, a down-home, real basic kind of guy who wore his jean-jacket all the time. I mean *all* the time. Same with his workboots. *All* the time. Naturally, this proved an easy target for his teammates who would inquire, "why not wear something else, something classier?"

The Coffey rebuttal was the essence of the man, plain and to the point: "I'm most comfortable in them. Just because I'm playing in the NHL doesn't mean I have to wear fancy clothes. I just want to be me."

Whereas Anderson hailed from British Columbia, Coffey grew up in the Toronto suburb of Malton and when the hockey season was over he'd gravitate home and hang out. This led to a story that gained circulation among our older guys that Paul would hang out at the Malton McDonald's hamburger place. The vets wondered, "What is Paul Coffey doing, hanging around at a McDonald's?" And they bugged him about that. The question was asked: "Jean-jacket, what do you do in the summertime — cruise up and down the main drag in Malton and hang out at McDonald's?"

It was hard for Paul to shake this. The older fellows were needling him to be one type of person and he resisted. Once, he told me, "Kevin, I don't want to be plastic. I don't want to be something I'm not. I want to be me." One thing about Paul, he stuck to his guns. He's always been himself and never pretended to be anything that he's not.

He did suffer, though, because of his shyness and the manner in which it was misinterpreted. He had a shyness that appeared to be a kind of cockiness and I remember one of our older players, Lee Fogolin, didn't particularly like Coffey early on. Matter of fact, a bunch of the guys didn't. Semenko, Dave Hunter and a lot of the guys gave him a hard time because he had this shyness that came across as arrogance.

That and his naivete toward professional hockey life got him into trouble at the start. At his first Edmonton training camp Paul walked over to his locker area and casually hung his clothes over three hooks. Unfortunately, two of these hooks belonged to a couple of vets. "Who does this kid think he is, taking up three hooks," was the comment.

While Paul's reply was candid, it was not the acme of diplomacy. He explained like a greenhorn, "I've got to hang my clothes up. I've got to put my jacket here, my shirt here and my pants here." Poor Paul had to learn the hard way and along the route, he took quite a ribbing. The notorious Philadelphia Spectrum incident is a case in point.

We were preparing for a game against the Flyers and had just concluded our warmup and returned to the dressing room. At a time like that most guys take their sweater and shoulder pads off until it's game time. Then, they put them on and go out on the ice.

Like the others, Coffey had removed his jersey and shoulder pads. Now we hear the warning "Five minutes on to the ice, five minutes!" So, we all get ready except Paul, after putting on his shoulder pads, puts his sweater on backwards. The big number seven with the name COFFEY is on the front and the Oilers emblem is on the back.

Pretty soon just about everybody in the dressing room realized the goof but not a word was spoken. Even after we trooped out onto the ice to start the game, nobody said a word. We just let him go while everyone was rolling. It wasn't until Paul actually was getting onto the ice that he noticed it by which time the club was cracking up. With an embarrassed smile, Paul looked up and down the bench as if to say, "Why didn't you guys tell me?"

C'mon, Paul — and lose a good laugh? "Hey," one of the vets said, "how could we not have a laugh at your expense. That's part of your job as a rookie."

Part of my job being a second-year man was to take our first draft pick out to dinner. This had become a club ritual and the previous year Pat Price had taken me to dinner at training camp in Edmonton. "From this point on," Price told me, "I want you to take the first draft pick out. So, Paul was my guest. We played a round of golf, shared a few beers and, in that way, he was welcomed to the team. By the time he came to training camp I had already known him. (Eventually, Paul's mom and mine became good friends as well.) And I liked him. He was a young single guy, like me, and pretty soon we were doing a lot of things together.

Musically, Paul's passion was Bruce Springsteen. The Boss was his favorite artist and one day a friend of a friend contacted Springsteen's father-in-law who in turn contacted The Boss. Springsteen wrote Paul a little note on a photograph, saying, "Paul — keep up the good work and hang in there." In addiiton, the father-in-law added a private note to Coffey, saying: "Bruce is a private sort of guy and he doesn't do this very often but in your case he made a special exception. After you read this letter, will you please destroy it?"

Paul never did. Instead, he framed it.

My link with Paul extended onto the rink as well and in his rookie year Coffey was teamed up with me for 20 or so games. We were either great or we were awful; there was no in between. It had to do with our mutual inexperience but we did complement one another because of our ability to move the puck.

One night we were playing the Hartford Whalers and after the first period Glen was all over us for what we thought was no apparent reason. (The rest of the fellows weren't too kind to us either.) Naturally, the tendency in a situation like that is to be mad at the coach. (Every player has an ego and we all feel we're above mistakes.) Now the second period is about to begin and Paul and I head out to the ice together, cursing Slats for the bawling out he gave us. "Who does he think he is?" I mentioned to Paul and then we went out and played a beautiful period. Every time we made a good play we'd return to the bench figuring that Slats must be eating his words. He even yelled over to us once, "Great play, you guys, now you're doing it. See, when you guys put your mind to it, you can do the job."

Ah, but there was still the third period and this time we were atrocious. The minute we walked into the dressing room Slats was all over us again so we made the trek from the shithouse to the penthouse and back to the shithouse all in one game.

Paul's climb up the NHL tree was more difficult than Wayne's in a lot of ways. To begin with, it's more difficult for a rookie to start on defense than it is up front simply because a forward can get away with more mistakes than a defenseman can. Some wiseguys in the media nicknamed him "Paul Cough-Up," which wasn't very nice but that's the way it goes; you have to take it.

Add to that the fact that Paul, like myself the previous year, was just so in awe of everything around him and when that happens, lots of times you forget to play your game. His rookie season was like a blur to him and he was just happy to get it over with, regroup in the summertime and start again.

But Paul's additional burden was that, unlike Wayne, Coffey felt a much tighter rein being pulled on him. Sather realized that Paul had all the natural talent in the world but that he could only allow one guy to have the free rein and that had to be Wayne. More credit should go to Paul for being able to make the adjustment and accepting Slats' rein-pulling as much as he did.

The adjustment for new guys like Paul and Glennie is never easy but it was particularly difficult for the Europeans. In our second NHL season, 1980-81, Jari Kurri became an Oiler. Not surprisingly, he couldn't speak much English. That was the bad news. The good news was that we already had a Finn on the squad, Risto Siltanen, so Jari learned English from him. (Later on Kurri became the interpreter for our latest Finn, Esa Tikkannen.) We had a third Finn that season — Matti Hagman, who had played in North America earlier.

Risto was the ringleader, the one who showed them the city and taught them what they had to know about life in North America. Unfortunately, they succumbed to the natural tendency that you find among foreign athletes in all sports — never mind athletes, just about *anybody* — and that is the inclination to form cliques with your own group of guys. In my estimation the Finns hung around a little too much together but, in fairness to them, it wasn't as if we were going out of our way to have them with us.

It was, in many ways, similar to the situation in baseball locker rooms where there are black and white cliques and those of the Dominicans and other groups. You have the black guys here and the white guys there. In the NHL, the Europeans are here and the North Americans there. The veterans here, the young guys there.

While these separations may have been natural, they were not good for the chemistry of our hockey club and it was essential — if we were going to be a *team* — for us to get beyond that.

Wayne led the breakthrough as far as Jari was concerned and a good thing, too, because out comaraderie would become a major strength of the Oilers. Talent obviously helps but you need that tight-knit relationship to win and, eventually, Jari became a part of our fabric but he didn't become one of the boys right away. There's a "lapse time" from the moment a new man joins the team and the time when he has finally proven himself and becomes accepted. For the time being, Jari was the new kid on the block but then he showed that he had the goods and everyone went out of his way to make him feel accepted because he was going to help our team win hockey games. That's all that really mattered.

Make no mistake, though, there *was* resentment, the typical anti-European kind that has been prevalent ever since Borje Salming broke in with the Toronto Maple Leafs. The resentment came from the guys who would be losing their jobs to the Finns. Fortunately, I wasn't one of them and I could concentrate on lifting this club from one that got wiped out of the playoffs in three straight to a team that might make a name for itself in the 1983 playoffs.

19

Down With the Canadiens! Are You Kidding? Nope!

When our club convened for the start of the 1980-81 season, many questions were being asked about us, not the least of which centered on our vigorous effort against Philadelphia in the playoffs. Was it a fluke or were we really a young club on the rise?

If my head was becoming a bit too inflated, a headline in the *Toronto Star* summing up prevailing opinion about the Oilers prospects immediately brought it down to size: GRETZKY IS EXCELLENT BUT OILERS LACK DEFENSE.

In our first season Gretz had been centering a line with BJ MacDonald and Brett Callighen until Brett went down with an eye injury in the home stretch. This time around there would be several experiments and, eventually, BJ would go bye-bye. MacDonald had been very effective in 1979-80 but BJ was one of the first guys to confront Sather as general manager and, as it turned out, his days became numbered. He decided to play out his option and a power struggle developed between the two.

Like so many disputes between player and management, this one centered on money. Glen thought he was being fair with MacDonald and BJ disagreed. The next thing you know BJ was traded to Vancouver and was never heard from again.

Gretz was heard from — plenty. He laughed at the "sophomore jinx." Said he didn't believe in it. "If you're a good hockey player one year, you should be a good hockey player the next season as well," he explained. "Guys like Guy Lafleur, Marcel Dionne and Darryl Sittler always play the same."

Sittler was a hard-nosed character who spared nothing in his attempts to check Gretz. On November 15, 1980 we played Sittler's club at Maple Leaf Gardens and Darryl was all over Wayne but Wayne still managed to score a power play goal. Others were zeroing in on Gretz, people like big Jerry Butler of the Canucks and Terry Ruskowski of the Black Hawks were the types who hounded Wayne. "They stick to you wherever you go," said Wayne. "I don't think you've got to be brilliant to follow a guy around a rink all game."

They may have followed Wayne but they didn't catch him too often although we had our troubles early that year, perhaps because there still was a leadership void. No one was really *the* leader. There were still some older guys who were in and out and there were others who had come into their own as special people. Lee Fogolin was one of them and he was one of the coming leaders but everyone sort of did his own thing and no one looked to one guy to do it.

Wayne led in terms of hockey ability but we all didn't turn to Wayne and say "What do we do next?" Everyone had his own job to do and that's the way it should be. Personally, I don't like the idea of saying that two or three guys have to lead. It's nice to have guys to take charge when the time comes — if they're capable — but it's tough on a team when everyone looks to a couple of players when times get tough. That puts a lot of pressure on those guys.

What I could feel in the second season was the definite youth movement. We went from a team with a high average age to one with guys who were 19 and 20. We were a big lumbering team at first but now the speed was more evident. We were no longer moving in slow motion.

On the other hand, we weren't exactly tearing up the league either. We were winning about the same amount of games as the year before but with the youth, we knew it would get better. In the meantime, changes were taking place in the front office that would have a long-range affect on the club. Bryan (Bugsy) Watson, Glen's old friend, had moved behind the bench with Billy Harris, the former Maple Leaf, the assistant coach.

By mid-season we had only 34 points, were in fifth place

(out of six) in the Smythe Division and were not progressing at the pace that suited Slats. Watson was removed and Sather went behind the bench. Gretz, as good as ever, was once again neck-and-neck with Marcel Dionne in the scoring race.

With Glen back behind the bench, the team slowly came around. Part of it had to do with his being positive. I've always been positive but I'm not one of those Norman Vincent Peale "Power of Positive Thinking" type of people. I don't sit home and make affirmations about how great I'm going to be. I just believe in myself and my talents. Slats tried to bring that little bit out of everybody. He'd say "Isn't that player great? Aren't the Canadiens great? Aren't the Flyers great?" Then, he would add, "What are you guys talking about? You're going to be better than those guys." And we'd sit and say, "What do you mean? I sure would like to be." Then, Slats would come right back, "You don't want to *like* to be. YOU'RE GOING TO BE."

The repetition of that — always being positive — began to work. With only ten games remaining in the regular schedule, we trailed Washington for a playoff berth but then we made our big push. Slats kept after us: "You just have to work at it. You have to dedicate yourselves. You have to believe it. You can do it if you want to."

And we did. We moved past Washington and kept on moving. Meanwhile, my game was on the rise and for that I have to tip my hat to Lee Fogolin. Fogie taught me a lot of things, not the least of which was patience.

He'd tell me, "A bird in the hand is worth two in the bush," which was another way of saying why gamble when you can back off and play your position. With words like that, he developed my game but the curious thing is that I might never have wound up being paired with Fogie had it not been for BJ MacDonald's falling out with Slats. BJ was traded to Vancouver late in the season for a defenseman named Garry Larivière who immediately was paired with Paul Coffey. Garry did wonders for Paul and, by the same token, Lee did wonders for me because when Larivière arrived, Slats paired Fogie and me together. From a hockey standpoint it was a match made in heaven.

Talk about chemistry between players, Fogie and I had it. We liked playing side by side. We both had a pride in the game and a pride in each other and, gradually, we developed a special bond. It may sound a bit corny but we were united.

Between the two of us we felt that no one was going to beat us. That was our attitude. One guy might get beat or get caught but the other guy would go out of his way to make up for it. He's not just going to do it for the team, he's going to do it for his partner because if his partner gets beat, then he looks bad. He'll do whatever he can to go above and beyond the call of duty to make up for it.

Mind you, there were no dramatics involved. No hugging and stuff. After the game it was just a nod. "Hey, I appreciate it." We had a quiet communication that way. From the very first day of training camp in 1979 Fogie took me aside and kept a special eye on me — on and off the ice. He had toughness, durability and, most of all, a love of the game. It all rubbed off, including some valuable lessons on what defense is really all about.

He emphasized the difference between a defenseman's role and the forwards. When we make a mistake, it *really* shows. You block a shot, make a good hit or break up a two-on-one and you get noticed but the highest compliment for a defenseman, he'd say, is to go unnoticed. When you stand out, there's an awfully good chance that it's because of a mistake. I remembered that.

Fogie and I became very close to the point of my becoming godfather to his son. I liked his down-to-earth approach to life. He was traditional, a fantastic carpenter, a top-grade mechanic. He could build a home from scratch, build furniture that is nicer than the kind you find in a showroom.

You could tell he came from good stock. His father, Lee, Sr., who played in the NHL, would frequently visit. It was amazing to see Lee, Jr., Lee, Sr. and the grandfather next to each other. It shows how mankind is getting bigger and stronger. The grandfather was a strong man but shorter and a little more compact. Lee, Sr. was a little taller and Lee, Jr., Fogie, that much taller — but they all looked alike. Ah, evolution!

And speaking of evolution, we evolved brilliantly in the final week of 1980-81. We landed in 14th place overall, well into a playoff berth for our second straight ticket into the Stanley Cup round. We lost only one of our last 12 games and three out of our final 17.

Wayne didn't hurt us. Down the stretch he began pulling away from Dionne. "Nobody can get points like him," Marcel lamented. "I can't get points like he does. He makes me feel like an old man." (Dionne was 29 years old at the time.) Gretz ran away with the scoring championship with 55 goals, a record-breaking 109 assists and a record-breaking 164 points. And he was nine years younger than Dionne!

How good was Wayne? Maple Leafs owner Harold Ballard made an offer: "I'd trade my whole team for the kid, and throw in the farm club, too." Our boss, Peter Pocklington, just laughed.

"I was offered $2 million for him but $10 million wouldn't buy him. There's no price on greatness."

The price on us entering the playoffs was not especially good. Our opponents in the first round would be just as tough as our 1980 opposition, only this time it was the Montreal Canadiens.

From 1976 through 1979 the Canadiens had won four straight Stanley Cups and the nucleus of that team was intact. Household names like Guy Lafleur, Steve Shutt, Serge Savard and Guy Lapointe were sprinkled through the Montreal roster. This was a very formidable hockey club, one that I had delighted in rooting *against* when I was growing up in Lachute. Now I was facing them in the playoffs.

If we were worried, Slats made sure our anxieties didn't last long. Another coach might have considered the Canadiens series a crisis but Slats thrived on this type of situation. (When things were running too smoothly he'd get concerned.) He was at his best in the so-called crisis. "Montreal has playoff experience," he said before the series opened at The Forum, "but we've got enthusiasm."

Did we ever. Our critics thought we had too much. Already, we were getting a reputation. A stigma developed about the looseness of the Oilers. It had started one night at Maple Leaf Gardens before a game. We rolled up a ball of tape and five or six of us played ball hockey, using the spare nets as a goal. Gary Dornhoefer, the ex-Flyer who was doing *Hockey Night In Canada* in color, couldn't believe what he was seeing. He remembered the Philadelphia days when Bobby Clarke and himself would be sitting in their stalls for two hours before a game concentrating and here we were playing ball hockey.

"What is this?" he wondered.

Others couldn't believe it either, especially when we continued playing ball hockey before our opening playoff game in Montreal. (One of the Montreal papers carried a photo of

Dougie Hicks and I playing ball hockey in the Forum hallway. *Sacre bleu!*) The Montreal people were flabbergasted.

They were just as amazed at Slats' handling of the team, especially the goaltending. Through most of the year our top goalie was Ronnie Low but we also had Eddie Mio and Garry (Scoop) Edwards. (Don't ask me why we called him Scoop. We should have called him Blinky because he blinked all the time. He had been around pro hockey for years and nobody could figure out how he lasted as a goaltender because he blinked every second.)

Neither Ronnie nor Eddie nor Scoop would be our goalie against the Canadiens. Slats was relying on a gut feeling and his instincts told him to go with an untried kid, Andy Moog. It was vintage Sather, about as long a shot as our chances going into the opening round. (We had finished 29 points behind the Canadiens during the regular season.) Eddie Mio had been hurt in the stretch and then Ronnie Low pulled up lame so he went with the kid from the Central League.

To say the gamble paid off would be the understatement of the half-century. Andy played phenomenally and that was one of the main reasons for our success in this best-of-five series. Then, there was the matter of pressure; it wasn't on us, it was on the Canadiens. And it didn't help them that at the very start of the series their goalie Richard Sevigny predicted, "Lafleur will put Gretzky in his back pocket!"

Not too smart.

Another positive for us was momentum (if you'll excuse the beaten-to-a-pulp expression, but in this case it *was* a factor.) We had finished the regular season on a roll. Our confidence was as high as it could have been under the circumstances and we were about to obtain that wonderful playoff commodity, clutch goaltending. Andy came in and stood on his head.

While he was doing that, he got a little help from his friends. He needed it. In our earlier two games at Montreal we scored a grand total of one goal. No way Moog would win for us if we didn't score for him but our new kids obliged in a hurry. Glenn Anderson and Jari Kurri beat Sevigny in the first while Slats encouraged us to keep taking the play to them. He figured that the Habs could be had by throwing them on the defensive. Glen figured that if we jumped into the lead and held it for a bit, the rabid Montreal crowd would turn on the Canadiens and screw them up even more.

He couldn't have been more right. We beat them 6-3 and right away we discovered chinks in their armor. Some of their aces — defensemen like Lapointe and Savard — didn't play particularly well and their age began showing. And as for Lafleur putting Wayne "in his back pocket," Gretz scored once and assisted on all of the other five goals.

Suffice to say, we had Lafleur's number — in spades. Davey Hunter was all over him like in the old days when Bugsy Watson would watch Bobby Hull. Lafleur couldn't do a thing. Every time he was on the ice, Hunter was on the ice, following him around. And Davey can be a pretty abusive guy, really aggressive. Worse for Montreal, the Canadiens didn't have anyone to counter that.

Big and tough, Hunter was stronger than Lafleur and could skate with him. So, what was The Flower going to do? The Canadiens tried to switch lines on us but Glen did an excellent job keeping up with them. And Moog kept making saves. The more saves he made, the more reassured we felt in front of him. We relaxed, realizing we didn't have to play defensive all the time and as we opened up, the Canadiens backed off. It was hard to believe that this wonderful Andy Moog had a 14-13 record with Wichita in the Central League and a 3.33 goals against average. Overnight, he had become a Canadian national hero — except, of course, in Montreal.

But could Andy Who do it again? The test came in Game Two and Moog passed it with as much ease as he had in the opener. Staked to a 2-1 lead after two periods (Coffey and Siltanen had scored for us, which shows you we had offense on the defense!), Moog shut the door on the Habs in the third. Kurri put the game away, thanks to Wayne's pass late in the third and we walked out of The Forum with an incredible two games to none lead.

The next morning the French language daily, *La Presse*, blazed a headline, GRETZKY MET TOUT LES CANADIENS DANS SA POCHE. I had no trouble translating it for the rest of the crew. "Gretzky put all the Canadiens in his pocket."

Now the series moved west to Edmonton and it appeared to the civilized world that maybe, just maybe, we had the Canadiens in our pocket. The signs of this unreal upset were becoming more and more evident. Lafleur had been neutralized. The older Canadiens looked really *old*. And to top it all, Montreal's goaltending was mediocre compared with the magnificent Moog. As a professional, I detetcted one other telltale sign that told me the Canadiens were finished — Guy Lapointe was fighting.

When a mild-mannered defenseman — truly a class act — like Lapointe starts playing policeman, you know your club is in trouble, deep trouble. To me, it was shameful to see what was happening to him. To this day, I don't know whether he was defending Lafleur, defending himself or if he was simply feeling the frustration of it all. Whatever the case, we still had another game to win if we were to win the series and 17,490 fans jammed into Northlands Coliseum to see just how big this bubble could become. Or whether it would, in fact, burst.

It was no contest. We dominated them in Game Three and Moog continued to play like Georges Vezina. "Maybe I was in a daze," said Andy, "but who cares, it was working."

Lafleur was invisible and Gretz all over the place. Wayne scored a hat trick and we just cruised at the end, holding a 6-2 lead. At the end the fans began a countdown and went out of their minds. Actually, I couldn't help but feel sorry for the Canadiens. Guys like Lafleur, Larry Robinson, Réjean Houle, Savard and Lapointe were names I revered growing up in Lachute — and they had just gone under.

It was, as the *Edmonton Sun* proclaimed the next day, INCREDIBLE!

20

We Still Had a Lot to Learn

The win over the Canadiens had all of Canada talking and our heads spinning. I don't know which was better — or worse. This much I knew: our next opponent would be the New York Islanders. And as great as the Canadiens might have been in the spring of 1981, the Islanders were even better.

How do I know? Very simple. The Islanders were the defending Stanley Cup champions. This was truly a challenge for our glorious leader and Slats took on the challenge with relish. Once again, he came up with a masterful psychological ploy; and he did it just before we were to take the ice for the opening face-off.

"Hold on, guys," he said. Next thing we knew, he had wheeled a television set into our dressing room at Nassau Coliseum. Slats flipped a switch and the screen lit up. Our eyes were riveted to the set and we had forgotten that, in a matter of seconds, we were supposed to be on the ice for the opening face-off.

Highlights of our Montreal victory began flashing across the set with a stirring musical background. *"This,"* Slats announced, "is what you guys play like."

We stood there with the hair on the backs of our necks standing up. For each Oiler to see himself overpowering the Canadiens as Tom Jones sings "The Impossible Dream" in the background was a truly inspirational experience.

So was the series against the Islanders, a team, by the way, very much like the 1985 Oilers when we won our second Cup. After beating the Flyers in the 1980 finals, the Islanders dominated every aspect of the NHL in 1980-81. Denis Potvin,

Mike Bossy, Bryan Trottier, Clark Gillies and Bill Smith were all in their prime. Unlike the aging Canadiens, New York was not fading. But we were not impressed.

Maintenance men and media folk who wandered around the bowels of Nassau Coliseum before the opening game were astonished to see our tape ball-hockey game being played as vigorously in the walkway near our dressing room as a playoff game on ice would be contested. They were equally astonished at the decibel count emanating from our dressing room. The older guard and I began introducing several varieties of rock music to the pre-game ritual. Until then music in the dressing room was virtually unheard of but, then again, a lot of things the Edmonton Oilers were doing had a touch of the exotic about them.

Taking the ice, we were as loose as could be. We were going out to play some hockey games and if we won some, great! We didn't look any further ahead than the game we were playing. On the other hand, the media took the series with infinitely more seriousness than we did. It was then that we received one of our strongest lessons in "the power of the press." Or, to put it another way, how a simple statement by a player can be sufficiently warped by a newspaperman to start a major "feud."

The fact that already we were being perceived as "cocky" didn't help matters. (I wish I had a dollar for every time I heard that term mentioned in relation to the Oilers. It reached a point that one might have gotten the impression that our real name was the *Edmonton Cockyoilers*.) But the issue was compounded by an innocent off-the-cuff remark uttered by Gretz in a sudden moment of joy after our first-round win.

"The thing that hit me first was, 'Geez, we beat the Montreal Canadiens — the Canadiens! — wow.' That's what I thought," Gretzky said. "We beat the best organization in the history of hockey. I guess that's something, isn't it?"

It sure was, considering that we had finished the regular season in 14th place overall, and that with all the kids in our lineup we were often treated by Slats like a bunch of summer campers. But the New York media, always quick to seize an angle for a story, pounced on something Wayne reiterated to a group of newsmen before the opening game on Long Island: "We had to be prepared mentally and physically *to beat the best team* in hockey."

Those five little words — *to beat the best team* — leaped into the minds of those New York reporters. How dare Wayne call the Canadiens and not the Islanders the best team in hockey. Even so distiguished a writer as the *New York Times'* Pulitzer Prize-winning columnist Dave Anderson entered the fray, pointing out that Gretz was in error, that the Stanley Cup champion Islanders remained the *best team in hockey* until defeated.

Anderson wrote: "For all his precocious genius on the ice Wayne Gretzky is indisuptably 20 years old in coping with the psychology of play-off diplomacy. By complimenting the Canadiens, he unthinkingly had insulted the Islanders."

In no time at all just about every New York hockey writer had jumped on the anti-Gretzky bandwagon and pretty soon the Islanders had grabbed the bait. "I think Gretzky got it backwards," barked Islanders defenseman Stefan Persson. Bryan Trottier added: "If he thinks Montreal is the best team, fine. It will only act as an incentive for us."

The *New York Post* headline screamed: ISLES WANT TO MAKE GRETZKY EAT HIS WORDS.

In a sense, they did. We got clobbered 8-2 in the opener. Whether he liked it or not, whether he was misinterpreted — which he *was* — or not, Wayne had a lot of explaining to do when the press converged on him after the game.

Gretz was magnificent. Unlike other superstars who frequently hide from reporters in the trainer's room after a defeat, he not only met the media head-on but addressed the question with his typical candor. Now, the reporters demanded, what *did* he have to say about the Canadiens being better than the Islanders?

No problem. Wayne had the answer and it was perfect. "I thought we beat the best organization in hockey. The same as when someone beats the New York Yankees in baseball. I know the Islanders were the best team in the NHL this season. But to all of us guys who grew up in Canada and watched the Canadiens rule the NHL for so many seasons, they were the greatest and to beat them was something we dreamed about doing. I'm taking nothing away from the Islanders. They have a good team, but Montreal is the best ever. This year the Islanders were the best team but it will take a long time to knock Montreal off the post."

Now it was time for us to knock off the Islanders — or at

least try. In Game Two we gave them a scare, taking a 1-0 lead on Glennie Anderson's goal in the first and later coming from behind to tie the score at 3-3 at the end of the second. But the Islanders had too much gas and our tank was running on empty. They scored three unanswered goals in the third and skated off with a 6-3 win. Did we ever look forward to the return home.

Northlands Coliseum was just what the doctor ordered. We completely reversed the flow — Wayne got a three-goal hat trick — and we wiped them out, 5-2. Could we do it again? Our juices were flowing and so were our forwards. We played the Islanders even through three periods of Game Four and went into overtime, tied 4-4.

For five very exciting minutes play ebbed and flowed without a score. As so often happens in sudden death, the winning goal would be scored on a break and the perpetrator would be a man who would be our nemesis for many years, defenseman Ken Morrow. The shot Morrow fired was not a particularly devastating one but somehow it handcuffed Andy Moog and went in at 5:41.

Were we downhearted? No.

Any suggestions that we were going back to Long Island on a sightseeing visit were dispelled in the second period of Game Five when we moved into a 3-2 lead and increased it to 4-2. It ended 4-3 for us and with that we had put the fear of God into the Islanders. Going back to Edmonton, they knew darn good and well that they had a *series* on their hands.

The seasoned vets like Potvin, Trottier and Gillies couldn't quite figure us out. Pressure? We laughed at it. Our bench was more like a collegiate fraternity than a big-league team. The kids on our team — me included — would cheer HERE WE GO, OILERS; HERE WE GO!! like it was a Saturday afternoon football game. And the beauty of it all was that this came perfectly naturally to us.

The city of Edmonton was higher than a kite for Game Six but we weren't quite up to it. We held them to 1-1 into the second period but then the Islanders broke the game open with a pair of goals. If they thought we'd quit, they were sadly mistaken. Mark scored at 5:31 of the third and we were right on their tails but it just wasn't to be — at least not this year. Duane Sutter scored for them and the game ended at 5-2 for New York.

Could we have beaten the Stanley Cup champions that year? Conceivably. We had the opportunity to tie the series in Game Four when Kenny Morrow torpedoed us in overtime. We scared them because they knew that we were running on emotion. ("It was tough to play them," said Denis Potvin. "They were all over the ice.") Which was true but we played way above our heads while they were at their peak and that was much better than us. If it had gone to a ten-game series we wouldn't have won because they had the one quality we still lacked — experience.

But I wasn't ashamed of our performance. We showed all the character in the world and, as Wayne pointed out, "The most important thing we did was create a winning attitude."

21

Hooray for Hollywood — Sometimes

We may not have beaten the Islanders but we did the next best thing — the Oilers made a name for themselves. It was as positive as it could be. Vibrant young skaters like Jari Kurri, Glenn Anderson and, of course, Gretz had given us a romantic touch that even the Islanders, who won the Stanley Cup again in 1981, didn't possess.

Surely, if a Hollywood script writer wanted to project a fascinating collection of characters for the screen, he'd just go to our lineup for 1981-82 and select Glennie and Gretz, Andy and Fogey but, most of all, Mark Messier.

To begin with, they'd fall in love with Mark's image. His motto is to live every day as if it's his last and he plays that way as well. If I were to choose one word to describe Mark it would be *fierce.*

Don Cherry made an accurate appraisal of Mark when he said, "Here's a guy who can fight, who can hit, who can score goals, who can set up goals and who knows what to do with his stick. He's got that *wild* look in his eyes."

Amen.

That wild look has been intimidating people for a long, long time and Mark isn't that old. Around Edmonton they tell a story about the time he was playing his first year pro for Cincinnati in the WHA and went up against the Oilers who had a pretty well-known young player named Dennis Sobchuk. The way Mark's father, Doug, tells it, the other guy started the fight. "Dennis thought Mark was one guy he could get some points with," said Doug.

It was no contest. A dozen punches for Mark, none for Sobchuk.

Bryan Watson, who was on Cincy with Mark at the time, often said that the bout helped steer Mark to Edmonton. "The fight made a hell of an impression on Slats and everyone," Watson explained, "and I could see why." The raw fury of the young man would eventually meld with his irresistible speed and powerful shot. Slats saw that and picked Mark on the third round of the entry draft, 48th overall. Mark once told David Staples of the *Edmonton Journal*, "In my mind I was going to be a hockey player and that was it."

When his father was playing minor pro hockey (Western League) for the Portland Buckeroos, Mark was the team stickboy. The family yarn is that Mark would bawl his head off and run after his father's car down the street if Doug left for the rink without him.

Eventually, Mark worked his way up the hockey ladder from the amateurs to the WHA and, finally, the NHL with us. It didn't take Mark very long to get a reputation as a mean sonofagun. He wasted some big names, wasn't very discreet when he suckered Jamie Macoun of the Flames and elbowed the Soviet ace, Alexander Kovin, out of his senses.

That's the kicker to Mark's game, the gravy part. It's the question that people raise about him, whether he's missing a screw or not. To me, that makes him a lot like Gordie Howe. You never know when he's going to turn on you. And he has the goods to back it up. This is what's made him a total hockey player. But Hollywood would love him for the other reasons. Mark Messier would *really* like to be Mick Jagger. "To be a rock 'n roll star and have the fans going crazy," said Mark. "Would that be a rush or what?"

He's done just about all the other glamor things. He owns a guitar, sings, surfs, would love to be a race car driver as well and travels around the world. Somebody once said that Mark runs over life like it was an enemy defenseman and in no time at all he became the soul of our team. "Fellas," he would say, "there's nothing to save it for. There's nowhere for us to hide out there so let's play with reckless abandon". He does everything there is to win — a lot like Tiger Williams used to be except with plenty more talent. And a lot better looks.

Staples tells a story about the time Mess, Mike Krushelny-ski, Dave Lumley and Dave Hunter visited Edmonton's General Hospital. Mess walked in wearing a yellow and black sweater with green pleated corduroy pants.

A nurse did a double-take. "He looks like a bumble bee," she said.

Lummer had a better response. "Turn if off! Turn it off!"

Mess laughed. "What? This sweater ain't bright."

Staples put the Messier charisma in perspective. "Of the four, Messier grabs people's attention. He talks the loudest, leads the way, signs the most autographs. The nurses with blush and pearls and lipstick are dressed as if they were heading out to a nightclub. They joke with him. And Messier loves it, loves the attention, the image."

Mark symbolized the attention we began receiving and a slow but gradual intermingling between ourselves and show business personalities like Hollywood star Michael J. Fox.

Like Glenn Anderson, Michael J. Fox hails from Vancouver. They not only grew up together but also played some hockey in the same group before Glennie went on to university. They didn't see each other for some time but on one of our road trips to California, Glennie phoned up Fox after a Kings game and we got together with him for a few beers.

We relaxed at Fox's place with the ease that we would have had we visited Gretz, and he treated Glennie and the rest of us like a bunch of long lost buddies, with a bit of sardonic humor. Said Fox to Glennie, "Here's a guy who, for years, didn't even know I existed and now that I'm a big star, he phones me up!"

We all laughed because he was joking, of course. "That's gratitude for you," added Fox. "But I forgive him."

Alan Thicke became another of our Hollywood friends. If we checked into Los Angeles a day before a game we'd phone him up and go over to his place. One night when Wayne and I were there Thicke's guests included Michael Douglas, Morgan Fairchild and a group called The Tubes.

Another time the entire team went to Muhammad Ali's house and, for that, we have to thank Mark. His uncle, Larry Messier, at one time had been a part of Ali's entourage and he arranged for us to meet Muhammed. The visit had a combination of fun and sadness to it.

Someone had tipped us off that it was Ali's birthday so we brought him a birthday cake. He chatted with us, showed the team around his estate and introduced us to his wife, Veronica, who was very gracious to us all.

What perplexed me were the two faces of Ali. On the one hand, he appeared mentally sharp, especially when he was taking fun photos with our tough guy, Dave Semenko. Muhammed seemed very quick, very capable in the repartee. But almost immediately after that he began talking real slow and everything he did was slow.

At the time he was really into religion and at one point brought out his little daughter's pink record player with a Donald Duck figure on it. Then, he brought out a religious record that a friend had recorded on a little 45 rpm disk.

What made this all so weird was the fact that we were in this enormous mansion filled with expensive trappings and there's Ali playing a record for us on a two-bit phonograph that was virtually inaudible. I asked myself two questions: Why is he playing this religious record for us? And why didn't he play it on his $50,000 stereo instead of on the Donald Duck phonograph?

When he did talk, we could hardly hear him and after a while he just sort of drifted off. My observations were that he's punch-drunk or that he's just having fun with everyone while in his own private world. After all, I figured, he's Muhammed Ali; he can do whatever he wants. He's into the religious thing and playing with everybody's minds. He realizes his power and what he can do with it.

For the short time that he fake punched with Semenk, he was smooth and still looked like a fine specimen of a man. I pictured him in his prime and could only see a man who was totally devastating. But I can't say that I was terribly upset when we finally did leave the place.

No less interesting among our Hollywood stops was the visit to Hugh Hefner's mansion. As a rule, Mister Playboy doesn't invite many people to his mansion, except for personal friends. (We were told that he only invites older men who won't prove a threat to his girl, a threat in the sense of taking his women from him.) When we were invited, we considered it an honor.

Before we went, I talked to the only other NHL player I had known who had gone to Hefner's mansion. That was Charlie Simmer, who had played for the Los Angeles Kings. Charlie was invited on the one night a year that girls can bring dates, the Midsummer Night's Dream Pyjama Party. Terri Welles (whom Charlie later married), a former *Playboy* calendar girl, brought Charlie along that night.

I went to Hefner's mansion along with Mark and Wayne. The information we got was that we hop in a limo and get out at a big rock at the mansion gate.

Why the rock? We were told that it was a security checkpoint. A camera was imbedded in it which conveyed pictures up to the mansion. The rock also contained a speaker system so you can literally talk to the rock. We were told that when we got to the rock, we should have the driver drive us in.

Being young, energetic young men, we were in a bit of a hurry to get to the mansion, if you can understand what I mean. We didn't want to wait around for a limousine.

Wayne said, "Let's do without a limo; let's just go!" I echoed his sentiments. Instead of a limo, we grabbed a cab and told the driver to take us to Hefner's place. But when we finally arrived at the gates, embarrassment consumed us and we felt silly driving up in a taxi when everyone else came in a stretch limo.

Nevertheless, we talked to the rock; the guy opened the gate for us and said, "Just have your driver bring you up."

We were now so embarrassed about rolling up in a little cab that we paid off the cabby and decided to walk the rest of the way to spare the humiliation.

Of course, we had the misapprehension that the mansion was just a few hundred feet up the road, so we started walking up the hill. The more we walked, the more we wondered why we had ever gotten out of the cab because we walked and walked *and* walked. And the more we walked, the more cameras we could hear focussing in on us from the trees. All along, Mark was saying, "If Hugh Hefner comes walking by in his pyjamas and that pipe, I'm going to sucker him!"

After the endless trek, we finally got to the mansion where Hefner's PR lady met us and commented, "You guys should feel honored to be here, because he rarely does this — but because of Mister Gretzky, he's making an exception."

Well, that was nice but even nicer were the dozen beautiful girls roaming around. What could we do but mingle, a little bit nervous but enjoying the remarkable scenery nonetheless. The best part occurred after we sat down to dinner. Who should march into the room but Hefner himself, in pyjamas, smoking his pipe, looking just like he does in his magazine.

Hef dropped over to chat with us and, suddenly, I had this sense of déjà vu. He was just like Ali, off in another world by himself, yet courteous at the same time. All that was missing was a Donald Duck phonograph!

As much as Gretz, Mess and myself enjoyed the Hefner visit, Hugh didn't quite have the same appeal to us as some of the other show business stars, particularly Johnny Carson. Probably because "The Tonight Show" has been around so long — and we all watched it as little kids — Carson had made a deeper impression on us than most show business personalities, male or female. As far as we were concerned, the height of fame in terms of being *visible* to the North American public was an appearance on the Carson show.

With that in mind, we'd needle Gretzky, "Wayne, you've accomplished just about everything, but you haven't *really* made it until the day you're invited and appear on 'The Tonight Show.' You have to be on with Carson to be a true star."

Sure enough, Wayne had made it so big in the NHL that one day he was notified that he was going on Carson. To say he was happy would be terribly understating the case. He was jubilant to the extreme.

"Kevin," he said, "have I made it or have I made it — I'm going on with Carson!"

We had just played a game against the Nordiques in Quebec City and were next scheduled to be in Bloomington to play the North Stars. But there was a two-day lapse, which meant there was enough time for Wayne to jet to the West Coast, do the show and then fly back to Minnesota for the game.

I should point out that Slats worked very hard at monitoring Wayne's appearances because the demands on him — not only from the city-to-city beat writers but from magazines and tv stations as well — were already enormous and growing faster. Sather wanted first of all to do what was best for the Edmonton Oilers but he also realized that Gretz had become an ambassador for hockey in general and something like a Carson show appearance would be a terrific PR boost for the NHL. Certainly, Glen would go along with it as long as Gretz got back to Minnesota in time.

Wayne asked me to go along with him and, of course, I was delighted. We were to fly from Quebec City to Toronto and then from Toronto to Los Angeles, do the show that night and then head back to Minneapolis. The problem, as so often happens with cross-country flights, was that we had to make a connection in Chicago which, under optimal conditions, can be maddening.

When we arrived in Toronto word had been circulating around the airport that a severe storm was raging near Chicago. What could we do? We sat in the plane for an hour, waiting for the storm to die down, then we learned that the plane was not going to take off after all. So, we're back inside, it's about 11 A.M. and we have to be in Los Angeles by 5 P.M. That meant we still had enough time to make another connection but it was now getting hairier by the minute.

Wayne and I went from airline desk to airline desk but we couldn't find another connection. By now, Gretz was starting to panic. The team had gone off to Minnesota and the two of us were stranded at the airport. I was disappointed because I knew how much this appearance meant to Wayne and I was aware that the NHL publicity people were talking up the appearance because this would be such a big deal for hockey in general.

Suddenly, Wayne got an idea, a brilliant brainstorm. Why not rent a Lear jet and fly directly to California, circumventing the trouble in Chicago. We checked it out and discovered, sure enough, we could do it for six grand.

Sure, six grand sounds like a lot of money but we're talking about a million bucks worth of publicity for the NHL. I mean you can't buy that kind of exposure. Seeing that this was a great promo for the league, Wayne phoned the NHL office and said, "I'm going on Carson but I can't get to California through Chicago. I want to rent a jet but it'll cost $6,000. I'll pay half and the NHL can pick up the other half. How do you feel about that?"

The NHL said no.

So, Gretz said, "I'm only getting $1,000 to go on Carson, I can't afford to pay $6,000 for this out of my own pocket."

Still, the NHL wouldn't budge. We couldn't believe that the league wouldn't shell out $3,000 to promote the NHL. We wound up eventually flying to Minnesota to meet the team with everyone saying "I thought you were going on Carson." We didn't tell anyone the story behind the story of why our California visit bombed.

Of course, that wasn't nearly as bad as the bombing we took on the ice that spring from the Los Angeles hockey club. It was, as they might say in Edmonton, a series that will live in infamy.

The 1981 playoff win over Montreal and the six-game series with the Islanders had had a very positive effect on our club even though we lost in six to New York. We opened the following fall like gangbusters and finished first in the Smythe Division, 34 points ahead of second-place Vancouver. A lot of people figured we had come of age as a hockey club and would be legitimate contenders for the Stanley Cup.

Our first challenge would be the Los Angeles Kings, who had finished fourth, 17 games under .500 and 48 points behind us. How did the Kings feel about us? Their captain Dave Taylor summed it up pessimistically. "We just want to keep it close."

They did — in an extraordinary way.

We jumped into a 4-1 lead before the game was ten minutes old but the Kings rallied — oh boy, did they ever rally! — and with less than eight minutes left in regulation time the score was tied 8-8. Then, Charlie Simmer scored for them and L.A. skated away with a 10-8 upset.

What happend to us? Several negative things. To begin with, we entered the playoffs in a slump, the worst time to have one. Next, our youth and inexperience began to show right after the game. We got behind the eight-ball and sort of panicked. From there on, we never fully bounced back.

To the Kings credit, their defense played well. In Jerry Korab, Jay Wells, Mark Hardy, Dave Lewis and Rick Chartraw, L.A. had plenty of experience behind the blue line. One thing we learned in Game Two was that the Kings' performance in the opener was no fluke. They fought us to a 2-2 tie after regulation time and it wasn't until 6:20 of sudden-death that Gretz put the game away.

Game Three was as ridiculous a playoff game as you can imagine (except maybe for Game One) and certainly should have been our lever for demolishing the Kings. We had a 5-0 lead after two periods and the situation seemed so well in hand that the final 20 seconds loomed as a huge yawner. Even Jerry Buss, the Kings owner, got so disgusted that he walked out of The Forum early in the third period with his team trailing 5-1.

Then, the inexplicable happened. Doug Smith and Simmer scored for L.A. to trim the margin to 5-3. Uh-oh. Mark Hardy made it 5-4 at 15:59. Still, we had our chances. Pat Hughes broke away with a minute and a half left but shot wide. The Kings pressed in the final minute and, finally, in the dying seconds, Steve Bozek pushed the rubber in and we had blown the 5-0 lead.

Hey, there was still overtime, so why worry. Mark almost put the game away early on but shot over the net. Now it was the Kings turn and they made good. Doug Smith won a face-off, sent the puck to Daryl Evans and, *red light*, we are in deep trouble!

How did we blow it? Good question.

Critics charged that we were too cocky, too relaxed. We just weren't a disciplined hockey team then. We had all this untapped talent but we were like the little girl with the curl; when we were good we were very, very good but when we were bad, we were horrid. It all came down to inexperience and the fact that we tightened up and got the jitters. Instead of relaxing when they began coming back, we did the opposite. We should have told ourselves, "No problem, we're under control, keep taking it to them." Instead, it was, "Oh, God, we have to get the puck out of our end. I don't want to be on the ice for a goal." Thinking defensive at a time like that was the worst thing in the world. We stood around, thinking defensive, and they scored goals.

The aftermath of that debacle provided an interesting insight into our young hockey club. There was no game the next day and, in order to find a practice rink, we bussed down the San Diego Freeway all the way to Culver City. I'll never forget it. Rain was coming down in buckets and we were all sitting in the bus with long faces on.

I was thinking, "We had such a good regular season: we think we're a great team, so what the hell happened last night?"

The guys were all sitting there, gazing at the awful, ugly day, looking at each other, wondering what happened. Finally, from the back of the bus, Semenk made a smart-ass remark: "Can you believe what we did last night?"

There was a pause and it was as if his remark touched everyone's funnybone. You had to laugh; that was the only way to look at it. Everyone joined in the laughter and while all this may sound very silly, it was good for us. The remark broke the tension and the monotony.

What followed was the game of our lives — at least until that point in the franchise's history. We fought, scratched and clawed our way to a 3-2 win and it made us so proud to come from behind and regroup like that. It showed a lot of character.

The problem was that we still had another game to play — the finale back in Edmonton the following night. The two teams chartered a jet and we flew together, the Oilers in the back of the plane and the Kings up front. Believe me, it was a great feeling for us to have won the game in L.A. and see their faces. We were sitting on top of the perch. We counted them out of it and that, in the end, was the biggest error of inexperience we had made all year. The thinking before Game Four was, "All we have to do is win this game in L.A. and then when we go back to Northlands, the Edmonton fans will win Game Five for us."

Say this for the Kings, they were better prepared entering Game Five. "We want to get them off their game and force them to play individual hockey," said Jerry Korab and he had the right idea. We got behind early and stayed behind. It was 3-2 Los Angeles at the end of the first and, incredibly, 6-2 for them at the end of the second.

The final score was a crusher, 7-4, and the post mortems ran well into the night and for several months thereafter. My theory is that the problems began at the start of the series and never were fully reversed. Had the same thing happened to us a few years later, we would have been mature enough to give ourselves a mental timeout and tell each other, "You guys see what's happening. Relax. Start over!" But we couldn't avert the panic and we never fully coped with the inexperience.

Coping with the press was another challenge. The media brutalized us, especially Terry Jones who earlier in the series had written that we were guilty of "The biggest choke in Stanley Cup history." After we were eliminated, Jones called us a bunch of "Weak-kneed wimps." I think what he was saying was that we played so badly in Game Five that it looked like we laid down and gave up but we certainly didn't give up. We were trying too hard. He took the worst possible shot at us and it stung the team to the core. The worst part was the knowledge that the "Weak-Kneed Wimps" line even made headlines in the *L.A. Times.*

They made a mockery of us. But we also had to face the fact that we lost, the press had a job to do, and under the circumstances, we had to expect to be subject to some ridicule.

But "Weak-kneed wimps." That was a bit much. Even in Hollywood!

22

The Fuhr Era Begins, Never to End

As William Shakespeare once noted, "Sweet are the uses of adversity." At first the taste of the Los Angeles loss was bitter but it would prove, in the long run, to be fruitful to us because we learned a major lesson in maturity and discipline. Burned badly though we were, the wounds would heal and the Oilers, as a whole, would emerge from the defeat a team with a mission. How long it would require to accomplish that mission would remain to be seen but, certainly, most of the elements had fallen into place.

If we needed any prodding — apart from Slats — we certainly got it from the media. Jones' verbal harpoons were only a few among many. One of the lessons we had to learn involved coping with the press and that we did. My lessons would be particularly involved because I would become a member of The Fourth Estate myself.

But before I ever sat behind a typewriter I had ample opportunity to digest the works of Jim Matheson and Dick Chubey, the two reporters who had been covering the Oilers from Day One in the NHL. Dick from *The Edmonton Sun* and Jim from *The Edmonton Journal* competed with each other and were a pair of contrasting personalities.

Superficially, Chubey was the more imposing of the two. He's a bigger man and was a bit (*is* a bit) louder than Matheson. Chubes likes to wear big fedoras and, at the beginning, guys on the team would make smart remarks about him when he'd come in the dressing room. That put him on the defensive and pretty soon he would have his guard up. You can't communicate as human beings when one guy has his guard up, or vice versa. I learned that the way you deal with Chubes is to treat him like a decent human being and, in return, he'd do likewise. Dick is a don't-push-me-because-I-can-push-back-harder kind of guy.

In the early days of the franchise, guys looked on Matheson and Chubey as the enemy — the way many athletes do the press. The thinking was (and is), those guys are digging for dirt and will try to sensationalize a story that really wasn't meant to be sensational. The Gretzky-Islander business in 1981 was a case in point.

Eventually relationships developed and some of the guys got to like Chubes more than Matty (maybe *trusted* is the better word) while others felt better with Matty. Personally, I trust them both. I can say things to Matty or Chubes "off-the-record" and they could still write a story without jeopardizing my credibility. Without hurting anayone, they could word it in a way that they still had a story.

Remember that both Dick and Jim were with us at the start and have been with us right up to the present so eventually relationships developed. The guys realized that they were pretty fair and would tell it like it is but I remember Chubey telling me that there was some concern at his paper because the editors thought he had become too close to the players. (I'm sure Matheson has been confronted with the same concern.)

For the hockey fan, they did the job. They told Edmonton what was going on, what the Oilers were doing each day, but as far as taking shots at us, that pretty much was left to those who didn't travel with us, columnists like Terry Jones.

When you have two papers in a city, there's obviously competition and a lot of times they try to out scoop each other. If Dick had a scoop, he'd ask me, "Keep that quiet!" and, of course, Matty has done the same thing. I always gave them the benefit of the doubt on the grounds that the guy in question had done his homework and deserved his beat.

I began to get a more intimate view of newspapering when *The Sun* asked me to do an occasional hockey column for them. It happened after I had begun doing a radio show and was getting known around the league as someone who could and would articulate his opinions. They realized that I had an ability to express myself and wondered whether I could present a behind-the-scenes kind of view of the Oilers.

It was an intriguing proposal but not one that I wanted to act rashly on until I had given it considerable thought. At first, I was concerned that the guys would be wondering what I would say and, of course, how Glen would react, so the first thing I did was talk to Slats and lay out the proposal just as they had made it to me.

Another genreal manager or coach might have been uptight about it but Glen's reply was, "If you can better yourself, by all means do it but remember that hockey should be your number one priority."

What I wanted to do in the column was present a side of the hockey club that the average fan doesn't see or read about in the regular newspaper stories. "You know, Slats, I won't jeopardize the good and welfare of the team or be controversial," I assured him.

He said, "Kevin, I never had any doubts whatsoever. What I'm concerned about is how much time you're going to spend on it."

I assured him that it would be a couple of hours of my free time on my days off. Instead of watching soap operas, I'd spend a few hours putting my thoughts down on paper. With that assurance, Slats gave me the green light and I went home to write my first newspaper column for the *Edmonton Sun*.

I tried to be humorous in my first piece, explaining what this jock was doing, dabbling in the field of journalism. Why not, since I already had the reputation of being a guy who had never met a microphone he didn't like. I typed the first column but then the *Sun* gave me a Radio Shack computer and I'd put it on that, sending it to the paper in rough form. Then, they'd edit the piece.

They must have liked the first column because they printed it exactly as I had written it except for spelling mistakes and misplaced commas and periods.

After that, they began giving me hints on style and journalistic grammar but the ideas for the columns remained my own. Pretty soon, I began opening my ears for the comments that went on between the players in the locker room and on the bus. I'd quietly take notes and use some of the thoughts for columns.

If there were any objections, I never heard it from my team-mates. On the contrary, they'd tell me, "Kevin, you can write just about anything and the real, true hockey fan is going to appreciate it. They want to know what goes on during the bus rides and what goes into taping sticks. The want to know what hockey players do."

What pleased me initially about the column was that people actually were reading it. They'd come up to me in the street after games and instead of saying "good game" or "bad game" they'd say, "I like what you wrote" or "That was an interesting observation." They liked me as the reporter as opposed to liking me as a hockey player.

At first I wondered how Matty would react to my column since I was writing for the competition. Did he think I'd deliberately hold back scoops from him? I didn't think it would be fair to do that and neither Chubes nor the *Sun* asked that of me although the fellows at the *Sun* would needle me with barbs like, "Of course, Kevin, you won't be talking to the *Journal*, will you?"

They never made that demand of me and if they had, I would not have accepted it. If something interesting came up, and Matty happened to be the first there, he'd get it before the *Sun*.

What I soon learned is that happenings that we on the team usually take for granted as commonplace are interesting to the reader. I was reminded of that by Dave Lumley who was recalling his early days as a Maple Leaf fan — especially a Davey Keon fan — in Toronto.

One day Lumley the kid happened to be at Maple Leaf Gardens when the Leafs had a practice. He must have ambled into the dressing room when Davey Keon had come out of the shower because he managed to see Keon in the nude. "Boy," said Lumley, "these guys are human!"

Then, Lummer, the kid, discovered that the team flew out of town lots of times after games in Toronto. Lummer recalled, "I never thought that these guys had to travel to play in another city. I just thought that they played in Maple Leaf Gardens all the time. I thought the Leafs were always the home team." Lummer's stories proved to me that just about anything I wrote about the Oilers would prove interesting to the reader.

The one area I avoided was controversy. The *Sun* wanted me to get a bit more controversial but I don't have that type of personality and I could never do that. More than anything, I didn't want the column to jeopardize the camaraderie I had with the players so I was very careful never to report on a game. I'd write about how our co-coach John Muckler was highly underrated and how I felt that Mark Messier is the second best player in the game. At the *Sun*, they called me Mister Positive although they didn't want me to take that tack all the time. You run out of positive things to say, no matter how great the team is.

It was when I started writing wonderful things about the Oilers training staff that the *Sun* said, "Hey, you've gone overboard. They might be good guys, but how great are they. We don't want to put words in your mouth, but let's find another angle. Let's not be positive *all* the time."

That's when I changed my tack and wrote a piece about refereeing. I didn't really take a shot at the referees but I explained the difficulty of the job. Next, I did a column about the NHL and how I thought the league could better market the game. I had watched Major League Baseball's commercials which said, "Baseball Fever, Catch It!" and it dawned on me that hockey should be marketed the same way. After all, we have the agility of basketball, the aggressiveness of football and the endurance and stamina of soccer, and the speed of no other sport. Hockey has everything in one so I did a piece on that.

One of my favorite columns had to do with the art — and pain — of goaltending.

> A not-so-funny thing happened recently in Winnipeg. Ouch. I took a shot on the foot and the agony made me think of just what Grant Fuhr in particular and NHL goaltenders in general go through in a 80-game season.
>
> You have to have a lot of respect for Grant.
>
> All you have to do is check his body — there are bumps and bruises everywhere. Even the best equipment in the world can't protect you when someone lets a howitzer go at your head from the slot.
>
> His body is like a patchwork quilt — red here, blue there, a mess everywhere. One shot in Winnipeg gave me the shivers. It was deflected and missed Grant's noggin by less than an inch. Only his reflexes saved him.
>
> It's bad enough physically, but it's no walk in the park mentally, either.
>
> Goaltending is arguably the toughest position physically, but is definitely the toughest mentally. There's no in-between. You

either win or you lose, you're either the hero or the goat. Forwards and defensemen can get lost in the crowd. Not goaltenders.

Fans often rate goaltenders on how many goals they allow. Not I. My criterion for greatness is measured by only one thing — wins. That's all that counts. And that makes Grant the best in the game today.

Mike Liut was considered great for a number of years; he was even considered as the MVP. But greatness has to be measured in wins. And Mike never won the big one.

I'll never forget the spring I was going to be drafted. I went to the first game of the final between the Habs and Rangers at the Forum. Montreal lost 4-1 and they booed Ken Dryden right out of the building.

The next night, Bunny Larocque was going to start, but Doug Risebrough nailed him in the head in warmup and Dryden was back in there. He stoned the Rangers and Montreal went on to win the Cup.

Tony Esposito was booed during his last few years in Chicago.

It's tough. The accolades, it seems, generally don't come until they retire.

A great goaltender is vital. Case in point: last year's playoff series between Montreal and Philadelphia. Montreal had the better series, but Ron Hextall was great for the Flyers. That was the difference.

You can't win without a superb goalie. That's what makes the Oilers so fortunate to have Grant Fuhr. But, despite all he's done, the respect that comes with being the premier player at his position didn't come until the Canada Cup.

Bumps, bruises. Eye-high slapshots from the slot. Boos. No respect. Geez, he can have it!

My appreciation of goaltending grew rapidly once Grant Fuhr signed on with the Oilers. The first black goaltender ever to stop pucks in the NHL, Fuhr made the jump to Edmonton directly from junior hockey and we were very fortunate to get him. When he was 18, while playing for the Victoria Cougars, Grant was being pursued by a dozen NHL clubs.

The Rangers were especially interested in Grant because their top goalie, John Davidson, had come up lame and the New Yorkers were shallow in goal. Add to that the publicity prospects of a black man starring for a Broadway hockey club. The ramifications for the Rangers — if they could land Grant — were enormous.

But our people had been scouting Fuhr as much as any club and the reports coming back to Sather were invariably enthusiastic. Jack Shupe, his coach in Victoria, offered an appraisal of Grant that holds up right through the late 1980s: "Fuhr has a really good temperament to be a goaltender. He's always easy-going and nothing seems to get him upset. You can score on him and he doesn't change outwardly whatsoever. I've always felt he was tougher and played better if he let in a soft goal. He really bears down then."

A general manager on the lookout for goaltending insurance couldn't ask for a more positive evaluation than that. Still, we already had a good, young goaltender in Andy Moog, so one might wonder why Slats would "waste" a number one draft pick on another when he might obtain a solid forward or defense prospect.

The answer has two parts. In this age of high-speed hockey, the two-goalie system is more important than it ever was and, therefore, you can't have enough netminding insurance. Also, of the players available when we drafted, Fuhr was the best.

Another consideration was our draft-picking position. We were eighth, right behind the Canadiens and immediately ahead of the Rangers. Conceivably, Grant would be picked in the first seven. (Actually, the selections went this way: 1. Dale Hawerchuk (Winnipeg) 2. Doug Smith (Los Angeles) 3. Bobby Carpenter (Washington) 4. Ron Francis (Hartford) 5. Joe Cirella (Colorado) 6. Jim Benning (Toronto) 7. Mark Hunter (Montreal).

Slats was aware that other junior goalies who had been drafted high in other years had proven disappointing under fire. In 1972, for example, the Canadiens drafted Michel Larocque sixth with much the same guarantees that we had heard about Grant but Larocque fizzled out in Montreal.

With the assurances of Barry Fraser and others on the scouting staff, Sather picked Fuhr. (The Rangers followed with James Patrick and the Canucks, who had also eyed Grant, went for Garth Butcher.) Vancouver scout George Wood, himself a former goaltender, had the same questions we all did. "A lot of outstanding junior goaltenders have been stuck right into the NHL pressure cooker and have never recovered," said Wood. "It requires a lot of maturity and adjustment to go right from junior to the top."

We'd find out soon enough and Grant, in turn, would

immediately be introduced to Oilers humor, even before he ever played a game in Edmonton. Our first meeting with the prospect occurred immediately after he had been drafted. The Oilers had a team in the annual Niagara Falls NHL Slo-Pitch Softball Tournament. We knew that Fuhr would be joining us so it was decided that some sort of caper was in order to "welcome" him to the fold.

A bunch of the players assembled at the hotel all dressed up in our ball uniforms. Each of us had plastered heavy helpings of black grease under our eyes the way the baseball players do to deflect sun rays. When Grant was ushered in, we handed him a bottle of white shoe polish to put under his eyes.

Grant took the prank well and, despite his shyness, he bonded well with the rest of the fellows. A lot of credit for that belongs to Ronnie Low who went out of his way to help Grant. This in and of itself demonstrates the special fraternity of our club. Ronnie, now that Grant and Andy were on the roster, would become low man on the Oilers, no pun intended. Yet Ronnie worked hard to help Grant improve his skills, taking the young goalie under his wing, teaching him the NHL ropes. Thank goodness for us, there was a Ronnie Low around because, quite frankly, I don't know if anyone else could have taken the responsibility, especially since goaltenders are a different breed.

What made Ronnie even a breed apart from everyone else was his attitude. Known to his peers as *Lowtide*, Ronnie was a classic. (He wound up playing more than a dozen years in the NHL.) He always gave undivided attention to practice and he helped teach Grant and Andy consistent work habits.

When I broke in with the club, Ronnie was a bit of a thorn in my side only because his name is Low and mine is Lowe. The difference was that he already had eight years of pro experience and his name was more recognizable to the fans, resulting in several fans calling me "Ron." (Years later, after Low had been traded, I stepped onto the ice at Vancouver's Pacific Coliseum and a fan yelled out to me, "Hey, Ron." Ah, the price of fame.) I survived those bruises to my ego sufficiently to gain a keen appreciation of Ron Low. To me he's living proof that good guys do finish first.

If was one thing for an older player who had been around to make the adjustment to Fuhr but it was much different for Moog. After all, Andy had become the toast of Canada after we had beaten Montreal in the 1981 playoffs and, since then, had established himself as a promising young goalie. Now, all of a sudden, here's Grant Fuhr.

If there were any personality clashes between the two youngsters, I didn't see any of them. Andy was intelligent enough to know that it wasn't Grant's fault that Slats had drafted him and brought him up to the big club. Nor was it Grant's fault that from the moment he stepped on the ice for us as a rookie, Fuhr never played a bad game. Not from Day One.

More than that, Grant was an ideal team player. To begin with, Grant said very little, so he never was going to get the pot boiling. It was virtually impossible to get into a personality clash with a fellow like him.

Both Fuhr and Moog did their jobs and when they weren't in the net, they were for the team. Sounds corny? Perhaps, but in those earlier, pre-Stanley Cup days, they both knew they'd each get plenty of starting assignments. So, the adjustment was hardly traumatic for either guy. Since Grant was a number one pick, he could have proven to be a problem, ego-wise, but he was quite the opposite.

At first Grant didn't even want to say two words. He wouldn't say shit if he had a mouthful. Grant gave you "yes," or "no," or "maybe" answers and that was about it. He was a dream to a defenseman like me because if he let a goal in, he figured that it was his fault and if I made a mistake, it was still his fault. Grant never pointed a finger of accusation at any of his teammates the way goalies do on other teams. You know, guys with big egos afraid to admit their own mistakes. Having him in goal was like having a board in front of the net.

Because he is black, Grant has been the butt of dressing room humor that — no matter what the bleeding-heart liberals might tell you — was good, clean fun and never, as far as I could tell, really disturbed Fuhr. He was nicknamed "Cocoa" and that has stuck with him until the present and he has been chided in other ways because of the color of his skin but never to the point where it was insulting.

Here's an example. On one road trip we had gone to Washington for a game with the Capitals. On the day before the game the club had to take a bus to the practice rink. On the way back, we passed a McDonald's hamburger place and, suddenly, twenty guys began shouting — very much like a bunch of five-year-olds — "McDonald's, McDonald's; we want to go to McDonald's!"

Our camp counselor, Slats, said it was okay although we

certainly looked like a bunch of Martians at the time. The problem was that the practice facility didn't have enough dressing room facilities, so we were still wearing all our uniforms which we would change back at Capital Centre. So, if you can picture this, with all our hockey gear on, we galumphed out of the bus and trooped into the McDonald's.

It so happened that this particular McDonald's was located right in the middle of an all-Negro neighborhood and every one of the employees in the hamburger joint was black.

Here we have 24 white guys — not counting Grant — wearing shoulder and shin guards, covered by the Oilers uniform, standing at the counter, dripping with perspiration and smelling from liniment. Semenk instantly sized up the situation, looked at the black help behind the counter and slowly turned to our goalie. "Grant," he said, "YOU better order for us!"

Before Grant could utter a word, the girl behind the counter said with a real down-home Southern accent, "You guys are *real* strange."

Semenk stepped forward and, with feigned hurt, replied, "And what's so strange about us?"

"The way you dress," she explained. "And the way you talk."

Semenk wasn't going to let a good routine go that easily so he turned to Wayne, whom he liked to call "Weas," and went on, "Wayne, you get up here and talk a little 'Weas' to this girl. Maybe she'll understand that."

By this time Slats was rolling on the floor with laughter and Semenk was urging me to talk French to her to really confuse things. The scene was fabulous, right out of "Candid Camera." Unfortuantely, we didn't have video equipment to film the looks on their faces.

Being a part-time journalist, I became more and more interested in the human element, be it in a McDonald's when we were fooling around, or sitting in a posh restarant dining with Gretz.

As the years passed and Wayne grew more and more as an internationally known personality, it became less and less possible for him to enjoy a meal in peace. When we'd go out, people would grab him to the point that he became genuinely concerned for his own welfare. Soon, it was almost like the Beatles. One day I mentioned to Gretz, "You're like Elvis, the way these girls are screaming and crying over you." All he wanted to do was avoid those situations as much as he could. And since Wayne and I were roommates, I had a first-hand view of the overwhelming attention and the thought crossed my mind once or twice that maybe it would be a good idea to change roommates.

I never did, though, because I soon became as oblivious to the attention as Wayne did. I figured, same as Gretz, that it's going to happen so why make a big deal of it. Once we got behind closed doors, we were safe. Or perhaps I should say Wayne was safe.

It wasn't bad in the hotel room. We had the phone turned off and the door locked and it was as safe as could be. I could have been in any other room and felt the same way.

In restaurants or similar public places, it became a large pain in terms of the pestering public. During the earlier seasons, Wayne would sign autographs at any time but then the crowds and the interruptions became impossible and he had to draw the line. One of his "rules" was simplicity itself: *"When I'm eating, I don't stop to sign autographs!"*

If a fan chose to break the rule, Wayne would reply: "If you let me finish my dinner then I'll be glad to sign the autograph for you and I'll sign as many as you like. But please show me enough respect that I can finish eating."

Poor Wayne. He could never understand why anyone would be so thoughtless as to interrupt his meal and it upset him when people did. "Wayne, Wayne, can I have your autograph?" are words that have made an indelible impression on my inner ears. Not to mention Wayne's response, "That burns me so bad!"

Being such a considerate fellow, Wayne always figured that I might be embarrassed that the fan only asked for his autograph and not mine so he'd always hand me the piece of paper to sign as well. "Wayne," I'd tell him, "you don't need to do that." But that's the way he was, upset that all those people were bypassing Kevin Lowe for Wayne Gretzky.

Wayne and I came to a parting of the ways as Edmonton roommates after we had lost the playoff to Los Angeles. After the summer I decided that I wanted a place of my own in the city. Nothing personal but I felt it was time to move on and Wayne understood. It was like changing a car only I wanted to change places.

I looked all over Edmonton and my one discovery was that I

couldn't discover a place to stay. The apartment business was booming all over town and I simply couldn't find a place downtown.

One afternoon I got a call from Mark Messier. "My dad's found this house," he said. "It's unfinished but we can take it over and finish it ourselves. This way we won't have to pay rent anymore and you and I can own our own place."

It was like when I bought my first car. I said, "Sure, I'll take it." So, we bought the place and moved in, so spontaneously it was ridiculous.

The difference between Mark and Wayne as roommates could be symbolized by their choice of sports on television. In a sense it also defines their personalities — Mark fiery, Wayne so relaxed. Mess loved to watch boxing on the tube and became passionate over the fights. I've never seen a person more excited about a boxing match than Mark.

Wayne, on the other hand, is a dedicated baseball fan and a true student of the game. I used to get a kick out of watching Wayne watch baseball on tv because of his insight into the sport. Not only was he extremely perceptive as an armchair analyst but he also knew what channel the games were on in just about every NHL city.

He could sit in an easy chair, armed with the channel-changer, and know what time they would come on and he would catch ITV Sports at 6:10 P.M., CSN Sports at 6:30 and CBC Sports at 6:45. He'd watch them all and even though he was seeing basically the same clips, it didn't matter. He was totally absorbed in watching sports.

That used to bug me so much because I'd get used to one program and then he'd switch channels — and switch again and again. "Wayne," I'd plead, "would you please leave it on one channel." But he'd be so absorbed in watching the next sports show — preferably baseball or basketball — that he didn't even hear me. Fortunately, Mark wasn't as interested in television. If a boxing match or stock car race came on, Mess would get involved, but otherwise he couldn't care less.

As for me, I liked soap operas in our early rooming-together days. Part of it had to do with our show business orientation. We had previously met performers from "One Life To Live" and through Alan Thicke, we met a lot of soap opera stars in Los Angeles, like Genie Francis who was a big star in "General Hospital." When Wayne met Genie he thought it was the greatest thing in the world. In his eyes she was the Gordie Howe of soaps.

The more performers we met, the more interesting it was to watch soap operas on tv. When we'd play the Rangers in New York, you could be sure that we'd visit the set of one soap or another but eventually this interest in the shows turned into addiction until finally I realized that I had had enough of "tune in tomorrow for another adventure of . . . ." It finally came to me that I had better things to do than watch soap operas. I decided I'd rather do something more constructive and one of those things was writing the column for the *Sun*.

Wayne stuck with them longer than I did. He got to know every plot on every show just the way he knew where every sportscast was. "Wayne," I'd ask, "what's happening on 'General Hospital'?"

Always, he'd have the answer: "Well, so-and-so meets so-and-so who is killing so-and-so who's in love with so-and-so . . . ." His knack for detail had my head spinning, especially with all his other activities. My conclusion was that the soaps were an excellent diversion for someone who was besieged by the world around him. In plain English, it was a good form of relaxation. He got away from himself while getting his head into those soaps.

Some Edmonton fans, meanwhile, may have gotten the impression that the Oilers saga was becoming an NHL soap opera. After all the promise generated by our upset over Montreal, the letdown in 1982 was not only a stunner but a source of soap opera-type ridicule. People were beginning to wonder whether this team that was filled with so much promise was ever going to deliver or whether the close-but-no-cigar scenario would run through the rest of the decade.

Glen Sather was wondering as well — and getting ready to take action if we didn't fulfill our potential pretty soon.

23

One Obstacle Before the Road to the Cup

Like an adolescent growing to maturity, the Edmonton Oilers took an enormous stride forward after our embarrassing loss to the Kings in 1982. We attacked the rest of the NHL with an arsenal that was without equal in the league, with Wayne, Mark, Jari, Glenn and Paul scoring like wild men.

The diversity in scoring was a particular blessing for Wayne because he had become such an obvious target in the earlier years that opposing coaches would torment him with checkers, knowing that if Gretz got blanked there was a darn good chance of stopping the Oilers.

Worst of all were the Boston Bruins and their superpest Steve Kasper. A solid young forward, Kasper built a reputation for himself solely on his ability to shut down Wayne. And how did he do it? By following Gretz everywhere. If Wayne had gotten married that year, Kasper would have shown up as best man at the wedding (or at least have tried to) and his penchant for proximity became a Kasper obsession every time we played the Bruins. The guys on our bench would say that we really should give Kasper an Oilers jersey because the way he tagged along with Wayne, he was like our sixth player out there.

While Kasper was effective in what he did, the Bruins also brought about a positive reaction from our club because they gave the other Oilers some responsibility. We realized that Wayne is a great player who will be subjected to this harassment for the rest of his career. The word was out: "Somebody has to do some work out there if we want to win some games and go on to a Stanley Cup." And in 1982 everything began falling into place and the sometimes cranky machine at last became finely tuned.

This, in turn, gave Wayne what had been taken away from him, his freedom of play. Now that all the other guys were playing so well, the opposition couldn't concentrate on checking just one.

Another area of maturation was the bench. Not only was Slats evolving as a superior coach but he began surrounding himself with aides who were able to relieve him of the burden of both managing and coaching while providing us with their own particular brand of knowledge.

John Muckler was one of those prime additions. A former professional defenseman, later coach both in the minors and the NHL, Muck brought to us an understanding of the game and its individuals. It would not be much of an exaggeration to say that Muck had an answer for everything. Naturally, a lot had to do with his rich background for this was a guy who paid his hockey dues in spades.

He broke in as a 16-year-old defenseman alongside Al Arbour with the team Detroit Hettche and then moved on to Baltimore of the old Eastern Hockey League. He might have lasted a lot longer in Baltimore than he actually did had the Carlin Ice Rink not burned down. Muckler's next stop was Charlotte, North Carolina at a time when Eastern League teams could be found all over the south in places like Nashville (Dixie Flyers) and Greensboro (Generals).

I remember an amusing interview between Muck and Dick Chubey when John recalled those days of traveling up and down the east coast in station wagons. "Then," said Muckler, "our owner invested in a $600 used bus. One day we were going to Philadelphia when I looked out and saw a flat tire. Well, we got that fixed and we're on the road again when a rod went through the motor. The owner bought a new bus. Same thing happened. He put a new motor in and it happened again. We went back to three station wagons."

Muckler said that the Paul Newman film "Slapshot," which examined minor league hockey in a somewhat bizarre way, was not far off the mark. That very same Eastern League was the model for "Slapshot" and the Newman character was patterned after John Brophy. And the team was modelled after the Johnstown Jets, then in the EHL.

"They filmed the movie in Johnstown, Pa.," Muck told Chubey. "We were playing there one time when a fan came after Brophy. The fan had a pipe or something in his hand so Brophy didn't take any chances. He whacked the guy's arm with his stick. The arm just went limp, broken all to hell. There was no lawsuit. Today they'd hang a guy for that. I even saw a woman fan knock a referee cold when she hit him with a broom. He wanted to sue, but they told him it was her first game and talked him out of it."

Muck also had the distinction of playing for and later coaching the Long Island Ducks at a little rink in Commack, Long Island. "Once," he recalled, "we had to call in the riot squad to clear the building."

Having survived those battles, the NHL was a breeze for Muckler and we found his style and smarts very reassuring. "Muck," we'd frequently ask, "what happened on that play?" And John would patiently reply, "Here's what happened . . ." and clear detail would follow.

"Muck, what do I do?"

"Here's what you do."

Sometimes players disagreed with Muckler's assessment but he would have the last word — "Let me show you on the video." This wasn't criticism; it was fact. This man is very cool, very calm. Gretz has said he's the smartest hockey man he's ever played for and I'll second the motion. Wayne has so much confidence in Muck's smarts that when he made a hockey video a couple of years ago, he flew John in for a day and paid him a salary just to get a better idea about the game.

Muckler blended perfectly with Sather. John was the ideal analyst and Slats was the perfect motivator. Muck handled the Xs and Os, preparing the team, getting the engine finely tuned, while Slats put in the gas and ignited the fuel.

Which is not to say that Glen isn't capable of drawing the Xs and Os or that John can't motivate; it's just that one was more capable in each of the fields than the other. Or maybe that's just the way they chose to do it; you handle this end and I'll handle that.

Whatever the case, it worked and my game kept getting steadier and steadier. Ironically, as the club kept revving up the offense, I was honing my defensive skills to sharpness and developed a reputation as a stay-at-home defenseman. In a sense I was going in the opposite direction of the team.

Fogie and I were playing solid defense and Slats also had us killing a lot of penalties, an assignment in which we took enormous pride. We figured that if we could kill every possible penalty it would allow the team to stay even with or ahead of the other guys. Through 1982-83, we were mostly ahead. Nothing says it better about how the campaign evolved than a series of headlines in *The Hockey News* throughout the season:

KURRI RELISHES HIS ROLE WITH OILERS.

ADOLESCENT OILERS ARE NEAR MATURITY.

HUNGRY OILERS FAT WITH JOY AFTER SUCCESSFUL ROAD TRIP.

NO LEASING SMYTHE LEAD FOR EDMONTON.

OILERS MESSIER ARRIVES RIGHT ON TIME.

And then the playoffs:

OILERS WASTE LITTLE TIME DISPOSING OF WINNIPEG.

OILERS EASILY EXTINGUISH CALGARY'S FLAME.

OILERS MAKE IT LOOK EASY AGAINST HAWKS.

Our rapid run through the first three playoff rounds should not have surprised anyone who had examined our regular season record. We finished first with a 47-21-12 mark and scored 424 goals, a big 74 goals more than the runner-up Canadiens. We made a mockery of the Smythe Division race. Second-place Calgary wound up 28 points behind us and scored 103 fewer goals.

One obstacle remained on our road to the Stanley Cup — the New York Islanders, a team which had already established a reputation as one of the class acts in NHL history. You name it, the Isles had it, from goaltending (Bill Smith) to scoring (Mike Bossy, Bryan Trottier, Clark Gillies, Bob Bourne and Bob Nystrom) to defense (Denis Potvin, Ken Morrow, Dave Langevin and Stefan Persson) to Al Arbour's coaching. Those were a few good reasons why New York had won three consecutive Stanley Cups and now eyed four in a row, a feat achieved by only two other teams in hockey history: the Canadiens of Toe Blake (1956-60) and the Canadiens of Scotty Bowman (1975-79).

True, the Islanders had finished the regular season sixth overall with 96 points — 10 behind our club — but we had no illusions about them being any weaker than they had been in 1980, 1981 or 1982. "What's important," said Mark, "is that they've won three Stanley Cups in a row. They know what they must do to prepare for a good playoff."

The series opened in Edmonton and just prior to the first game Slats tried a bit of underdog psychology. He met the press wearing a casual sports shirt, pullover and blue jeans. Chubes suggested that Slats looked like he was holding court on farm market prices behind the haystack, not addressing the media on the matter of the National Hockey League's championship series.

"Yes," drawled Sather, "it'll be the *Big Apple* against the *Poor Little Country Boys*. Think about it; they've got the most fans, they come from the richest area in North America, they're the three-time Stanley Cup champions. I mean some of our guys haven't even played pro hockey as long as they've been winning Stanley Cups."

If Slats was trying to lull the Islanders into a false sense of security, it didn't work. All you had to do was pick up the papers to read the put-downs. "We want to beat them more than anything," said Clark Gillies. "You know why? Because they think they're the greatest thing since the invention of sliced bread."

Or Bob Bourne: "The Oilers are so damn cocky. The thing that really bugs me is that they don't give us any respect. The Flyers respect us. So do the Rangers and the Bruins. Edmonton doesn't respect anyone. There isn't any team we want to beat more. If we win, it will be the sweetest victory we've ever had."

The opening game on March 10, 1983 provided a vivid example of how two factors — excellent goaltending and patient disciplined checking — can save a vastly overwhelmed team from defeat. On that night we came at the Islanders in offensive ways. Not one line or two lines but everyone and Bill Smith was out of his mind.

With Smith holding fast from the opening minute, the Islanders only needed one break to turn the game in their favor. At 5:36 of the first period pesty Duane Sutter beat Moog and the Isles sat on the lead for the next 53 minutes, or until Ken Morrow found the open net after Slats had pulled Andy in the third period. On this night the irresistible force met the immovable object and the latter emerged the victor. Slats summed it up as well as anyone when he said, "The Islanders didn't fold when the pressure was on."

We pressured them again in Game Two, this time taking a 1-0 lead before the game was nine minutes old. But they were stifling Gretz, Mark was playing with a damaged shoulder and the Islanders, to their credit, would not be daunted. They struck back with three straight goals in the first period, led 5-2 into the third and held us off after Glennie scored at 4:48 of the third. The game ended 6-3 and we headed for Long Island a lot less optimistic than we had been at the start of the series.

There was no denying our firepower and our speed but the Islanders commanded one vital area and it became more and more apparent as the series wore on and they took over. It was experience. "They have eleven regulars between the ages of 28 and 32," pointed out our assistant coach Ted Green. "Of the guys we have playing in the finals, three are 28 (Lee Fogolin, Dave Lumley and Pat Hughes) and one is 32 (Willy Lindstrom). That makes a difference."

We hung tough again in Game Three, the first at Nassau Coliseum. It was 1-1 after two periods but Bob Bourne put them ahead for good at 5:11 of the third. They got three more and left us with a 5-1 loss. In between the third and fourth games, the NHL held an awards luncheon at the Marriott Hotel across from the Coliseum. Although we were down by three, we still were not out. I remember Slats sounding almost defiant when he made a short speech from the dais. He concluded by asking us to stand before the audience and then he toasted us with a glass of wine. Through it all, though, you could sense the feelings of hostility between the two clubs. A very real, very intense rivalry had been kindled.

With their discipline, opportunism and goaltending, the Islanders were a bit too much for us this time around. In Game Four, they scored three goals in less than two minutes, starting with Bryan Trottier's score at 11:02 of the first and our goose was cooked — almost. Jari Kurri got one back early in the second and Mess got another with less than a minute left in the period.

We pressed like the dickens in the third but Smith was giving absolutely nothing away. With more than a minute to go, Slats pulled Andy and it looked for a moment like we might organize something in their end but our old nemesis, Kenny Morrow, broke free with the rubber and sent it into the empty net at 18:51. That was it.

At least we had done something no Edmonton team had done before — we did reach the Stanley Cup finals, but it was no solace in the immediate aftermath of defeat. Once again there was a lesson to be learned from defeat. To some of us, it was provided during the long walk down the corridor between the two clubhouses at Nassau Coliseum. Long afterward, Wayne remembered it well: "We were all dejected and down. We walked by the Islanders' dressing room. They were celebrating and their guys had ice packs on their shoulders, their jaws, their knees. A lot of them would have operations. We realized then what they had done to win. We said to each other, 'Hey, now we know what it takes. You gotta put your face in front of slap shots, take a punch in the face, you gotta sacrifice — that's what winning is.' "

No more lessons were necessary.

24

"We Did It!"

Following our defeat on Long Island, there was some speculation that, once and for all, Slats would give up his coaching portfolio. His other titles included "president" and "general manager" so it would not be an exaggeration to say that he had a lot of work to do just handling the administrative end of our operation. But anyone familiar with the Sather spirit knew instinctively that he would be back behind the bench once more in 1983-84.

"One thing I hate to do is give up," he said as we jetted back to Edmonton from New York. "I don't like to stop when a job is still unfinished. I feel we can win a Stanley Cup. I feel if we hadn't played a team with the experience of the Islanders, we could have won. The Islanders didn't make any mistakes."

Glen was determined not to make any either as he prepared for 1983-84. The nucleus of the club remained intact but on November 5, 1983 Sather made a trade that went virtually unnoticed but would ultimately have a direct bearing on the first championship season. He sent Tom Roulston to Pittsburgh for Penguins center Kevin McClelland.

Anyone who scanned the statistics on McClelland could hardly get excited about the deal. Before being traded to us, Mac had played in 24 games that season and scored only two goals and four assists. The Penguins thought so little of him that they had demoted Mac to their Baltimore Skipjacks farm team before Slats rescued the big guy and had him center our checking line. He performed commendably over the regular schedule but the best from Mac was yet to come.

The best from many others was evident all season. Once again we blew past everyone in the Smythe Division and finished with the best record in the league, 57-18-5, but not far behind was the team that had embarked on what its management called THE DRIVE FOR FIVE.

Impressive as our regular season numbers had been, they still were not enough to muffle the skeptics, especially when we reached the 1984 finals and went up against our nemesis from Long Island. The "Drive For Five" had brought New York through an exceptionally tough three rounds but they *were* the champions and, furthermore, they had whipped us in every game we had played against them that season and, of course, in the previous playoff.

I can't begin to tell you how much aggression had built up in us concerning the Islanders. Sure, we all felt very confident on the eve of the opener at Nassau Coliseum but there was that question mark in the back of our minds. And the press continued to remind us that they had beaten us ten straight.

The leaders on the team — Mark, Wayne, Fogey and myself — knew that we had the ability to beat them and as long as the other guys felt that way, we would. The bottom line was that by this time we really hated the Islanders. We hated them because they got so much publicity and they were "The Almighty Islanders." The feeling had spread throughout the NHL that because they had won four Cups in a row they couldn't lose, that they didn't know how to lose. We wanted to put an end to that.

Bear in mind that our enmity had nothing to do with their personalities. Our dislike had everything to do with the fact that they were in our way. Mostly it was directed at Denis Potvin and Bryan Trottier. As it happened, we directed a lot of attention — plenty of physical play — at those two.

Another object of our disaffection was Bill Smith. His antics had bothered us for years but, here again, there's that dichotomy between disliking the guy as an opponent and your feelings about him as a person off the ice.

I remember seeing Smitty after a hard-fought game in which he had swung his big goalie stick at a few guys. But the off-ice Bill Smith I saw was hardly the hateful guy I had clashed with an hour earlier. He had had a couple of beers in the dressing room, was completely relaxed and as he walked past us, he turned and said, "Hi, fellas, how are you doing?" as if he was our buddy. As he left to meet his wife at the van, he made some comment about the rain and then took off. I said to myself, "This can't be the same guy who was just on the ice."

On the ice Smitty was still a winner but we felt that Grant Fuhr had lifted his game enough to be in Bill's class. We knew they didn't have the scorers we had but they might have had a better defense going into the finals. Of course they were capable of playing a disciplined brand of hockey whereas we were still being criticized for not being able to match them in that department.

"We can beat them," Muckler insisted, "but we all have to play a perfect brand of hockey and abide by our systems. Otherwise, we're not going to beat them."

To me it boiled down to not allowing the Islanders a one- or two-goal lead because they'd sit on it the way they did the previous year. We had to play tight hockey and hope to capitalize on our speed. Doing a checklist of various factors — speed, scoring, goaltending — I felt we had more checks in our column than they did but they still had the major check, which was the discipline.

In order to beat the Islanders system we employed more intense video work than ever. Slats had hired Roger Neilson, the former coach who had become known as "Captain Video" because of his belief that you can't look at too many film clips. The morning of the opening game we studied a number of things. For example, we learned something about Smith that would be helpful later on.

We watched how Smith had trouble handling the puck behind his net. We figured that if we shot the rubber hard enough around the boards we could full-court press into one corner of the ice and keep the puck in. Once we got into their zone, we figured, everything would be all right.

We also went over a list of guys to watch out for. Clark Gillies and Bob Nystrom headed that section because they'd lay you out if they got the opportunity. We wanted to take advantage of Morrow because the intelligence we received was that his knees were hurting. On the video we saw an example of Morrow stumbling as he pivoted so we figured we could take advantage by going down his side. Since he was hurting, we wanted to hit him when we got the opportunity. We wanted to work his side rather than Denis Potvin's.

Muckler handled the videos but all the coaches and some

scouts — Green, Neilson, Lorne Davis, Garnet Bailey — would collaborate and we'd get a finished product. Glen would end the meeting on an inspirational note with a power-boost speech. He said we should "believe in ourselves" and not be intimidated by the Islanders. "You guys are the best team in the NHL," Slats insisted, "if you just use your heads and play the way we're telling you to play. You're going to win and you're going to win easy."

Some coaches could say those very words to a team and nobody would believe them but Slats had an ability to say them so that our guys believed it and believed in themselves. When he spoke I got goose bumps. I wanted to get on the ice right away. We still had ten hours before the game even started but I wanted to get out there and play right away. So did Wayne, who was feeling an enormous amount of pressure going into this series, maybe more than anyone.

A lot of people remembered how we had been beaten in four straight the previous spring and how Gretz had been held in check by the Islanders. They were wondering, "Is Gretzky really great or not?" I think Wayne figured that he might go down as one of the greatest regular season players ever, but not a great all-around player. He put that pressure on himself, but none of the guys ever felt that way. It was the press, constantly harping on the theme: "Let's see how great Gretzky really is."

Our feeling was that if Mark played well, that would give Wayne a little more opportunity, but basically we only wanted to do our own jobs as best we could. It was also no secret that we were beaten in 1983 by superior goaltending so we wanted our man to at least match Smitty this time around.

Slats' choice was Grant although it never mattered to me whether Grant or Andy was playing. I had equal confidence in both of them. Oh, I know a lot of people believed then that Grant made bigger saves but I thought Andy could be more of a spectacular goaltender than Grant. They were both perfectly sound.

When we finally arrived at Nassau Coliseum that night I experienced more nervousness than ever. Throughout the season and the first three play-off rounds we were building up for the Islanders. Now we were there. We were like kids at Christmas. There's not much anticipation in June but come December 1st, you start preparing for it. By December 24th, the adrenalin really gets flowing.

The nervousness manifested itself in many different ways depending on the individual. Fogie was setting next to me at Nassau and for two hours before game time he was going through his ritual rock. Although Fogie is not an overly nervous person he did have this thing in the room as he dressed for the game. He'd rock back and forth on the bench. And the more nervous he got, the more he rocked.

I don't know how anyone could do this for two hours but Fogie did it. He'd stop for a little while and then start rocking again. When it got closer to game time Mark and I started doing the talking. I'm the type who likes to talk all the time. It gets me up and I also feel that I can review what the coaches have told us. On that night I repeated that we were to dump the puck around the boards. "Let's work on their injured defensemen," I said, "Let's really take it to Trottier, Bossy and Potvin. Let's disrupt Bossy, get him off his game. Let's give him the stick whenever we can."

"Let Gillies sleep. Let's not wake him up. Don't be running him." I directed that remark to Dave Lumley because Lummer always liked to take a shot at Gillies for whatever reason. I tried to get everyone upbeat. Pretty soon everyone was fired up but I still liked to overplay the adrenalin factor. I think I would have been a better football player than a hockey player because I play on emotion a lot. Mark is pretty much the same way.

We knew we had to get to Bill Smith. We weren't plotting to run him over but we did discuss the possibility of distracting him and Lummer was summoned for that task. We're talking about an inadvertent stick behind the leg. Or if an Islander defenseman was carrying him to the net, Lummer would just keep going through. Let the defenseman push you into Smith, fall on top of him and take your time getting up. Talk to Smith. If you run over him, skate by again and say, "Beware. I'm coming back!"

Whether it would work or not was a moot point but we certainly had to try something. At last the warning buzzer was telling us it was almost time to get on the ice. This was it, the start of the opening game of the 1984 Stanley Cup finals. We *had* to do it this time.

Once the puck was dropped there was every indication that we had a replica of Game One, 1983 on our hands, although I felt that we were more in control than in the previous play-offs. In 1983 we played on emotion and desire. This time we were still that talented bunch of kids but more in control of ourselves and the game. I felt that even if we fell a goal down we could or would come back.

But as the game unfolded in that first period I became more and more anxious. My anxiety stemmed from the fact that while we were playing good hockey, we weren't scoring any goals. In the earlier series we had scored a pile of goals against Minnesota on the same amount of chances only now we were up against Smitty and he was playing so well.

Then, it happened.

Slats had the checking line on the ice for us and the play moved into the Islanders end. Up until then there had been precious few defensive lapses but one major letdown was about to occur. Fortunately for us, it happened to the Islanders. The puck was in the left corner and Brent Sutter somehow got himself twisted around as Kevin McClelland sprung himself loose with the puck. Since he was off to the left side and not in such a good scoring position, the shot itself didn't at first appear terribly dangerous.

In truth, it was a very deceptive shot, quick and with a perfect trajectory. Mac wasted no time with the release and it skimmed right inside the right post before Smith could move his left skate in front of the gap. The red light flashed behind the New York goal and we were up 1-0. When I saw the puck cross the goal line the last thing I figured was that this would be the only score of the game. I thought that Mac had broken the ice and now things would be wide open. Everyone felt the same way. It would be ridiculous to think the Oilers would get a shutout and only score one goal.

Mac's goal gave us the added boost we needed but we knew that we couldn't open the game up or we'd be in big trouble. Along the bench the guys kept saying, "Keep pounding away, but don't open it up!" We knew that if we sat back on it, it would be all over.

Give the Islanders credit. They were relentless from the time Mac scored until the final buzzer. They were afraid to lose and, like ourselves, were totally committed to the cause. They wanted that fifth Cup and they were willing to do anything to win it.

But Grant Fuhr was in the way.

I won't say that Cocoa played the greatest game of his career that night but he was every bit as good as Bill Smith was in the 1983 opener at Northlands Coliseum. Anyone who knew Grant could tell that he was at the top of his game on this night because he was challenging the Isles, coming far out of his net if necessary, using the angles when necessary and instinct at all times. At 7 P.M. that evening nobody could have convinced me that the game would finish 1-0 but at 11 P.M. that was the final score in what was the biggest victory for the Edmonton Oilers until that time.

Why was it so pivotal? Because up until that time, although we were finishing first in the Smythe Division by a country mile, there were many many critics who doubted us and especially doubted that we could get the Islander "jinx" off our backs. Our position was not unlike that of earlier Islander teams. Thoughout their championship run there were those who doubted their chances and that doubt served as a motivating force as they constantly proved to everyone that they were, in fact, the best. That's what made them great; they never settled for anything less and now, having beaten them in that big game, we began feeling the same way. Once you've tasted victory, nothing else is acceptable but, as we soon discovered, the Islanders were still feeling the same way.

The feeling in our dressing room after the 1-0 classic was interesting, to say the least. To begin with, we all knew that we had a long way to go. Naturally, we were excited but it was *controlled* excitement in the sense that nobody was going berserk over the win. The sobering part was that we played the game of our lives and still could only scratch out a 1-0 win. Furthermore, the Islanders had shut down Gretz again.

We were more contemplative than we should have been under the circumstances, wondering what was in store for us the rest of the way. We played on that theme a little too much and this carried over into Game Two and proved more damaging than helpful.

Not that Slats was at fault. As soon as we trooped into the visitor's dressing room after the win Glen closed the door to reporters for a moment and said, "What did I tell you guys? You proved to yourselves that you could do it."

Then he reached into the propaganda machine. "But let's remember when we're talking to reporters that we're just happy we won a hockey game against the mighty New York

Islanders. *We* know we're going to win the Stanley Cup now, but don't you tell anyone that. You tell them that we're just lucky to win a game and we're just happy to be playing in the same rinks as them."

Looking around the room, I could sense that some of us — especially Mess and myself — were having a tough time controlling our emotions. By contrast, Grant was as calm as ever. To him the 1-0 shutout was "Oh, well, just another game. That's what they pay me for." Even Kevin McClelland, who scored the only goal, downplayed it. Someone mentioned to him, "You're a national hero. Everyone in Canada saw you score that goal. And they're all pulling for the Oilers. That makes you a national hero like Paul Henderson."

Kevin brushed off the compliment. "I don't care who scored the goal," he said. "I'm just gald we won and glad to be here in the NHL and part of this team."

Many thoughts were coursing through my head that night as I rested my head on the pillow and ran the game through my mind. My overall reaction was that we not only controlled the Islanders but we had them running around in their own end. We had never seen that before.

We won the game on goaltending and one goal and that goal came on aggressive play. The Islanders were lacking that aggressiveness and they weren't very emotional. What they did have was a couple kids who showed youthful spark. Little Pat LaFontaine, who had just come from the U.S. Olympic team, was much faster and better than I had anticipated. Their other new Olympian, Patrick Flatley, had already earned something of a reputation for strength, having collided with big Barry Beck of the Rangers in an earlier series. Beck went out with a severe shoulder injury which eventually ended his career. I had seen Flatley bowl over Beck and I thought, "Holy jumpin' jiminy! Barry Beck is thirty pounds heavier than I am. I'm going to have to watch this Flatley fellow."

But when it came down to it, he wasn't as big and strong in person as I thought he would be. We had a few good collisions. He had his share of them and I had my share but, basically, none of the Islanders hit our defensemen an awful lot. I recall myself giving more than taking. But when Game Two came around we did the taking and the Islanders were giving — grief.

Why, after we had played so well in the opener, we got

blown out so quickly in Game Two was a matter of serious discussion by our high command and, as always, there were simple and complicated explanations for such a defeat.

Losing 6-1 after such an excellent opener was a bit much. The Islanders stormed at us from the very beginning and had us back on our heels before we could muster any effective counterstrokes. They outplayed us. Period.

And the press killed us. I don't mean the Edmonton media, I mean *everyone*. In the 6-1 defeat they conjured up visions of Oilers debacles past and seemed to wrap up the series for the Islanders in one neat little journalistic package.

The point they seemed to miss was that every team, no matter how good, will experience off-nights — even in the Stanley Cup finals. That's the beauty — or tragedy — of sport, the unknown factor. We experienced our "down time" in that game and Slats was wise enough not to allow it to cloud his thinking.

When we got back to Edmonton, he sat down with us and made a couple of telling points. "Hey, you guys, you only wanted to win one game there anyway. And we never said we'd win two."

He knew we had another thing going for us that was not a factor in playoffs past. The NHL altered the format for the finals so that the next *three* games would be played at Northlands instead of the usual two. Then, if more games were necessary, they would revert to Long Island.

Glen replayed a tape of Game One and showed highlights of things we had done well in Game Two. He briefly showed us some technical errors we had committed in the second game — he never shows the mental lapse stuff because that's just something that happens.

On the flight home, I had plenty of time to review my own game. My standard begins with whether or not we win the game. If we lost, then my game is not relevant. My standard starts with goals-against. The primary objective is to have no goals scored when I'm on the ice. Then, I move to the next rating section, scoring opportunities for the other team.

I feel good if the defensive part is clean. Then, I get to the offensive aspect of my game, maybe setting up a goal, a couple of good shots on net or a couple of quick outlet passes that might result in a two-on-one or a good pass up the middle to whomever. Finally, there's the aggressive part of it, throwing in a few blocked shots and a couple of good hits that might spark the team. I'm especially thinking of a hit that will give the club a mental lift, like one right in front of the bench or a good open-ice hit or finishing someone off in the corner. If I can do all that in a game then I've had a "10."

In Game One, our 1-0 win, I gave myself an "8." My offense was not what it could have been. That was such a defensive game and we were killing so many penalties that I spent a lot of energy on the defensive aspect. I didn't think much offense. My "10" game was on the way — at Northlands.

Coming home was a tonic to us despite the fact that the media had jumped off our bandwagon. We didn't start all that well and for the second straight game the Islanders took the lead, I realized then that we all had to get more involved offensively if we were going to win. Me included. Glen suggested that the defensemen should follow up the play a little more. Once the forwards got into the New York end the defensemen had to be involved to help sustain the pressure. The thought clicked in my head the way you put a cassette into a deck.

The play started with Glennie Anderson moving toward the Islanders zone. As their defense concentrated on him, I instantly got the message: "Move up!" I broke down the left side and Glennie saw me and sent the pass that put me one-on-one with Smith.

Now I'm thinking, "What did they tell me about Smith?" And the message came back to me: "Make a move on him, don't just shoot!" Denis Potvin was the defenseman on the play and he gave me enough room to cut in. He figured for sure that I was going to shoot.

He must have figured me for a defensive defenseman who would just make a dumb play. With that in mind, I came down, faked the shot, then brought the puck to my backhand and slid it into the open net as Smith went sprawling.

The feeling was sheer ecstacy. My first recollection was being so tired, yet delirious. Mark, Glennie and Fogie surrounded me with Fogie yelling to the crowd. I was trying to scream but I was too tired even to get into it. The team feeling was "Now we're back to even; let's get this game our way."

Still, the Islanders were giving nothing away and once again they went ahead of us. But Mark scored another titanic goal for us. It was the kind that has not been forgotten by many Oilers or followers of the team because of its timing and execution.

New York had had a good grip on the game after moving ahead and Smith was formidable in goal. But Mark showed that he had a lot of Bobby Hull — speed, strength — in him as he motored down the left wing, one-on-one with defenseman Gord Dineen. Next he made a play that provides a perfect example of why he'd be (after Wayne) the most sought-after player in the NHL if you were starting a new franchise. With a couple of shifts, Mark breezed around Dineen and in virtually the same motion blasted the puck past Smith.

From that point on we never looked back. I remember noticing Mark right after his goal. He simply couldn't contain the jubilation, the excitement. None of us could and certainly not the fans. Everyone could sense that we were beginning to take over and now we wanted to stick it to them. The Islanders' tight defensive shell was slowly but surely being peeled away — and they were getting tired. Meanwhile, we were running on all 18 cylinders. Now it was only a matter of time before we opened the floodgates and it all started — just as we had said earlier it should by zeroing in on key players — with a check on Potvin in the corner of the rink.

The Islanders captain seemed to be wilting and we just pounded at him with our artillery. The softening-up process had worked. Denis was stripped of the puck and — BANG! BANG! BANG! — just like that, the puck was behind Smith. In no time at all — or so it seemed — we had wiped them out 7-2. (How quickly our 6-1 defeat was forgotten.) For the first time we had *completely* outplayed them and despite the momentary fatigue after scoring my goal, I played on an endless source of energy.

Once, Bossy led a three-on-me rush with Trottier and Anders Kallur moving along with him. I stopped them cold at the blue line, forcing Bossy to make a bad pass. Andy Moog, who was sitting there on the bench, shouted, "They didn't even get a shot on net. They didn't even come close to getting one." By now the adrenalin was overflowing, not just for me but for every Oiler. And it just spilled over to the next win, 7-2 again. Now Gretz had found his groove, even scoring on a breakaway, which had always been his nemesis. There was no stopping us now. One more and we had them — and the Cup.

Our plan was "Let's do what the Oilers do best" and that was to take it to them right off the opening face-off. There were a number of reasons not to lose including our desire to wrap up the series in Edmonton. Add to that the ego factor on both a team-wide and personal level.

For the latter we can thank the media which always like to make comparisons. How many times did we hear the Trottier-vs-Gretzky question raised? Or who's better, Bossy or Kurri? Not to mention the ongoing battle with Bill Smith. Of the three, the Oilers-Smitty War was the most intense.

It had its roots years earlier when the Islanders were riding high and Smith took a swipe at Gretz and knocked him down behind the New York net. (Even some of the Islander writers took Wayne's side in that one.) We regarded Smitty's move as reckless; he could have hit him in the face. From that point on we developed a genuine dislike for Smith so it was kind of neat now to be rubbing it in.

The Gretzky-Trottier comparison is interesting because of their diverse styles. There were times earlier on when reporters might have given the nod to Trottier, which started to perturb Wayne but Gretz has never been jealous of anyone.

There may have been a time when Trottier was better defensively and on face-offs but that was long, long ago. Wayne is the greatest player in the game, so how can you compare the two? Trottier is going to go down as a great player but it's not conceivable that he was better than Wayne. Of course, until we won our first Cup, the dissenters were still putting down Gretz. I remember Wayne saying he's never going to have the question mark removed from himself until the Oilers win a Cup. Bobby Orr played on Cup-winners and so did Gordie Howe and Jean Beliveau. The greats who were truly the greats were able to lead their teams to Stanley Cups, so Wayne really wanted to do that.

Finally, we have Bossy vs Kurri. In my estimation a lot of people haven't given Bossy his just due. When he came to the Islanders, they said he couldn't play defense. He learned, but never got credit for his defensive capabilities. Jari is a super hockey player, a good two-way player, probably better than Bossy, but Jari can never escape the stigma that he's made it because he's been Wayne's right winger.

On the other hand, didn't Trottier set up Bossy a lot? That's the reality of it all. You just can't do things alone. Bossy-Kurri? Two great hockey players. You couldn't go wrong with either. Except in the spring of 1984 Bossy was being stifled and we were heading toward hockey's Holy Grail.

For a time it appeared that the series would end the way it had begun — with a Grant Fuhr shutout. It was 4-0 for us and I was bubbling with joy. My defensive game was never better over the entire playoff and we were cruising toward the finish line when in an incredibly short time LaFontaine scored two goals for them, both against me and Fogie. I remember coming to the bench and being really upset and Muckler telling me to just calm down because we've got the game in hand. I said to myself, "Geez, I can't believe this just happened!" We had been in complete control. Now it's 4-2 and they're back in the game.

Up and down the bench it was like, "All right everybody; it's not over. The Islanders are back into it." This was a very strange feeling, particularly for myself. I hadn't been on for any goals and then, all of a sudden, two goals in one shift. Then, John Tonelli had a breakaway for them. Grant stopped him but it was like the old Islanders were coming back to haunt us. The old question was coming into our heads: the Islanders have always bounced back. Are they doing it now?

Just as quickly we tightened up and they were stopped cold and now the clock was winding down and so many things were going through my head that I couldn't think straight. But some thoughts crystallized before the final green light flashed. "I set out all my life to win this and, lo and behold, we *are* going to win it!" I wondered what my teammates were thinking.

Another thought came to mind: "I'm so proud of all the guys. Everyone in Canada is seeing us do this. Everyone who watches hockey in North America is seeing us do this." My heart was pumping so hard that my mind sort of slowed up and slowed up.

Now the clock was down to the final seconds "five. . .four. . .three. . .two. . .one." WE DID IT!

I was on the ice when it happened. Andy Moog came over and I jumped on him. Then, things began to blur. I don't remember what happened to my gloves or my stick or anything like that. Mark threw his stick and his gloves in the crowd. Being the only French-speaking player on the team, I was hustled right into the French studio for an interview so by the time I got into the dressing room the place was filled and I could barely get in. Unfortunately, I couldn't bask in that 30-second or longer period after the game and just be with the guys. I'm sorry I missed that. Frankly, I was disappointed to see all those people in the room so soon.

Fresh in my mind were the faces on the defeated Islanders. A year earlier we had been the vanquished shaking the hands of the victors. This time it was reversed. I'll never forget the emotion in the faces of the Sutter brothers, Duane and Brent. Both were crying. Potvin was like a soldier, like a general of an army in battle, admitting defeat in his intelligent, straightforward way. I could see that in his face. Clark Gillies' face told me, "It's been a great career for me, and we've had our day, but it seems all to be ending."

I felt genuinely sorry for them because I knew exactly what it was like to be in their shoes. Even though Smitty was not on the line — he never shakes hand with the enemy, win or lose — I didn't even feel any special rancor toward him although I was pleased that we had put it to members of the eastern media who had questioned our abilities.

By now the champagne bottles were popping left and right and I fulfilled my lifetime dream, slurping the bubbly from Lord Stanley's mug. And with that, I learned another lesson. Don't drink too much champagne so soon after a game!

I had sweated a lot during the game and had not had any other liquids in me when the bottles were being passed around. So, I had a big swig here and another swig there — and no water going into my system. I got drunk a lot quicker than I would have under normal circumstances. From that point on, I can't remember much of what happened, except for the family involvement.

My sister Nancy phoned me in the Oilers dressing room telling me how excited and pleased everyone was and shortly thereafter my mom made her way into the dressing room and we hugged. This was something very special because for me the win was for my whole family but particularly for my mom. Because dad had died at such an early age mom raised me by herself. She had come to all my junior games and was a huge supporter of mine. So a large part of it was for her but parts of the joy were also for the others. Let's put it this way; there's enough excitement in winning the Stanley Cup for the entire family. Everyone reaps the benefits and everyone can enjoy it.

To an outsider watching the festivities it would be hard to imagine that a touch of sadness could intrude on the Cup celebration, but in my estimation an element of the camaraderie is lost with the instant surge of the tv cameras, the microphones and the pen-and-pencil guys. Ideally, what we should have done was shut the doors to the room to anyone but the players, coach, and the scouts. We all should sit back for a moment and contemplate the wonderful thing we had just accomplished. You really need to do that from a team viewpoint.

It would have been nice to have been able to spend a few minutes with Slats but there never really was time. We had a hug, a handshake and "Hey, we did it, all right!" Then it was off to the next person and me running around like a chicken with my head cut off.

From that point on until about three days later, I can't tell a hell of a lot of what happened. I know I had a lot of fun — but don't ask me what I did!

I do know this much: WE DID IT!!

(Lowe Collection.)

(Lowe Collection.)

Me, at age 4, wearing the tools of ignorance before I got smart.

People who've said I look like an altar boy were right. That's Mom on the left and Dad on the right.

(Lowe Collection.)

I was the only English-speaking kid on this team. That's me with the Captain's 'C' at a pee wee tournament.

(Lowe Collection.)

It was always nice to have your name on the front of your jersey. Notice my brand new CCM gloves.

225

(Lowe Collection.)

It's always gratifying to work with the disabled. This is a 1979 Christmas party.

(Lowe Collection. Photo by Jackie Northam, *Edmonton Journal*.)

That's Kid Kevin on the bench with a young Slats mulling over some magical move.

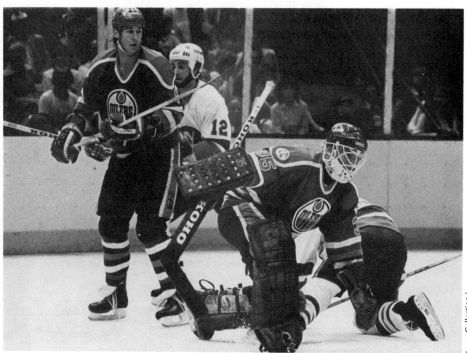

(Lowe Collection.)

That's me in my first pro season, with goalie Andy Moog and Duane Sutter.

(Lowe Collection.)

Enjoying our first post-season vacation with Gretz and Dougie Hicks.

(Photo by Bruce Bennett.)

Islanders' celebration, Oilers dejection in 1983.

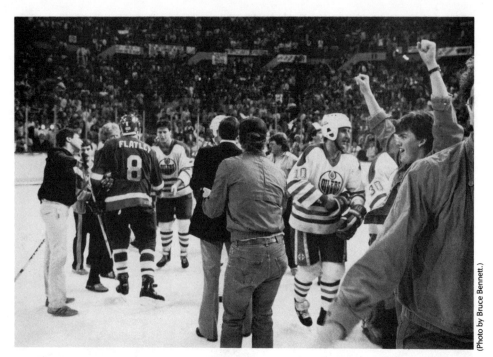

The tables are turned in '84. It's our turn to celebrate.

(Photo by Bruce Bennett.)

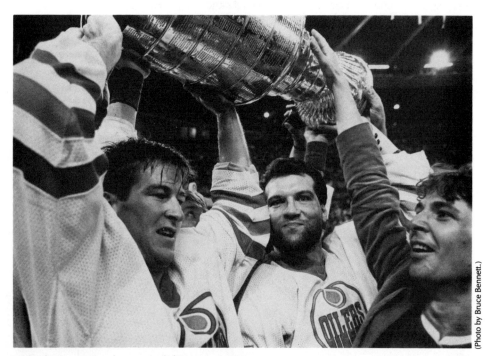

Me and Dave Semenko — we did it again in '85.

(Photo by Bruce Bennett.)

(Photo by Bruce Bennett.)

Slats: Our leader.

(Photo by Bruce Bennett.)

Just doing my job!

Messier in 1988.

(Photo by Bruce Bennett.)

Celebrating our victory in '88.

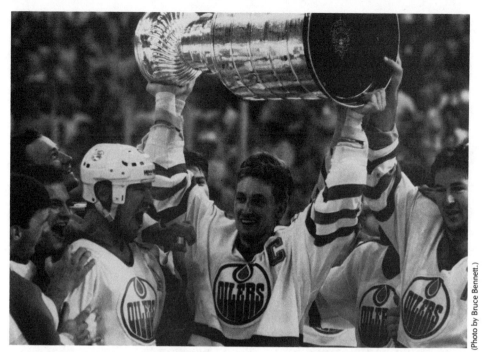

(Photo by Bruce Bennett.)

Mess, Gretz and I hoist the Cup in '88.

(Canapress Photo Service.)

Pocklington and Gretzky at the press conference announcing the Great One's trade to L.A.

25

You Can't Take That Away From Us

The expression "The grass is always greener on the other side" certainly had meaning for us. When we won that first Stanley Cup in 1984, the Edmonton Oilers had stepped to the "other side" — the champion's side — and liked it. But as the Islanders had learned, once you have a mortgage on the Cup, you still have to pay your dues. Even more so.

No longer were we pretenders to the throne, we were rulers of the NHL realm and what that meant was that 20 other teams would be taking dead aim on ice every game of the 1984-85 season. Now we were expected to win and if there was a letup, the media would jump on us faster than they ever had before. Everyone wanted to upstage the champs. When we went to Boston, the Bruin writers would say the home club played its best game of the season. On Long Island, the Islanders were at their feistiest against us. And so it went. All of which proved that it was going to be darned hard to remain champions.

If I needed any reaffirmation I got it from Billy Carroll, a defensive center we had acquired from the Islanders. He said that during their four-straight Cup run on the Island, the club *had* to come to play every night otherwise it would be in big trouble. We now knew that if we wanted to remain top banana we had to be fired up for all 80 games.

Carroll told me that we might have even had it a bit harder than the Islanders because of our glamorous image. He said the Islanders never were quite the media heroes that we had become. That, I'm sure, was a function of having Gretz on our side and the fact that, as a team, we were considerably younger than the Islanders. The evidence of our youthfulness was everywhere but nowhere more than in the dressing room where the music blared as if it was coming from a disco.

The orchestrators, essentially, were Messier, Lowe and Coffey although many others — Ken Linseman in particular for a short but significant period — produced tapes. A song called "Jeopardy" was a big hit for some time.

As the older players left the club in the first two years of the franchise, the young guys played more of it and the decibel count climbed. The few who were bothered by it would just go off to another room or had the ability to shut it out of their minds. Davey Hunter, a big country and western fan, didn't like our choice of rock but he saw how much it fired up the other guys so that was good enough for him. Eventually, even he got into it.

Certain guys — Glennie, Mess, Wayne, myself, Paul and Semenk — would get outwardly excited by the music. We'd put on "Jeopardy", which has a real nice beat to it, and all of a sudden everyone would be clapping to the music. It was spontaneous. Guys would be standing around, taping their sticks, adjusting their equipment, doing routine stuff when the music would get going and everyone would start to clap.

Even the guys who one wouldn't figure would get so involved because they were the older guard actually were moved by the music. Fogie, for one, liked rock 'n roll although he doesn't look like a rock 'n roller. It really got him fired up and Randy, the doctor, who some thought was out of place on the team, was the same way.

The Gregg case is interesting because of his intelligence and background. He played on the Canadian Olympic Team and played hockey in Japan before he came to us and people would say, "What the heck is a full-fledged doctor doing with these hockey players?" But I have the answer to that.

Intelligence is not only education and upbringing; it's an ability to deal with all aspects of life. Intelligent people are capable of rubbing elbows with dignitaries and policitians as well as with guys who run the factories. Randy is that type of guy. Outwardly he might have looked out of place and he might have been out of place but to us he wasn't out of place. He was just another guy playing the game.

Randy's closest friend on the team was another defenseman, Donnie Jackson, who had an image of being a big tough guy and hardly the type one would expect the doctor to hang out with. But this odd couple didn't seem that odd once you realized that Donnie is a very intelligent guy, very capable in business and very witty and that Randy could see those qualities in him.

Another one of Randy's friends was our Czech import, Jaroslav Pouzar. For a while, Pouzar needed all the friends he could get because he didn't initially make a big hit with the team. He had come to us with a big advance billing, a member of the Czech national team who would be the answer to Wayne's perennial left wing problems. (Jari was no problem on the right side.) On the surface, Pouzar looked good. He dazzled in pre-training camp, skating well; he was big and strong. The word was, "This guy is fantastic." But then the season started and he disappointed everyone. It reached a point where he wasn't even dressing for games. Poor guy, he could hardly speak English and no one understood him. (We eventually learned that he had a lot of frustration building up in him and a lot of the guys disliked him for it.) Some thought: "We've got another European; it's just a matter of time and he's gone."

Just when his situation appeared hopeless, Pouzar turned it all around. He threw a party, invited some of the guys over — I don't think many wanted to go but they obliged on the grounds that he *was* a teammate — and the gap was closed in a matter of hours. We got into the Czech tradition of knocking back a few vodka shooters. That did it. There's nothing like sharing a little drink with a potential friend to find out what he's all about as a person.

After a few drinks, we saw a different side of Jaroslav, a lighter side, and we liked it. From that point on we found a new appreciation of our Czech and even when we wasn't playing, he was now a part of the team. In time, he would move the Oilers to new heights in the most unlikely way imaginable from a Czech with broken English — with a speech. But I'll get to that shortly.

Now that we were defending Cup champions, a new sense of confidence was being shared by the team. Although Winnipeg enjoyed a superb season (43-27-10), we easily finished first once more (49-20-11) and dominated the scoring. Our offense was so strong that Paul Coffey finished in fifth place among scorers, ahead of aces like Mike Bossy, Denis Savard and Mario Lemieux. On top, naturally, was Gretz with 73 goals, 135 assists and 208 points. Not bad for a young man who shuddered every time he got into an airplane. And when you played for the Edmonton Oilers, brother, you did a *lot* of flying.

By this time, Wayne's aversion to flying had been mentioned around the league but I doubt that many outsiders realized the depth of his anguish. It was more than just "trouble with flying," it was paranoia. Wayne realized this and even saw a few psychiatrists about it. Whenever possible, Gretz avoided flying and, occasionally, the results were a bit strange.

Once, he was in New York for a post-season awards presentation and then was to return to Canada for a golf tournament that I run. First, he headed for LaGuardia Airport to catch a plane. As he was getting on the plane he decided, "I just don't want to fly." So he rented a limousine and drove all the way to Lachute, Quebec for the tournament. Ten hours in a limo just to avoid a one-hour plane trip.

Another time we were in New Jersey for a game with the Devils and then were to fly down to Washington to meet the Capitals. We were staying at the Hotel Glenpointe in Teaneck, New Jersey and when we got up the next morning a bad snowstorm was brewing.

Slats phoned in to say that our flight to Washington was cancelled but we still had to get down there. But how? We were standing in the lobby trying to figure out a solution when someone said, "How about taking the train?"

All of a sudden Wayne's ears popped up. "Yeah, yeah, yeah," he said, enthusiastic in a way I had never seen before. "Let's take the train."

We finally drove all the way into Manhattan and caught a train out of Penn Station. This tickled Wayne no end. He had a smile on his face from ear to ear whereas the other guys were kind of bummed out. Their half-hour flight to Washington had turned into a three-hour train ride.

It was fun for Wayne but a brief respite. After Washington, we were back on the plane again and he faced his usual torment with take-offs and landings. (If there's no turbulence he's okay once the plane reaches cruising speed.) On take-offs, he sits in his chair and holds the seat in front of him. He looks out the window and has an expression that asks, "Am I going to be all right?"

On trips within Canada, Gretz rides with the pilots. (FAA regulations forbid this in the States.) They reassure him and he has the added advantage of seeing what's happening. He'll go up to the cockpit right after the take-off and by now all the Air Canada pilots know him. Some days he's so tired that he just passes out and falls asleep but if there's any sign of turbulence, he'll wake up and break into a cold sweat. Then, he'll go right up front and sit with the pilot.

As for the Oilers on ice, we seemed to be operating on automatic pilot right into the playoffs. Los Angeles, which had been a problem in the past, was up for the best-of-five series and the Kings made it interesting, to say the least. They forced us into overtime in the first game at Northlands before Fogie got the winner at 3:01 of sudden death. We beat them 4-2 in the second and then finished the series in L.A. Once again we went to overtime before Glennie put it in only 46 seconds into sudden death. Next it was the Winnipeg Jets. Down they went in four straight, the closest being the third game which we won 5-4. Gretz got the winner. By the time that series was over Grant had a seven-game winning streak.

So far we had been challenged but not severely tested. The next round — the Campbell Conference championship — put us up against Denis Savard and the Black Hawks. Northlands was the site of the first two games and they were laughable, 11-2 and 7-3 for our side. The series resumed at Chicago Stadium which did not intimidate us in the least. We always went into Chicago and dominated the Hawks. If you talked to Doug Wilson or Bob Murray anytime the Oilers were coming to town, they'd moan, "Oh, no, these guys are back." They simply couldn't put it together against us.

Their goaltender, Murray Bannerman, fronted a pretty good team and had been voted top goaltender in the conference but he couldn't stop a beach ball against us — until we got a bit overconfident. We went into Chicago thinking we'd walk all over them as we had in previous playoffs but they got a couple of goals and started believing in themselves.

They knew they couldn't skate with us so they realized that the only way to stop us was to bang bodies and it became very physical from Game Three on. Al Secord and Curt Fraser, a couple of tough forwards, played well for them and by the time Game Three was over, and they had a 5-2 win, they weren't frightened of us anymore.

Chicago Stadium, which can get pretty crazy, really was wild for the next game and the Black Hawks helped matters by giving us their best shots. The final score was 8-6 and some people in the land of journalism began getting the notion that we could be taken.

I could understand why it would make a good story but the fact of the matter was that we were not worried. As much as they were hitting us, we were hitting them just as hard, if not harder, and their defense was wearing down faster than ours. But just to be extra cautious, we went to our ace-in-the-hole upon our return to Edmonton. That was the Grand Hotel.

This place had a bar (not the classiest joint in town) which had come to our attention through the Edmonton Eskimos who had a tradition which was rooted several years back in the club's history. They called it "Grand Night." After a Monday practice, all the veterans and rookies would get together at this tavern, drink beer, play games and pick on the rookies. It was just the boys night out. And since my brother, Kenn, is trainer for the Eskimos, he began telling me stories about Grand Night. So one evening I checked it out and realized that the night was a great move and that the Oilers should do likewise.

So one night the Oilers came to visit and found this big pool hall and tavern where we could sit in the corner and not be bothered. The fact that no one in town knew about the place except the local regulars appealed to the boys and they agreed that it would be the ideal spot for team meetings and team beers. (At just about any other place we'd surely be disturbed but here we could play a little pool, relax and not worry about being bothered.)

Charlie Huddy's theory is that we went to the Grand Hotel "because we belong here" and after the two losses in Chicago, we began to think (humorously, of course) that he was right. So, we convened at the Grand Hotel before Game Five, relaxed, got good and mad at ourselves and then went out and clobbered Chicago, 10-5.

We were still winning the physical battles but the Hawks tried desperately to knock around Paul Coffey. They did just about everything illegal to Paul until he finally blew a fuse and wound up in the penalty box more often than he should have.

Paul could fight, but we didn't need him in the box.

The Hawks didn't pick their spots. Behn Wilson, one of their bigger defensemen, laid some heavy punches on Semenk in one fight and it hurt some of our guys to see him lose the fight although he, himself, didn't get hurt. The thing that bothered me and Mess was that we both knew how good a fighter Semenk was but he really didn't defend himself against Wilson and was just hanging on. Part of that was that he had been hurting a bit with a bad shoulder.

Whatever morale booster the Wilson fight meant for Chicago, it certainly didn't affect the series. We returned to Chicago Stadium and destroyed them 8-2 and marched into the Stanley Cup finals for the third year in a row, but for the first time against a team other than the Islanders. This was interesting.

Facing us in 1985 was a Philadelphia club that had fooled a lot of the "experts" during the regular reason. With a relatively unknown rookie coach named Mike Keenan behind the bench, the Flyers started the schedule with a bunch of kids who were not very well known around the league. Peter Zezel, Rick Tocchet and Lindsay Carson were not exactly household words in the NHL, nor was Ilkka Sinasalo. But we got to know them pretty fast.

The series opened at The Spectrum and we knew it wasn't going to be easy because Philly had beaten us throughout the season. For some reason, we were never totally prepared to play them and there'd be ten or twelve guys on our club who really wanted to beat them because they had something to prove, and there were eight or ten others who said it was just another game, let's not get excited about it. The guys felt that when the time comes — that is playoff time — we'll really go out of our way.

I knew that in the games where they had beaten us, bad penalties hurt us in just about all the games, so it was a matter of us being a little more disciplined and intense.

So, what happened? First of all Glennie Anderson missed the plane and right away the buzzing started. When we got to Philly, the bus driver who was supposed to take us to the practice rink managed to get lost. When he finally got his directions straight, the bus wouldn't start so we all got out of the bus and sat down on some grass to relax. "Hey, you guys, GET OFF MY LAWN!" was the next bit advice we got from the unhappy homeowner whose grass we were creasing. Turns out the chap was kidding and even invited some of the guys into his house to watch tv. Meanwhile, Mess and I pulled out our baseball gloves and tossed a ball around — all this when we should have been practicing for the Cup finals!

Finally, a truck filled with our equipment arrived and took us to the practice rink. After practice the bus was late again. We got back to the hotel so late that even Glennie Anderson was there. What else could possibly go wrong now? I'll tell you: the hotel's rooms only had one bed in them so we had to find another hotel. But our bus was gone so we had to round up cabs. The Flyers couldn't have done a better job of sabotaging us if they had planned all this nonsense.

The next night, May 21, we launched our defense of the Stanley Cup — and fell on our faces. We skated as if we were in quicksand; I've never seen guys skate slower than we did that night and Philly knocked us off, 4-1. Everyone said the same thing after the game: "I can't believe how tired I am. I just couldn't get going."

How bad were we? Usually, on the day following a game in the finals, Slats and Muck would go over the previous night's game films. You should have seen the look on Glen's face when he walked into the meeting room. "It was so bad last night," he chortled, "I don't even want to show you guys the films."

Brilliant psychology.

If I do say so myself we were brilliant in the return engagement at The Spectrum. Disciplined, fast, creative. You name it, we executed it and we had to because Pelle Lindbergh was sensational in the nets for Philly. We won because we played it hard and smart. "Tonight," said Fogie, "we were ready. We made damn few mistakes in our end and that's the name of the game."

As an added surprise to shake things up, Slats tossed a complete unknown — at least unknown to the Flyers — into the lineup when he dressed Esa Tikkanen and put him alongside Gretzky. Tik was goofier than anything but he was fresh and played extremely well.

Philly hung tough. We held them to 2-1 right down to the wire and finally choked them off with an open-netter. Apart from our solid effort in the comeback, the talk of the series was Tikkanen's appearance and the fact that Slats played him so much. That's what made the papers. What *didn't* get into print was an episode involving our Finish rookie and a break with team tradition. WE SHAVED HIM!

Tik, it should be noted right up front, was not your average introverted European rookie, as Jari had been when he arrived in Edmonton. Tik's appearance, attitude and demeanor made him seem more like a North American than most North Americans. To some of us, he was almost too outgoing, a happy-go-lucky kid who appeared just a bit cocky to the civilized world. He needed to be put in his place so The Shave was ordered.

This in and of itself was a surprise but the biggest upset of all came about when someone asked for the shears and who should walk in carrying the scissors but the owner of the Edmonton Oilers, Peter Pocklington himself! Which goes to show what a transition Peter had made. Six years earlier he wouldn't have even known our rookies and now he knew all about this one, including the fact that Tik needed to be taken care of — or else.

Returning to Edmonton, we felt a lot better about ourselves. The Northlands ice, smoother and faster, is more suited to our game and I figured that if our defense could keep the Flyers in check, it would only be a matter of time before Gretz got going. What surprised me in Game Three was just how far and how fast he would go in so short a period of time. In the first period he had seven shots on goal and scored three, two within 15 seconds before the game was 100 seconds old. And you wonder why they call him The Great One.

We beat them 4-3 but the Flyers showed us that they were a club that wouldn't toss in the towel. For the first two-thirds of the game, we followed the coach's game plan but in the final period, we became undisciplined and the Flyers almost took it away from us. Fortunately, we had built up a 4-1 lead and the bottom line, after all was said and done, is that we came out on top. We did what we had to do, a hallmark of the Oiler champions.

In our favor was Keenan's strategy of going with four defensemen. As the series wore on they were getting tired and they simply couldn't cope with our speed. Whenever possible we worked on Brad Marsh, Doug Crossman and Ed Hospodar, who had replaced the injured Brad McCrimmon.

Hospodar got himself on our blacklist when he clocked our Mark Napier but I give the guy credit; he went after our toughest guy, Kevin McClelland, as well, which showed that he would take a stand. Hospodar hit McClelland one of the hardest hits I've ever seen but Mac got up and skated away.

Mac's recovery was symbolic of our hockey club, especially in Game Four. The Flyers hammered us in the first period, rushed into a 3-1 lead and didn't look at all like a tired team. Philly discovered that it's a three-period game and by the 21 second mark of the second period Glennie had tied the score at 3-3. Next it was Grant's turn to grab the spotlight after Tocchet popped out of the penalty box into a breakaway. Grant stopped him cold and then Gretz put us ahead to stay with the next two goals.

If nothing else, the win demonstrated that when necessary we could work as hard as any club. Our character showed through and so did our conditioning. The Flyers were deteriorating fast. Marsh was getting weary, we limited Mark Howe's offense and the Flyers were not handing out any more thunderous bodychecks.

With the series virtually sewn up, the media became hard-pressed for angles. One of the better tidbits involved the Flyers demand — brand new in that playoff — for water bottles on top of the nets so that goalies could get a drink during the respites. Slats thought it was a ridiculous idea and suggested that if the Philly people wanted that why not have a picnic lunch as well — some fried chicken, or cheese and crackers.

Obviously, Glen and Mike Keenan were not hitting it off and the personality clash continued through Game Five. We ran away from them in this one but tempers became frayed near the end and Keenan and Slats did quite a bit of jawing, much more than you usually see and something I never saw between Slats and Al Arbour.

By the time the fighting had ended our lead over the Flyers was so big the game was no longer in doubt and when the clock ran out we ran out as we had the previous year but the feeling of joy wasn't quite the same. (Is it ever after the first Cup? The Islanders say the first one will always be special to them.) I was a little more controlled the second time around. Instead of running around, I sat at a desk with a bottle of beer and watched all the excitement, but got excited at the same time. I savored the moment so that I would have a good memory of it years down the line.

As I sipped my beer, I contemplated the difference between the two Cup wins. In 1984 the win was too good to be true because we hadn't won before and the win had more of an impact. This time, because we played so poorly in the first game, it felt good that we were able to come back. There was relief along with the satisfaction of still being champions. Another difference was in the celebrating. This time I knew the right places to go to and the places to avoid.

Over the next few days we brought The Cup to a number of Edmonton bars and I think just about everyone in the city had a chance to sip out of it. What bothered me was a letter which appeared in the *Edmonton Sun* a couple of days later saying, "Why aren't the Oilers bringing the Cup to the hospitals to see kids?"

I thought it was very selfish of anyone to write something like that. Sure, I understood the person's motive but the Oilers do plenty of charity work over the season and put in an awful lot of time. The celebration was spontaneous and completely without format so the fact that we brought the Cup to various bars should not be construed as an attempt to avoid hospitals and places like that. The letter bothered me.

Once again we had heroes galore. Wayne, Grant, Mark, Mess and Glennie, to name a few, were brilliant but the lesser lights were as significant as any of the superstars. Jaroslav Pouzar was one of them.

Remember my mentioning something he had done that was so terrific. Well, it happened after we had lost the first game to Philly. Pouzar actually delivered an impromptu speech to the team, one which had surprising impact.

"Hey, guys," he said. "I don't have many years left as a hockey player because I'm getting older and it's really important to me to win the Stanley Cup championship and the only place I'm going to do it is here in Edmonton. Like I say, I don't have a lot of time and you guys don't know how close you are. You can't see beyond your own noses now so go out and win it."

On the surface the speech didn't seem like much but we all knew that Jaroslav wasn't holding anything back and everything he said was coming from the heart. In retrospect, it played a significant part in our winning.

I was as happy for Jaroslav as I was for Gretz, Mark and the rest of the guys. Here we had fellows still under 25 and they already had two Stanley Cup championships under their belts. I hoped that they appreciated it as much as I did because I knew there were a lot of people in the hockey business who envied us, some of them in The Hockey Hall of Fame.

One I thought of was Bill Gadsby, a defenseman like myself, who toiled brilliantly in the NHL for 20 years with Chicago, the Rangers and the Red Wings. I thought of Brad Park, another superior defenseman — now also a Hall of Famer — who spent more than a decade in the NHL. Neither of them ever sipped champagne from the Stanley Cup.

I returned to Lachute that summer a very happy and grateful young man, wondering whether we were capable of winning three in a row.

26

Murphy's Law, Oilers Style

According to Murphy's Law, anything that can go wrong will go wrong. Perhaps that explains why we didn't win our third straight Stanley Cup in 1986.

Certainly, the catalogue of mishaps in 1985-86 was bigger than most, starting even before training camp had begun. Mark Messier cracked up his Porsche and right away the Oilers were in the papers again. Dave Hunter was in and out of jail and every report on the Oilers chances for winning another Cup suggested that we could be our own worst enemy.

The coaches harped on it and harped on it and again. Maybe too much. We were aware of it so why overplay the situation? Have a little trust in us. Not that management wasn't in our corner. Slats always said he would back the guys to the bitter end and he certainly stood behind Hunter.

Despite the early setbacks we got off to a good start and ran neck and neck with the Flyers for the best record in the league. But Murphy's Law always seemed to intrude. Early in the season Philly goalie Pelle Lindbergh was killed in a car crash. It was a terrible episode and Pelle's name was dragged through the mud for drinking and driving. Right after the accicent we arrived in Philadelphia to play the Flyers. It was their first game since Pelle's death and a memorial service was held prior to the face-off with Pelle's mentor, Bernie Parent, on the ice to give a speech.

Parent, a member of hockey's Hall of Fame, gave a moving speech which got a lot of us to stop and smell the roses. I was thinking about Lindbergh as Parent talked. Pelle was a guy who had been on the top of the world, driving a $130,000 Porsche and — bang! — it was all over.

As Parent spoke, a lot of our guys looked down our blue line at all the faces of good friends and thought about the good times. A lot of guys must have said to themselves, "Someday this will come to an end. Let's appreciate it a bit."

The game followed Murphy's Law all the way. It was 2-2 in the second period and just a great game between a pair of evenly matched teams. Then, with about ten seconds left in the second period and the face-off in our end, Mess moved in for the draw. I was there so what I'm saying is based on what I witnessed first hand.

Mess jumped a bit on the draw so he was thrown out of the circle. He stepped back and said, "What are you talking about? I can't believe you're doing this." With that he was given a two-minute penalty and since we already had one man in the penalty box that gave Philly a two-man advantage. They scored two power play goals and that to all intents and purposes ended the game.

This was a classic example of officiating ruining a perfectly good hockey game. What kind of point were the officials trying to prove? I say prove it in a game that's less important.

We recovered, of course, and marched through our division but there were other obstacles and other examples of Murphy at work against us. Take the game against the Russians.

The NHL had arranged for us to play Soviet team immediately after our Christmas break. The timing was awful but what could we do? That was the only time the game could be scheduled so we went along with it. Slats let some of the guys go home for the holiday and as much as we were disciplining ourselves to be prepared for the Russian game, we had two days off when we didn't practice. We came back, practiced once and played the Russians. Trouble is, you can eat a lot of turkey and the rest of mom's cooking in two days. So, by the time we took the ice against the Soviets, we were rusty.

Could it have been done differently? Sure, in Russia. But Slats couldn't say. "All right, I'm going to keep all you guys here and you're not going to get any time off for Christmas!" We needed the rest. Besides, our main goal was to win the Stanley Cup.

Naturally, we wanted to beat the Russians for the sake of the NHL, for ourselves and for the city of Edmonton and it was disappointing that we lost. We were outclassed but the fact is that we didn't go about the game as if it were a do-or-die situation. We went at it as though the NHL were forcing us to play. And that was too bad because generally we weren't like that. It went against the grain of most of our characters.

Paul Coffey took the most heat because he was quoted across the country saying that he didn't even want to play the game. Frankly, it's a credit to the talent on our club that the game wasn't a complete blowout. It was a 5-3 game but we were never in it from the start.

From a professional viewpoint, I was impressed by the Russians, their conditioning, their skills. But they rely too much on skill and too little on emotion and, as far as I'm concerned, emotion in sports plays a large part in determining who wins. The Soviets are not more skilled shooters but I think they're better puckhandlers. There are not a lot of teams who have as many skilled players as we did. By skill, I mean the ability to skate at top speed while handling the puck. A lot of guys in the NHL cannot do that because they're not trained to do it. The Soviets are.

As much as the loss to the Russians stung, it soon was forgotten and we got back to the business for which we were being paid — finishing first and defending The Cup. If the loss to the Soviets hurt us, you couldn't tell by the standings. We dominated the league, finishing with 56 wins, only 17 losses and seven ties for 119 points, best in the NHL. Philly was second with 110 points.

Even with those glorious numbers, a couple of disturbing things were happening. Just at the trade deadline our rivals from down the highway, the Calgary Flames, had pulled off a major trade, sending defenseman Steve Konroyd and left wing Richard Kromm to the Islanders in return for left wing John Tonelli.

Slats went public charging that Flames general manager Cliff Fletcher had conspired with his Islanders counterpart Bill Torrey against us, the theory being that Tonelli could really damage the Oilers in a playoff series. (In the long run it appears that Torrey got the best of the deal.) Whether the Tonelli deal affected us or not is questionable but he arrived in Calagary after we had completed six of our eight games with the Flames.

In those six games, we had beaten them 5-3, 6-4, 5-3, 4-3, 6-3 and 7-4. In February we tied them 4-4, but they still hadn't beaten us up until April 4 when we played our last regular season game against them. It was played at The Saddledome and they really took it to us, this time with Tonelli in the lineup. The final score was 9-3 Calgary but our feeling was that we could still handle them in a playoff should we meet down the road.

Perhaps we underestimated the psychological effect of that game. For the Flames, such a lopsided win gave them a big emotional boost going into the playoffs. (If we had beaten them, 9-3, our reaction would have been, "So what else is new?") But the Flames looked upon it as a turning point and we looked at it as just another game. I thought it was pretty naive of Calgary to think that the victory was the beginning of a new era for them. Enter Murphy's Law once more.

Our first round opponents were the Vancouver Canucks and we simply outclassed them in every way. It was the easiest playoff series we had ever had and it lulled us, softened us and generally did everything but prime us for what lay ahead. I remember sitting on the bench for Game Three saying, "I can't believe that this is a Stanley Cup playoff. This is not what I grew up watching or fantasizing about. This is ridiculous." There were only eight or nine thousand fans in the Pacific Coliseum, which can hold almost twice that number and while we were shellacking them, the play was horrendous. Even in past preliminary series which we won, at least the opposition like Winnipeg and L.A. made us work. We had to battle every step of the way which sharpened us for the series ahead. As the series wound down, I remember thinking, "Ho-Hum, who's next?"

Meanwhile, in the other Smythe Division semi-final, the Flames took Winnipeg in three straight but the Jets at least took Calgary to overtime in the final match before losing. Were we concerned? Not really.

After two straight Stanley Cup championships and three trips in a row to the finals, we had built up a lot of confidence in ourselves. The feeling was that, yes, the Flames series would be a battle but we had beaten them six out of seven times during the season and we had all the confidence in the world.

What the Flames did have — as we would later learn — was a good coach in Badger Bob Johnson and a game plan that worked. They had enormous desire and intensity and that made a difference. Whatever it was, they had a new-found confidence and it was manifest in Game One in our rink. Calgary not only took the contest, they took it good — 4-1. They started young Mike Vernon in goal and he played the way a young Andy Moog once did in 1981 against the Canadiens. That win started them believing that they could win the series.

Even when we came back to beat them in Game Two, it was hardly convincing. We won 6-5 but we needed overtime. Then, they beat us again in Game Three, 3-2, for a 2-1 series lead and people started talking upset. We squelched that with a 7-4 win at Calgary and all seemed right with the world now that the series was tied at two apiece and we were returning to Northlands.

Home ice was no advantage. They ran up a 4-1 win and it became apparent that Vernon coud do the job for them. The city of Calgary was braced for the kill on April 28, 1986 but we wouldn't let it happen. Having beaten them 5-2, we once again came back to Edmonton secure in the knowledge that we would play Game Seven in front of friendly fans. Friendly, that is, if we made a game of it.

At first we didn't. As if to prove that their three wins were not flukes, the Flames jumped into a 2-0 lead but we fought back and tied the score before IT happened.

What was to become one of the most publicized hockey events of the year began innocently enough behind our net. Steve Smith, our big young defenseman who had replaced the injured Fogie, was behind our net in the left corner looking to make our standard fast-break play. That means the puck goes up the ice pretty quick. Unfortunately, Steve kind of bobbled the puck a bit and he never did get good wood or a handle on it. Since he knew the objective of the play was to do it as quickly as possible, he moved the rubber without having all the control he should. The puck just sprayed off his stick, hit the back of Grant's left leg and went into the net. Just like that!

A lot of guys on the bench didn't even see it and the question went around, "What happened?" Muckler was saying, "What the hell happened? How is the puck in the net?" When we make this fast-break play, the first thing we do is look up the ice. The players on the bench have a tendency to look up the ice, too, to see if anyone else is breaking. The fans do, too, because they know the play is coming. Everyone was looking ahead and they didn't see the puck go in the net. But it *was* in and the red light provided confirmation if we had any further doubts.

Smith was stunned, then devastated. When he returned to the bench he underwent several emotional stages. The first was embarrassment for what he had done. The second reaction was hope. If you put the puck in your own net in a 7-0 game, you don't worry but this was 2-2 in the seventh game and now Smith was hoping that it wasn't the goal that would cost us the series. Another reaction was if this is the seventh game (which it was) and if this is the deciding goal (which it was at the time), then I can't believe it happened. I could see that in Steve's face as he came to the bench.

At first, when he arrived at the bench, he seemed pretty well relaxed. Then, all of a sudden, he broke down in tears. (Had it been a regular season game he wouldn't have broken down because these things happen; hockey is a game of mistakes.) Given the timing, his mistake had much more impact than it might have under other circumstances.

Still there was more than half a period to go, plenty of time for us to rebound and get the goal back. Shortly thereafter there was a delay when the referee got hurt and I said to Mark while we skated around, "We've always liked to do it dramatically, so what better way than this. It's 3-2 in a seven-game series. We're going to get a goal. I think you'll probably get the winner in OT. You or Gretz."

Mark chuckled and said, "Yeah, this is great, isn't it?"

The feeling was "What kind of play was that; what a horseshit goal. It was just a goal. We're down. So let's get another one." Soon after that we had four or five good scoring opportunities but we just couldn't bury it behind Vernon.

Still, we didn't panic as the third period wore on because we had that Oiler confidence. No matter how far down we are in a game, we always feel we can come back, if we get a few breaks. But we weren't getting breaks in this series. Then, it was down to the final minute and still we were behind. We were coming. Everyone felt that way until the very end but the green light ended that possibility. And when it was over, everyone said, "I can't believe we didn't get our goal." We were coming. We had them but we didn't get the goal that we always got in the past and now we were on the wrong end of the hand-shaking line.

Minutes later, the dressing room scene was surreal. Naturally, the fall guy was Smith who was broken apart. He was in tears from the time the play happened to a good two hours after the game. At first, Steve was off in an area by himself but then Peter Pocklington told him that he had to face the press, suck it in and take it like a man. He went out there and met the media.

Slats met the press as well and said, "We gave them a game plan and they didn't follow it." He was right. Some guys might feel differently. In this series we followed the game plan in the games we had won. We played well, discipline-wise, and dominated Calgary. But in the games we lost, we didn't have any sustained forechecking. We had a set forechecking system but the guys refused to do it. It was like years before when the Islanders used to gobble up all our passes in the slot. The Flames were doing the same thing. The players were refusing to do what the coaches said. Why? That's a good question.

Perhaps our guys were simply all caught up in the series. Maybe it was having so much success doing it our way. A lot of times you play the game with a narrow-mindedness that keeps you from seeing what's going on around you. We just weren't adapting to what the coaches were pointing out to us.

For the next two months we analyzed the series but for Kevin Lowe, journalist, there was some instant analyzing to do since *The Sun* had wanted me to do a column on the seventh game, win or lose. Trust me when I tell you that it wasn't easy.

The Sun had a new guy handling my column and he was at Northlands that night. He approached me rather tenderly after the debacle and asked, "Would you like to do something?" At first I said no. Then I figured, why not? As Bryan Watson pointed out years earlier, "Life goes on." So I sat down and wrote out the column. It was headlined: A BITTER END TO A BRILLIANT YEAR — GIVE THE FLAMES CREDIT.

Perhaps one line in the column said it all. I was talking about breaks in hockey and noted, "They just got one more than we did."

Other journalists were considerably tougher. Terry Jones crucified Smith, calling his pass one of the biggest blunders in pro sports. I though he was extremely unfair in victimizing the kid but what Jonesy did was minor in the Unfair Department compared with what was to come the following week in *Sports Illustrated*.

The most devastating part of the article, which was co-authored by Armen Keteyian and Donald Ramsay, was a paragraph suggesting that the Oilers had been the subject of drug-use rumors. Without any substantiation, the authors went on to say: "One former Oiler insider told SI that at least five team members have had 'substantial' cocaine problems. Three sources told SI they have seen Oilers players use cocaine or marijuana at parties in Edmonton and other NHL cities. . . ."

As soon as the magazine hit the stands there were reverberations in the press right across the continent. By this time, Gretz and I had left for vacation and were in Phoenix. Glen called and suggested that we make a statement. Wayne said, "I don't want to touch that one with a ten-foot pole."

I thought about it a bit. I was really soured and was ready to make any statement saying, "Hey, I know the guys on this team. I don't know what kinds of problems baseball or football has but I know that sort of problem doesn't exist in the NHL. Let's be realistic; this is Edmonton, not South America."

At first I was a little bit hot; then I talked to two people about how I should go about this. Glen said, "This has been an awful shot to our team. We've had some bad slights and some bad image problems, but this is the worst. The next thing in line is that we're murderers or that we beat our kids up."

He said it was important for the guys to make an effort over the course of the summer to uphold the image of the Oilers.

My first reaction after that was to remember when Dave Hunter was getting raked over the coals in the press. (He was convicted three times in less than two years for driving while impaired.) I really wanted to write an article about it. I wanted to tell Dave Hunter's side of it, to describe the hell he was going through. No one knew Dave Hunter's side of it. I talked to a few people and they said, "Kevin, if you touch that, you're just dragging the story out one more time. You're just giving people one more opportunity to talk about it. Let sleeping dogs lie."

I remembered that from the Huntsy thing, and it did blow over pretty well. That's the way I approached the SI thing — let it die. But the article was a shot at the NHL and who was a better target than the Edmonton Oilers right after we were beaten by Calgary.

With the winning and the glory and the success comes all

the other stuff. That article was part of the other stuff. But we knew what had to be done. It was like the song said, "Pick yourself up, dust yourself off and start all over again."

And hope that Murphy's Law applies to the other guy.

27

Back on Track

Most of us spent the summer licking our wounds and wondering what Slats would do about the team. He had several options: a massive shake-up with trades galore; a few choice moves here and there; or sticking with the status quo.

In retrospect, he did the right thing. Nothing.

Those who thought he might panic were dead wrong. Glen stayed calm and cool through the whole, ugly mess — even when it came to putting down *Sports Illustrated* for running with a story that had absolutely no basis in fact, was completely unsubstantiated and lacked even one credible witness to back up the anonymous charges.

But those of us who knew Slats well realized that he doesn't make decisions rashly. He makes moves that will benefit the team and that's how he handled the aftermath of the Calgary defeat. He would let the season unfold and deal with the problems as they occurred. My feeling was that we should forget the Flames series and, instead, look at the fabulous season we had had.

What I worried about was that the guys might try too hard in compensation for what had happened. My answer was, "We had a setback but let's realize our potential and our talent. Let's go about the rebounding in an organized manner." If we got off to a good start, the criticism would be extinguished. Wins can do wonderful things when it comes to blocking out boos.

I knew I was right because all the talent was in place. Mark, Paul, Wayne, Jari and Grant were still young and getting better. I could see Steve Smith improving a lot, provided that Slats didn't give up on him for his mistake. This would be a very pivotal personality move. And I was looking to Craig MacTavish to get better for us, as well as Mike Krushelnyski.

Mike had come to us two summers earlier in a deal that was somewhat surprising since Slats dealt Kenny Linseman who had had an excellent play-off for us when we won the first Cup from the Islanders. But Slats wanted a big guy and Kenny was small although he often acted like a big man.

A lot of us missed Linseman because he was one of the better characters on a club that respected characters. Kenny, otherwise known as "The Rat", was one of the great arguers in Oiler history, one of the most opinionated players we have ever had. Kenny's problem was that he didn't know when to be opinionated and when not to be and he sometimes overstepped those boundaries.

He was also one of the sharpest businessmen we had ever met. Whenever we went on a road trip, Linseman would bring an enormous briefcase with him filled with all his business papers. Semenk would look it over and say, "Kenny, what have you got in your briefcase — your bankbook?" Someone would try to steal the briefcase as a prank but I always suspected that the guys were a little bit jealous of the fact that he had interests other than hockey.

Kenny was one of the few people who could get Gretz upset. There was one big game with Calgary when Kenny kept taking dumb penalties and even though we were dominating territorially, they were winning 3-1. Panic started to set in and Wayne was getting a little upset, which was totally out of character. But in the second period, when Kenny returned to the bench after yet another penalty, Wayne turned to him and said at the top of his lungs, "IF YOU TAKE ANOTHER FUCKING PENALTY, I'M PERSONALLY GOING TO KILL YOU!" Kenny had made Wayne snap, but then The Rat proceeded to set up two goals, then take a vicious crosscheck in front of their net to score the winner.

Wayne went over and apologized to him after the game. "Kenny, I'm sorry. It was in the heat of the action. I saw things slipping out of our hands. I thought you were the cause of it."

Well, he *was* the cause; he was the cause of the victory. With Linseman gone, we needed production from others and we got it from several sources, not the least of which was MacTavish.

This case demonstrates the similarity between Slats and Al

Davis of the NFL Raiders. Davis loves to give opportunities to football players who are rejected by everyone else. His club became the Bideawee Home of Football and ours became the Devils Island of hockey.

Everyone knew that MacTavish had been in trouble for drunken driving, but Glen would be the first to admit that many of us had had a few drinks and then driven a car. Craig was just the unlucky one who got caught. He paid his dues and now he was free and Slats was the one to give him a chance.

Why not? Craig's personality was a gem and he was a good player. Because the guy made a mistake, should he be persecuted for life? I don't think so and the rest of the team felt the same way.

Getting MacTavish was a spectacular move, like a dream come true. When he came to us everyone went out of his way to accept Craig. We just wanted to make him feel at home and he was obviously delighted with the response he received. Once, on a trip to Boston, he showed how he felt about us by bringing the entire team to his off-season home a half-hour from Boston. It was a big Cape Cod house right on the water. We had steamed clams, steak, fish, the works. He put on a feast for 30 guys that had to set him back a pile of bucks but it was his way of saying thanks for being taken into our fold. And by this time, the fold had gotten good and tight since the nucleus had been around since 1979.

I had been there so long I could tell my teammates just by their superstitions alone. Charlie Huddy, for instance, would put on one skate before the other and one shin pad before the other — the same order every time. As long as Semenk was with the club, Wayne was always second to last going out for the warmup, but he was always first after the goaltender going out for the start of each period. If Semenk wasn't in the lineup, Wayne would be last.

My buddy Fogie would lay out all his equipment and roll up his socks in a perfect fashion, everything arranged as neatly as possible. Lee had it laid out like a mother would lay out a child's clothes. He had the socks rolled up so he could easily roll them up his leg. One time, the guys sewed up the sock at the bottom so that when he tried to put his sock on, he couldn't get it up. Everyone watched quietly and then delivered a good laugh.

Like the others, I've had my own superstitions, mostly concerning equipment. If things are going well I refuse to change equipment, a stick or skates, no matter how broken down they may be. I keep wearing them until they fall apart.

Wayne's superstitions are subtle. After each period he grabs a glass of Gatorade and a glass of water. He sips the Gatorade and just before he's about to put his skates on, he takes one sip of the water and throws it in the garbage can. He has to toss it a good 15 feet. It's a big garbage can and he gets it in most of the time. Lots of times he hits the rim and the water spills all over the place.

None of our guys are as wild as the former NHL goalie Gary (Suitcase) Smith. He'd come into the room after every period and take all of his equipment off — every piece from the jersey on down — and then put it right back on again. He used to wear six or seven pairs of socks.

Fogie came closest to being a throwback to the Gary Smith era. Lee had played for the Buffalo Sabres when Punch Imlach was still running the club and there were few martinets who could match Punch for old-style hockey. Fogie would tell us that before a game there was no music in the Sabres room, and the guys used to sit for two hours in their stall. Just sit. When it came to game time, the team would throw their equipment on and go out on the ice. Nowadays, guys are playing ping-pong even up to 15 minutes before warm-up.

Maybe this joie de vivre couldn't produce a winner with other clubs but it worked for us. As Ronnie Low once put it, "I've never been around better people or had more fun. It was that way right from the beginning and we had natural leaders in Wayne and Mark but people outside the team didn't realize it. Fogie was great, too."

Ronnie understood how we were able to maintain this camaraderie. "It's the way the Oilers treat their young players. Veterans always set the rules for the new guys. Peer pressure is the best way to keep things in order. It's impossible for a new player to set his own standard around this club. What's good enough for Messier and Gretzky and the other real stars — they're all veterans now — is sure to be good enough for the rookies. The best players are the best people, that's why."

Among "the best people" coming back to us for 1986-87 was Ted Green, our assistant coach, who had taken a year off to go into private enterprise and was now returning. With Green, Muckler and Slats, we had as fine a triumvirate as you could find. They knew what they wanted in order to get us back on track and it was simply articulated in a *Hockey News* headline a week before the season opened: SATHER WANTS 'WE' TO REPLACE 'ME'. The coaches weren't interested in individual records; they wanted more teamwork than ever. "All I want," said Slats, "is to win the league, win the Stanley Cup and not to lose too many games."

In particular, we didn't want to lose many — if any — games to the Flames. Their playoff triumph had heightened (at least in the media) a rivalry that had had a very positive tilt in the direction of Edmonton — until the spring of 1986. But now that the Flames had gone to the Stanley Cup finals, the rivalry would take on a new texture in both of these interesting cities.

Curiously, they are like twin cities, 250 miles apart, almost the same size and both wealthy because of the oil business. Even the physical features and silhouettes of the cities are very much alike.

As a heavily involved participant, I always tried to downplay the rivalry. Both teams tried to because anyone who knew anything about the histories of the cities certainly didn't want the rivalries to spill over to hockey simply because it could get out of hand. And it has.

People would frequently ask us about our feelings about the Flames and we'd offhandedly reply that it was good competition and they're in second place in our division and we play each other eight times and let's not make too big a deal about it. But as much as we said that, we couldn't kid ourselves. It was there. You'd walk into a shopping mall and someone would say, "My sister-in-law is down in Calgary and I hate her because all she talks about is her Flames." Your next-door-neighbor says, "Great game last night. I don't care if you guys win another game, just beat Calgary whenever you play them." Like it or not, there was a natural hatred and the crazy thing about it is that half the citizens of Calgary and Edmonton are related.

As far as the players were concerned, there wasn't much resentment from our end but they may have resented the fact that — until 1986 — we always won and they may have hated us because of it. We got all the press. Edmonton has made Alberta famous; the Calgary Flames haven't. As long as Gretz is around, the Oilers will always be the team in Alberta regardless of whether the Flames win or not.

Whatever fire exists between the teams is fanned by the media. The Calgary scribes love their team just as the Edmonton scribes love theirs. Down in Calgary, the media live in their own little environment and they don't hear about the Edmonton Oilers. Once in a while they'll hear about Wayne Gretzky but it's all Calgary Flames territory.

As you might expect, our games with them have been particularly rough over the years and the playoffs merely intensify the aggression. There's a fine line between aggressive hockey and dirty hockey. It's all right to run somebody over but it's not all right to maim him. By that I mean things like sticks in the eyes and swinging sticks. When sticks are recklessly swung in an attempt to injure, it's outrageous, but the game is so emotional that sometimes a player has difficulty staying on the right side of that fine line.

I would be somewhat of a hypocrite if I said I never used my stick because in the heat of the action, you're bound to slash a guy or two. If a guy is beating you wide, cutting to the net, the natural thing to do — as Kent Douglas, the onetime NHL-er used to say — is to "cut him down." You have to cut him down but you can do it in a manner that's not going to maim him but will compel him to think next time.

My attitude is that if someone uses his stick on me, I'm going to use mine right back. Maybe that's not the smartest philosophy because it almost cost Ted Green his life, but it's just a natural defensive instinct. I would never purposely attempt to injure someone unless I had a reason for it. I'm certainly not beyond reacting but I would never initiate anything like that. When you're dealing with human nature, with emotions and tempers rising rapidly in a fast-paced game where players carry sticks, some nasty things can happen. So, my philosophy is: don't cross me because I'm not beyond using my stick.

Many players feel that way so if no one starts the stickwork, then you don't run into a problem. Unfortunately, the amount of stickwork has grown over the years. Just look at Gretz. He gets worked over pretty bad and has to wear extra padding on his arms because they're getting whacked so badly.

Isn't there a rule that says slashing isn't allowed? Slash and, technically, you're breaking the rules. But it's accepted. A player is going around you and he gets a two-hander; if the stick doesn't break, it's fair. If the stick breaks, the referee calls a two-minute or five-minute penalty. If the stick doesn't break, there's no justice at all.

People wonder why hockey teams need enforcers and the answer is that if there wasn't all this stickwork and the possibility of someone beating up a Gretzky, then you wouldn't need an enforcer. Guys like Wayne get worked over so badly that, eventually, someone has to do something about it.

I've seen Wayne fight when he was cornered — and fight very well — but what good will that do the Edmonton Oilers or Wayne Gretzky? So, sad as it may seem, you need someone else to do the fighting. We had Semenk, Kevin McClelland and any number of others, if necessary. Paul Coffey could handle his dukes but we didn't want him wasting his time with fighting; he was too valuable to us on the ice to have him vegetating in the penalty box.

Unlike Gretz, Paul was not the soul of harmony as we embarked on the climb up to the top of Mount Stanley. Unlike Gretz, Paul did not have the same fine tuning with the media that Wayne had from the very start; nor was he always on the same wavelength with Slats.

Paul's media problem stemmed from the year when he didn't win the Norris Trophy and Rod Langway of the Capitals did, the result was based on votes by members of the Professional Hockey Writers' Association. Paul felt that his not winning the Norris was an injustice. He took his rejection by the writers hard. To him, not winning the Norris was a shot at him personally. He not only felt *he* deserved it but that it was ludicrous that Langway won.

Eventually, he turned it around, won the Norris twice, broke Bobby Orr's goal-scoring record for defensemen and began getting the attention that he felt he deserved. He developed a positive relationship with the media — but not necessarily with his coach.

The new season had hardly begun when the guns in both the Sather and Coffey camps began to roar. Slats fired the first volley after the third game by first saying, generally, "I can't defend guys when they're playing horseshit. If a guy's playing bad, he should own up to it." Then Sather was specifically asked about Paul and replied: "I'd say he's not playing as well as he's capable. I'd say he's trying to get his game into shape. But, Paul has always been a slow starter. Every year he seems to be slow to get out of the chute. I told him it would be interesting to see if he played in October and November the way he's played the rest of the season."

Paul's counterattack was not a short one, but he concluded, "If he starts pointing fingers, that sucks. It's pretty shallow. I'm sick of it. Seven years, it's been the same thing, game in and game out. We should be treated a little better. We don't need to be treated like. . . ."

The skirmish made headlines in the October 15 edition of the *Edmonton Sun* and over Dick Chubey's piece in *The Hockey News*. BLEEP, BLEEP, SUPERSTAR COFFEY SOUNDS OFF.

Slats extinguished the fire almost as soon as it blazed and refused to take any disciplinary action against Paul despite the harsh words spoken. "He's an athlete with a great deal of pride," Glen explained, "and when you criticize someone like that, you expect a certain amount of backlash. I consider it a situation where a guy was a little upset and as far as I'm concerned, it's over."

Despite the hullabaloo, we got back on track and soon established that we were once again the class team of the NHL. (The proof, at the end, would be our overwhelming dominance of the division and the league.) We became an angry team. The loss to Calgary compelled us to focus on our goals again. Muck told us that we "have to be ten feet tall on the ice," meaning that we had to sacrifice more to turn a loss into a victory.

Meanwhile, off-ice, Slats was tinkering with the machine. He swung a deal with Phil Esposito of the Rangers, which sent Donnie Jackson and a college player named Mike Golden to New York for the rights to Reijo Ruotsalainen, the talented Finnish defenseman who was playing in Europe. We were told that Reijo might be available to us later in the season.

Just before Christmas we suffered a real shocker when Semenk was dealt to Hartford for a third-round draft pick. This was tough to take because Dave was one of the originals and I had always thought he'd finish his career in Edmonton, but trades are part of hockey and Slats has always believed that it was wise to change about 15 percent of the team every season. With typical humor, Semenk quipped as he left, "It's about time I got some attention again."

Semenk had been seeing less and less ice because Slats had taken a liking to a young tough kid, Marty McSorley, who had many of Dave's qualities. But if that didn't shake me up there was the deal later in the season that sent my pal Fogie to the Sabres, along with Mark Napier, for Normand Lacombe and Wayne Van Dorp. Glen next re-acquired Jaroslav Pouzar, who had been playing in West Germany, and to add more quality to the lineup obtained slick Kent Nilsson from Minnesota for a draft choice.

We entered the homestretch fine-tuned for a rush that was a part of our tradition dating back to our very first year when we won eight of our last ten games to make the playoffs. First place was virtually clinched. With an eye toward the Stanley Cup which had been wrested from us the previous spring, Slats summed up the pre-playoffs thinking with a simple declaration: "We're ready to roll."

28

Out of Our Way, Please

To regain the Cup we would have to re-discover the formula for beating the Flames. Where once we had treated our Alberta neighbors with a touch of disdain, the 1986 playoff experience had changed our view of Bob Johnson's team. What's more, our games with them — particularly in the first half of 1986-87 — had taken on a completely different flavor than in the earlier seasons.

Calgary whipped us 6-3, 3-1, 6-4 and 6-5 in our first four games before we finally turned the tide, 5-3, in the fifth match-up. It was our only win over them. They came back and beat us twice with the last game coming out a 4-4 tie. Over the course of the year we had learned to *hate* the Calgary Flames and we reached this mental state the hard way. Or, to put it another way, we discovered that not hating a foe can have very unpleasant results. We learned that from now on we had to treat games against the Flames as a special event and not something to dismiss out of hand.

The Edmonton Oilers do not like losing. We don't single out our victories but we do remember the defeats. The more we lost to Calgary, the angrier we got. We looked ahead to the playoffs, understanding that there was every possibility that we'd meet the Flames for the second time in two years. This challenge whet our competitive appetites, something that Slats had anticipated. That explains the spate of trades he had made and what changed the complexion of the club that had been beaten by the Flames in 1986. Kent Nilsson fit in neatly with Mark Messier and Glenn Anderson. Reijo Ruotsalainen gave us added firepower on the point and Marty McSorley demonstrated that he could be every bit the enforcer that Semenk had been.

I don't for a moment mean to suggest that I was happy about the trades or anything but saddened by the departure of some very good friends. Getting traded is analogous to being the last player picked for the sandlot team when you were a kid. It's kind of embarrassing and difficult to pick up and leave your home, friends and teammates.

In some cases, the trade is a blessing. Semenk was hardly getting any ice time with us but Hartford immediately put him in the lineup. Same with Fogie in Buffalo. Another friend of mine, Pat Hughes, had been with us, then Buffalo and finally St. Louis and said he didn't mind the moving all that much. Like the professional he was, Pat made the necessary adjustments.

Seeing what happened to Semenk and Fogie got me to wondering how well I'd be able to make the adjustment if I ever got the word that Slats had sent me elsewhere. Should that happen, there's not much I could do about it but go. My other choice would be to quit, which I wouldn't do.

I consider myself fortunate to have played for one NHL team the length of my career. That's more (or perhaps less would be the better word) than Walt McKechnie could say. This was a big-leaguer who had to keep his suitcase ready at all times. Over 16 years in the bigs, McKechnie played for eight different teams. I'm surprised he didn't score half of his 214 goals into the wrong net.

Each March, most of us get a bit antsy in anticipation of the trade deadline because, unless you're a Gretzky, there's always a chance that *you* might be the one to get the hook. Some guys can be awfully cool about it while others find sleeping difficult.

When our franchise was a bit younger, we had a player who got the heebie-jeebies as the trade deadline approached. With 24 hours left before all deals would officially cease, he would become the ultimate nervous wreck. When the phone rang, he jumped. Fortunately for him, the calls were all friends.

Usually, a trade is made for good reason. The deal for Semenk made sense because Hartford had lost one of its rugged players, Torrie Robertson, and needed beef right away. Other times deals are made out of pique. For any number of reasons, a coach might take a disliking to a player and, despite his proven ability, have him moved. On the other hand there are often players who find a coach intolerable and try to have a trade made. When Ted Sator coached the Rangers, his disciplined approach (the players might use a more powerful word) didn't go over well with fellows like Mark Pavelich, Barry Beck and Ruotsalainen. They all got out of New York in one way or another but only one of them, Ruotsalainen, ever returned and had impact in the NHL.

That's not a knock at Beck or Pavelich. Some players thrive in certain environments and wilt in others. Take Kent Nilsson; when he came to Edmonton, he had already earned a reputation as a floater but with the Oilers he worked hard and was a key factor for us in the spring of 1987. Bobby Smith was another case. He virtually wasted away in Minnesota but found himself in Montreal and seemed to change his work habits from disinterested to hard-driving.

Of course anyone familiar with the North Stars situation in the past few years would have to question the decline of that once-powerful franchise. Even when they had a roster filled with solid players, the North Stars would easily become unglued. Get them down a few goals and they quit and start pointing fingers at each other. Yet on another club they might turn out to be excellent team players.

Sometimes the adjustment to a new bunch of guys is difficult. I remember when I was involved in the Canada Cup after we had developed our keen rivalry with the Islanders and suddenly found myself with an enemy like Bob Bourne or Mike Bossy. It was quite obvious when the group was thrown together that the Edmonton and New York players didn't like each other, but that feeling soon changed.

All it takes is a few beers over a table with lots of hockey talk and the animosities evaporate. I've seen it happen dozens of times and it was no different with Team Canada. When you play against the Islanders, you hate them, but when you sit across the table from them, you find that you have everything in common and that they're not bad guys after all. In the fraternity of hockey players, I can honestly say that I've never met a guy I didn't like. It didn't take me long to realize that Bossy, Brent Sutter and John Tonelli are among the greatest people you'd ever want to meet.

But friendships were put aside as the 1986-87 regular schedule was completed. Despite all the shuffling and the problems with Calgary, we still finished with the best record in the league (106 points), six more than runner-up Philadelphia and eleven more than the Flames who finished second in the Smythe Division.

We would open our challenge for the Cup against the Los Angeles Kings on April 8, 1987 at Northlands. Now it was time for Slats, Muck and Teddy to prime us for the big run. This meant a few intense practices which would better integrate our recent acquisitions into the flow.

Under Slats, our practices had become revolutionary. He developed fast, fluid motions; everything was executed at game tempo, high speed, with lots of movement. It was just like the Soviet style of practice. (In the traditional NHL practice the guys stand around all the time. They would do breakouts and three-on-twos and that was it. No movement of players. Glen emphasized fluidity with everyone crisscrossing. If you're a leftwinger you don't have to stand on the left side all the time.)

Every month Slats or Muck would throw in a new twist and we'd have to work on it until we could almost execute the play with our eyes closed and at a really fast pace. Sather believes that if you go at game tempo for 45 minutes, you accomplish the same thing as you would if the guys stand around for two hours.

Slats makes the practices so interesting that there have been very few times when I've stepped on the ice and said, "Oh, no, I have to go out there *again!*" In general, practices are exciting because we're creating something. It's almost a form of art. We have a five-man flow drill which is really fun to do because when we're having a good day and everything clicks, you get a good rush out of it, a good high. The passes are sweet and right on the sticks and, most of all, there's a feeling of accomplishment as a professional.

To keep each other sharp, we usually challenge each other. In every practice you see the natural competiveness of the athletes surface. The shooters challenge the goaltenders; the defensemen challenge the shooters to beat them; we do things to keep everyone sharp.

Of all the players, the goaltenders usually like practice the least. These are guys who stop 35 to 40 shots a game and then they're facing 350 shots a practice, which is frightening. On the one end, you have guys like Glennie and Mark working on their shots, shooting to score — they'll shoot high and often hit the goaltender in the shoulder — and the goalie will come out of it with a bruise the size of a grapefruit. The goalie says, "I'm paid to stop pucks in a game, not in practice." But the question is, how can a guy stay sharp if he's not playing in practice?

By far the best goalie I ever saw in practice was Ronnie Low. He tried to stop every shot directed at him from the time he stepped on the ice to the time he got off the ice. His philosophy was, "They're paying me to stop pucks, so I'll stop pucks in games or practices."

Ronnie was an extreme case and not your average goalie. Then again, it would be difficult to find an "average" goalie because they are all so different.

The most "different" goaltender we ever had was a character named Don Cutts, a native Edmontonian, who played for us in my rookie season, 1979-80. The best way to describe Cuttsy would be to call him a goaltending beatnik. He looked like he had come to us directly from the Woodstock festival and to add to that, he was a drummer on the side.

Cuttsy prefaced every sentence with the opening "Hey, man. . . ." He used it for any and all occasions and was quite popular in the short time that he played for the Oilers. But we did get the impression that he meant to go to Woodstock and somebody dropped him off at the rink by accident.

My most vivid memory of Cuttsy involved a game at The Forum in Los Angeles and on that night he was playing pretty well. Without any notice, he called Fogie over to him for a discussion. The dialogue went like this:

Fogie: "What's wrong, Cuttsy?"

Cutts: "Hey, man, it's my eyes, my eyes!"

Fogie: "What?"

Cutts: "I can't see."

Fogie: "What do you mean, you can't see? You're playing nets!"

Cutts: "I can't see the clock. I don't know what's wrong. There's something wrong with my eyes."

Fogie kept looking at this strange cat, wondering why he didn't just take himself out of the game. But for Cuttsy, that would be too simple. He just preferred driving Fogie nuts with his "It's my eyes, it's my eyes!" routine. (Cuttsy, by the way, played in a grand total of six games for us and had a 3.57 goals against average. Not bad for a drummer.)

Cuttsy was just a dim memory as we opened the playoffs against the Kings. Grant and Andy gave us as good a goaltending unit as any club in the league possessed and Slats could feel comfortable starting either of the guys. With the addition of Nilsson, Ruotsalainen and Moe Lemay, we seemed to have as solid a lineup as ever although the media wasn't too sure.

Prior to Game One, Slats took umbrage with a reporter who suggested that the Oilers lacked depth. "Right now," countered Glen, "we have two extra defensemen (Steve Smith, Jeff Beukeboom) and two extra forwards (Moe Lemay, Mike Moller) and we can call guys up from Halifax (AHL) if necessary."

The depth wasn't very apparent in Game One. The Kings stunned us 5-2 and brought back memories of a Los Angeles upset not all that long ago. If any good came from the defeat it was that it gave us a loud wake-up call. We responded the next night with a 13-3 drubbing and pushed our way — believe me, it wasn't all that easy — through the next three games, winning 6-5, 6-3 and, finally, 5-4.

"This," said Mark, "is a better team than last year."

Nilsson was beginning to dazzle on the line with Mark and Glenn, proving again that Slats had this special knack for recruiting so-called "losers" from other teams. An earlier case, Craig MacTavish, was playing the best hockey of his life for us. "There isn't a deeper team in the league than Edmonton," added Craig.

Some observers might have figured that Calgary boasted a lot of depth and that we'd get another stiff series from the Flames. The entire province of Alberta had been anticipating another classic playoff like the 1986 seven-gamer. So were we — but the Winnipeg Jets got in the way.

Winnipeg went into the Saddledome and beat the Flames twice. By the time Calgary recovered it was too late. After six games the Flames were gonzo so it would be the Jets facing us and not Calgary after all.

We had taken Winnipeg in four straight two years earlier but this was an improved Jets team with better speed and a superstar in Dale Hawerchuk. Nobody wanted to sound cocky or even give a hint that we would take this club for granted. Gretz reminded us what had happened the previous year against Calgary. "The Flames got on a roll and beat us fair and square," he pointed out. "Then they got a taste of that this year."

Whether it was a "jinx" or not is debatable but once again we had Winnipeg's number. One, two, three, four and the Jets were out. They pushed us in the opener — a 3-2 win on Glennie's overtime goal at 36 seconds — and then it went 5-3, 5-2 and 4-2. On May 5, 1987 we were ready for the Red Wings.

Our mistake was in thinking that Detroit would be easy. The Wings had just slipped past Toronto in seven games and didn't appear to be very formidable but Jacques Demers is a special coach and he produced as airtight a system as any average club could devise against us.

And their system worked, to the tune of a 3-1 slap in our faces right at Northlands. Demers' discipline was excellent. In the second game they worked just as hard, got some better-than-average goaltending and gave us another hard time. Although the final score was a deceptive 4-1 in our favor, the Red Wings stayed close until the end. The next two games at Joe Louis Arena were equally tight but we had a little too much in every department. We edged them 2-1 and 3-2.

One of the Red Wings' plans was to hit us as much as possible and to a certain extent they succeeded. It was an incredibly taxing series what with Detroit's defensive checking, the overwhelming heat in Joe Louis Arena and the physical play. But once we got back to Edmonton we skated and won the series 6-3. We were one series away from redemption, looking ahead to the same club we eliminated in 1985, Mike Keenan's Philadelphia Flyers.

With a 46-26-8 record and 100 points, Philly earned their way into the finals. Enroute, they beat the Rangers in six, the Islanders in seven and Montreal in six. The latter series produced headlines all over the place because of the brawling. We knew the Flyers were tough but they had an added element that could make life difficult for us — Ron Hextall in goal.

As a rookie that year, he inspired a lot of interest because of his aggressive goaltending and his habit of shooting the puck, like a defenseman, out of his zone up to the forwards. The Flyers had been rejuvenated under Keenan two years earlier and now with people like Tim Kerr, Peter Zezel, Rick Tocchet,

Brad Marsh and Mark Howe in their lineup, they figured to be better than they were in 1985, if only because of the experience.

The Flyers were an excellent example of the trend toward parity in the league. As Bob Johnson explained, "The league is so even now, you can't expect to win unless you're at your best."

He should know; his Flames weren't going to get a crack at us this time because they hadn't been at their best.

Philly, we knew, would be different.

29

How Sweet It Is — Again

"We want to get even with them for what they did to us in 1985," said Peter Zezel on the eve of the 1987 Stanley Cup finals.

There was a revenge motive on our side as well. We wanted to atone for the 1986 humiliation. "Losing to Calgary has been on our minds all year," said Gretz.

Not since our 1984 collision with the Islanders had we faced a team that offered such an interesting contrast to the Oilers. Our speed, artistry and flair were balanced on the other end by the boisterous, lunch-pail style of Philadelphia. Many journalists were fascinated by the possibilities of red-hot Hextall taking on the likes of Wayne, Mark, Glennie, Jari and now, our newest offensive threat, Kent Nilsson.

If that wasn't enough, Slats and Mike Keenan provided as intense a coaching rivalry as you'll find in the NHL. More than a few people remembered the nasty ending of the 1985 play-off when the two were screaming at each other from the benches. Ho-boy, this would be a dilly.

For the first game, at Northlands, May 17, Slats had to ensure that we weren't rusty. Having disposed of Detroit in five games, we had a much longer lay-off than Philly. Add to that our penchant for getting off on the wrong skate. We had lost opening games to both Los Angeles and Detroit. Glen didn't want it to happen again — and it didn't. I helped see to that.

With the score tied 0-0, I picked up an offensive rebound in front of Hextall and set in motion the play that would eventually result in Gretz, camped to the left of the net, putting a rebound through a scramble in front of Hextall. The goal held up through the end of the period but we couldn't do anything with Hextall in the second. Meanwhile, Brian Propp fired a high shot off left wing at 16:08 of the second and it was a new hockey game after two.

Even though the score was tied, I could tell that we had an advantage over them. We were getting second and third chances against Hextall. They weren't getting those chances against Grant. They weren't going to win the game that way. Sure enough, Glennie got a quickie before the third period was a minute old. Seven minutes later, Gretz skimmed a magnificent pass to Paul and he whizzed it past Hextall. The fourth goal by Jari was icing. The 4-1 score held through the end. "We knew we couldn't afford to lose the opener to Philadelphia," Gretz said when it was over and I heartily concurred.

But the Flyers had to worry about our overwhelming offense. Not only were all the forwards moving in high gear but Paul was at the top of his game and I was feeling pretty good myself. "We've got to get in their skating lanes," suggested Brad Marsh — but he didn't say how.

There's an old expression, "You can't hit what you can't catch" and that was the Flyers dilemma. Our speed was awesome but, on the other side, so was Hextall's goaltending. He kept them in the game until late in the first period when Philly was tagged with a too-many-men-on-the-ice penalty. Right at the buzzer we had the Flyers defense in disarray and Brad McCrimmon, holding on for dear life, was given a two-minute penalty. So even though the score was tied, 0-0, we entered the second period with a five-on-three advantage.

Gretz finally put us ahead with 45 seconds gone and that should have been a springboard for even more goals but Hextall closed the door and the Flyers pecked away as they had in the first game, only this time they forged ahead with two late goals in the second.

The scenario for the third period featured overwhelming offense against impenetrable goaltending. (We outshot Philly, 15-5, in the third period.)

For more than eleven and a half minutes Hextall gave us nothing but grief. Then, Glennie did what he does so well, combining speed, intricate skating and a deft shot for the goal.

The play began with Randy Gregg's pass that sent Glennie winging. He dipsy-doodled past Dave Poulin and Doug Crossman before slipping the puck past Hextall. That goal sent us into overtime.

Gretz demonstrated why he is The Great One on the winner. He orchestrated the rush into the Flyers zone and could have shot or passed once inside the blue line. Then he detected Paul moving up and sent him the puck. Paul could have shot as well but he noticed Jari wide open 15 feet out from Hextall. The pass was perfect and so was Jari's shot, in at 6:50.

The following is a part of what I wrote about the game in my *Sun* column the following morning:

> If 40 hockey players proved anything last night, it's that the fastest game in the world can also be the greatest game in the world.
>
> People keep asking me what I expect from the Philadelphia Flyers. Well, I expect exactly what we've seen during the first two games — outstanding hockey in every facet of the game. After all, these aren't the *Broad Street Bullies* of the bad old days.
>
> This series features hard-hitting, tight-checking, up-and-down hockey, hockey the way it's supposed to be played. And, I'd like to think Game 2 made up, at least in part, for what happened during the pre-game warmup for Game 6 of the Wales final. It doesn't erase it, but it certainly puts it on the back burner.
>
> The Flyers have already paid the price when it comes to foolishness. They know they're not going to intimidate us and we know we're not going to run them out of the rink. I don't think either team even wants to try.
>
> Playing last night made me realize just how much we missed out on last year. The fans were really into it. They were on a different wavelength.
>
> More than anything, this is fun.
>
> It's one classy organization against another classy organization for all the marbles.

If we thought the series was over, a second look at the headline on another *Sun* story might have altered our thinking: FLYERS HAVE JUST BEGUN TO FIGHT! We would soon get a trench warfare feel for that in Game Three but first there was time for a brief respite from the battle. The NHL throws a Stanley Cup luncheon in the midst of the finals and this time was no different.

Both teams get together along with a bunch of other hockey people and the talk is rich with anecdotes. Slats was in fine form on this day, telling stories about his playing days in the NHL.

He told one about the time he played for the Rangers and was sitting on the bench, as he did for much of his NHL career. Coach Emile Francis finally ran over and called his name. Glen began to leap over the bench but was stopped in mid-air by Francis who was shouting, "No, no!"

Slats sat back down and was told to go to the trainer's room to sharpen teammate Jean Ratelle's skates. "I guess," said Slats, "I'm the only player who's ever gone from the bench to sharpen skates then got back in the game."

Francis then laughed about the day Madison Square Garden officials decided to have a huge safe installed so that the Rangers could store valuables during the game. The security force wanted a small number of people to know the combination and Francis begged off. "I didn't want to know and told them so," said Francis. "Then I walk into the room [where the safe was located] and there's Slats on his knees in front of the safe. All of a sudden the door pops open. So I told them to take their $25,000 safe back."

Meanwhile, the Flyers were taking the series back. Not right away, mind you, but in an exceptionally gutsy manner. With the game almost half over, we had built up a 3-0 lead and seemed capable of pouring it on but this business about Philly never quitting was for real. They came back with two late in the second, tied it in the third and then went ahead to stay on Brad McCrimmon's goal. Some wise guy put it well after our 5-3 defeat; "The Oilers seem to have difficulty coming from ahead!"

After Game Four we were feeling pretty good about ourselves again, especially me. Jari gave us a 1-0 lead at 5:53 but late in the period we were hit with a penalty. With Mark in the box, Gretz and I broke in on Crossman and Propp. Gretz slowed on the right wing side, drawing the two Flyers to him. Then, he slipped me a pass and I backhanded the puck inside the right post. It was the winning goal as we breezed ahead 4-1 and had visions of the Cup as we returned to Edmonton for the (hoped-for) clincher.

Everybody in Edmonton thought the Fat Lady had sung already. The mayor announced plans for a victory parade after

Game Five and champagne was shipped to Northlands. But nobody told the Flyers to lie down and be gracious about it. "All we can do now," said their captain Dave Poulin, "is break the series down and take it piece by piece."

We had the first two pieces — goals by Jari Kurri and Marty McSorley. Marty's goal would have crushed most teams but the Flyers showed us something, namely, that they had exceptional recuperative powers. They got one late in the first and after Marty put us ahead by two early in the second — this really should have killed them — they came back again, scored twice and left us dazed and terribly impressed after two. Next thing we knew Tocchet had banged in a Propp pass, Hextall stiffened and the champagne went unopened. Our feelings were not soothed by a headline in my own paper before we embarked for Philadelphia.

THE OILERS CHOKED.

Returning to The Spectrum was the last thing any of us wanted to do but the Flyers left us with no other choice. Game Six would be the toughest of the set. The best clue was the look on their faces. We had let them off the hook and now they were beginning to believe that they could beat us. Hextall was making a good case for that point.

He had given us cause for revenge, having smashed his stick against Nilsson's leg late in Game Four, but we shouldn't have needed any such prodding. The Flyers got all the prodding they needed from The Spectrum fans. Normally intense, Flyers fans were loud beyond the thinking level during Game Six. For someone on the ice in an enemy uniform, it was like playing against two teams — Philadelphia and the fans.

To neutral newspapermen — and even some Edmonton chaps — the series was one of the all-time winners. Terry Jones said it ranked with the best in more than two decades. Surely it would if it went seven games but we were determined to end it on Broad Street. We had given them a little sniff and now it was time to take it away.

No such luck, despite my heroics. Just after five minutes of the first Gretz and I were out on a penalty-killing mission. Wayne got the puck and I sped toward Hextall. Propp checked me but not soon enough and we got that important first goal. Except with Philly you need that important fourth goal as well. Kevin McClelland got another for us late in the first and the fans were momentarily taken out of the game.

Lindsay Carson got Philly on the board in the second and we got nothing. No sweat; we still had a goal lead. It held up until 13.01. With Glennie in the box for high-sticking, Propp tied the score and the place went positively mad.

Experts talk about the ebb and flow of a hockey game but it is impossible to anticipate some changes in momentum. Certainly the Flyers, in a losing situation, managed to completely turn the tide of that game with a vengeance. It was like getting hit with a lightning bolt; there was absolutely nothing we could do to prevent it, nor the winning goal by J.J. Daigneault at 14.28. I would have liked to have seen a seismograph in The Spectrum right after the red light flashed.

The trip home was long in more ways than one. Skeptics said we'd lose. One of them was Jacques Demers, who told the press that he had predicted Philly in seven games all along. Personally, I couldn't wait to get at them again. Mark said, "We've never been so up and so positive."

As a kid, growing up in Lachute, I would fantasize about playing in a seventh game of the Stanley Cup finals. Now it was happening and I experienced a childhood sensation, that of the Kevin Lowe who couldn't stay in bed on Christmas morning in anticipation of the tree, the gifts, the glorious day.

Now it was here. Northlands was overflowing and, this time, just about everyone was on our side. "We have to believe in ourselves," said Slats, "and play a confident relaxed game."

Which is just what we did.

Philly's early goal did not faze us in the least. With the game still young, Glennie, Nilsson and Mark played ping-pong with the puck with Mark backhanding the last excellent pass from Kent into the right corner. Even the sensational Hextall couldn't be all over the net at once and had to concede that perfect goal.

Hextall wasn't conceding much else. He stood on his head in the second until we beat Philly at their own game. Tikkanen won a battle in the corner against Crossman and got the puck to Gretz. He saw Jari 25 feet off to the left and fed Kurri. He beat Hextall before he could move. Edmonton, 2-1 after two.

In the third period we smothered them. Period. They had two shots over 20 minutes and we forced them into mistake after mistake — but we couldn't fatten the lead. That is, not until 17:36 when Glennie took a Charlie Huddy pass and bombed a slapshot that went right through Hextall's pads. The valiant goalie could hardly get up but everyone else in North-lands was on his or her feet. We had squeezed the last breath out of the Flyers. We knew it. They knew it and, certainly, the fans knew it.

There would be no more false alarms with the champagne. We had earned our third drink from the Stanley Cup. Even Mike Keenan admitted that when he said, "The Oilers played a fabulous game."

30

The Paul Coffey-Andy Moog Saga

So many things about our third Stanley Cup celebration were similar to the first two. The champagne was still bubbly. The main cast of characters — Gretz, Mess, Glennie, Grant — remained the same and the general staff, headed by Slats and Muck, was still in place.

But there *was* a difference. To the superficial viewer it would go unnoticed amid the backslapping and Cup-sipping, but it was there and it manifested itself around Paul Coffey. At a time when everyone else was enjoying the moment, Paul was making it abundantly clear that he was not the happiest Oiler.

This was not a slip of the tongue between Cup and lip, either. On network television and in conversations with reporters, Paul wondered whether he had played his final game as an Oiler. The problem, in his eyes, was Slats, and a summer of rest and relaxation would not change his tune.

In September *The Hockey News* would print a verbatim transcript of an interview with Paul which had taken place during Team Canada's training camp. Referring to Glen, Paul said, "A lot of things were said that hurt me personally."

Paul also freely discussed the possibility of being traded: "If they [the Oilers] don't want me to play hockey anymore, that's fine."

This was merely the tip of the iceberg. As summer turned to fall the Coffey-Sather relationship would grow even colder. Little did any of us know how prophetic Paul had been when he wondered whether he'd ever play in an Edmonton jersey again.

But before all of the holdouts and question marks which would arise in the 1987-88 season neared, there was first the summer of 1987 and the Canada Cup — or in my case, the non-Canada Cup.

Peter Pocklington had offered the team a trip to Hawaii if we won the Cup, and quite a few of us took him up on the offer. These post-playoff gifts, or incentives, always came up first at the traditional Oilers "Stanley Cup Playoff Dinner" which Pocklington hosts on the eve of the playoffs.

The players had begun a tradition, from the occasion of our first pre-playoff dinner, of needling Pocklington for these little — and sometimes not so little — added fillips. One year it would be a complete set of golf clubs, the next a request for a special, extra big diamond in the Stanley Cup rings if we won. Well, in 1987 it was a trip to Hawaii.

I had traveled quite a bit over the summers with Mark, Wayne and Glenny; but for the first time I spent some vacation time with — in addition to Gretz, Mess and Glennie — Esa Tikkanen, Craig MacTavish and Davey Hunter, which was fun and different. But while we were cavorting in the islands, I remember thinking to myself one day, "Geez, it's practically time to start working out again," and feeling down about it for just a moment. Normally I love working out, but we had played a lot of hockey that year — 100 games with the playoffs just finished — and the Canada Cup would be coming up in no time. I was suddenly conscious of how tired I was, and for the first time ever post-season, I was really hurting. All the way back in November I had taken a hit from Brent Sutter in a game against the Islanders. What felt at first like a groin pull just continued and continued to bother me, ultimately through the rest of the season. I only missed three games over the season, but it turned out that the injury was more threatening than we had originally supposed.

Turns out I had *osteitis pubis*, which, simply put, means an inflamed pubic bone. It's common among pregnant women and runners! And it is only treatable with anti-inflammatory drugs and *rest*. I couldn't rest during the season, so I took the anti-inflammatories and played.

Come summer I was warned that osteitis pubis can stick around for as long as two or even three years, and that the only thing which would probably calm and eventually cure the inflammation was rest. My doctor strongly advised against playing in the Canada Cup, but said that I could finally resume riding my stationary bike, which had been forbidden since the injury was diagnosed. So I dragged that stationary bike around with me all summer — home to Lachute to see mom and the family and back to Edmonton for my charity golf tournament. All that while I held off deciding about the Canada Cup, hoping that the tell-tale discomfort would go away. But it didn't, and finally, just before the time to report to Canada Cup training camp, I told them I wouldn't be able to make it. I felt bad, because I enjoyed playing the Canada Cup series, but hoped that the additional six weeks' rest would calm the inflammation down.

And it did. By the time I reported to the Oilers' training camp, I was back in shape and, best of all, the pubitis had disappeared!

I had been active in other ways during the summer, though. I negotiated, with a little help from my financial adviser Mark Hall (former Oilers Director of Marketing and nephew of Hall of Fame goaltender Glenn Hall), a new contract with Edmonton. I did it a little differently than the guys who would be hold-outs in just a few short weeks.

There's no doubt in my mind that, by the time we won the third Cup in 1987, the Oilers had to be one of the most underpaid clubs in the NHL. Considering what we had accomplished, and comparing our salaries to the rumors of what others were being paid, there was no question of it.

Hockey is the only major sport today in which salaries are not made public. Up to this point I'd always believed that was right, but for the first time I realized how handy a negotiating tool public knowledge of salaries could be: it would remove the inevitable cloud of rumor and innuendo and allow you to make a direct comparison between yourself and similar players. Plus, I'm sure the uncertainty of not knowing what was true and what was apocryphal concerning other players' salaries only made the situation tougher and more complicated for the guys who would hold out later on.

In my case, I evaluated the potential in Edmonton — playing for the team, the off-ice opportunities which existed such as endorsements and charities, the small-town atmosphere and fraternity-like aura, and the business ventures. I was the first

Oiler drafted and I also scored the first NHL goal for the team. Slats had already made it clear to me that if at all possible, management wanted me to play out my career there. Plus, if I stayed in Edmonton, I knew there was a good chance of being with a Stanley Cup-winning team for a couple of more years.

Knowing all of this enabled me to deal realistically with the enticements — the potential American dollars if I went instead to a team in the States (where it would also cost me a hell of a lot more to live) or holding out for really, *really* gigantic bucks. But what's another $50,000 or $100,000 a year, if your sanity's involved, or if you help to destroy a winning tradition that is being carefully nurtured.

There is a sign in the dressing room of the Canadiens that mentions passing on the torch. We don't have a sign in our room, but we have this big metal door leading into the coach's room. There is a sticker on that door for each year we've made the playoffs — one year it was an "I Love The Oilers" (with a heart for the word "love") sticker. And for every year we've won the Cup, there's a tiny Stanley Cup sticker placed on the right-hand end of the "annual" sticker. That door is now half-way filled with those stickers, and that's the door the players all bang on to signal that they're ready to start the period. I bet that door ends up in the Hall of Fame some day, after all those wins.

I have always enjoyed being a part of that evolving tradition and although I've thought once or twice about playing one day for the Canadiens (another winning tradition) and of being close to my childhood home (Lachute is only about a 40-minute drive from Montreal), I quite simply felt that Slats and company made me a perfectly fair offer, and we inked the deal early in the summer. I haven't a shred of regret, either, despite all the hold-outs which were about to take place.

The groundwork had actually been laid during the 1986-87 season. There was more grumbling and note-taking among the guys on the team that season than I ever remember. We kept it quite secret, though. Slats might have had some idea, but I don't think anyone — particularly the media — had any idea of how rife the discussions were. All of the vets now had a good idea of how discrepant the salaries were and how meager the gratuities were for the superstars. But everyone also realized that the goal was to win the Cup, to rebound positively from 1986, and that required pulling together and not letting management or the youngsters and newcomers feel that there was division on the team.

But many of us were aware that — if and when we won the Cup — there were going to be several contracts re-negotiated. Still, I'm certain that few of the guys actually made up their minds for sure until the Canada Cup series. Canada Cup 1987 proved that not only were the Oilers players the best in the NHL, they were unquestionably among the best in the world. That clinched it.

As Canada Cup ended, the rumbling began in earnest. While Paul Coffey was the only one who had vocalized the possibility of holding out in the late spring, when fall and training camp came, there were actually a small horde of hold-outs.

One unhappy chap was goalie Andy Moog. Our oldest goalie in length of service, Moog had played out his option with the Oilers, but he could not be signed by another NHL team without the Oilers being compensated. Andy and Slats would go to war and, like Paul, the goalie would never play for Edmonton again.

One by one, the storm clouds gathered. Kent Nilsson had resisted all bids for him to return to the club for 1987-88 and instead ended up in Europe, this time in Italy instead of his native Sweden. Reijo Ruotsalainen also opted to leave the NHL and the Oilers, while veteran Randy Gregg finally chose the Canadian Olympic team. Even Glennie Anderson held out briefly, although he was back by late September. With the end of the Canada Cup, Mess disappeared on a jaunt to West Germany, leaving no phone number and no doubt causing Slats to begin tearing out his hair. Free agents Mike Krushelnyski and Moe Lemay refused to report to training camp, and finally, Paul stuck to his initial prediction and was nowhere to be seen. It began to look as though "that old gang of mine" was really breaking up.

"I'm not going to camp," Paul asserted immediately after Canada Cup. "I'm not going to be there until this thing is worked out — and we're a long way apart."

In Paul's corner was his agent Gus Badali, a veteran players' rep who over the years has handled Gretz, Dale Hawerchuk and innumerable other NHL people. Before very long Gus and Slats would become as friendly as Punch and Judy.

Meanwhile training camp was under way, and I was finally

without the debilitating effects of the pubic bone problem. The hold-outs had created a situation where guys who previously didn't get that much ice time were now working out like gang-busters because there were so many absentees from the regular lineup. So, as usual, there was a positive side to the situation.

Then we started our exhibition season, and it was a crusher. Here we've barely recovered from playing 100 games (and some of the guys had just left Team Canada) and have potentially another 100 to look forward to, and we have to play 11 exhibition games in rapid succession. Of course, the Oilers are now in great demand and — all in the cause of helping the league — we end up going to Timbuctu and back. After three home games in exhibition, we played six road games in eight nights, hitting such exotic hockey locales as Indianapolis, Houston and Dallas along the way.

Wayne had wanted to get a decent respite after Team Canada, but ended up joining us in Indianapolis. After all, that's where he had begun his professional career. Gretz felt he owed it to the Indianapolis fans, and besides, the exhibition games raised money for the league and the fans wanted to see The Great One. While we were stumping the continent in exhibition, Slats was on the phone constantly, trying to locate Mess as well as talking fast and furiously with Gus Badali in Toronto. Finally, in the midst of all this, Andy Moog called a press conference in Edmonton to announce that he would join the Canadian Olympic team. Slats was furious, feeling that the team should at least have been warned of the impending announcement.

Although I honestly didn't blame any of the guys for holding out for more money, I have to admit I have never truly understood Andy's reasoning. Had I been in his place, I'd have been happier to be "Goalie 1A" as Slats called him (saying that he had two number one goalies) on a Cup-winning team than be Number One on a losing team. But obviously Andy felt it was more important to chance it somewhere else in the hopes of playing more and being top goalie.

Quite frankly, I had as much confidence when Andy was in the nets as I did when Grant was there, and I think he's a great goaltender. True, Grant handles the puck a little better, but Andy had a kind of cockiness, a confidence, that was an asset at times. And Moog was also the sentimental favorite of the Edmonton fans, partly because of certain unfortunate remarks

Fuhr had made about the hometown crowd when he was in the midst of his "sophomore slump." But obviously Andy needed a new challenge, and ultimately he would get it.

Then, when the season opened at home against Detroit on October 9, 1987, everything came together. Krushelnyski came back, although he didn't play the first game; Lemay returned but was sent to the minors, and Mess suddenly showed up out of the blue, playing the first game cold! In fact, as we started regular play, the only major figure we were missing was Paul (Moog, too, but with Grant in the nets, Andy's absence wasn't felt yet).

Throughout all of Paul's hold-out, I never once talked with him about it in detail, but I know that the situation was tough on Wayne. Because he and Coff had been so close, so compatible on the ice, and because he knew Badali, Wayne sort of got stuck in the middle of the negotiations. I got a running account from Gretz: "Well, I talked to Slats" . . . "I talked to Coff today — he seems to be getting there" . . . "They're not close at all; geez, I don't think he's coming back." The emotions fluctuated from day to day and it was obvious that it wore on Gretz to be in the middle of it.

For Paul it must have been awful. Despite the fact that I have a special understanding about the media because of the column I do, I think that their attitude that Coff was being selfish and glory-seeking was unfair and untrue. Paul's a great competitor and sitting it out had to bother him terribly. Here he was skating with a Junior B team in Ontario, playing with kids who earn $19 a week and trying to stay in shape.

Then the mud-slinging began in earnest, with Pocklington reportedly questioning Paul's courage and Coff saying that after management's remarks there was no way he could ever come back. The situation degenerated into one in which there was no way anybody could back down or come to some amicable compromise. And somehow in the middle of all the name-calling and threatening, the media decided that Badali had caused it all.

Although there was endless discussion in print and on TV about what sort of team the Oilers would be without Paul Coffey, the fact was that the season had started and this was the team that was. It was a lot different than if we had begun the season with Paul and then he got traded. But we had been through training camp without him, and the defense had adapted to the current personnel: the team which began the season was a "given."

Of course, realistically, our power play suffered a bit over the season because Paul had that ability to bring the puck out of our zone and he had such a good shot from the point. But it was Wayne and Jari who had to make the biggest adjustment, because they played with Coff so much. Paul could always spot Wayne up high and give him that good outlet pass that would break Wayne out.

But from a coaching point of view it was easier. Our concept of team discipline had been well implanted in the Philly playoff series and, truth be told, it was easier to implement the discipline without Paul and his sometimes overly creative offensive talents. When I speak of the discipline, I'm not thinking about 20 guys but about the five players on the ice at any given moment: playing their positions, not missing their assignments and reacting according to how the coaches wanted them to play.

Still, there was a 100-point void on the team, and it was taking time for Mess and Krushelnyski to get back into the game. Without consciously discussing it, the defense knew that it would come under scrutiny in Paul's absence. But, rather than taking a negative attitude or defensive posture, it proved to be the chance for players like Steve Smith to play a lot and show his stuff; for Charlie Huddy — one of the most underrated talents in the league as far as I'm concerned — to prove that Paul Coffey hadn't created him (Charlie had been Coff's defensive partner for some time); and for me it was a chance to become slightly more involved in the offensive aspect of the game.

I think I spent more time up ice in the 1987-88 season than I had in all of my previous eight campaigns. Every time I would do something uncharacteristicly offense-oriented, it seemed to be mind-boggling to everyone but me! After all, I had been a forward briefly as a kid, and I had always felt that I had the potential to get more involved in offense. But when there are snipers and offensive defensemen on a team, you do what you have to, and up to this season my role had been to stay at home and play a defensive game.

Then in November it happened. Paul, long-time Oiler Davey Hunter and Wayne Van Dorp were traded — to Pittsburgh, for 20-year-old Craig Simpson, 18-year-old Chris Joseph, Moe Mantha and Davey Hannan. It was touted as the "trade of the decade" by some, and, of course, the name mentioned most frequently was that of Paul Coffey.

At first the judgment was that Pittsburgh had come out ahead in the deal by acquiring Paul. But by the season's end the odds were all on our side, as the Pens would once again be out of the playoffs, while we had acquired a huge dollop of youth. Best of all, Craig Simpson had blossomed into a 50-plus goal scorer.

It would be almost two full months before the Oilers would play the Penguins again, and we would face Paul Coffey in a strange uniform. In the meantime, more contract furor arose, as Slats and Grant Fuhr's agent Rich Winter would virtually come to blows.

While it was true that many of the Oilers had been underpaid compared to other NHL-ers, Grant Fuhr may have been one of the most grossly underpaid stars in the whole shooting match. Since player salaries are basically secret, "guesstimates" had been flying all over the place: Grant was only making about $110,000 a year on his current contract which had three years left to run . . . No, it was more like $200,000. No matter what the numbers were, everyone finally conceded that Grant's salary was considerably smaller than nearly any other top-ranked NHL goalie, and Slats had been negotiating with Winter the whole time he was also trying to deal with Paul.

Shortly after Coff was traded Slats and Winter became involved in a name-calling shoving match: "He called me a liar," said Slats. "It was the silliest thing I've ever seen."

Winter later tried to make light of the episode; "During discussions over contracts things get heated . . . I'm not one to threaten anybody."

While we tried to play hockey, the public noise over the contract dispute went from silly to crazy. Vancouver writer Tony Gallagher alluded to Glen as "Uncle Tom," and Slats in turn threatened to sue Gallagher, calling his remark racist. Luckily for all of us Grant refused to hold out during the negotiations, and finally Slats, Winter and Grant announced the signing of a new, reportedly six-year contract at a salary that everybody agreed was satisfactory. One shudders to think what would have happened to the team had Fuhr sat out the season, since the contract wasn't announced until the last six weeks of the campaign. In fact the hullabaloo over Grant's contract negotiations caused no disruption to the team, other than that the media were constantly asking us questions about it. He had the wholehearted support of the fans and the press, and there was much less noise about the fact that he was in the middle of an already existing contract than there had been for Mess and Paul.

At virtually the same time that Slats and Winter were shoving and throwing verbal abuse, Wayne Gretzky finally succumbed to injury. On December 30, with less than two minutes remaining in a 6-0 trouncing we gave the Flyers, Wayne sprained a knee. It was ironic that he sustained the injury while scoring his 573rd career goal, which tied him with Mike Bossy. It was doubly ironic that after missing a month of play, Wayne came back and injured an eye nine games later while trying to outdo Gordie Howe's career assist mark.

While Wayne was out with his injury, the team met Paul Coffey as a Penguin for the first time. This had to be one of the biggest games in the history of the franchise. It was as big as if Wayne and Mess had come back playing against us.

The game took place in Pittsburgh and Gretz and Mario Lemieux were now neck and neck in the scoring race, so the whole team wanted to have a good game for Wayne. It was a good chance for Mess, too, to go head to head with Mario. It was even the Oilers defense versus Paul Coffey. The game was being televised back home and the press was out in full force. Let's face it, it was a big deal — not the end of the world, but a nice little challenge.

Ironically, as we skated around before the game, I thought I spotted Paul's mom, Betty, in the crowd. As I circled a second time I realized that it wasn't Betty, but it reminded me of the fact that probably the two people most affected by the infamous Paul Coffey trade had been his mom and mine. Over the past few seasons they had gotten quite close. My mom was a widow and Paul's mom was alone a lot because of her husband's work, so the two had taken to attending games together and staying in close touch when they weren't visiting Edmonton. In fact mom had told me that right after the trade, Betty had called her, saying, "Does this mean we can't be friends anymore?" Of course, mom had replied, "We'll always be friends, no matter where the boys play."

This memory prodded me into recalling an uncanny talent Paul had possessed: he could *always* instantly spot anyone and everyone he knew in a crowd. This wasn't just because he knew where their seats were, but because he somehow could just see them. Whereas I would be concentrating so hard on the game to come that I could barely see anyone in the stands, not even my mother, Paul would skate over to me and say, "Well, I see Betty and Jessie over there," and sure enough, he'd point them out.

While it was still a shock to see Paul in a Penguins jersey, I was prepared for it, since I had seen him for the first time since the trade at the morning skate. Most of us also shook hands with Davey Hunter before the game started. But then it was down to business when the puck dropped. Mario was playing well, Paul and Mess were playing well. Then the guy who stole the limelight from the whole shebang turned out to be Davey Hannan, as he scored three goals in the third period! How hilarious. Ultimately we won the game, although Paul and Mario played well, and I felt that it was a kind of statement the team made: we were just fine without Paul Coffey.

After the game the team went out together and Paul and Davey Hunter dropped by. We picked up immediately as though they had never been gone, and I was delighted to hear that they were both happy. Paul felt he was making a big contribution to the team and Davey was happy too, because he had begun to see a lot less ice time in Edmonton, while Pittsburgh had acquired a good, experienced player.

Almost a month later Paul made his first appearance at the Northlands Coliseum in a Pittsburgh jersey. The press had been hyping the event for several days, and since we were in a home stand, they had tried to question a lot of the players as to how they thought the fans would react to Paul's return. Most of us were noncommittal, but I think it was Craig MacTavish who finally predicted that the crowd would boo him.

Well, when Paul's name was first announced, the fans gave him a cheer, but it wasn't long into the match before Craig's prediction came true, and sure enough, for the rest of the game he was roundly booed every time he'd touch the puck. But the biggest shocker of the night was that the predicted Gretzky-Lemieux confrontation never took place.

Mario had just overtaken Wayne in the scoring race, so everyone expected the game to be a shootout since Gretz had missed the game in Pittsburgh. But in the first period Mario got a puck in the eye and left the game and incredibly Wayne suffered his eye injury in the same game and in the same period, too. At first they thought that Dan Frawley of Pittsburgh had shoved his stick in Wayne's eye, but it turned out that it was Jari's stick which inadvertently inflicted Wayne's second injury. What a night! Well, we did win the game, nevertheless.

As it turned out, the upheavals weren't over, either — not by a long shot. The Olympics ended and veteran defenseman Randy Gregg was signed on with the team again — which was super as far as I was concerned. But it also meant that Andy Moog was through with his Olympic stint and Edmonton still had the right to compensation if another team wanted to sign him.

As the traditional March trade deadline rolled around, Slats performed another of his astounding trade coups. Andy Moog went to the Boston Bruins — where ironically he would have to settle for "Goalie 1A" slot again with hot veteran Reggie Lemelin — for young netminder Bill Ranford and promising left winger Geoff Courtnall. Once again we had new bodies to work into the club.

For the first time since 1981 Wayne did not win the scoring championship, as Mario Lemieux took advantage of Gretz's absence to win the Art Ross Trophy for the first time. And unquestionably Gretz's linemates had to adapt, as did the power play. But the positive aspect of it all was that Wayne got a good month's rest, which he needed; and it gave Mess the opportunity to really be the leader and scorer that he is.

Also for the first time since 1981, the Oilers did not finish in first place. Instead, while we tried to play disciplined hockey amidst all of this craziness, a blistering Calgary club nabbed the first place slot in the Smythe Division while we came second, and we came in third in the league overall, behind the Flames and Montreal. Here we were, the Stanley Cup defending champs, but all of a sudden there was a lot of talk about Calgary trouncing us and a Calgary-Montreal Stanley Cup final.

That was annoying — and it hurt. But I would soon hurt even more.

31

The Second-Place Oilers Are Hurting, Especially Me!

We were at home against Montreal on March 9 — almost a month before the playoffs would start. It was the third period when I went to hold Mike McPhee from forechecking my partner. I put my left hand in his stomach and twisted it kind of strangely. I knew instantly that I had done something wrong, but when you're in the middle of an intense game, you're so keyed up that you're almost numb. I thought that I had stretched tendons or something, and didn't find out until the next morning that a small bone at the base of my thumb, near the wrist, was actually broken.

The doctor told me that I might be able to play again in about three weeks as long as I had some protection on the arm, and I thought he was talking about an Ace bandage or something! But naturally, he was talking about a cast.

The cast that was put on was a bit of a high-tech marvel. In the first place it wasn't made of the old plaster wrappings you think of when you think "cast." Instead, it was made of a lightweight substance — almost like fiberglass or some sort of plastic. It was also structured so that each day my arm was hooked up to an EBS (electronic bone stimulation) machine which promoted rapid healing. This machine is more advanced than the ultra sound which has been used for years to increase circulation and decrease inflammation in injuries. I would "plug" myself in each day!

For the first few days after the injury I simply took off from

289

my normal practice routine and rode my trusty stationary bike. I owed it to myself and the team to stay in shape — after all, if there was a chance I could play, I didn't want to make a fool of myself and be a detriment in the playoffs. I would never opt to be injured as a means of getting time off, but I had to look at this situation positively, so I viewed it as a chance to get lots of rest and prepare for the playoffs.

Then, when I finally began practicing with the cast on, it didn't feel too bad. I wasn't worried about throwing a check, or even taking one — the cast would actually protect me. But I could tell that I would be limited in handling the puck, limited in anything I tried to do with my hands. So I needed an edge. I would have to get to the corner a little faster and be a little stronger, rely on my legs a bit more. I needed to have the puck in my possession a lot less and would have to get rid of it a lot faster. My passing would be off, my wrist shot from that side would be practically nil and I wouldn't flip the puck 100 percent. That may sound like I wasn't going to be able to contribute much, but what it really meant was that I had to be absolutely sure I was in proper position at all times and ready to do my job. I just wouldn't put any pressure on myself to score, as I had in the 1987 play-offs. I would just stick to a conservative defensive strategy.

I was determined to play before the season ended — somehow that was really important if I were to play in the playoffs — and I made it into the last game of the season, against Los Angeles. The joke was that everybody thought I would have no trouble playing with the cast because I scored a goal that night! The truth was that Mess scored the goal for me. He passed the puck so hard onto my stick that it just ricocheted into the net, and I had virtually nothing to do with it except that my stick was in place.

As far as the team and the pending playoffs were concerned, however, preparation had actually begun weeks before the first game, which would be against the Winnipeg Jets this year. One of the luxuries of being a winning team in the regular season is knowing that you will be in the playoffs and being aware from experience that you should start building that playoff frame of mind in the last weeks of the regular season. This happens in little ways; the guys simply start verbally revving each other up — "It's time to start putting everything together" ... "Gotta' start getting your rest, guys" ... "Let's see more commitment."

As soon as the regular season is over, the team figuratively wipes its forehead and says, "Well, that's all over . . . thank goodness." Then there are a few days of cramming, as though you were studying for your finals in school. The practices pick up in intensity and focus, but most of all this is where the use of videos comes in.

The Oilers don't really use video that much during the regular season. The fact is, it's practically useless then. If you're only meeting a team three times a season, watching videos of its "special teams", for instance, is meaningless. Maybe they were missing their best point man, perhaps they were at the end of a long road trip — what you see on the tape of one game really tells you nothing more than what the team did that night.

But once the playoffs start, you're going to see two teams play each other several times, and general trends or game plans become much more apparent. This is where video tape can be useful.

John Muckler and Teddy Green are the masters with the video tape. They'll point out aspects of a team's game plan or consistencies in their special-team strategies and then we'll discuss ways of adapting. That's the key: rather than hanging on to one set game plan, like a bully clinging to a club, Muck and Greenie will work on showing us how to adapt, to change. They stress a club's strengths and weaknesses: it might be for one series they'll say, "Defensemen, in this series you have to move the puck quickly," whereas in the previous series it was, "We want you to hang back and force their forwards to you . . . with good puck control."

We don't pay too much attention to statistics per se. The media will put so much emphasis on a team's power play, for instance. In fact there may only be a difference of 10 goals between team one and team 13 over an 80-game season — which is virtually insignificant. There are also important elements which are *not* factored in to the special team stats. The time at which a power play occurs and the score at the time of the power play can have an enormous effect on whether that power play succeeds, but nowhere are those elements part of the standings. If we're winning 8-1 at home and there are three minutes left in the game and we get a power play, odds are that we won't score. If we should get a penalty against us at that moment, we might well be scored upon, because we have this huge lead and the players will say,

"We have a big lead and only three minutes left, let's go out there and nobody get hurt." It's not that we don't work, but simply that we have space to conserve energy for another time.

As for home-road numbers, they are highly overrated as a factor in the playoffs. In fact, they can work against a team. If you start a series on the road and win one out of two, there's a good chance that the team will loosen up as it goes home, feeling confident that the home crowd and familiar ice will help win the game.

We had a nucleus of veterans on the club who had experienced all of these factors and won three Cups by learning from those experiences. *Could* this combination of experience, talent and fresh faces "put it all together?" Yes. But *would* the team coalesce to win it all again? I hoped so.

For the first time in several years, I sensed that there was more of a question mark heading into the playoffs than there had been for some time. Maybe it was my own doubts about my ability to perform playoff-caliber hockey because of the wrist that filtered off onto my beliefs about the club. Normally I'm a very confident person — I'm aware of my capabilities and my shortcomings and have learned to live with them, but the wrist could definitely throw a bit of a monkey-wrench into the works.

Because Wayne had lost the scoring race for the first time in years and because the team placed out of first for the first time in years, there were other questions being publicly posed. Certainly our somewhat lackluster performance late in the season (the Rangers literally blew us away once in March, and we lost one to our former nemesis, the Islanders, among several less-than-stellar performances) added to the air of uncertainty.

As I had mentioned, the team had a pre-playoff dinner sponsored by Peter Pocklington at which we would negotiate for extra incentives — gifts we would receive if we won the Cup. The results of our 1987 "gifts" backfired on us in 1988, in a way which disturbed the team.

In early March, just before tax preparation time, the players who had been on the 1987 club received T-4 tax forms for the golf clubs and Hawaii trip we had been awarded. We were going to have to pay taxes on our rewards! We received the forms on a game day, and the guys were quite upset. But Wayne, Mark and I decided that this was not the time to broach the subject, and we agreed to keep silent. Problem was, we lost that game. Still we decided not to bring up the T-4 forms with management, and sure enough, we lost the next game, too.

It would be embarrassing to think that a club with this maturity and experience could lose because of some petty tax charges, but the fact was that we were losing games. Our trainer got wind of the team's disgruntlement and must have whispered something in Slats' ear, because the next day Glen came to us and said, "Look, if that's what's bothering you, forget it. We'll take care of it, somehow." He also tried to explain that no matter how they were categorized, sooner or later gifts were taxable items, but not to worry.

The result of the T-4 fiasco, however, was that when the 1988 pre-playoff dinner with Pocklington came to pass, the team decided en masse not to ask for any Cup-winning extra incentives. We had decided to make a statement of sorts: the rewards weren't worth it, if we had to pay penalties on them. But our silence shook Pocklington up so badly that the next day Slats approached several of us and said, "Geez, guys, since you didn't ask for any special gifts, Peter thinks that you don't want to win!" We hastened to reassure Glen that it was in fact the reverse: we were committed to winning for the sake of winning itself; we didn't need to line our pockets with extras. All of this simply added to the air of uncertainty which seemed to surround the 1988 Oilers. Once again we would have to prove ourselves.

The media was picking up on this uncertainty, too. They were questioning everything, and some of it was ridiculous. Wayne had recently announced his engagement to Janet Jones, a talented dancer/athlete and budding starlet (she had just appeared in "Police Academy Five"). Suddenly the media began predicting that Wayne's performance would deteriorate, even suggesting that he had lost the scoring race because of his infatuation with Janet (had they forgotten his injuries and missing 16 games?). This guy has been super-motivated for more than eight years — the best of his time and perhaps the best ever — and they think that a relationship would obstruct Wayne's desire to succeed? On the contrary, Janet has had a positive impact on Wayne's life — the impending marriage had given him another reason to want to play well and has enhanced his feelings of security and stability.

So on the eve of our series with Winnipeg, the local press

was saying things like "We hope you win, but . . ." instead of predicting that the Oilers would be a shoo-in for the 1988 Cup. The only problem was that, while they were posing the possibility of our losing the Cup (largely because they were already predicting our demise at the hands of the first-place Calgary Flames), they were already giving us the series against the Jets.

This is always a mistake — one which we had learned to avoid several times. Never, never award a series to one team before the fact, because all it does is give the projected loser fuel and incentive to win. True, at that moment, Winnipeg had never won an NHL play-off game against us, but rubbing that fact into their collective noses could simply boost the club's morale into that dangerous "there's-a-first-time-for-every-thing" mode.

As for me, aside from the constant questions concerning my cast and the state of my arm, the only other question the media wanted answered was "Who would you rather have faced in the first round . . . Winnipeg, Los Angeles or Vancouver?" The answer, although I wasn't going to say so the media, was "none of the above!"

I would rather not have met a divisional rival first at all, because no matter how the rest of the world perceives a division, the reality is that, because of rivalries and familiarity, the intra-divisional games are the toughest. The series against Winnipeg would be tough regardless of past history or present personnel — just because we were divisional rivals.

In fact, for some time the rivalry between Winnipeg and Edmonton was more intense than the warring which would develop between Calgary and the Oilers, because the Jets and Edmonton had a "thing" going on in the WHA, before ever joining the NHL. Add to that the fact that Winnipeg would be *driven* up against the wall to win a playoff game — after all the Jets hadn't won a playoff game from us yet — and you knew the series would be rough.

"WINNIPEG WILL SHOW NO RESPECT TO OILERS . . . WILL PLAY THEM TOUGH" blared the quote from Winnipeg coach Dan Maloney. This was a young and hungry club, and no doubt the coach figured his public bravado — along with the team's gusto, guts and game plan — would throw the Oilers off and win games.

Winnipeg played the series pretty much as we had prepared for and expected, but *harder* than we anticipated. In fact, they played with perhaps more determination than any other team we would face in the playoffs. They had a definite game plan and it was apparent that it was to throw us off our plan.

The Jets were incredibly tenacious and, while it was obvious they were more concerned with getting Wayne, Mess and Jari off their games than with distracting Kevin Lowe, it was also apparent that each and every Jet had an assignment for one individual while on the ice. Even though they lost the first two games at our Northlands Coliseum, Winnipeg was striving to be effective and to ignore past history.

But while we had to work hard to win, what was happening to our team was enormously reassuring. First, the discipline was in full force. One of Winnipeg's tactics was to try and involve us in the little pushing and shoving matches that precede face-offs (I call them "scrums," from rugby) or follow blown whistles — and the guys were ignoring the goads. Secondly, the veterans who had appeared to slump in the regular season were coming to life: Glennie Anderson had three goals and two assists in Game One and Kurri scored the game winner in Game Five. Thirdly, the youngsters were flying: "Simmer" (Craig Simpson) scored the game-winners for Games One and Two. It wasn't so much that Winnipeg was failing as that we were finally "putting it all together."

After winning the first two at home, we moved to Winnipeg Arena, where we were somewhat shocked to find that the games were not sold out. This was really unfortunate: the media had done such a thorough job of reminding everyone that Winnipeg had never won a playoff game against the Oilers that the fans stayed away in fair-sized numbers. This could only affect the Jets more than it would us. Worst of all, the fans missed witnessing a first — the Jets finally beat us in Game Three. It was a thriller, too, as we trailed 3-0 at one point, came back to tie it 3-3, and then lost it (6-4) as Ray Neufeld and Thomas Steen each got a goal and two assists, and their rookie Randy Gilhen scored the game-winner.

A word here is appropriate concerning Dale Hawerchuk, the Jets superstar. I have grown to respect Dale more and more as I have watched him. I used to think that he was simply an offensive talent, but over the years he has acquired that ingredient that takes a player from star to superstar: he has become the quintessential team player. For instance, in the 1987 Canada Cup, Dale realized that he would have to take a back seat to some of the other scorers, but instead of getting all pushed out of shape and pouting, he adapted to a team role. He became a checker and did whatever was necessary to contribute to the welfare of the team. That is stature in a player, and Dale has it now. It's rough on individual stars when a team loses a series because they often have to bear the brunt of the blame for the loss. It's easier, when the team wins, for a "superstar" to remind the press that the triumph should be shared with the other guys; but when the team loses, the star can't very well remind the media that the loss should be shared equally with the other guys, now can he?

Even though the Jets had won the third game, the Winnipeg fans didn't seem to acquire any faith in their team, as Game Four was far from a sell-out (and remember, Winnipeg Arena is not that big to start with), which had to be demoralizing for the Jets players. Even so, they took an early and commanding lead, and by 1:52 of the second period, we were losing 3-0. This was one of those classic playoff games in which your goalie literally keeps you in the game. Grant was outshot 29-15 in the first 40 minutes of play, but he was stupendous. This enabled us to regroup and go into overdrive, which resulted in an Oilers 5, Jets 3, win and we were on our way home just one game away from winning the first series.

A potentially dangerous spot for us. We led the series three games to one and we were at home. The Oilers of the past might well have gotten smug and complacent, but we had learned over the years that giving in to our own worst tendencies was what would cause us to lose hockey games — not the other team!

Believe me, Winnipeg was determined — determined to goad us into reaction and retaliation. We, on the other hand, were even more determined not to respond. The result was that we won the game on power plays — at one point we had four power play goals and opened up a 5-0 lead, on our way to a final score of 6-2.

We had won the first series and would now face the powerhouse Calgary Flames in the Smythe Division finals. But I was now hurting even worse than I had been when the playoffs started.

Late in the first period of Game Five we were in control of the game and had a commanding lead. A Winnipeg player tried to go around Craig Muni and did put the puck by him.

Craig went to play that man and I went into Craig's corner to get the puck. Stupidly, my guard was down — probably because of the lead and the lateness of the period — and suddenly husky Ray Neufeld came out of nowhere and blindsided me.

A lot of people thought at the time that I had re-injured my wrist, but in fact I hit my head against the glass with such an impact that I was out cold for a few seconds. The next thing I knew I was down, then I had the familiar tingling, numb sensation of reviving.

It was a few minutes after recovering, while sitting on the bench, that I realized I had a pain in my side — kind of like a charleyhorse. The period ended soon and after the between-period rest, I thought I should continue the game. We often say, "If you're not in the game, get a hit or give a hit, but rattle yourself to wake up!" I thought maybe the hit would shake me into the game. Well, my head was definitely into it by now, but the body was getting slower and slower. My first shift in the second period I went into the corner and some big winger — either Andrew McBain or Neufeld again — came in to hit me. I turned my body completely out of the way. I was forced to protect myself and would be for the rest of the playoffs. It would take another set of X-rays — *after* the Detroit series — before the broken ribs would be spotted by the doctors. We thought we were only hiding a couple of bruised ribs!

Concentration and singlemindedness were my stock in trade; would this double dose of physical distraction throw me off? And how were the other guys going to do as underdogs?

32

Snuffing Out the Flames

There's an old expression, "Don't believe *everything* you read in the papers."

Even as a newspaperman myself, I have to say it makes sense.

This was proven beyond a shadow of a doubt on the eve of our long-awaited, much-heralded — and speaking for myself eagerly anticipated — Smythe Division final series with the Calgary Flames.

Had the Edmonton Oilers believed what was written, we might have been tempted to hoist the white flag of surrender over our dressing room at The Saddledome and simply mail in the four losses.

It wasn't only the Calgary media or the horde of out-of-town writers from other NHL cities who wrote us off; the pessimism about the Oilers came from our own home town as well.

Cam Cole, who writes a page one column for the *Edmonton Journal* sports section, headlined his pre-series piece, FLAMES BETTER UNDER CRISPY, and then proceeded to predict a Calgary victory.

"The Oilers lost something this season," Cole concluded, "and beating Winnipeg doesn't prove they've got it back."

On the basis of the regular season standings, it was only natural to predict a Flames victory. Calgary finished six points ahead of us — interestingly, the Islanders finished first, six points ahead of the Devils, and look what happened to Bryan Trottier and Company — had beaten us two years earlier in the play-offs, led the league in goal-scoring (397 to our 363) and had the rookie-of-the-year in Joe Nieuwendyk. They also had pressure on them.

"There's pressure on us to win the first two games in our building," said Terry Crisp, "but we dealt with pressure in the last two months of the season. We answered the bell."

Normally, we'd take a regular scheduled flight to Calgary but because it was the playoffs, we chartered south. During the trip some of the guys read the dire predictions about us and collectively agreed that, yes, we *are* the underdogs. My view was that, favorite or underdog, it's all irrelevant. In 1986 we were favored and it was a tough series. Same thing in 1984. No matter what the odds, this would be a tough series as well. We *believed* it was going to be tough.

Another aspect of our reaction was plain resentment toward those Edmonton writers. Granted, they were not on our payroll, but everyone knows that no matter how objective the press tries to be, they usually have a fondness for the local team. Ironically, the only guy who called us to win was Terry Jones, the same guy who had indelibly labeled us "weak-kneed wimps" when we were younger.

If the anti-Oilers reaction stung, it also stimulated us. We were going to be motivated by the betrayal of the press.

As for the Flames, we knew we could beat them but we admitted we were in for a tough battle. And since I had been through plenty of these Edmonton-Calgary battles before, I was an ideal target for media questioning. The standard question from the reporters was, why should 1988 be different for us than 1986?

The answer was in preparation. Two years earlier we had not been as prepared as we should have been because we had handled them rather easily up until then. They played us as well as they could that year while we were firing on only three cylinders. This time we were ready. What we required was composure and discipline. With our game plan, some luck and the usual excellent goaltending from Grant, I felt we could beat them. If nothing else, we had something to prove.

One of the media's favorite points of comparison was defense. They liked the Flames because, as the writers put it, Calgary's defense "is much more mobile" than Edmonton's because we no longer had Paul Coffey. The Oilers-without-Paul-Coffey issue had surfaced so many times that it was coming out of our ears. We had thought the argument had long ago been dead and buried but no, the press resurrected it for the playoffs. I'm not denying that Gary Suter and Al MacInnis were one-two in defensemen scoring in the NHL but I was surprised that the point was made so often at this time. (In the end, the Calgary series would be the last straw on the Coffey question.) As it happened, we neutralized Suter and MacInnis and this was one of the pivotal points in tilting the series our way.

Our pre-game strategy before the opener did not concentrate so much on the Flames weaknesses as it did on our own game plan. We were aware that the press said the only real weak link in Calgary's armor was goalie Mike Vernon and we knew that Vernon had some potential soft spots, but we didn't devise a strategy around exploiting that. We did blueprint a way of defusing their power play and now we eagerly awaited the opportunity to put our plan to the test.

Terry Crisp put it best for both camps when we arrived in Calgary. "The guys are getting antsy. You can only watch so much video, and we can only tell them the same things so many times."

Opening in Calgary turned out to be a blessing for us. The demands made on the Flames by their hometown fans put pressure on them long before the opening face-off. They were planning a Stanley Cup victory parade and they hadn't even won a game yet! The souvenir hawkers were peddling Stanley Cup key chains and other Calgary-winning objects as if the series were a fait accompli. What a lot of folks seemed to have overlooked was the fact that we were still the champions until proven otherwise. And nothing the Flames did in Game One proved otherwise!

We exchanged power play goals in the first period — Mark first for us and then McCrimmon for them — and then settled down to a tight playoff game. Of the first five penalties in the second period, we had three but neither team scored. Then, at 18:04 our Norm Lacombe got hit with a major. This was Calgary's chance to bust open the game but their power play failed.

We knew that we had to put pressure on MacInnis and Suter. Of course, every other team knew that; the difference was that we *executed*. There's one thing knowing what to do and there's another having the players to execute. We had three excellent penalty-killing units who hounded them, Gretz and Mark; Gretz and Jari; MacTavish and Hannan. It was a good team effort in the sense that we had lots of line changes. The best thing a team can do during a penalty-killing situation is to get two or three line changes. It's no good to have your best unit out there for a minute and a half. The trick is to get a good flow going and as soon as you ice the puck, you make a change. You get fresh troops out there. Guys were now giving up ice time for the good of the team and we demonstrated that by killing off the major to Lacombe. This gave us the 1-1 tie early in the third and increased the pressure on them.

The way Grant was saving us, all we needed was a break to open the game but it didn't happen until well after the mid point in the period. Gretz broke in and threw a shot off Vernon's glove and then the goal post. We kept up the pressure and Jari finished it off 20 seconds later. That goal sent the Flames reeling and Wayne polished them off for good with a breakaway at 16:18. It ended 3-1 for us and we were higher than a kite. Conversely, the other guys were feeling mighty low.

So, why did the "underdogs" win? Superior goaltending didn't hurt and the penalty-killing was fabulous. Thirdly, Calgary showed inexperience.

They were unprepared and overanxious. They were cocky and they underestimated us. They had gotten wrapped up in the whole the-Stanley-Cup-is-in-the-bag picture that was being painted in their town. The Flames were caught up in the whole thing. When they lost the first game, everything got turned upside down for Crisp. You have to have an experienced team to be able to sit back and say, "All right. Okay. What happened?"

We had a similar situation a year earlier when the Red Wings beat us in the opener at Edmonton. We were supposed to win but we didn't and then we retooled and straightened out the situation.

One dilemma Crisp had that Slats didn't was with personnel, especially John Tonelli and Paul Reinhart. Let's start with Reinhart, who had been with Calgary for a long time. This is a great talent but the guy had suffered an injury problem for the past few years and 1987-88 was no different. He played only 14 games all season but they nevertheless shoved him back into the lineup. Believe me, it's awfully difficult to miss most of the season and come back and get into the swing of things. On top of which it could be devastating to the rest of the club because Reinhart was displacing a guy who had played all season long. Why make a strategic change at that time when everything had gone so well with the Flames all season *without* Reinhart? It made no sense at all.

Another mistake was benching Tonelli. As an Islander, he proved to be a major clutch player. He could have been a major force in this series for Calgary. He could have hurt us but he was in civvies which was quite all right with me, but it was evident that Tonelli was upset with being benched and it was evident that there was animosity between him and Crisp. Going into Game Two all was not peace and happiness in the Flames camp.

We were laughing. Quietly, of course. "I don't think we've had a bigger win in the history of our hockey club," said Gretz. (I still think Game One on Long Island in 1984 was bigger).

What had been pressure on the Flames prior to Game One was now PRESSURE going into the second contest at the Saddledome. It was best reflected by this story. An ambulance rushed to a downtown parking spot at the foot of the Husky Tower. As the siren wail abated, two paramedics rushed inside. An onlooker took in the scene and then quipped, "I guess another Flames fan committed suicide!"

Terry Crisp certainly wasn't joking when he growled, "The cannons have to be firing when you're in a war but our cannons were non-existent!"

Crisp didn't name names but it was obvious he was talking about Suter, MacInnis, Nieuwendyk, Mike Bullard, Joey Mullen and Hakan Loob, the big guns. But they were silenced, at least partially, because our gunners were willing to check as well as go to the net. We knew we weren't going to win on talent and desire alone. We had to make sacrifices and Gretz and the guys were willing to make them.

Just as we suspected, Calgary came at us with a rush in Game Two. They had us 3-1 by the middle of the game but we tied it, 3-3, by the end of two. They had one more gasp; Tim Hunter, of all people, put them ahead at 4:04 of the third. Remember I told you about Reinhart. Well, he was guarding Jari, one-on-one with four minutes left in the period, when Kurri zipped past him and shot a 30-footer to the far side past Vernon. It was all tied up again, ready for overtime.

Now you may ask, doesn't what happened so far indicate

that Vernon was a weak link in the Calgary chain? Not really. He wasn't playing badly but he wasn't making *the big save*, which is what makes or breaks a team in the playoffs. Grant, on the other hand, was making them for us.

Slats' advice was not elaborate. "Play to win. Go after them. Don't hold back!"

We didn't. The shots were six-to-two in our favor when referee Bill McCreary caught Mark for tripping at 5:57 of overtime. And we still pressed *them*. Gretz went one-on-one with McCrimmon, passed off to Randy Gregg but Vernon stopped him. We had the penalty all but killed when Steve Smith moved the puck to Jari. Using the boards, he got it up to Wayne and he was off and running. Gretz blasted it high and to the far side and Vernon could only wave as it went by.

Normally, when a guy shoots from way up there, he shouldn't score. On the other hand, the goaltender will say, "God, he blew it over my shoulder." Let's face it; that *was* a tremendous shot.

Also, a tremendous win.

"It was," said Wayne, "the biggest goal I ever scored."

Perhaps. But this much is certain: there isn't a player who can rise to his level. And to score a shorthanded goal. Why, the only thing that could be better would be winning it in Game Seven or something like that.

The Flames, no doubt about it, were rattled. And Crisp was being second-guessed from Red Deer to High River. What would Badger Bob Johnson have done differently? Wouldn't he have motivated them in a more positive, calmer way?

I could see that they didn't adapt to how we were playing. They didn't adapt to our power play and our penalty-killing. They played a free-wheeling game that reminded me of us in our undisciplined immature early years. You can't do that in the playoffs and get away with it, but they didn't have the discipline and now with the series moving to our town, it was going to be very interesting to see how Crisp would try to reverse the tide.

"It's up to us to make sure we do the same thing in Edmonton that they did to us in Calgary," said Crisp.

The gap between games provided the second-guessers with a field day. Didn't the Flames trade themselves to a Stanley Cup? This was an oft-asked question. Remember, in March Cliff Fletcher dealt Bobby Hull's kid, Brett, and Steve Bozek to

St. Louis for Rob Ramage and Rick Wamsley. "The Flames say they have all the right players," needled John Muckler. "Fletcher says he's got the perfect team now."

On paper, maybe. So far, Wamsley hadn't played and Ramage was not exactly giving us fits. On the other hand, the absence of Paul Coffey was not exactly killing us. Even the Flames could see that. "Coffey was the kind of guy who could kill you," said their assistant coach Pierre Page. "But you could take advantage of his being up ice all the time. With Coffey in the lineup, you could get two-on-ones and three-on-twos against them."

Until Game Three the series was surprisingly calm and virtually free from so much of the tumult we had grown accustomed to over the years. This "Phony War," as it were, would end with a bang — or should I say "with a spear" — in our first game at home.

The episode was not unlike so many which have occurred in play-off games down through the years; a controversial collision leads to an injury and accusations are hurled left and right. What made this particular incident even more complicated was the goal that was scored right after the victim went down.

Calgary's Mike Bullard was the victim. Marty McSorley was the aggressor. However, I am by no means suggesting that he was guilty. First, let's examine the developments leading up to the spear because, as is so often the case in hockey, an infraction is triggered by an earlier act of violence, but that first assault is sometimes overlooked.

Marty had been hit heavily by Gary Roberts who followed through by smashing Marty's head into the glass. By the time Marty got to the bench he was dazed, I mean out of it! In a situation like that, the victim — and make no mistake, McSorley *was* the victim at this point — wants retribution, particularly if no penalty is called on the play. It's the eye-for-an-eye theory and anyone who tells you he's never experienced that emotion is full of applesauce. What you feel is "I want to get someone on the opposition, *anyone*, right now!"

I am speaking from personal experience. Several years ago, I found myself in a nasty vengeance mode after being victimized by Carey Wilson, who was then with Calgary. I had gone into the corner and Wilson — who knows whether he did it intentionally or not — pushed me from behind and I went face first into the boards. Now that's an awfully dangerous play and there was no penalty called, which thoroughly enraged me. (I was lucky to get my hands up in a "bumper" position to cushion the blow but I could have suffered a broken neck. Anything could have happened.) Meanwhile, Wilson just skated away but I wasn't about to allow him to escape unpunished. I followed him around until he finally went to his players' box. As he was going in, I did what Marty did. I speared him and got a five-minute penalty.

The difference, in Marty's case, is that as he came back to the bench Bullard just happened to have leaped over the boards to get into the play, and that's when Marty speared him.

As Bullard went down, Charlie Huddy had the puck and shot it past Vernon. The goal stopped the play, but then linesman Gord Broseker went over to Andy Van Hellemond and explained what had happened. Then, the debate got even more heated. The Flames wanted the goal disallowed.

I could see where the Flames were coming from but Van Hellemond was not about to disallow the goal and he later explained why: "Gordie was the one who saw the play. By the time he let it run through his mind, he turned to see where the puck was and it was in the net. My question to Gordie was, did he blow the whistle before the goal went in and he said 'no'."

Naturally, the Flames yelled and screamed that the goal should be disallowed but Van Hellemond overruled the objections because no whistle had sounded before the puck entered the net, which would have been the only basis for not counting it.

What do I think of the incident in retrospect? As a member of the Edmonton Oilers, I believe in protecting and defending my teammates. It so happens that Marty was my stallmate and I can vouch for the fact that he was pretty well rattled by what Roberts had done to him. I don't for a moment condone foul play but human beings do make mistakes and I'd say Marty made a mistake. Heck, he himself admitted it after the game, saying, "I know I shouldn't have done it because I put our team in jeopardy with a major penalty. But I was disoriented. I was on our bench doubled over, trying to clear my head when I got back." Slats added, "Marty sort of passed out."

Because the victim was a scorer like Bullard, quite a fuss was made about it but had the victim been a less gifted player such as Tim Hunter, there might not have been the same to-do. For sure, the stickwork has to be prevented in the league and I have no quarrel with the three-game suspension that the NHL eventually doled out to Marty. As for Van Hellemond, he reacted as quickly as possible and handled it well.

What remained to be seen was how the Flames would react to the situation since it was clear that the goal would count and they now were on a five-minute power play. But we had them completely flummoxed and Mark and Jari had better chances than their power play specialists. Vernon stopped Mess but Glennie put in the rebound and we were up, 3-1.

McSorley's spear brought the expected retaliation from the Flames. It is questionable behavior and something we talk about, especially during the playoffs. The key is to initiate not retaliate. You shouldn't react to a situation if it's going to jeopardize your team by causing a penalty situation. A guy smacks you in the nose; it hurts; it's embarrassing but you shouldn't smack him back right away. You have to wait for your opportunity. You have to suck it up.

Of course, if something like that happens to Gretzky, it's *bad* and something has to be done about it. But if he's not injured, you sit back and think about it even more. You store the facts, concentrate on the business at hand. We've got to score a goal, that's more important. From our angle, the most important thing of all was winning three in a row and just as vital as that was keeping our cool and our mouths shut as well.

Sure, the Edmonton papers had started shouting SWEEP after we had won the first two games at Calgary and we let them do the talking; we vowed to keep a low verbal profile. This was very important to our 1988 strategy. We emphasized one game at a time. We wanted to play in an organized fashion and not get carried away with premature Cup parades or champagne in the dressing room.

The experience the previous year — when everyone indulged in premature Cup celebrations — really had burned the players when we returned to Edmonton, leading the Flyers three games to one. I can't imagine people being so dumb and inconsiderate as to do something like that. It upset us and then the series blew up in our faces. We tried to tone everything down and not get caught up in it. Having learned that lesson, we weren't about to even think sweep because we had the three-game lead. All we wanted to do was play as flawless hockey as possible because, to us, the upcoming game is always *the* game.

Nevertheless, sweep mania had swept across Edmonton and the papers ran with it at full speed. The Battle of Alberta was being waged in Edmonton's favor in the games department but not in the area of insults. Calgary columnists like Larry Tucker never stopped needling us or, more particularly, our glorious leaders.

He told one about a Calgary cop who stopped Terry Crisp and asked him, "What's two feet long and hangs from a blankety-blank?"

"I don't know," Crisp replied.

"Glen Sather's tie," the cop replied.

Or the sign carried by a Flames fan. "I'd rather have a sister in a brothel than a brother who's an Oilers fan."

Cliff Fletcher remembered the advice he had received the first day he arrived in Calgary from Atlanta to operate the Flames. "A man came up to me on the street," recalled Fletcher, "and said, 'It doesn't matter how well you do, as long as you beat Edmonton.' That tends to give you some idea of what's at stake in this series."

On the ice the baiting was at a minimum from our end because we realized that we had been guilty of foolish needling in the past and it had come back to haunt us. We had grown up and learned that we had wasted good energy with that kind of after-the-whistle stuff so there was a conscious effort not to get caught up in it. We wanted to be machine-like, the way the Islanders were when they were winning Cups. Still, you're not going to tell an Esa Tikkanen to keep his mouth shut all the time.

Our feeling before taking the ice was something along the lines of W.C. Fields' "Never give a sucker an even break!" We had no intentions of losing hold of our advantage and we showed it in the first period with four goals on our first nine shots. Crisp yanked Vernon and inserted Wamsley. I was reminded of the wonderful Satchel Paige comment, "Never look behind because someone might be gaining on you."

The Flames did gain on us but not enough. We beat them 6-4 and trooped into a dressing room that had a bit more of an air of celebration than your normal second-round triumph. We had earned the right to let off steam. Calgary was never in the series and this the team that was favored or, at worst, figured to be a "pick-em." We had thrown a loop around the so-called "experts" who had put us down before the opener. By now their mouths were wide open saying, "What happened?"

Badger Bob Johnson had one good explanation: "Edmonton got a lot more mileage out of its world class players than Calgary did out of its 20 players. I thought Mike Vernon played well — but he's not Fuhr."

Happy as we were, we didn't want to get caught celebrating too early. Let's face it, good as it was, beating the Flames did not yet win us the Stanley Cup. I didn't want to give in to celebrating with wild abandon. The winning was accomplishment enough. I saw no reason to get extraordinarily crazy about the whole thing. But it was all so hard to believe.

In terms of performance, we played better as a team than ever before. At least that's what some of the guys thought. One thing was certain, we had produced one of the biggest wins in the Oilers history. And this triumph produced a summer of post-mortems in Calgary. One local television show, "On Sports," had four CFAC commentators on to discuss the series. One of them, Grant Pollock, said, "The Flames had dissension in their dressing room. Many people don't realize there were problems in the dressing room. They weren't a team."

We were. Now it was time to underscore the point against Detroit's Red Wings.

33

"C'mon, You Mediocre Bums!"

I was not the least bit surprised to learn that we would be facing the Red Wings for the second year in a row. A year earlier they had demonstrated that Jacques Demers was a quality coach, handling several first-rate players like Gerard Gallant, Greg Stefan and Bob Probert, just to name a few. They had finished strong at the end of the regular season even without their captain Steve Yzerman, and then marched right through their first two rounds.

Not that I harped on who our next opponent would be. That would not be like me. I spend very little time thinking about anything beyond *now*. Why bother? It's a waste of time. The farthest I like to think ahead is to the next game. Deal with the present, I say, and don't bother trying to create the future. So which team we'd wind up playing in the Campbell Conference championships was of no particular concern to me. I wanted to play whoever was there when we got there.

What did concern me were my injuries and the increased attention I was receiving. It was starting to wear on me mentally. Here I was trying to put the whole injury business out of my mind and people were always asking me how my hand and my ribs were. By now I was getting my casts changed regularly and a new one had to be put on before we took on Detroit.

I expected some heavy hitting from the Red Wings. What scared me the most about them was that they wanted another shot at us after what we had done to them in the 1987 playoffs. I respected Gallant a lot because he's a feisty little guy who can score goals and who made it to the top. He deserved the captaincy when Yzerman got knocked out of the lineup. Probert is not only rugged but he's a lot better hockey player than most people think. For me, the one-game-at-a-time thing was in full force. There would be no bragging and little to say. I would leave that to others. And when there are coaches like Slats and Demers around, the words fly like snow in the Arctic.

Coaches love to play games with the press before a series, especially these two guys. Demers, who is really dedicated and works hard, is a past master at manipulating the media. But because Jacques has done so well wherever he's been, he gets a lot of publicity that he really doesn't deserve. No one — not even the coach — should be singled out from a team that's doing well. But in Detroit, they're referred to as the Demers-coached Red Wings instead of the Yzerman-led Red Wings. Unfortunately for them, Yzerman, who is one of the better inspirational leaders in hockey, would miss the first games of the series. He's a tough young man, but even without him Demers could dress a veteran like Mel Bridgman who also is rugged and has a good hockey head on his shoulders.

There's a lot more braininess in hockey than the average fan believes and, of course, we get an overdose of it from all the commentators on *The Sports Network (TSN)*, *Hockey Night In Canada* and some of the characters in the States.

One of the most visible in Canada is Don (Grapes) Cherry, the former Bruins and Rockies coach who is about as outspoken as they come. We on the Oilers were very aware of that because Grapes put down the Edmonton defense at the start of the playoffs, describing us as "medicore."

This defense, as now constituted, included myself, Steve Smith (who had made tremendous strides since the 1986 Flames episode), Charlie Huddy, Randy Gregg, Craig Muni, Marty McSorley (occasionally), Jeff Beukeboom and Jim Wiemer. Now when Cherry insults us as "mediocre," it tells me one of three things. He's doing some rabble-rousing for the sake of getting headlines. He hasn't seen enough of us lately. Or he is in error. (Or, as some might put it, being stupid.)

The toughest thing about Don's accusation was that he has a large following and he states his mind whether it's valid or not. It's his point of view, but people don't see sports commentary or news reporting as that, be it in the papers or the electronic media — they see it as gospel.

Don Cherry is just an individual who has a point of view that's colorful and who is employed by television networks to state that point of view. But he's not the President of the United States or the Prime Minister of Canada; he's not making a political speech that the whole country is going to live and die by, but unfortunately people think of it that way.

I guess the best thing is that those guys are forced to swallow their words sometimes. He pays the price and he admits his mistakes sometimes, which I don't mind, either. He'll make a statement about an individual or a team, and if he's proven wrong, he says, "Hey, I made a mistake."

Another character of the airwaves not unlike Grapes is Howie Meeker, who is something of a legend in Canadian hockey broadcasting. Meeker played right wing for the great Stanley Cup-winning Maple Leaf teams in 1947, 1948, 1949 and 1951 and over the years has become a terribly opinionated NHL commentator. I find him far too quick to jump in and criticize rather than analyze situations. It's typical of Meeker to say, "Oh, this kid shouldn't even be in the league. He should be in the minors."

Perhaps the kid in question needs a bit more coaching. Imagine how the poor rookie must feel to hear what Meeker is saying about him.

Regarding Cherry, we were more amused than hurt by what he said because we took the comment at its source. None of the players believed him for a minute.

What a great line to play around with though, and that we did. Whenever we wanted an incentive boost, one of the guys would bark, "Well, we'd better get our 'mediocre at best' defense going here." Or, "C'mon, you *mediocre* bums!"

It was a pretty hefty statement for Cherry to make but there was always the possibility of refutation by demonstration; so we demonstrated just what defense is all about and the Red Wings were the unfortunate witnesses — and victims.

We held Detroit to a goal in Game One at Northlands and beat them 5-3 in the second game which got spicy when Red Wings goalie Greg Stefan skated behind the net to clear a stray puck — just as our Craig Simpson charged after it. Simpson hit him hard, snapping his head back. Detroit had lost a goalie (Stefan was replaced by Glen Hanlon) but gained some argument-fodder, the claim being that there was something less than fair about Simpson's maneuver.

As so often happens in a controversial play like this, there were some who would suggest that Simpson could have avoided the collision, but I think it was quite evident to everyone, Detroit included, that Simpson was just skating in there; he didn't hit Stefan on purpose. He just ended up skating in there and Stefan turned around and they ran into each other. There was no attempt by Simpson to collide with Stefan, in fact he made an attempt to get out of the way. The one defenseman, Chiasson, who didn't even see the play, then cross-schecked Simpson, which was foolish because we ended up getting a five-on-three and scoring a goal — and there's the problem with retaliation instead of initiation. . . .

There's a whole tradition about a team protecting its goaltender, and you have to respect the player and the team for doing that, but in a situation like this one, where it was obvious to everyone that it wasn't done on purpose, that kid Chiasson had to evaluate the situation. "We're already down a man, I can skate up to Simpson and tell him I'll take his head off next time, but I don't know if I really should go over there and cross-scheck him right now, because I'll undoubtedly get a penalty. . . ."

Hanlon didn't buy any of the "accident" version of the episode. He chopped at Glennie, slashed and pushed Simpson in the face and hacked Tikkanen on the back of the leg. "Steff and I are very close," Hanlon later explained, "and I just couldn't handle it. To me, it was tough to see him get hit like that. It was hard for me to keep my composure. I had revenge on my mind."

Fine, but we were the beneficiaries and left Edmonton for Detroit with a two-games-to-none series lead. The series heated up as expected in Joe Louis Arena. Figuratively and literally. The Detroit rink was hot and we sweated buckets. We also faced a determined Red Wings team that was bent on a physical game. Although Gretz got both goals in our 5-2 loss, he was the target of a lot of hitting.

"He's not an untouchable," said Probert. "I'm sure there are a lot of players who treat him as an untouchable, but part of my game is bumping and grinding and, in my eyes, he's no different than any other player out there."

Probert was the same fellow who had gained notoriety

because of his alcohol-abuse problem. The Red Wings management had been working closely rehabilitating Bob and that season (in which he played super hockey) they supervised his taking pills daily which would cause a negative reaction should he take any alcoholic beverage. Once when someone took a run at Steve Yzerman, who played in Game Three, Probert warned Gretz that that made him an open target. Gretz responded by playing even harder, which was so typical of him.

Shortly thereafter we suffered an unfortunate setback — the loss of Charlie Huddy who suffered a severe charleyhorse in his left thigh when kneed in the first period by Tim Higgins. The win fortified the Red Wings thinking that rough hockey might give them a chance in the series.

Detroit is a fairly physical team, they skate well and they have big guys. They figured they could wear us down by playing man to man and dishing out a few lumps. They tried to get a reaction from us, and they thought that would throw us off of our game plan. They underestimated us, because by the third or fourth game when they realized we were not waivering, they became frustrated.

We expected that from them, or from any team that wants to win the Stanley Cup. The Red Wings knew that they would have to take us out of our game plan. They say "if we don't beat them on the ice than we'll beat them in the alley." That is why you have to be extra disciplined during the play-offs. We take some extra lumps when the ref is not looking, but we are men enough not to retaliate. That is one reason why we win in the playoffs.

Wayne knows that every time he is on ice, and particularly during the playoffs, there is someone wishing to put him in the hospital. He understands this and he plays in a way which keeps him out of traffic and away from the corners and the boards where the heavy hitting takes place. The only way to really get him is to make a run at him. The rules do not allow for this. How are they going to do it? Is someone going to go up to him and pummel him, hit him over the head, kick him, crosscheck him into the goalpost? That will not go unnoticed. The guy will get a ten-minute penalty, and maybe a ten-game suspension for intent to injure, and in a night or two, Wayne will be out there again doing his stuff.

We did our stuff thereafter, but it wasn't all that easy in

Game Four. We had a 3-2 lead late in the third period when Probert scored on a power play sending the game into overtime. In the sudden death Probert had two more chances and almost put us away. It was a case of close-but-no-cigar. At 11:02 the cigar went to Jari who took a pass from Tik and beat Hanlon with a 25-footer.

The game was ours because we have guys who can finish it off. Who better than Gretz or Jari? Or Mess? If there was one area that needed some fixing at our end it was the penalty killing. The Wings were especially effective on the power play and were scoring on shots from close to the net. For Game Five we'd have to make an adjustment.

We did — with a little help from Mark who broke a 2-2 tie as we cruised to an 8-4 win. It was typical Mess, getting himself up for a big game because we didn't want to have to go back to Detroit anymore.

If there was any "downer" over a four-games-to-one series victory, it came the morning after when a story broke in the papers that a few Red Wings, including Probert, were caught drinking and missing curfew the night before Game Five. Demers went on to blame those players for the loss.

My first reaction was that it was unfortunate that such stuff had come out in the media. It gave management an excuse for the loss when the bottom line was that the Red Wings faced a more talented, more experienced team — and a more determined one.

Losing is humiliating enough. We felt that ultimate humiliation the year we lost to Calgary when *Sports Illustrated* had the gall, the audacity, to write the article defaming the Oilers. The stories about the Red Wings after we eliminated them reminded me of that.

No matter. We didn't allow the-Red-Wings-stay-out-late story to get us down. There were more important things on our minds, like laying out the welcome mat for the Boston Bruins. The 1988 Stanley Cup finals were about to begin and we had business to attend to and another piece of silver to pursue.

34

Short-Circuiting the Bruins

The month of May was already past its mid point when we opened our final defense of the Stanley Cup. Everything about me ached, not just the ribs or the arm. I knew there weren't many games left in me and I wanted to get this thing over with as soon as possible. Even mentally, I was starting to wear. I was sick and tired of being hurt and tired of being sick and sick of being tired.

Our opponents, the Bruins, couldn't have been feeling too sprightly either. They had just weathered a tiring seven-game series with the New Jersey Devils and then had to fly to Edmonton for Game One at Northlands.

The Bruins had gotten this far on a combination of strong checking, Ray Bourque and some excellent goaltending from our old foe, Reggie Lemelin, the former Calgary Flame. But Bruins coach Terry O'Reilly also had Andy Moog in his goaltending tandem and had used him to spell Reggie over the course of the play-offs. When O'Reilly decided to start Andy against us in the first game, the sense of drama went up a notch.

It had to, if for no other reason than the conflict between Andy and Slats which eventually resulted in his being moved from Edmonton. It was clear that Andy felt animosity toward Glen but I don't know whether Glen lost any sleep over him.

The Edmonton fans reacted warmly to Moog when he skated out onto the ice for the first time in a Boston uniform, which didn't surprise me. Andy had been well respected and liked as an Oiler and the applause showed it.

As for the wisdom of O'Reilly's move in starting Moog, it was a good ploy. If he played well, O'Reilly could go back with him again and if he didn't play well, O'Reilly could bring in Lemelin, his number one guy. Jim Schoenfeld did the same thing with Bob Sauve — putting him in occasionally for Sean Burke — for his Devils.

We didn't care who they put in because we figured anyone short of Grant Fuhr we could beat and we were right. Thanks in part to our "mediocre" defense, we limited Boston to only 14 shots, got two goals and beat them 2-1. We gave them a firsthand lesson in how the series was going to be. They showed some inexperience, took some foolish penalties, which is not the way to win big games. We were confident that we could methodically break down the Bruins assets and one of them was Ray Bourque, who had won the Norris Trophy (and would win it again). We decided to play him clean and hard and try to tire him out.

We knew that the Bruins were going with only four defensemen and that the fifth defenseman, Allan Pedersen, would only play occasionally. We had beaten Philadelphia in two Stanley Cup finals when the Flyers basically used four defensemen and they tired at the end. When you get too tired, you're susceptible to injury.

By contrast, Slats was working our young defensemen into the lineup with sensitivity and good sense. Despite the 1986 experience, Steve Smith was encouraged and gradually became a force with us. By the time we reached the 1988 finals, Smith had begun to remind me of a young Larry Robinson. He skates well, moves the puck and is capable of throwing the big check like Larry did in his early days.

Steve was just one of several outstanding players for us as we moved ahead of the Bruins two games to none. In the second game, Boston managed only 12 shots on Grant Fuhr (we had 32 at Reggie Lemelin) as we beat them 4-2 and thereby were able to head for Boston with the kind of cushion we wanted.

As usual, Wayne was dominant in the second game as were Glennie and Mark. But slowly but surely it was becoming apparent that still another superior offensive force was coming to the fore for us, our other Flying Finn, Esa Tikkanen. There are times when he runs around like a kid with too much sugar. He's got a lot of energy and it's all positive and now he was becoming a leader, showing he was willing to go that extra mile to win.

Watching him play, I felt like I was looking at a Bull Terrier who wanted to fight the Great Dane. The Terrier barks up the Dane's leg and gets swatted and gets up and keeps coming back for more. Esa was just as aggravating to the opposition in a strong, feisty way.

Considering how well the pieces were falling into place — by this time Steve Smith was outplaying Ray Bourque — it was quite possible that we could fall into the overconfidence trap. Fortunately, the discipline was maintained and there was a nice mix of new players. (Remember Slats' desire to change 15 percent of the roster every year.) The new guys wanted to win the Cup badly and this anticipation grew as we flew to Boston. As long as the anticipation grew with every win, it made the entire crusade that much easier.

Enroute to Game Three there was some talk among the reporters that our club might have trouble in Boston Garden. They were misled. We had overcome the Boston Garden mystique. True, the ice surface there was considerably smaller than at most NHL rinks but the beauty of our club was in its adaptability. We examined the Bruins and understood what made them successful — a grinding style — in the Garden and played that style. We could do it because in addition to Gretz, Jari and Glennie, we had players who could grind as well as the Bruins. Instead of three passes, we could adjust to making only one on the smaller ice. We were not intimidated by the Garden when we walked in for Game Three.

Just as I had expected, we made an admirable adjustment to the 191-foot-by-83-foot Garden ice. The score was 1-1 in the second when none other than Marty McSorley became involved in yet another controversial play.

It began when Marty collided with Michael Thelven, the Boston defenseman. The ramming took place at center ice and Thelven went down and seemed in bad enough shape for the Bruins to send out for a doctor and then a stretcher. Yet no penalty was called on the play and there was no evidence that Marty had hit him illegally. There wasn't even a two-minute penalty.

In any event there was a sufficient delay while Thelven was being removed for both clubs to calm down and continue what had been a nice, tight hockey game. When we lined up for the ensuing face-off, who was on the ice for Boston but none other than Jay Miller, the Bruins enforcer. He was right next to Kevin McClelland. It could have been a gasoline-and-lighted match situation but Mac was determined to stay cool.

Miller, on the other hand, was guilty of poor judgment. First of all, as soon as the puck was dropped, he went after Mac, who had nothing to do with the Thelven injury. Mind you, the pressure is on a guy like that when he gets on the ice in Boston Garden. He knows the fans are expecting that of him so he's got to do something to make his mark. But that does not excuse poor judgment.

Instead of playing it smart the way Semenk would have, Miller immediately reacted to the incident. He went after Mac. He got his penalty and we got the goal. And we got the game. First, it was Tik on that power play. Then, Glennie and Tik again. Esa wound up with the hat trick and we skated off with a 6-3 win.

That was delicious. What was distasteful, however, was the post mortem. O'Reilly blamed the officials and Miller was used as the scapegoat. How could they make it seem that that one incident and the resulting goal be the "turning point" of the series? But that's what many in the media were making it out to be and it was totally absurd.

I was flabbergasted when I picked up the papers the next day. Many articles referred to the Jay Miller-Marty McSorley-Michael Thelven-Kevin McClelland incident, and there was little said about how well the Oilers were playing. Our jelling as a team was magnificent and the commitment was more intense than ever, not to mention the willingness — as Mac showed when he ignored Miller's senseless attack — to put up with a lot of crap in order to reach the objective. We were playing so well the Bruins could not get going.

OILERS TASTE CUP.

The *Edmonton Sun* headline was a bit premature. Yes, we had a three-games-to-none lead. But no, we had not won Game Four and hence, still had not tasted the champagne.

The game that *could* have been the final match turned out to be one of the strangest in NHL history if only because it was never completed. Boston Garden was a mess that night of May 24, 1988. It had been an extremely warm spring day and the Garden, which was not equipped with air conditioning, was like an oven. The warmth produced fog on the ice and we frequently had to skate around just to dissipate the fog.

Still, we managed to get into the second period and after the Bruins had taken a 3-2 lead, we came back and tied the score. About 37 minutes of the game had already been played when *it* happened. A couple of seconds earlier I had been preoccupied on our bench, arguing with a Boston fan. Just then, the arena lights went out. Shortly thereafter the emergency lights provided some glow so I figured that it would just take a few minutes before we got going again. But then I saw the Bruins skating toward their dressing room and the referee said something about tacking the remaining time from the second period on to the third period.

Now we were being herded to our dressing room where there were no lights but the guys thought this was all very funny. A couple of people found flashlights and then a tv cameraman walked in and flicked on his portable light. We started getting out of our sweaters, treating the respite as if it were a normal between-periods rest. Some guys undid their skates, others fiddled with their sticks. We all awaited further developments. Then, the word came through that it could be a generator problem and that would mean an even longer wait than first anticipated.

Some of the guys began getting out of their gear. They put on dry underwear because it was so hot and wet in the building that our underwear was just soaked through and through by this time. But not me. Once my equipment is on, it's there to stay. I sat around thinking that we would be playing sooner or later. But then someone drifted in with the first news that the game might *not* be resumed that night; it might be continued the next afternoon.

With every minute, I was getting more annoyed because I was still intent on finishing the game and still hadn't taken my stuff off the way most of the other guys had. Finally, I said the heck with this, and peeled my equipment off while people were drifting in and out of our room. It was getting ludicrous by now with even some fans making their way into our quarters.

The more time elapsed, the less we wanted to play the game and when we finally were told that the game would be put off to a rematch in Edmonton, I said all right, I'll get a good night's sleep, go home, have a good rest and be ready for Game Four-A.

If the delay was fruitful in any way it was that there was still a possibility that Charlie Huddy, who had been out with an injury, might return. Everybody was happy about that because Charlie had played so well before he had gotten hurt. He had a big grin on his face as we jetted west to Edmonton. As we touched down, I got the feeling that it all was a blessing in disguise. We were still up by three games and now we would be able to conclude the series at Northlands.

Another plus was that the extra days meant that my mom could fly out to Edmonton and see the potential Cup-clincher. She had done a detour to see my sister who was having a baby but once the baby was born, mom had time to catch a plane for Edmonton. (She had told me that "I want to see you win and I'd like to be able to see you win," so she was to get her wish.)

By the time we had concluded our last practice before Game Four-A everyone was feeling good about what we had achieved so far but we were also trying to downplay the black-out business because the press was making so much of it. As usual, the media were looking for controversy more than for the basic fact that we were playing great hockey.

They also started talking up the "Dynasty" issue. It was difficult for us to talk about ourselves in that respect but we felt confident that we would be right up there with the best of them — four Cups in five years. And then if we could win yet another one, we'd be even higher on the list. That was all part of our goal. So, the feeling as we left the rink was, "Hey, we have to win this hockey game. If we lose, we go back to Boston and who knows what could happen there." We knew from 1987 how easily a thing can slip out of your hands. It bothered me thinking about how we had let Games Five and Six slip away from us a year earlier.

So, here we were at Northlands on the threshold. For a short time the Bruins made a game of it, leading 2-1 in the first, but with five minutes remaining Esa tied the score and early in the second we went ahead. It was 4-2 for us with ten seconds to go in the second period and Gretz had the puck. We were yelling for him to shoot but characteristically he looked for the ideal play. As the seconds ticked off, he noticed Craig Simpson driving the slot. Gretz put the puck on Craig's stick and it was deflected past Moog with two seconds remaining. We had a 5-2 cushion with 20 minutes to protect it. I didn't think Grant or anyone, for that matter, would let us down.

Sports Illustrated said it "was more coronation than competition" and I suppose that describes what was happening. The Bruins, pretty tired by now, managed one more goal but we matched that and then the clock wound down and Northlands went mad once more.

EPILOGUE —
Are We for Real, Or What!

I went out on the ice with 30 seconds left in what would be our final game of the 1987-88 season, one filled with tumult, upheaval, doubt and, ultimately, confirmation of what we had known all along — that the Edmonton Oilers were *champions*.

My arms were aching and my ribs pained but the balm of victory soothed all wounds at that moment. As we approached the end of the game I hoped that we would have the pleasure of a celebration not marred — as it had been in the past — by fans indiscriminately dashing out on the ice interrupting what really was a momentary private exaltation.

The final seconds approached and I looked to the bench. I fixed my eyes on the guys who would be winning the Stanley Cup for the first time, just to see their reaction. I knew from personal experience that there is one goal for a first-time winner and that's to hoist the Cup.

I suddenly remembered my youth. A kid plays hockey for one thing, to win the Stanley Cup. You play in the back yard, in the front yard. You play road hockey or shinny hockey. Whatever you play, you dream of hoisting the Stanley Cup. I recalled how intensely our newcomer, Davey Hannan, had talked about it; how all he wanted to do was carry that Cup, get it in his hands and carry it.

In that final game Keith Acton had replaced Davey and on this night of celebration, Hannan was in civvies but I couldn't help thinking of him when it was over and the jubilation was at its peak.

I remembered how much he wanted to get that Cup and hold it in the air so I called him from the bench after it had gone around and just about all the guys had picked it up. I said, "Hey, Hanner, stay right here!" And I went and got the Cup and brought it over to him and he was excited about that.

The newcomers intrigued me. I looked for Craig Simpson. I looked for stuff that I had missed in previous years. The best thing about the Cup as you win them more often is that you're much more aware and observant as to what goes on normally. In the earlier years I was so in the middle of it that when the celebration was over I'd say, "Geez, what the hell happened!"

This time I knew. I looked at Craig MacTavish, a guy who had once spent time in jail but had come back to play great hockey and then go on to win a Stanley Cup. And at Keith Acton, who was buried in last-place Minnesota and, all of a sudden, finds himself playing in Edmonton and helping us go all the way.

The new guys were all a little bit leery of taking the Cup and skating with it. Everybody was urging them, "Go get the Cup!" And they'd sheepishly reply, "Can I?"

And then the on-ice celebration was over and we were in a dressing room that was packed with media and more media and family and friends. I couldn't move, couldn't get from one side to the other. Then the champagne was flying.

So were the quotes. A standard question from the reporters had to do with greatness. Over and over again people were asked to put us in a quality perspective. Mario Tremblay, who had played for five Stanley-Cup-champion Montreal teams, told John Short of the *Edmonton Journal*: "They're a little better than we were."

Red Wings coach Jacques Demers put it another way: "As a coach, when you lose to them, you say they're great — you have to. But watching them in the finals, close to the ice, and also watching them from above, I can come to only one conclusion — they are brilliant."

My belief is that we're one Cup away from being recognized as the greatest hockey team of all time. Winning the Cup for the fourth time is just one more confirmation and it puts the team one step closer to documenting its greatness. Obviously, there have been many great teams in the past and many talk about the Montreal team that won five straight Cups, from 1956 through 1960. Right now, I'd say we're equal to the Islanders of the 1980-83 era and the Canadiens who won the four Cups from 1976 through 1979.

To be a part of this experience meant a lot to me, particularly because of the obstacles this season, the change in personnel, my injuries. It was a personal, mental and psychological battle that I had with myself. The personal battle I'll remember for a lot of years and it will make me a stronger person.

I did not choose to make much of my injury for a lot of reasons and, fortunately, it was pretty much kept quiet from the beginning of the playoffs right down to the end. I liked it that way. I'm not one to complain about wounds and I certainly didn't want to get into any whining syndrome no matter how much I may have been hurting. That was simply between me and my body.

But once we had won the Cup the newshounds got on my case and one day I woke up and thought my ribs had their own press agent, they were getting so much attention in the press. Check out some of these headlines that appeared following our victory:

BROKEN RIBS KEPT SECRET BY LOWE.
LOWE PLAYED WITH BROKEN RIBS.
LOWE'S RIBS TAKE A BREAK.

I even tried to conceal the rib problem from the rest of the team but Gretz began talking about it to guys like Dick Chubey when the reporters started coming around for the after-game "color" stories. "Know what it takes to win Stanley Cups," Gretz told Chubes. "Guys like Kevin, that's what it takes. Not only did he play the entire playoffs with a cast on his hand, he played the last two rounds with three broken ribs. I didn't even know his ribs were broken until the second game of the finals. He didn't tell anybody but I asked him one day in practice, 'How come your sweater's so big?' He said, 'I have broken ribs'."

As a matter of personal preference, I shun the hero's role. That's not Kevin Lowe, but once the rib business got out, I had to answer a lot of questions and, by this time, there was no point ignoring the issue.

Yes, I had three broken ribs on my left side, I admitted to the media. At first I thought they had been bruised but since they didn't improve during either the Calgary or Detroit series, I sensed it was something worse. When I donned the flak jacket for extra protection, some hockey people sensed that it was worse than it appeared. John Davidson, the ex-goalie who had turned broadcaster, had asked me about it. He knew but I requested that he not go public and John obliged me.

The wrist injury may have brought about the rib breaks. I had been reaching with my wrist when Ray Neufeld hit me and hurt the ribs. After that I was off-balance quite a bit and couldn't hit with my left side. And I couldn't sleep on either side for a month. When I did get hit by guys like Bob Probert and Cam Neely my body would just cringe.

Among the more difficult situations was fighting for the puck and trying to be strong while doing it. Handling the puck was a problem because of the wrist and I was trying to protect the weak parts at the same time. Simultaneously, I had to keep the mental struggle from tilting in the wrong direction. While the temptation to say, "I can't stand it anymore" was there, I overcame that temptation by urging myself on with, "Hey, Kevin, you can do it."

I did it, and that's why the celebration had added meaning to me. We ended up partying all night after the win and into the next day. In previous years I could go for four or five or six straight days of festivities. This time I was pooped by the second day of celebrating, which was a Saturday. I figured that on Saturday night I'd get a good night's sleep but when Sunday came around I was pooped again so I thought, well, another good night's sleep should put me right but Monday came and I was pooped again. I couldn't get out of the rut. I was really tired and the body was demanding some rest time. After that, I began to sleep all right.

Once the partying simmered down, I had more time to reflect on our accomplishment and how I reacted to it. I got a great deal of satisfaction out of the Stanley Cups but I don't really gloat over that part of my life. I use it as a motivational tool.

It doesn't take long for the glow of the Stanley Cup to wane. I know that the minute we step on the ice for the new season the opposition won't care about the fact that we won the Cup. They'll respect it even less and go after us that much more.

I learned from past experience that we'd get the respect and praise for a month or so after the season but once summer comes and the teams start signing players and the exhibition schedules come out and they start announcing training camp rosters, the other teams think *they* are going to win the Stanley Cup next year.

Which means that we have to go out and prove ourselves all over again. . . . We'll have to put the Stanley Cup victory behind us and look ahead to the next one.

Anybody connected with hockey will tell you that the bottom line is the Stanley Cup. That's the greatest. Since 1984, and after only we've nine years in the NHL, we've won it four times so, I ask you, are we for real, or what!

The Battle that Won the War

Kisha Ciabattari

A number of hockey analysts believe that the Oilers 1988 Stanley Cup victory was facilitated in large part by the club's victory over Calgary in the Symthe Division finals. That the 1988 Edmonton-Calgary series was pivotal to the Oilers success cannot be disputed. But how and why was it accomplished in merely four games? Hockey scholar Kisha Ciabattari believes Game One was, as Wayne Gretzky puts it, "the best played by the Oilers." She examines this game and the follow-up in exquisite detail, to further illuminate the path of Glen Sather's team en route to the 1988 Cup.

With all due respect to the Stanley Cup finalist Boston Bruins, the Stanley Cup was won on the eve of April 25, 1988 when the Edmonton Oilers completed a four-game sweep of the Calgary Flames.

And with all due respect to the National Hockey League's most durable team over eighty regular-season games, The Flames were through on April 21 when forgotten point-defender Wayne Gretzky wandered past the northernmost contour of his penalty-killing assignment, greeted a Jari Kurri bank pass, and swatted a high-to-the-glove-side bullet past Mike Vernon at 7:54 of overtime.

The play had begun innocently enough. Gary Suter was lugging the puck up the left-wing boards, as is his habit, and tossed it into the right-wing corner. Hakan Loob, after making his customary loop up the right wing, chased down the loose puck with Oilers defenseman Steve Smith in nearby pursuit.

The Flames, after going 1-for-9 in the series opener, abandoned their slants, curls and floods in neutral ice for a heartier, safer entry into the Oiler zone, and it was working well for them. John Tonelli had replaced Joe Nieuwendyk on the unit as the high man, but instead of sneaking into the high slot for a late pass or ghosting in and out of the enemy box, Tonelli, like a country dog, pounced on the bone tossed in his corner with strict instructions to take a bite out of any Oiler who got in his way. The Flames, as a result, were now operating at a whopping 66.7% after going 2-for-3 on the power play. Order had been restored.

Mike Bullard posted himself on the right-wing circle and Al MacInnis pulled up on the right point. The Flames in overtime on the power play. A natural. The Flames, who were expected to win, expected to win, which must have been MacInnis' reasoning when he saw the top half of the circle yawning and took two dooming steps in deep. He had dropped a few times on the power play in Game Two and had scored on a 5-on-3 to put the Flames ahead, 2-0 in the first period. Here was a chance to win the game and tie the series. Except Smith got to the puck first. And then Kurri had it on his forehand and banked it beyond Bullard, beyond MacInnis, as it rolled toward a rendezvous with the puckmaster himself, who had, with a lighthearted scorn of his team's predicament deep in their zone, decided to take a stroll. Gretzky, who never appears to be moving forward but who perpetually arrives, sauntered off, puck-in-tow toward the horizon while MacInnis, nursing a pulled groin as it was, scrambled hopelessly after him. Suter, in a dead run up the middle of the ice, tried to catch Gretzy and cut him off. But Gretzky, for whom time seems to come again, was gliding into the future as he leaned to his left and Vernon leaned to his right and dashed the Flames' dream of a Stanley Cup.

If the Flames and the critics were stunned, they should have known better. The Oilers, who annually disprove their tag of free-wheeling wimps who win on individual absentminded ability rather than on a conscious, cooperative efficacy, gave new meaning to the term "winning ugly" when they slopped around the trough with the Philadelphia Flyers for seven games the previous spring. Ron Hextall's performance notwithstanding, it should have been over in five. But the Oilers, who have dangled on the precipice of the abyss and have learned how to keep from toppling into it, survived the Flyers and put that wisdom to good use in the 1988 Smythe Division finals.

The Oilers lay low and tight-lipped and were smart enough not to be stupid about a Calgary power play that was not merely good but had been downright giddy. Behind closed doors they methodically addressed the problem of Paul Coffey's absence and the tactical task of launching the attack which fell to Steve Smith, Kevin Lowe, Randy Gregg, Craig Muni, Charlie Huddy and Marty McSorley. During the regular season the transition game had sputtered. Long passes were chopped down in center ice and Oilers defensemen fell under a siege of heavy forechecking when they tried to carry the puck out. And it was no secret that the Flames' dump-and-chase and forecheck within a 2-1-2 stratagem had proved a jewel all season.

Bob Johnson was gone and the Flames no longer squirmed within the ever-vigilant confines of endless schematas which drearily reinforced that no matter who you are, you always have to approach the other side of the red line with a healthy dose of paranoia if Wayne Gretzky is peering at you across from it, regardless of power play statistics and Smythe Division rankings. But Mario Lemieux's deification as The One and Gretzky's fall from grace to the status of, simply, The Other nurtured the Flames' sense of superiority. Gretzky had lost the scoring title, the Art Ross Trophy, and ouch, the irreplaceable Paul Coffey. The Oilers were not getting that flow from their own zone. Their well-intentioned, hard-nosed but brittle hulks had trouble crossing the blue line let alone joining the attack as the fourth man. The Flames, on the other hand, had Suter, MacInnis and Reinhart. When the Flames derailed what was to be the Oiler's third consecutive joyride down Jasper Avenue, the defense had dominated the scoring. Loob had had a brilliant '88 campaign, outscoring every Oiler but recent acquisition Craig Simpson, who had never played a shift of NHL playoff hockey. Joel Otto, everyone agreed, would again neutralize Mark Messier. Kurri would self-destruct as he did in '86 amid the deluge of punches, jabs and shoves. And Fuhr, well, Fuhr could be dealt with. And so the Flames dismissed the Oilers and focused on themselves.

With officials enforcing the rule book consistently throughout the 1987-88 season, the Flames cultivated the League's best power play. The unit of Loob, Nieuwendyk and Bullard up front with Suter and MacInnis on the blue line terrorized penalty-killing teams. Point defenders could scarcely afford to move up on the point for fear a quick pass to the circles would result in a 3-on-2. With Loob cruising the off-wing circle, Nieuwendyk sneaking around the crease, behind the net and into the high slot and Bullard shifting with Nieuwendyk out of the right-wing corner, it was impossible for a box to move itself up and prevent either Suter or MacInnis from walking in for a shot. How could the Oilers afford to be aggressive? And the Flames, operating on the assumption of superiority, would be concerned with the Oilers power play.

"You've got to be able to play the game now," Gretzky told the *Edmonton Journal.* "That's probably why they [the Flames] traded Sheehy. I think Cliff [Fletcher] probably could see the rules would catch up to a guy like him."

The Oilers opened Game One with Sather's new unit of Geoff Courtnall, Mark Messier and Norm Lacombe, which provided a perfect balance of elements for the teams' first clash. Messier's quickness in both directions and his two-way talents could adjust to any early theme suggested or he could dictate the tempo all by himself. Lacombe's tireless boardwork, punishing hits and darting ability could force turnovers, provide picks and impede attackers. Should Messier win the draw, Courtnall could use his speed to race ahead for a breakaway. They could play it any way. Crisp countered with Perry Berezan, Joel Otto and Joe Mullen to launch what Gretzky would later refer to as "the greatest game in Oiler history," a microcosm of which was Period One.

The Oilers were all business when Messier won the draw and subsequently settled into their own zone facing a mild 1-2-2 forecheck by Calgary. The Oilers, simultaneously looping Lacombe and Messier from right to left wing, with Courtnall jumping off the left wing boards across the circle, managed the precise response to what Calgary gave them, rather than force the play. The Oilers would alternatively flood the lanes until the ice opened up for them, or would, if under heavy attack, move the puck swiftly to backchecking Oiler forwards. If a second Flame were to appear, the forward would skate up to the circle, pulling off the forechecker, and drop the puck back to the defenseman moving out from behind the net.

The Messier line managed to get a jump on the Calgary forwards in the neutral zone and Lacombe and Courtnall soon found themselves with a two-on-one across the crease. Joe Mullen had let Courtnall slip through his fingers at the Oilers blue line, and Paul Reinhart had abandoned the left post to join Otto in a skirmish for the puck on the sideboards, freeing up Lacombe. Messier sent a pass to Lacombe's stick which he flicked off Vernon's left pad. Messier's line set the tone for subsequent Oiler shifts, with every defense pair pinching in, holding off a second forechecker, when the Flames bothered to send one in, and standing up on the blue line. No matter who Glen Sather sent over the boards, they forechecked, they raced back into the neutral zone to greet the Flames, they bashed and accepted hits to make a play, they buzzed all around the Flames who were in a somnambulistic haze.

The Oilers power play connected at 11:49 when Messier moved behind McCrimmon and Reinhart for a tap in of Esa Tikkanen's point shot. Gretzky, curling from behind the net, had passed out to Kurri in the slot, forcing McCrimmon to move up, leaving the left post unguarded. Overall the Flames' penalty killing was respectable in Game One, but Gretzky took full advantage of the low defenders' propensity for following the wing all the way up the boards. Gretzky would carry and join Tikkanen and Smith at the point to create a 2-3, while Messier and Kurri would be slung low at each post. When the low defender pursued, Gretzky would shoot the puck to Messier who would throw it across the crease to Kurri.

Conversely, the Oilers box would fan out at the points and stay in tight around the net. Lowe and Muni and Gregg and Smith patrolled an area rather than followed the puck, while Hannan and MacTavish, Gretzky and Kurri, and Messier proved wonderful little pets for MacInnis and Suter, who spent the night on their heels. Only McCrimmon scored for the Flames, a point shot that squeaked through Otto's screening legs through Grant Fuhr and so the teams entered the second period tied at one apiece.

The Flames, on five consecutive power play attempts from the latter part of the first period early on into the second, could not score a goal, nor get past the Oilers' 1-1-2 unit with any degree of comfort. There were long passes to no one, and a series of tactical retreat maneuvers that failed to pull the Oilers off-stride. The Oilers' pursuit in their own end rendered the

Flames an awkward, tentative unit to the extent that a five-minute major to Lacombe was a gleeful endeavor for the Oilers and a nightmare for the Flames.

When the Flames were able to break through, Fuhr was there, stopping a Mullen breakaway at even-strength, a handful of deflections by Otto in the slot on the power play.

The Flames line of Gary Roberts, Lanny McDonald and Tim Hunter did some hitting, but their hits were discordant, isolated. The Oilers were not banging for its own sake, but for the collective goal.

"In the past we wanted to win the fights and we didn't want to get punched," Steve Smith told the *Journal*. "Now it's a complete team concept. To take a hit, to make a play. Or to take a punch to create a penalty or power play for ourselves. I think we're taking pride in that."

The teams scratched and clawed through the second, with Calgary getting the better of the play in the latter half of the period. But in the third Tikkanen slipped behind Bullard and sent Kurri down the right wing boards for a high blast over Vernon's glove-side shoulder just inside the post. Moments later Kurri, who made some of the finest passes of his career, found Gretzky sneaking off all alone for a breakaway score and a 3-1 victory.

The backchecking of Kurri and Tikkanen and the latter's bellicosity were critical, as was the inspired play of Hannan and the sheer doggedness of tireless Craig MacTavish. Mike Krushelnyski, reduced to the fourth line, won a handful of face-offs in the latter stages of Game Two and deftly tucked the puck to Kurri in center ice before the right wing deked Reinhart and tied that game at four.

Marty McSorley didn't make the mistakes that you thought were just around the corner, moving the puck calmly and withstanding the pounding of Calgary forwards. The Oilers didn't make the mistakes the Flames had counted on, and Gretzky and Kurri proved to be themselves, which was more than the Flames could bear. No matter how tight-checking the flow, Gretzky would find a way to gain the offensive zone, not with a Savard-like pirouette, but like a bent straw he would stop and cut and the Flames would drift hopelessly back.

To speculate that the Flames "lost" a series that was theirs to win is to proceed from the assumption that got them in trouble in the first place. A video monitor reiterating the Flames' deadly power play would have proved a useless piece of technology had Messier, Kurri, Gretzky and Fuhr not proved again to be the best players in the world. Had Glenn Anderson, struggling offensively, not put to forechecking use his God-given speed (with which he later terrorized Ray Bourque in the Stanley Cup finals), the result might have been different.

It is a cruel irony for Calgary that the rule book catapulted them to the top of the League during the regular season via an invincible power play, but rendered them defenseless against the brilliance of Gretzky and Kurri. The Flames, who have considerable talent of their own, would have trashed any team this side of the Central Red Army with their game plan. Any other team. But not the Edmonton Oilers.

Was Crisp outcoached? Sure, but it wouldn't have mattered. Maybe if Nieuwendyk hadn't been chasing Bossy's regular-season ghost he would have corralled one of two great passes by Loob to the high slot instead of watching them bounce off the heel of his stick or maybe if Mike Vernon were as good as Grant Fuhr, the Flames would have had a chance.

Or maybe, as Reinhart suggested after the series, the Flames would have won if they had Wayne Gretzky.

APPENDIX II

Dynasty?

Stan Fischler

As successful as the Edmonton Oilers have been, Glen Sather's club remains challenged by one constantly repeated question: does Gretzky & Co. comprise a hockey dynasty?

There would not be any doubt about it had the Calgary Flames not knocked the Oilers from the 1986 Cup competition after Edmonton had won two straight previous championships.

"We did not want to go down in history as one of the great teams who ended up winning only two Stanley Cups in a row," says former Oiler Paul Coffey, a victim of the 1986 Calgary uprising.

The belief among some hockey scholars is that to be considered a true NHL dynasty, a championship team must win at least *three straight Stanely Cups*. Thus, Edmonton's wins in 1984, 1985, 1987 and 1988 obviously are impressive, but they lack the essential "dynastic" quality of three in a row. The inference being that there is a difference, however subtle, between *greatness* and *dynasty*.

"This has to be acknowledged as one of hockey's great teams," says Kevin Lowe. "Who can argue with that?"

Nobody. But that does not persuade skeptics that a great team is to be equated with a dynasty. In terms of putting Stanley Cup wins together, the Oilers must resemble a magnificent team of yesteryear, the 1950s Detroit Red Wings.

"Like the Oilers of today, we had some truly superior players," says New Jersey Devils vice president Max McNab, who played for those 1950s Red Wings, "it's just that we never could win three Cups in succession."

If the Edmonton nucleus is Wayne Gretzky, Mark Messier, Kevin Lowe, Jari Kurri, Glenn Anderson and Grant Fuhr, the Detroiters boasted Gordie Howe, Ted Lindsay, Sid Abel, Red Kelly and Terry Sawchuk, all Hall of Famers.

"We looked as though we were good for a long run of Cup wins when we beat the Rangers in the 1950 finals," McNab recalls, "but Toronto took it away from us the next spring and temporarily disrupted our momentum."

In the 1952 playoffs, Detroit won eight straight games on the way to the Cup and appeared on the threshold of a dynasty. But only a year later the Boston Bruins knocked them out of the play-offs in the opening round, four games to two.

Nevertheless, Detroit rebounded handsomely and won the Cup in 1954 and 1955. Like the Oilers, the Wings had won four Stanley Cups in a very short time, and had dominated the league for half a decade. But their bid for a third-in-a-row failed when the Montreal Canadiens defeated them in 1956. With that loss went Detroit's hope for a dynasty; that is, under the "Three-In-A-Row" definition of same.

Will the Oilers go the way of the Red Wings and never win that third Cup in succession? Certainly, Edmonton's chances for winning three or four in a row are good, but the words uttered by Oilers' co-coach John Muckler in 1985 are more pertinent today than ever: "If we keep working and keep our heads and don't get 'Fat Cat,' there's no reason why we can't do it."

In 1986 the Oilers lost their heads and may even have been "fat cat." But Glen Sather et al. weeded out the dissidents, especially Andy Moog and Paul Coffey, and infused the team with effective replacements such as Craig Simpson and Keith Acton.

Plenty can happen, though, when it comes to repeating a championship. Nobody knows that better than Kevin Lowe.

"Until you've been through it," says Lowe, "you have no idea how tough it is to win the Stanley Cup — let alone two Cups in a row."

The Oilers realize they are being compared with the Canadiens, who once won *five straight* Stanley Cups (1956-1960), and followed that with a run of four straight (1976-1979) — as did the New York Islanders (1980-1983).

"The Edmonton Oilers *are* a dynasty," concludes Red Wings coach Jacques Demers, "and one of the greatest teams ever."

The Greatest Trade in Sports History

When Edmonton hero Wayne Gretzky was traded to the L.A. Kings in August 1988, it marked the biggest deal in sports history. The only superstar similarly involved in such a trade was the inimitable Babe Ruth, moving from the Boston Red Sox to the New York Yankees on February 3rd, 1920.

By comparison, the Ruth deal was small potatoes. The Red Sox paid $125,000 cash for Ruth but that was long before the Babe had reached the peak of his career. So the avalanche of money and players involved in the Gretzky transaction thoroughly dwarfed the Ruthian transfer, or any other for that matter.

For the next decade at least, fans, critics and professional hockey people will debate the merits of the trade and why it was made in the first place. It seems clear than above all there were compelling financial reasons behind Oilers owner Peter Pocklington's decision to trade the Great One. And although the entrepreneur piously claimed he hated to see Gretzky go, there were other reasons for Pocklington to make the trade. To whit:

- With Gretzky in the lineup, the Oilers were so dominating they bordered on boring.
- Imagine a team that won four Stanley Cups in five years and still the Oilers had trouble filling Northlands Coliseum, even with Gretzky leading the way.

- In terms of production, Gretzky has peaked. In June 1987, he talked freely of retiring.
- Pocklington will save more than $1 million in payroll costs without Gretzky.
- With Gretzky gone, previously overshadowed stars, Mark Messier and Glenn Anderson — two underachievers — are likely to improve their production and take over the leadership on the attack.
- Pocklington realized that the Oilers survived the loss of Paul Coffey and can do likewise without Gretzky.
- The new Oilers will re-invigorate Edmonton hockey fans and the players themselves.
- And, finally Glen Sather has always believed in annual roster changes. With his new young aces like Jimmy Carson and Craig Redmond, he has planted the seeds for more championship teams.

What impact did Wayne's wife, Janet Jones, have on the move? Although Janet denied that she influenced Wayne's switch from Edmonton to Los Angeles, insiders believe that she did in fact inspire Wayne to look to L.A. when it had become apparent that Pocklington was determined to trade him. During a visit to New York in 1988, Janet chatted with Shirley, who came away from the conversation with the feeling that, given her druthers, Janet would rather be in L.A.

What will the deal do for the Oilers and Kings? In terms of Edmonton, the Oilers have the nucleus of a team that could dominate the NHL for another decade. As for Gretzky, he could turn L.A. into an imposing hockey club. To understand why, we must hark back to the only deal in NHL history comparable to this one. In November 1947, Max Bentley was the Gretzky of his day and was dealt from the Chicago Black Hawks to the Toronto Maple Leafs in then what was the biggest trade in hockey history. The Black Hawks received an entire front line of Bud Poile, Gus Bodnar, and Gaye Stewart, as well as a compete defence pair of Bob Goldham and Ernie Dickens, all for Bentley.

Chicago went nowhere. With Bentley in the lineup, Toronto won Stanley Cups in 1948, 1949 and 1951.

If Gretzky brings even one Stanley Cup to California, it will be the best deal the Kings ever made. But for this decade at least, Glen Sather and his Oilers are the winners.

Stan Fischler
August, 1988

Records and Statistics

Edmonton Oilers Play-off Records

MOST CONSECUTIVE YEARS STANLEY CUP FINALISTS: 3 (1983, New York Islanders won series 4-0, 1984, Edmonton won series 4-1 over Islanders. 1985, Edmonton won 4-1 over Philadelphia)

MOST CONSECUTIVE PLAY-OFF APPEARANCES: 9 seasons (1979-80 through 1987-88)

MOST CONSECUTIVE STANLEY CUP CHAMPIONS: 2 (1983-84, 1984-85) (1986-87, 1987-88)

MOST GOALS, ONE TEAM, FOUR GAME SERIES: Edmonton: 25 (Oilers vs Chicago, 1983 Conference Finals. Edmonton won series 4-0 and outscored Chicago 25-11)

MOST GOALS, BOTH TEAMS, FOUR GAME SERIES: 36 (Edmonton vs Chicago, 1983 Conference Finals)

MOST GOALS, ONE TEAM, FIVE GAME SERIES: Edmonton: 35 (Edmonton vs Calgary, 1983 Division Finals. Edmonton won series 4-1 and outscored Calgary 35-13)

MOST GOALS, BOTH TEAMS, FIVE GAME SERIES: 52 (Oilers vs Los Angeles, 1987 Division Semi-Finals. Edmonton won series 4-1 and outscored Kings 32-20)

FEWEST GOALS, ONE TEAM, FOUR GAME SERIES: Edmonton: 6 (Oilers vs Islanders, 1983 Stanley Cup Finals. New York won series 4-0 outscoring Edmonton 17-6)

FEWEST GOALS, BOTH TEAMS, FOUR GAME SERIES: 23 (Edmonton vs Islanders, 1983 Stanley Cup Finals)

FEWEST GOALS, ONE TEAM, FIVE GAME SERIES: Edmonton: 16 (Oilers vs Detroit, 1987 Conference Finals. Edmonton won series 4-1 and outscored Detroit 16-10)

FEWEST GOALS, BOTH TEAMS, FIVE GAME SERIES: 26 (Edmonton vs Detroit, 1987 Conference Finals)

MOST GOALS, ONE TEAM, ONE GAME: Edmonton: 13 (Oilers vs Kings, April 9/87. Edmonton won 13-3)

MOST GOALS, BOTH TEAMS, ONE GAME: 18 (Edmonton vs L.A. Kings, April 8/82. L.A. won 10-8)

MOST GOALS, ONE TEAM, ONE PERIOD: 6 (Oilers vs L.A. Kings, April 9/87 1st period. Edmonton won 13-3) (Oilers vs Winnipeg Jets, April 6/88, 3rd period. Edmonton won 7-4)

MOST GOALS, BOTH TEAMS, ONE PERIOD: 8 (Edmonton vs Chicago May 12/85, 1st period. Chicago won 8-6 and had 5 goals, Edmonton had 3 goals) (Oilers vs Winnipeg Jets, April 6/88, 3rd period. Edmonton had 6 goals and Winnipeg had 2, Edmonton won 7-4)

MOST OVERTIME GAMES IN FINAL SERIES: 1 (1987 vs Philadelphia, Jarri Kurri scored at 6:50 overtime in game 2)

MOST CONSECUTIVE PLAY-OFF VICTORIES: 12 (May 15/84 through May 7/85)

FASTEST TWO GOALS, BOTH TEAMS: 13 seconds (Oilers vs Chicago, May 7/85, 1st period. Scorers: Glenn Anderson, Edmonton 6:21; Bob Murray, Chicago, 6:34; Edmonton won 7-3)

FASTEST TWO GOALS, ONE TEAM: Edmonton 7 seconds (Oilers vs Winnipeg April 6/83, 1st period. Scorers: Ken Linseman 14:10; Dave Hunter 14:17; Edmonton won 6-3) (Oilers vs Chicago, May 7/85, 3rd period. Scorers: Jari Kurri 19:36; Glenn Anderson 19:43; Edmonton won 7-3)

FASTEST THREE GOALS, BOTH TEAMS: 31 seconds (Oilers vs Philadelphia, May 25/85, 1st period. Scorers: Wayne Gretzky, Edmonton, 1:10, 1:25; Derrick Smith, Philadelphia, 1:41; Edmonton won 4-3)

FASTEST THREE GOALS, ONE TEAM: Edmonton: 1 minute, 48 seconds (Oilers vs Winnipeg, April 6/83, 1st period. Scorers: Ken Linseman 14:10; Dave Hunter 14:17; Wayne Gretzky 15:58; Edmonton won 6-3)

HIGHEST SHUTOUT GAME: 1-0 over N.Y. Islanders May 10/84

MOST GAMES HOME TEAM WINLESS: Edmonton:3 (Lost 1986 Division Finals to Calgary 4-3; Calgary took 3 in Edmonton, Edmonton took 2 in Calgary. The home teams combined for 5 losses.)

MOST CONSECUTIVE GAMES WITHOUT BEING SHUT OUT: 89 (May 12/83 through May 26/1988)

MOST OVERTIMES, ONE PLAYOFF YEAR: 3 - 1984

MOST OVERTIME GOALS SCORED IN A SERIES: 2 (1980: Edmonton vs Philadelphia, Bobby Clarke at 8:06 Flyers; Ken Linseman at 23:56 Flyers) (1982: Edmonton vs Los Angeles, Wayne Gretzky at 6:20 Edmonton; Daryl Evans at 2:35 L.A. Kings) (1984: Edmonton vs Calgary, Carey Wilson at 3:42 Calgary; Lanny McDonald at 1:04 Calgary) (1985: Edmonton vs Los Angeles, Lee Fogolin at 3:01 Edmonton; Glenn Anderson at 0:46 Edmonton)

2. Edmonton Oilers Regular Season Records

MOST GAMES WON IN A SINGLE SEASON: 57 (1983-84 season)

MOST GOALS SCORED BY ONE TEAM IN A SINGLE GAME: 13 (Oilers vs New Jersey, November 19/83. Edmonton won 13-4) (Oilers vs Vancouver, November 8/85. Edmonton won 13-0)

MOST TOTAL GOALS SCORED IN A SINGLE GAME: 21 (Oilers vs Chicago, 11/85. Edmonton won 12-9)

MOST PENALTY MINUTES IN A SINGLE GAME: 135 (Oilers at Calgary, November 15/84. Edmonton received 10 minors, 7 majors, 2 10-minute misconducts, 1 match misconduct and 5 game misconducts)

MOST PENALTY MINUTES IN ONE PERIOD: 110 (Oilers at Pittsburgh, January 19/80 2nd period. Edmonton received 5 minors, 8 majors, and 6 game misconducts)

LONGEST UNDEFEATED RECORD AT HOME: 12 (October 5/83 through December 3/83. 10 wins, 2 ties)

MOST TIED GAMES IN ONE SEASON: 16 (1980-81)

FEWEST LOSSES IN ONE SEASON: 17 (1981-82, 1985-86)

FEWEST GOALS AGAINST IN ONE SEASON: 284 (1986-87)

MOST POINTS IN ONE GAME: Edmonton: 8 (Wayne Gretzky, vs New Jersey November 19/83, 3 goals, 5 assists. Oilers won 13-4; Wayne Gretzky vs Minnesota, January 4/84, 4 goals, 4 assists. Oilers won 12-8; Paul Coffey, vs Detroit, March 14/86, 2 goals, 6 assists. Oilers won 12-3)

MOST GOALS IN ONE SEASON-TEAM: 446 (1983-84)

MOST GOALS IN ONE SEASON-PLAYER: Wayne Gretzky: 92 (1981-82)

MOST SHUTOUTS BY A GOALIE: Grant Fuhr: 6

LEAST AMOUNT OF GOALS ALLOWED BY GOALIE IN A SEASON: (Andy Moog: 111 (1984-85)

MOST GOALS SCORED IN ONE SEASON INCLUDING PLAY-OFFS: Wayne Gretzky 100 (1983-84)

MOST ASSISTS IN ONE PERIOD: 4 (Gretzky 2/4/83, Kurri 10/7/83, Messier 1/4/84, Gretzky 10/26/84; Gretzky 10/15/86, Gretzky 2/18/87)

MOST CAREER HAT TRICKS: 43 (Wayne Gretzky)

MOST CAREER HAT TRICKS INCLUDING PLAY-OFFS: 50 (Wayne Gretzky)

MOST TIMES VEZINA TROPHY AWARD WINNER: Grant Fuhr: 1 (1988)

MOST CONSECUTIVE GAMES WITHOUT BEING SHUT OUT: 229 games (3/15/81 - 2/11/84)

MOST CAREER SHORT HANDED GOALS: 55 (Wayne Gretzky)

MOST CAREER POWER PLAY GOALS: 125 (Wayne Gretzky)

MOST GAME WINNING GOALS: 61 (Wayne Gretzky)

3. Edmonton Oilers All-Star Selections

1980-SECOND TEAM: Wayne Gretzky

1981-FIRST TEAM: Wayne Gretzky

1982-FIRST TEAM: Wayne Gretzky, Mark Messier

1982-SECOND TEAM: Grant Fuhr, Paul Coffey

1983-FIRST TEAM: Wayne Gretzky, Mark Messier

1983-SECOND TEAM: Paul Coffey

1984-FIRST TEAM: Wayne Gretzky

1984-SECOND TEAM: Mark Messier, Jari Kurri, Paul Coffey

1985-FIRST TEAM: Wayne Gretzky, Jari Kurri, Paul Coffey

1986-FIRST TEAM: Wayne Gretzky, Paul Coffey

1986-SECOND TEAM: Jari Kurri

1987-FIRST TEAM: Wayne Gretzky, Jari Kurri

1988-FIRST TEAM: Grant Fuhr

1988-SECOND TEAM: Wayne Gretzky

4. Edmonton Oilers NHL Award Winners

HART MEMORIAL TROPHY (MOST VALUABLE PLAYER)
Wayne Gretzky: 1980, 1981, 1982, 1983, 1984, 1985, 1986, 1987

JAMES NORRIS MEMORIAL TROPHY (OUTSTANDING DEFENCEMAN)
Paul Coffey: 1984-85, 1985-86

EMERY EDGE AWARD (PLUS-MINUS LEADER)
Charlie Huddy: 1982-83
Wayne Gretzky: 1983-84, 1984-85, 1986-87

ART ROSS TROPHY (LEADING SCORER)
Wayne Gretzky: 1981, 1982, 1983, 1984, 1985, 1986, 1987

LADY BYNG MEMORIAL TROPHY (MOST GENTLEMANLY PLAYER)
Wayne Gretzky: 1979-80
Jari Kurri: 1984-85

JACK ADAMS AWARD (COACH OF THE YEAR)
Glen Sather: 1985-86

LESTER B. PEARSON AWARD (OUTSTANDING PLAYER AS SELECTED BY THE
NHL PLAYERS ASSOCIATION)
Wayne Gretzky: 1982-85, 1987

CONN SMYTHE TROPHY (STANLEY CUP MVP)
Mark Messier: 1983-84
Wayne Gretzky: 1984-85
Wayne Gretzky: 1987-88

5. Edmonton Oilers Team Standing Since 1972-73

Season	GP	Won	Lost	Tied	GF	GA	Pts	Standing
* 1972-73	78	38	37	3	269	256	79	4th
* 1973-74	78	38	37	3	268	269	79	3rd
* 1974-75	78	36	38	4	279	279	76	5th
* 1975-76	81	27	49	5	268	345	59	4th
* 1976-77	81	34	43	4	243	304	72	4th
* 1977-78	80	38	39	3	309	307	79	5th
* 1978-79	80	48	30	2	340	266	98	1st
1979-80	80	28	39	13	301	322	69	4th
1980-81	80	29	35	16	328	327	74	4th
1981-82	80	48	17	15	417	295	111	1st
1982-83	80	47	21	12	424	315	106	1st
1983-84	80	57	18	5	446	314	119	1st
1984-85	80	49	20	11	401	298	109	1st
1985-86	80	56	17	7	426	311	119	1st
1986-87	80	50	24	6	372	284	106	1st
1987-88	80	44	25	11	363	288	99	2nd

*Denotes Alberta Oilers WHA

6. Kevin Lowe Personal Stats

REGULAR SCHEDULE PLAYOFFS

Year	Team	League	GP	G	A	TP	P/M	GP	G	A	TP	P/M
1979-80	Edmonton Oilers	NHL	64	2	19	21	70	3	0	1	1	0
1980-81	Edmonton Oilers	NHL	79	10	24	34	94	9	0	2	2	11
1981-82	Edmonton Oilers	NHL	80	9	31	40	63	5	0	3	3	0
1982-83	Edmonton Oilers	NHL	80	6	34	40	43	16	1	8	9	10
1983-84	Edmonton Oilers	NHL	80	4	42	46	59	19	3	7	10	16
1984-85	Edmonton Oilers	NHL	80	4	21	25	104	16	0	5	5	8
1985-86	Edmonton Oilers	NHL	74	2	16	18	90	10	1	3	4	15
1986-87	Edmonton Oilers	NHL	77	8	29	37	94	21	2	4	6	22
1987-88	Edmonton Oilers	NHL	70	9	15	24	89	19	0	2	2	26
NHL & Oilers Totals		NHL	684	54	231	285	706	118	7	35	42	108

7. EDMONTON OILERS STANLEY CUP CHAMPIONS

Four Stanley Cups
Glenn Anderson
Grant Fuhr
Randy Gregg
Wayne Gretzky
Charlie Huddy
Jari Kurri
Kevin Lowe
Kevin McClelland
Mark Messier

Three Stanley Cups
Paul Coffey: '84, '85, '87
Dave Hunter: '84, '85, '87
Andy Moog: '84, '85, '87
Jaroslav Pouzar: '84, '85, '87
Mike Krushelnyski: '85, '87, '88
Esa Tikkanen: '85, '87, '88

Two Stanley Cups
Lee Fogolin: '84, '85
Pat Hughes: '84, '85
Don Jackson: '84, '85

Willy Lindstrom: '84, '85
Dave Lumley: '84, '85
Dave Semenko: '84, '85
Jeff Beukeboom: '87, '88
Craig MacTavish: '87, '88
Marty McSorley: '87, '88
Craig Muni: '87, '88
Steve Smith: '87, '88

One Stanley Cup
Pat Conacher: '84
Ken Linseman: '84
Bill Carroll: '85
Larry Melnyk: '85
Mark Napier: '85
Kelly Buchberger: '87
Moe Lemay: '87
Kent Nilsson: '87
Reijo Ruotsalainen: '87
Keith Acton: '88
Geoff Courtnall: '88
Dave Hannan: '88
Normand Lacombe: '88
Bill Ranford: '88
Craig Simpson: '88

INDEX

Abel, Sid, 49, 335
Acton, Keith, 322-23, 335
Adams, Charles F., 24, 26
Adams, Jack, 34-39, 42, 47, 50
Aeros. *See* Houston Aeros
Alberta Amateur Hockey
    Association, 6, 10
Alberta, hockey in. *See* Hockey,
    history in Alberta
Alberta Oilers, 53, 77, 82, 83-84.
    See also Edmonton Oilers
Ali, Muhammed, 180-81, 183
Allan Cup, 10, 30, 31
Allan, Sir Montague, 10, 32
Anderson, Glenn "Glennie", 1,
    151, 153, 154, 157-59, 160, 163,
    170, 176, 178, 180, 202, 208,
    218, 233, 236, 238, 239, 241,
    242, 251, 262, 266, 267, 268,
    270, 271, 272, 275, 277, 278,
    281, 295, 312, 316, 317, 318,
    333, 335, 338
Arbour, Al, 38, 42, 48, 54, 203,
    205, 241
Arbour, Ty, 19, 21, 22
Art Ross Trophy, 132, 141, 288

Badali, Gus, 91, 92, 93, 281, 282,
    283
Baldwin, Howard, 73, 84, 85, 86,
    95, 99, 100, 101, 105
Ballard, Harold, 103, 105, 169
Beck, Barry, 216, 264
Beliveau, Jean, 146-47, 220
Benning, Jim, 153, 195
Bentley, Max, 31, 52
Beukeboom, Jeff, 267, 310
"Big Four", 14-15, 16
Birmingham Bulls, 86, 101, 118,
    119, 123
Black Hawks. *See* Chicago Black
Hawks

Blackman, Marty, 59-60, 66, 73
Blades. *See* New York Golden
    Blades
Blazers. *See* Philadelphia Blazers;
    Vancouver Blazers
Blues. *See* St. Louis Blues
Bossy, Mike, 132, 174, 205, 213,
    219, 220, 235, 264, 286, 333
Boston Bruins, 24, 54, 55, 57
    Oilers *vs.*, 202-3, 315-21, 327
Boucher, Frank, 11, 22, 23, 26,
    50-51
Bourne, Bob, 205, 206, 207, 264
Bourque, Ray, 315, 316, 317, 333
Bowman, Scotty, 139, 205
Bozek, Steve, 186, 303
Broadbent, Harry, 20, 21
Brophy, John, 203-4
Brownridge, R. "Bob", 63, 64, 66
Bruins. *See* Boston Bruins
Bucyk, Johnny, 38, 42, 43-44, 45,
    48, 52
Buffey, Vern, 65, 70
Bullard, Mike, 302, 304-5, 328,
    330, 332
Bulls. *See* Birmingham Bulls

Calder, Frank, 23, 35
Calgary all-star team (1895), 4-5
Calgary Broncs (hockey club), 30,
    66
Calgary Cowboys (hockey club),
    85, 88, 102
Calgary Flames, 205, 246, 247,
    307, 308
    Oilers *vs.*, 240, 248-52, 257-58,
    267, 269, 270, 288, 298-308,
    327-33
Calgary Stampeders (hockey
    club), 31, 42, 63

347